A PREVIOUSLY UNPUBLISHED STORY FROM FUJINO OMORI!

SPECIAL CHAPTER

AN ELF'S STORY

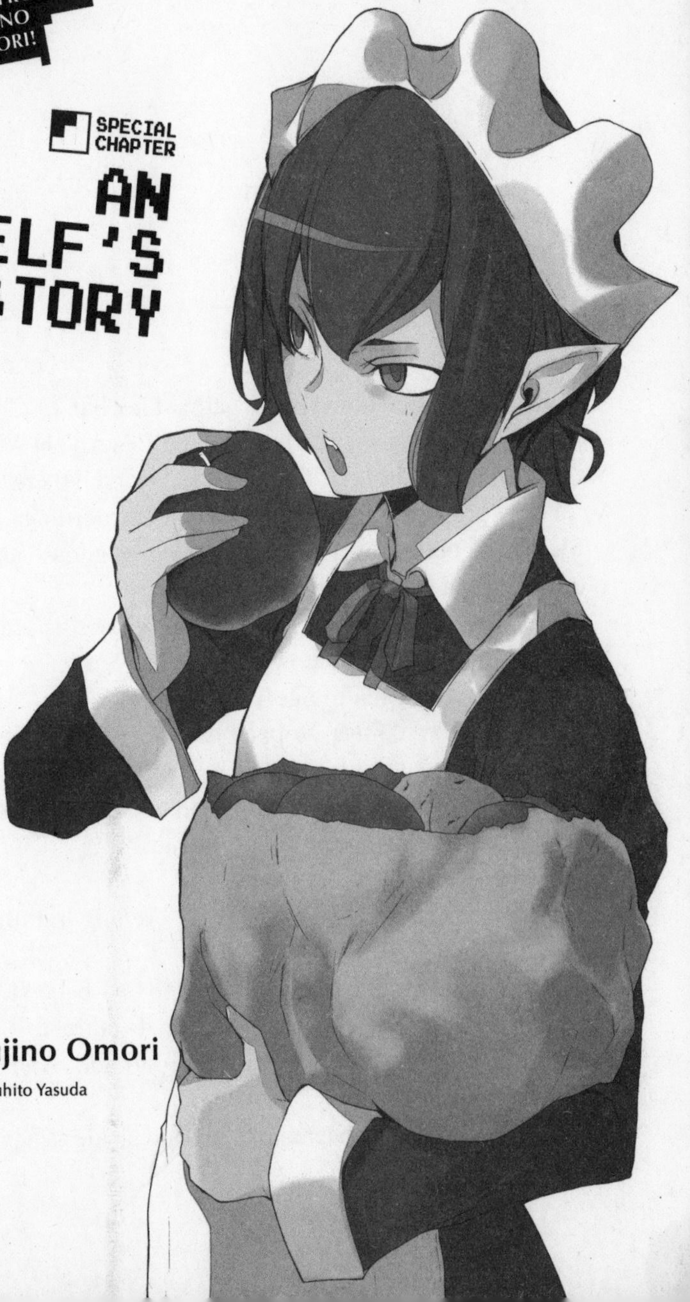

Story: Fujino Omori

Illustration: Suzuhito Yasuda

The elf, Lyu, looked down at the palm of her hand.

She was standing inside the bar, The Benevolent Mistress. She was a member of the staff that lived and worked there. All of them were busy preparing for the day early in the morning.

Many cat people were busy opening windows and cleaning around her, but Lyu was frozen in place.

"Lyu, something wrong, meow? You've been spaced out since yesterday...Feeling sick, meow?"

"No, my apologies...I'm fine."

The cat person, Ahnya, stopped to talk to Lyu while carrying a table in her arms.

Even while speaking to the girl with a long tail swishing at her feet, Lyu didn't take her eyes off her hand.

...This hand was held.

Memories of an incident in the early evening last night swelled within her chest.

An item belonging to an acquaintance had been stolen—when she recovered the knife from a prum and returned it to Bell, he grabbed her hand while showing his gratitude. And Lyu didn't reject it.

Memories of the past began to bubble up inside as her expression softened.

Lyu was once an adventurer.

She belonged to a Familia and spent each day in Orario surrounded by allies.

"Seriously, annihilating five adventurers at once...It was their fault for provoking you, but you went too far, Leon!"

"My apologies, Alize."

They were sitting on the roof of a building. On this day, Lyu was brought up there to receive a lecture from one of her allies—one that was fond of high places—in her Familia.

Elves, beautiful and proud, had a complex where they wouldn't allow someone they didn't approve of to touch their skin. While it wasn't true for all elves, that was how Lyu had been raised to think, and it occasionally got her into trouble.

"'Lyu' is such a pain to say!" Her ally had once said with a teasing grin on her face. She began referring to the elf as "Leon" ever since.

"Well, I thought your hunch was pretty good. After all, I refuse to get my own pretty hands dirty."

The human girl reached out to grab Lyu's hand and brought it up to shoulder height.

Lyu had a habit of physically knocking away the hands of anyone who tried to touch her. It was a sure bet that she would react like that if a stranger tried it. The only exception was the girl sitting before her. Lyu didn't push her away.

She had grabbed her hand the day they met and led Lyu back to the Familia with a smile on her face.

Lyu recognized the girl's pure spirit and lightheartedness before her instincts told her to retaliate.

"Indeed...you are beautiful. Always facing forward, you are nice enough to interact with anyone without discrimination. I have a very deep respect for you."

Lyu made this statement with the utmost sincerity, but the girl only blinked a few times before blushing.

Her rosy cheeks flushed to match the color of her gorgeous red hair.

"Saying such embarrassing things with a straight face...This is why I have a weak spot for you serious elves..."

Whispering under her breath and tilting her head slightly to the side, the girl tried to mask her shyness and practically shouted, "Are you listening, Leon?!"

"Remember this well! If a man ever holds your hand, no matter how ugly his face or weak his body is, you have to keep him! Because a guy you'll truly accept is impossible to find! Rare monsters will be easier to spot, for sure!"

The girl's fingers were just in front of Lyu's face. Now it was her turn to blush.

"Must I?"

"You must!"

Lyu took her ally's declaration to heart and carved it into her memory.

The two of them looked out over the city of Orario, a clear blue sky over their heads.

Lyu emerged from her precious memories of days gone by and returned to the present.

She thought about Bell as she looked at her own thin, white hand.

White hair and ruby red eyes, he was still a young boy and couldn't be relied on for much of anything. However, she sensed a spirit as pure as his white hair through the few conversations they shared.

Could this white-haired boy with the worry-free smile be the fated partner that her ally had spoke of back then?

But, this boy was...

Lyu got back to work with her former ally's words ringing in her ears. That is until she happened to see something out the window.

Her coworker, Syr, was giving a lunch to the boy, Bell.

Her coworker had been giving the boy a lunch to take with him into the Dungeon every morning for a while now.

Syr's pink cheeks were glowing with happiness, but Bell seemed embarrassed as he took the lunch from her hands and smiled back at her.

"...Alize, I am unable to do this."

Lyu smiled as she watched the two humans outside.

Not only was Syr her coworker—she was also her savior. There was no way she could even attempt to steal someone away from her.

Her former ally's name on her lips, Lyu took quick steps to leave the area.

$\boxed{*}$

Early morning, a few days later.

Lyu was in the kitchen making a lunch.

—Syr was pathetic when she overslept.

"Delay Bell as long as you can!" she had said in a panicked voice running up to her, but it was pointless. Lyu knew that Syr's trial-and-error method of making the boy's lunch took at least an hour.

Feeling that it was her duty to cover for her coworker's mistake, Lyu went to the kitchen to make the lunch herself before greeting Bell in front of the bar.

"Ah...Lyu?"

"Mr. Cranell, Syr is currently busy with preparations...She asked me to deliver this to you," she said as she handed the boy a small basket with the lunch inside. Bell was on his way to the Dungeon and accepted the basket without much thought—until a strange smell wafted up from within, making his face squirm.

...Must have overdone it in my haste.

Lyu had made a sandwich. She put vegetables and meat, along with a raw egg, between two wildly sliced pieces of bread and toasted the whole thing. Everything was burnt, bread and every other ingredient.

While she had experience making jerky and other dried foods during her time as an adventurer...when it came to making fresh food, Lyu's skills were horribly lacking.

Damn it, she swore to herself as she desperately tried to come up with an explanation to give to the boy standing in front of her with a forced smile on his face.

"M-Mr. Cranell, Syr was not the one to make this...n-no, she hasn't been feeling well today..."

Bell watched as the normally succinct Lyu struggled to speak.

He took a burnt lump of sandwich out of the basket. Lyu's eyes opened wide as the boy took a big bite out of it.

"...T-today's seasoning, it's rather unique..."

Lyu's spine straightened as stiff as a board as she watched the boy take another bite, black flakes sticking to his chin. She opened her mouth to speak, but no sound came out.

In the end, all she could muster was a shy smile.

"Thank you for taking the time to prepare this for me. It was delicious...please tell Syr for me."

More than likely, Bell knew.

He knew that Syr didn't make the sandwich, that it was Lyu.

So, his words of gratitude were intended for her, the one standing in front of him.

—You have to keep him!

Her ally's words echoed from the back of her mind.

Lyu hid the smile that was about to bloom on her face by tilting her head down.

"Yes...I will tell her."

Bell went down the street with the basket, carrying the rest of his lunch clutched in his hands. Lyu watched him go, narrowing her eyes as he disappeared into the crowd.

"This is a problem...I'm a little happy."

Lyu went back inside the bar with a smile on her lips.

From that day forward, she watched the boy from afar as she supported her coworker's endeavors.

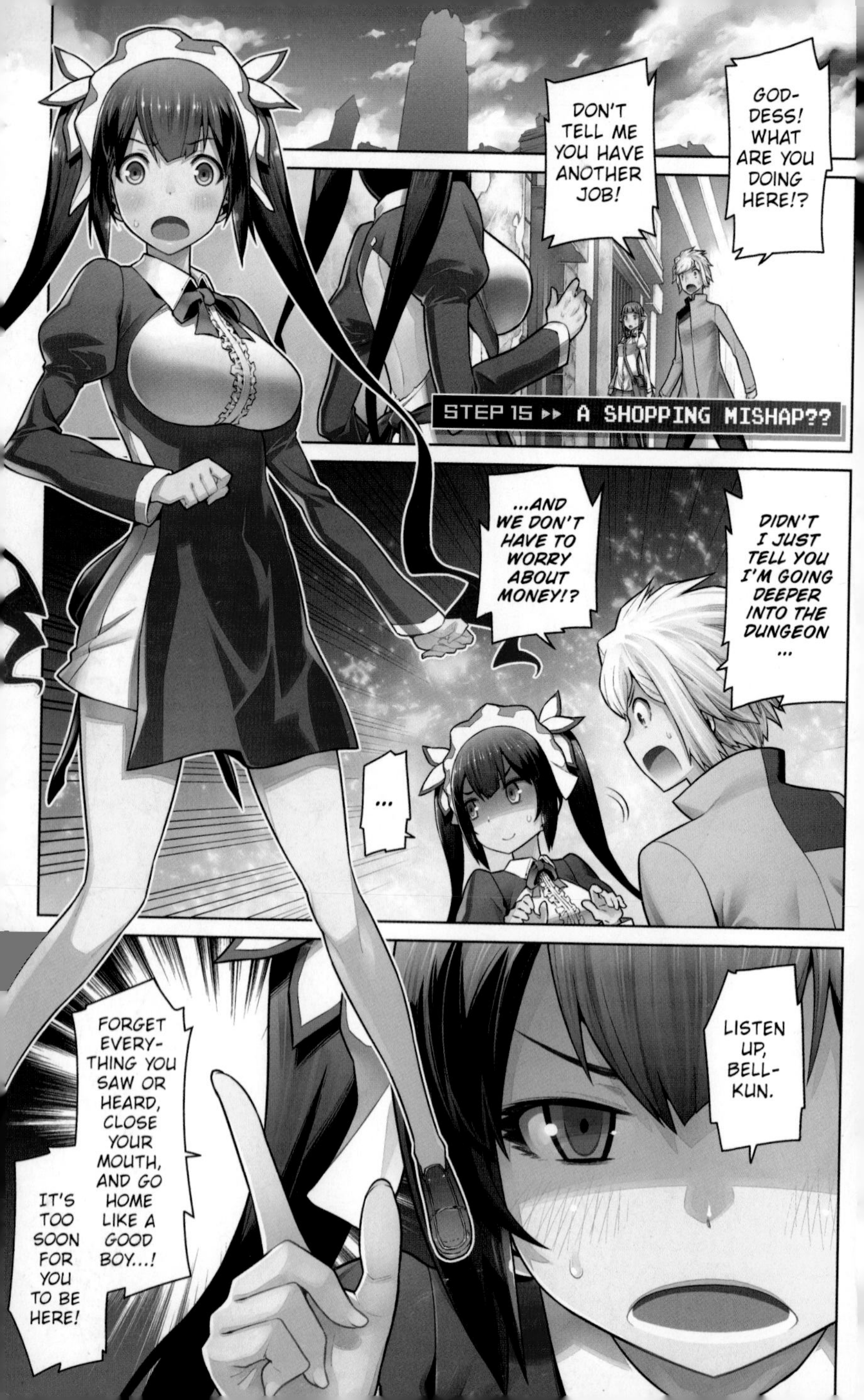
GOD-DESS! WHAT ARE YOU DOING HERE!?
DON'T TELL ME YOU HAVE ANOTHER JOB!
STEP 15 ▸▸ A SHOPPING MISHAP??
DIDN'T I JUST TELL YOU I'M GOING DEEPER INTO THE DUNGEON...
...AND WE DON'T HAVE TO WORRY ABOUT MONEY!?
...
LISTEN UP, BELL-KUN.
FORGET EVERYTHING YOU SAW OR HEARD, CLOSE YOUR MOUTH, AND GO HOME LIKE A GOOD BOY...!
IT'S TOO SOON FOR YOU TO BE HERE!

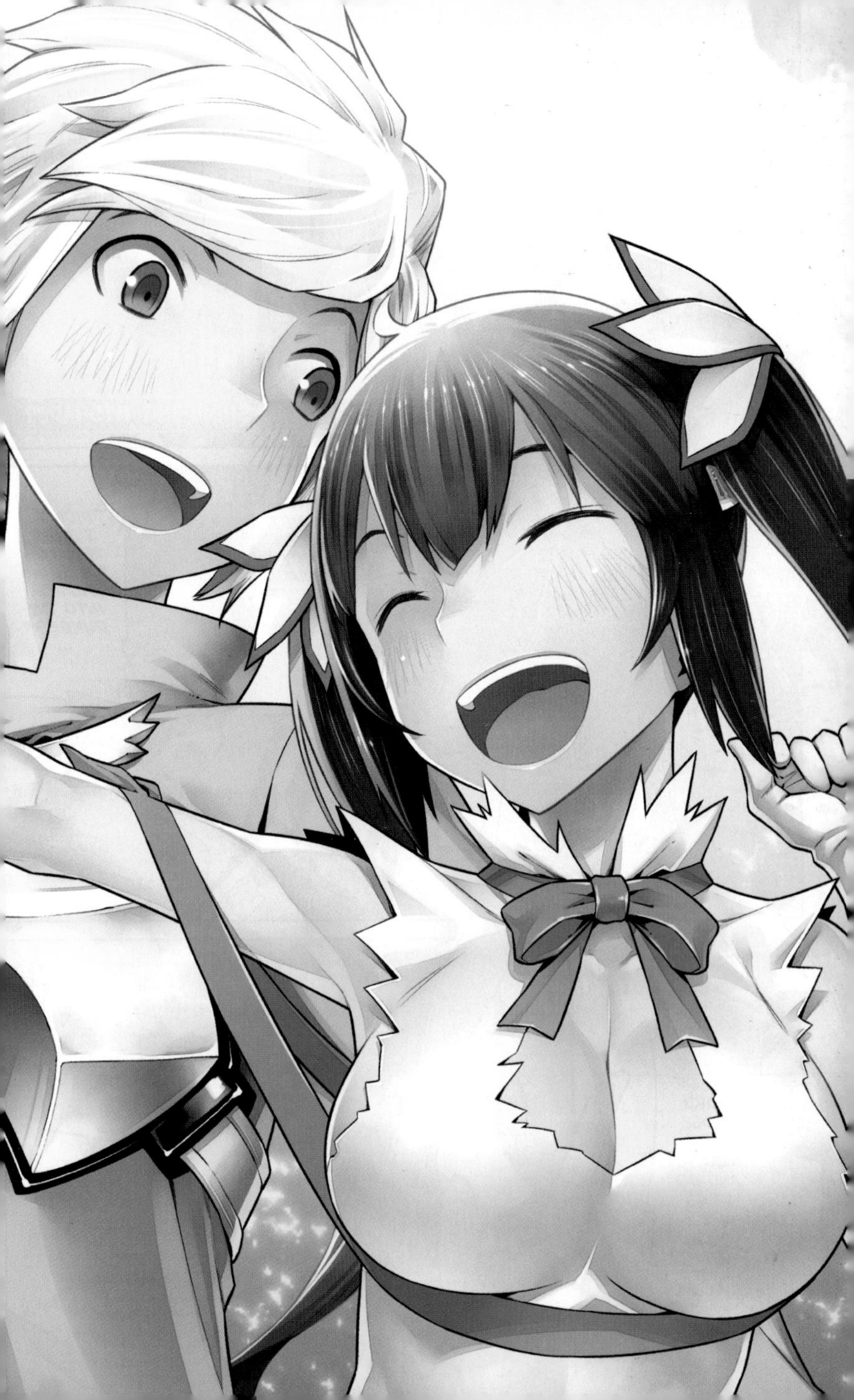

Is It Wrong to Try to Pick Up Girls in a Dungeon?

ORIGINAL STORY
FUJINO OMORI

MANGA ADAPTATION
KUNIEDA

CHARACTER DESIGN
SUZUHITO YASUDA

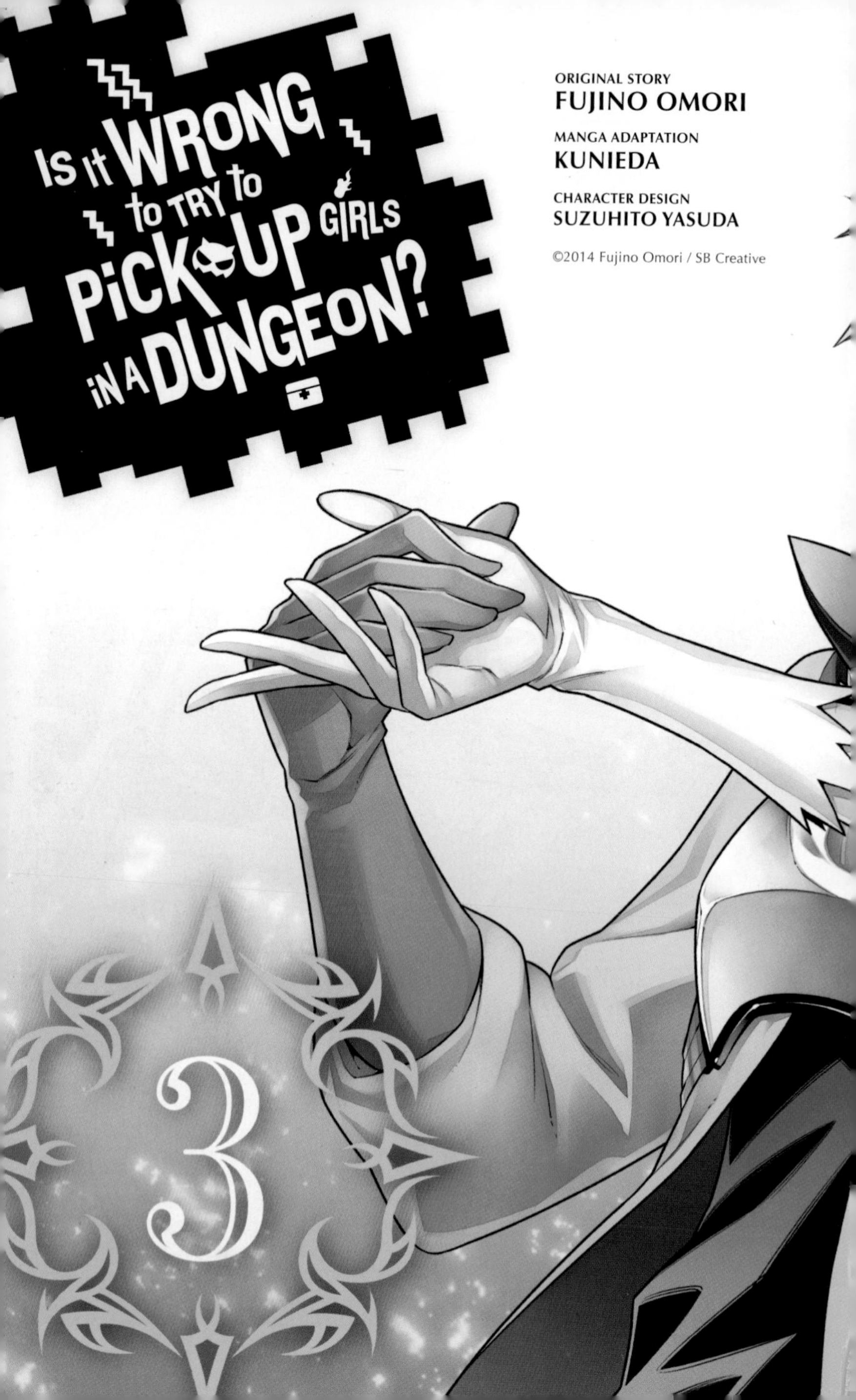
3

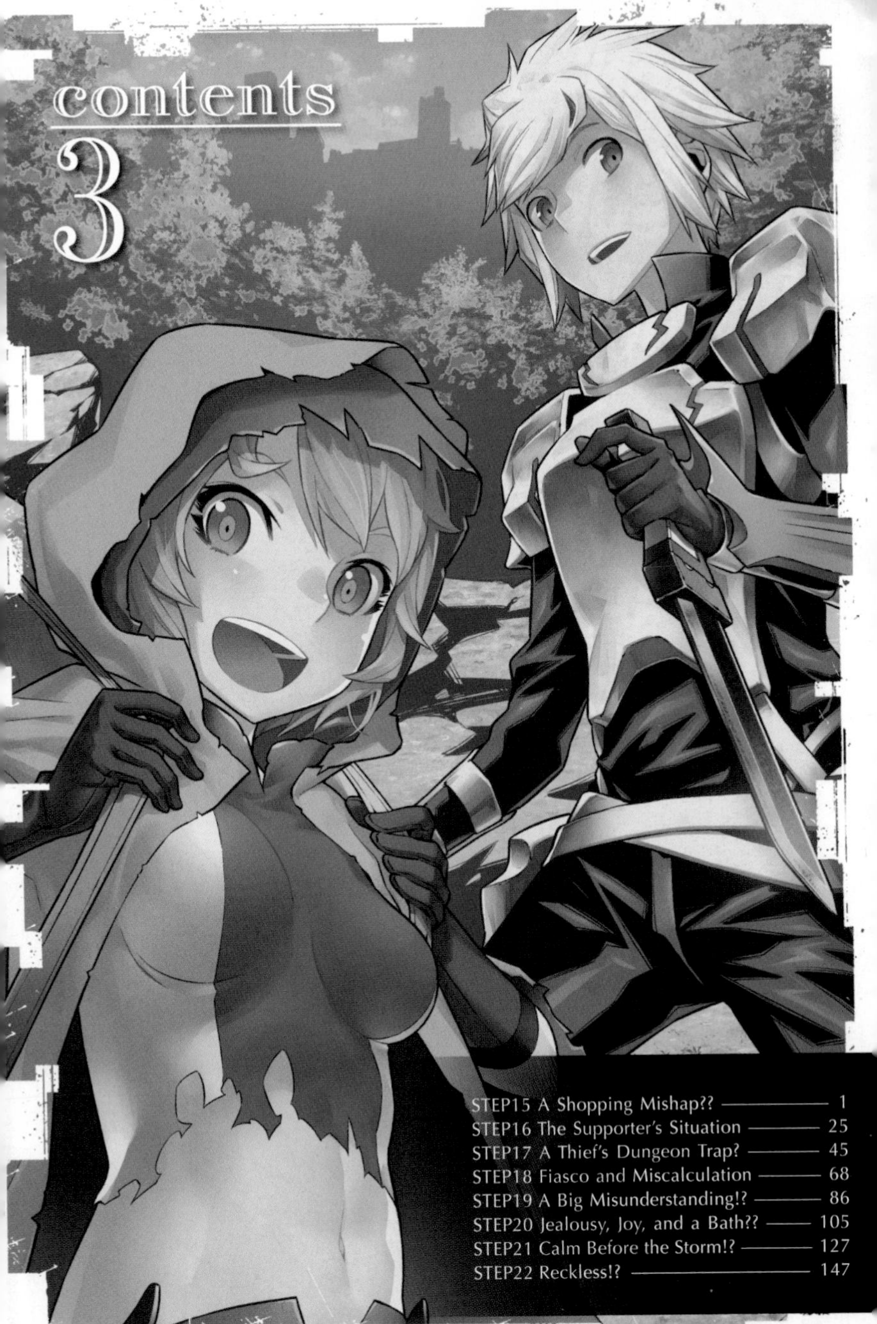

contents 3

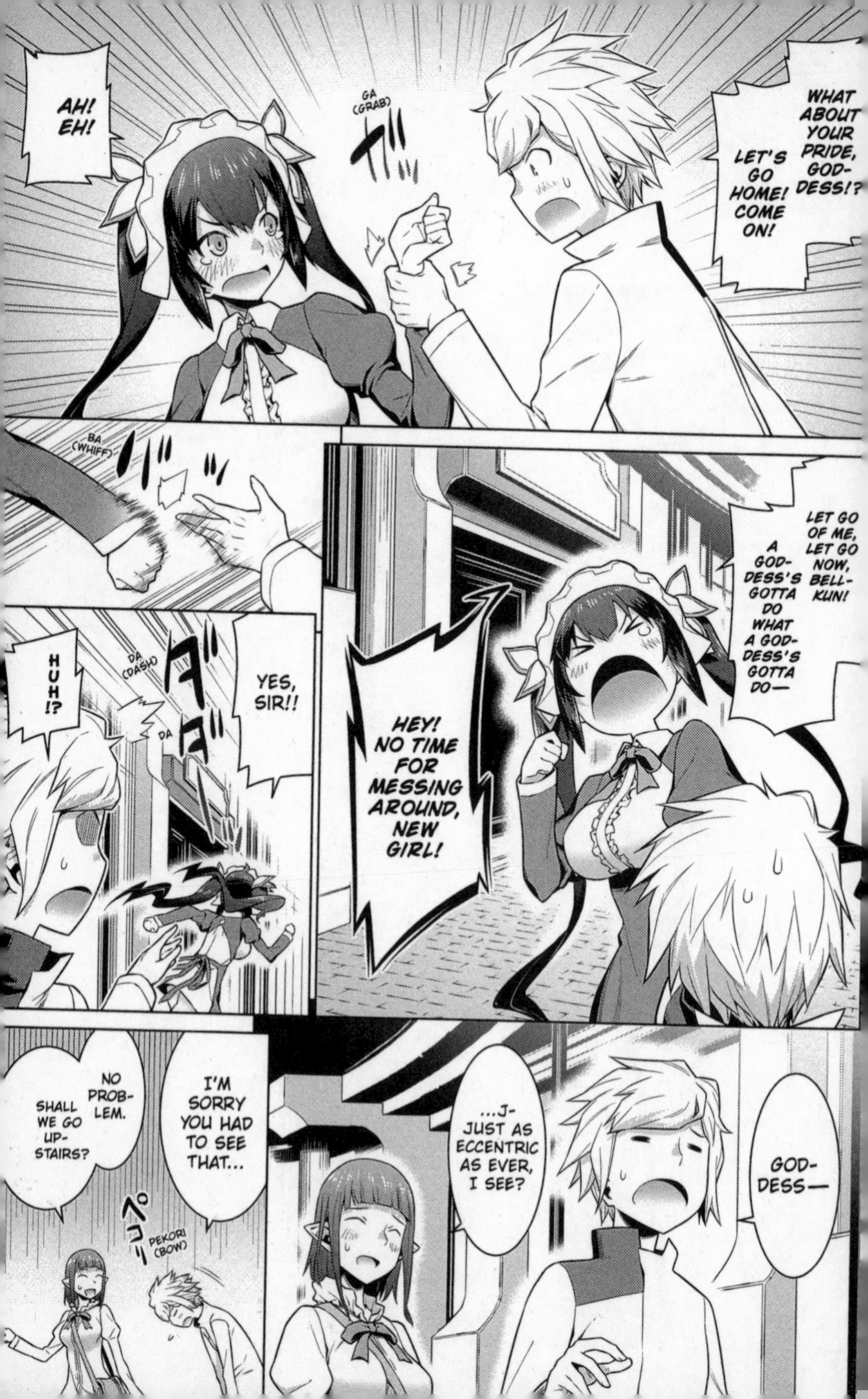
WHAT ABOUT YOUR PRIDE, GOD-DESS!?
LET'S GO HOME! COME ON!
GA (GRAB)
AH! EH!
BA (WHIFF)
LET GO OF ME, LET GO NOW, BELL-KUN!
A GOD-DESS'S GOTTA DO WHAT A GOD-DESS'S GOTTA DO—
HEY! NO TIME FOR MESSING AROUND, NEW GIRL!
YES, SIR!!
DA (DASH)
DA
HUH!?
GOD-DESS—
...J-JUST AS ECCENTRIC AS EVER, I SEE?
I'M SORRY YOU HAD TO SEE THAT...
NO PROB-LEM.
SHALL WE GO UP-STAIRS?
PEKORI (BOW)

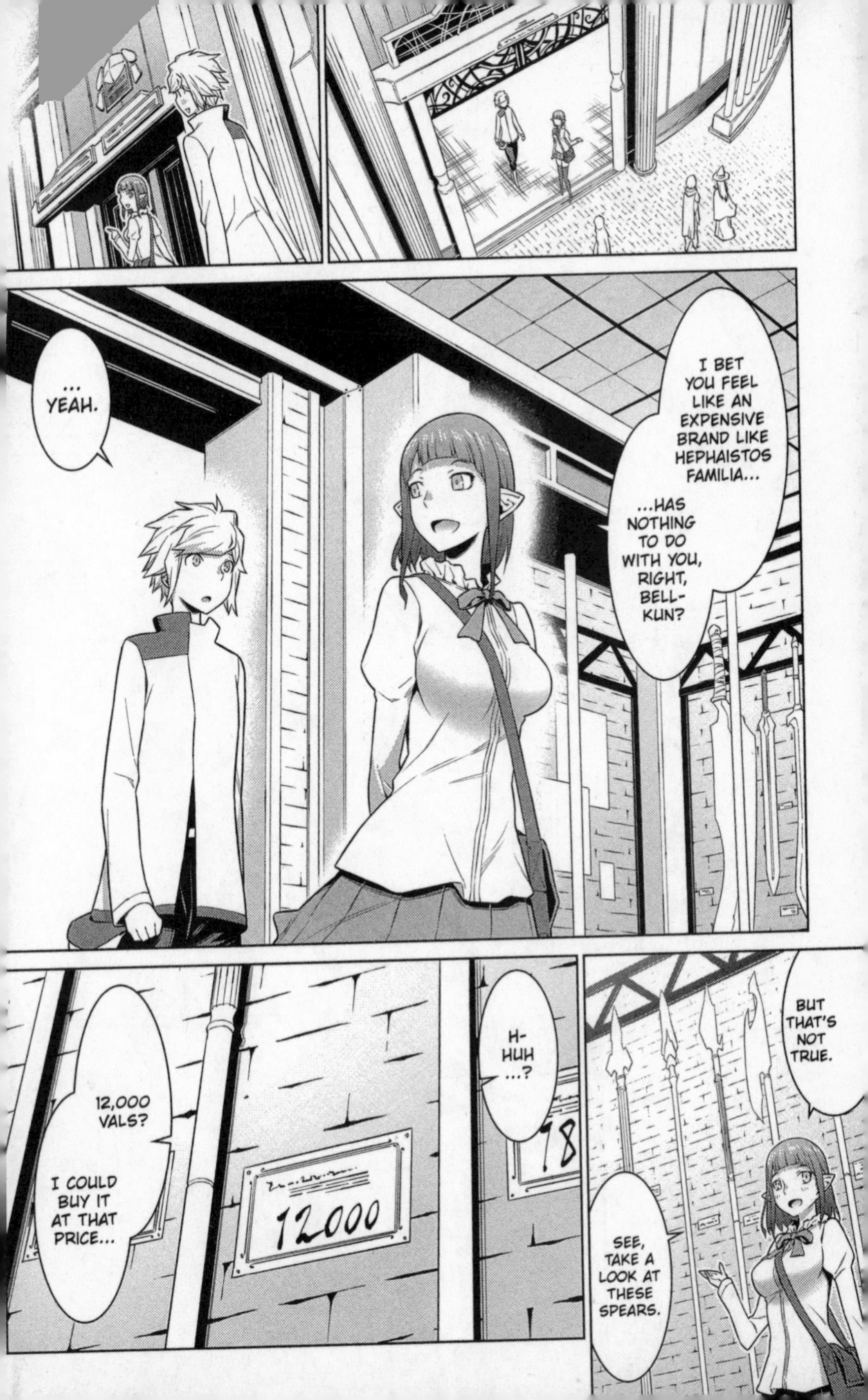
I BET YOU FEEL LIKE AN EXPENSIVE BRAND LIKE HEPHAISTOS FAMILIA...
...HAS NOTHING TO DO WITH YOU, RIGHT, BELL-KUN?
...YEAH.
BUT THAT'S NOT TRUE.
SEE, TAKE A LOOK AT THESE SPEARS.
H-HUH...?
12,000 VALS?
12000
I COULD BUY IT AT THAT PRICE...

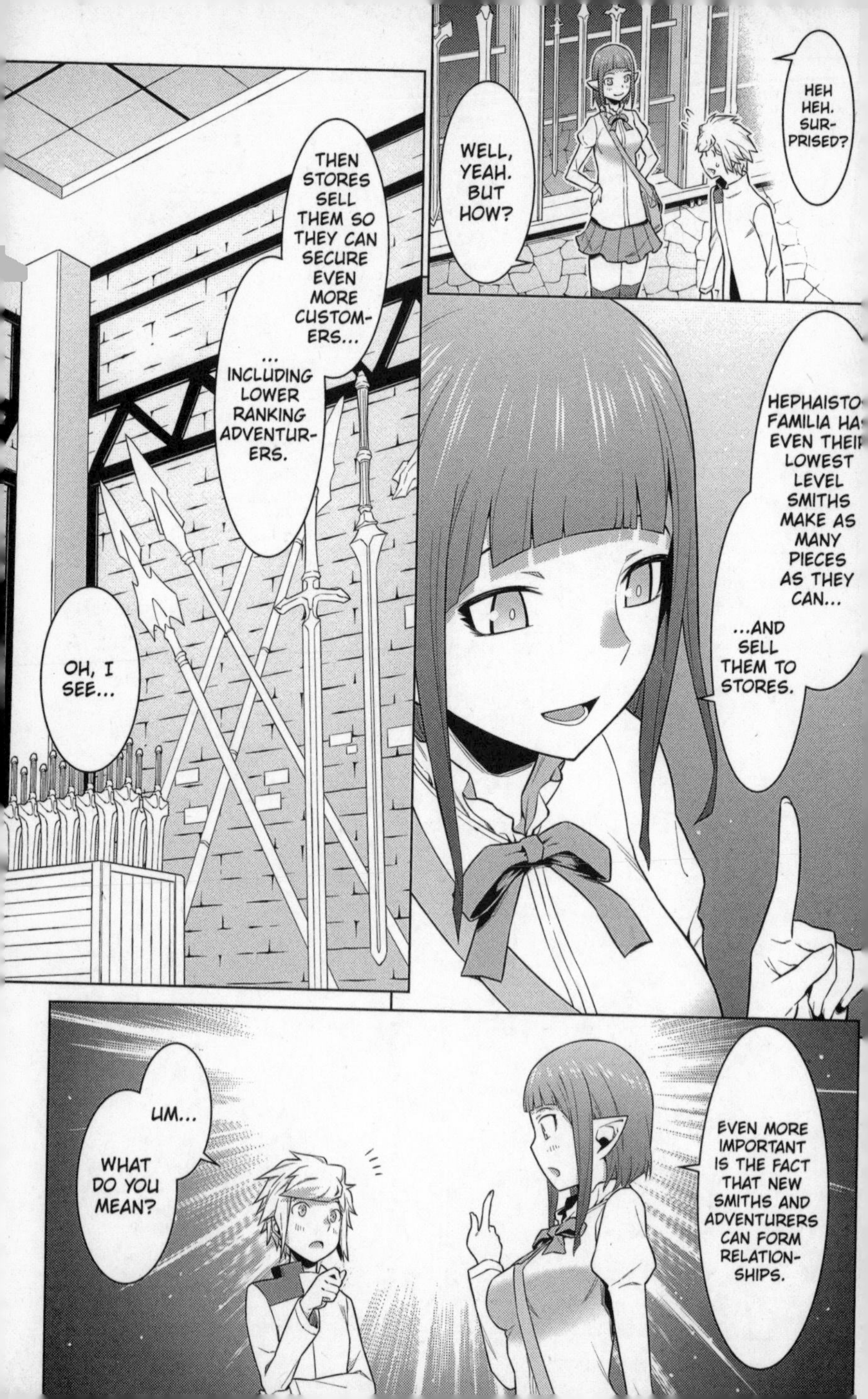
HEH HEH. SUR-PRISED?
WELL, YEAH. BUT HOW?
HEPHAISTO FAMILIA HA EVEN THEI LOWEST LEVEL SMITHS MAKE AS MANY PIECES AS THEY CAN...
...AND SELL THEM TO STORES.
THEN STORES SELL THEM SO THEY CAN SECURE EVEN MORE CUSTOM-ERS...
...INCLUDING LOWER RANKING ADVENTUR-ERS.
OH, I SEE...
EVEN MORE IMPORTANT IS THE FACT THAT NEW SMITHS AND ADVENTURERS CAN FORM RELATION-SHIPS.
UM...
WHAT DO YOU MEAN?

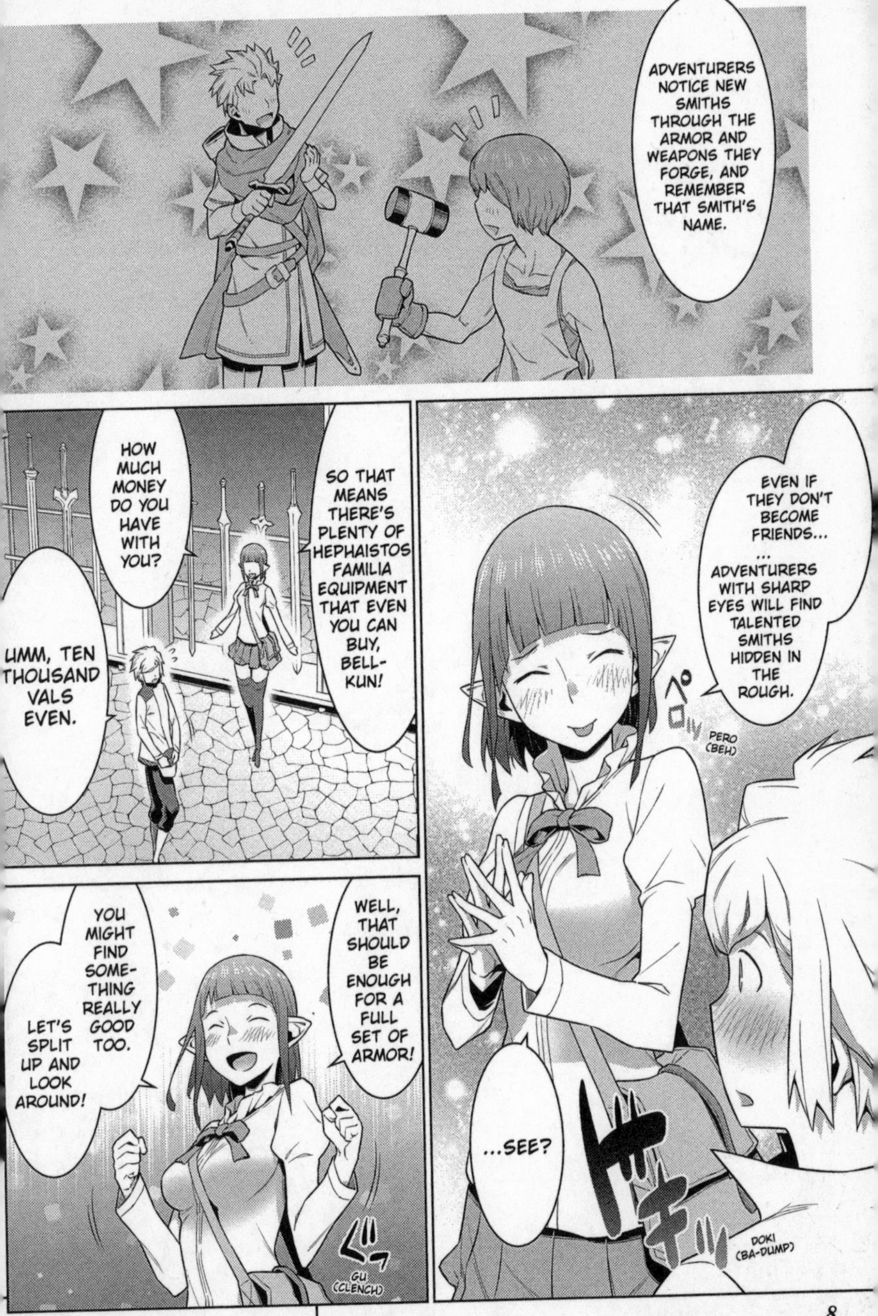
ADVENTURERS NOTICE NEW SMITHS THROUGH THE ARMOR AND WEAPONS THEY FORGE, AND REMEMBER THAT SMITH'S NAME.
EVEN IF THEY DON'T BECOME FRIENDS... ...ADVENTURERS WITH SHARP EYES WILL FIND TALENTED SMITHS HIDDEN IN THE ROUGH.
PERO (BEH)
...SEE?
DOKI (BA-DUMP)
SO THAT MEANS THERE'S PLENTY OF HEPHAISTOS FAMILIA EQUIPMENT THAT EVEN YOU CAN BUY, BELL-KUN!
HOW MUCH MONEY DO YOU HAVE WITH YOU?
UMM, TEN THOUSAND VALS EVEN.
WELL, THAT SHOULD BE ENOUGH FOR A FULL SET OF ARMOR!
YOU MIGHT FIND SOMETHING REALLY GOOD TOO.
LET'S SPLIT UP AND LOOK AROUND!
GU (CLENCH)

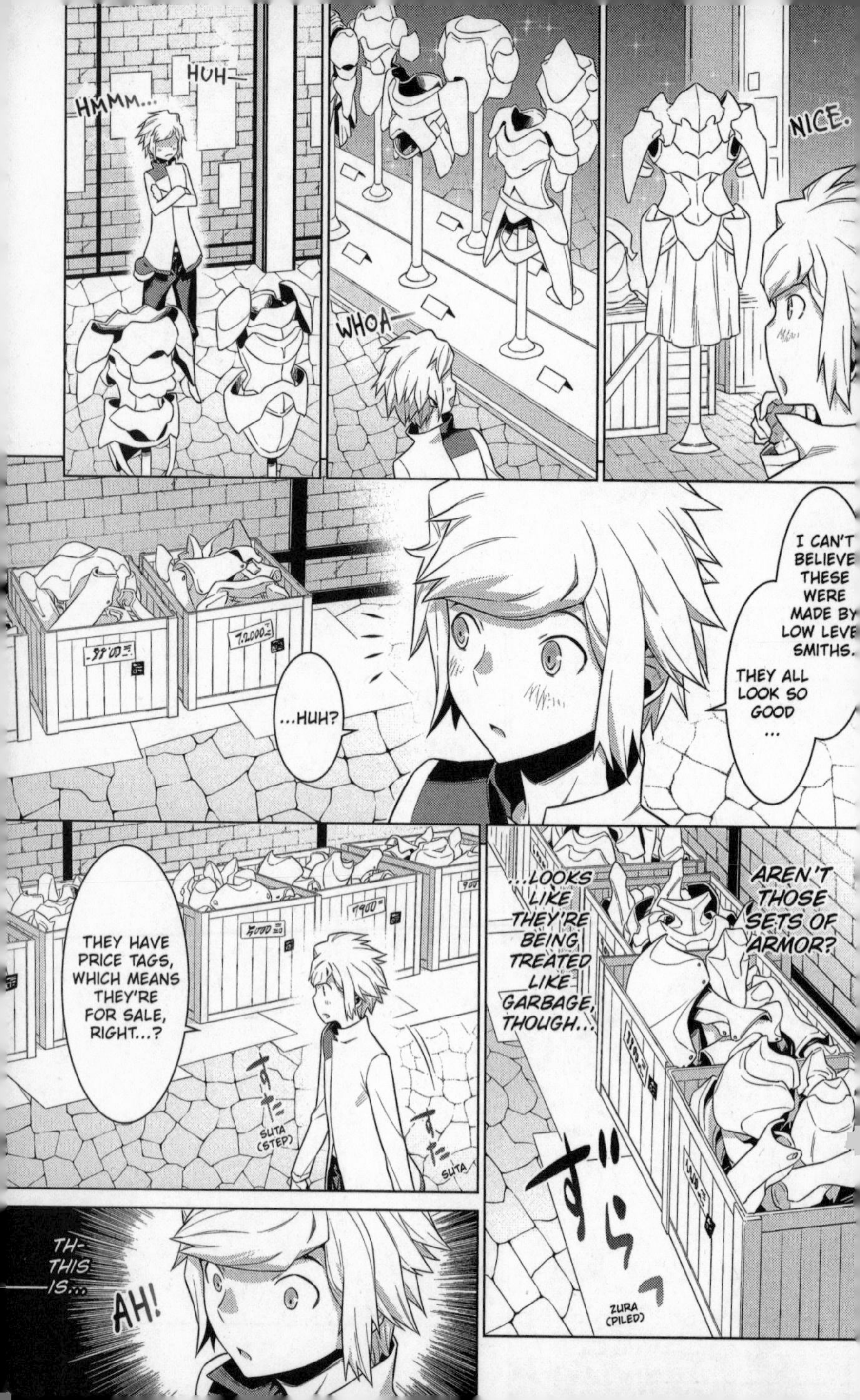
NICE.
WHOA
HUH
HMMM...
I CAN'T BELIEVE THESE WERE MADE BY LOW LEVE SMITHS.
THEY ALL LOOK SO GOOD ...
...HUH?
AREN'T THOSE SETS OF ARMOR?
...LOOKS LIKE THEY'RE BEING TREATED LIKE GARBAGE, THOUGH...
ZURA (PILED)
THEY HAVE PRICE TAGS, WHICH MEANS THEY'RE FOR SALE, RIGHT...?
SUTA (STEP)
SUTA
TH-THIS IS...
AH!

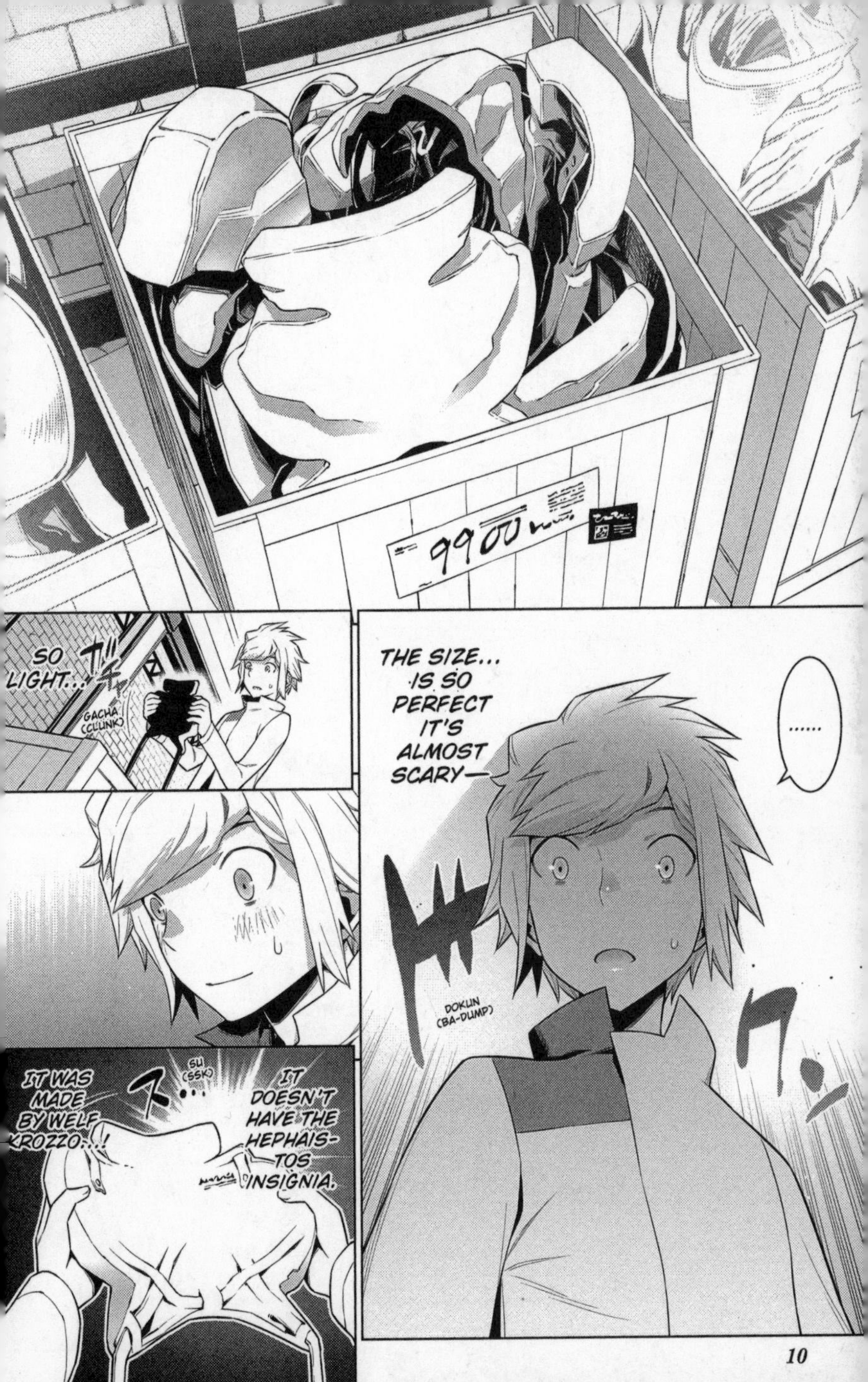
9900
THE SIZE... IS SO PERFECT IT'S ALMOST SCARY—
......
DOKUN (BA-DUMP)
SO LIGHT...
GACHA (CLUNK)
IT DOESN'T HAVE THE HEPHAIS-TOS INSIGNIA.
SU (SSK)
IT WAS MADE BY WELF KROZZO...!

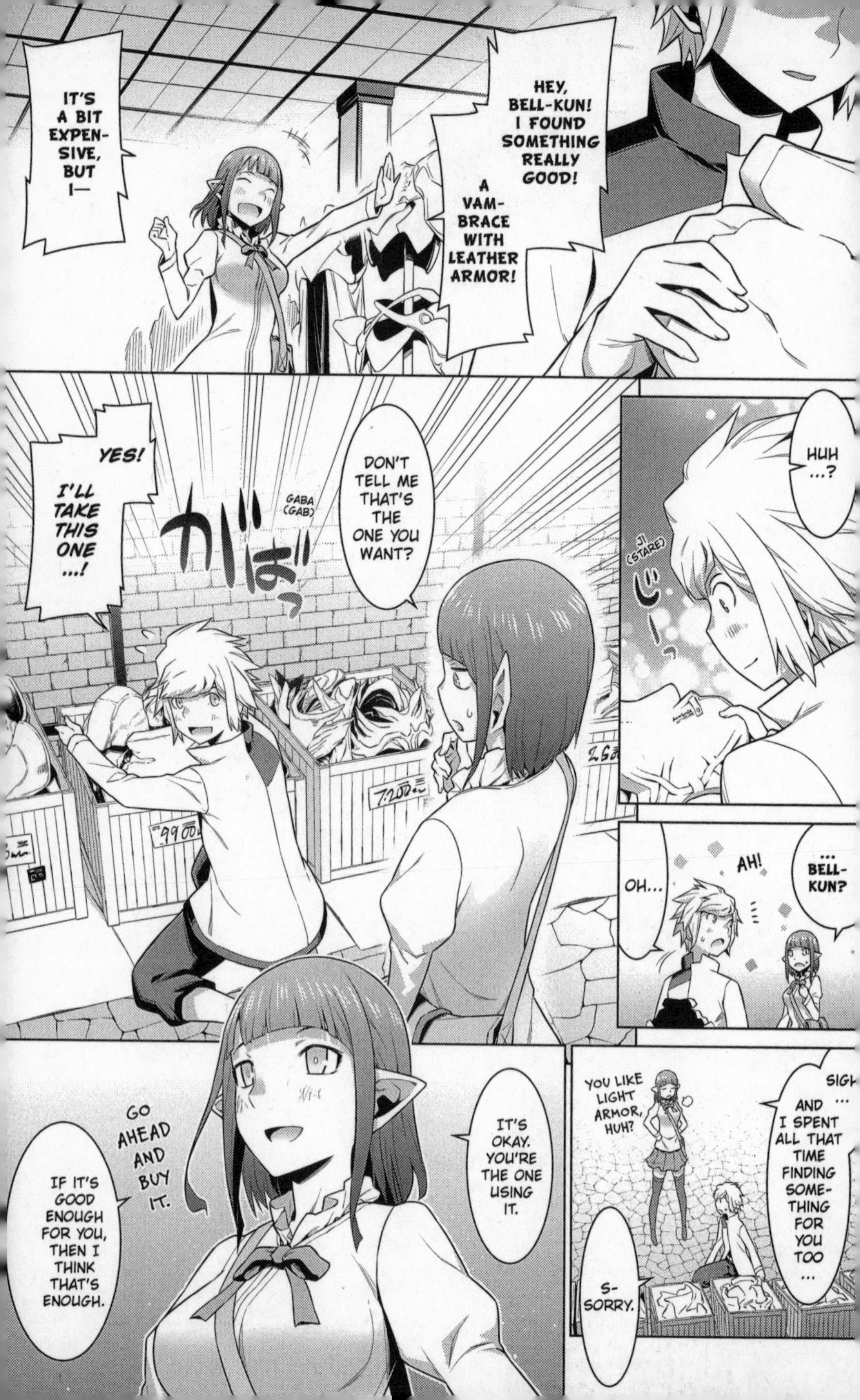
HEY, BELL-KUN! I FOUND SOMETHING REALLY GOOD!
A VAMBRACE WITH LEATHER ARMOR!
IT'S A BIT EXPENSIVE, BUT I—
HUH ...?
JI (STARE)
じーっ
... BELL-KUN?
AH!
OH...
DON'T TELL ME THAT'S THE ONE YOU WANT?
GABA (GAB)
がばっ
YES!
I'LL TAKE THIS ONE ...!
SIGH ...
AND I SPENT ALL THAT TIME FINDING SOMETHING FOR YOU TOO ...
YOU LIKE LIGHT ARMOR, HUH?
S-SORRY.
IT'S OKAY. YOU'RE THE ONE USING IT.
GO AHEAD AND BUY IT.
IF IT'S GOOD ENOUGH FOR YOU, THEN I THINK THAT'S ENOUGH.

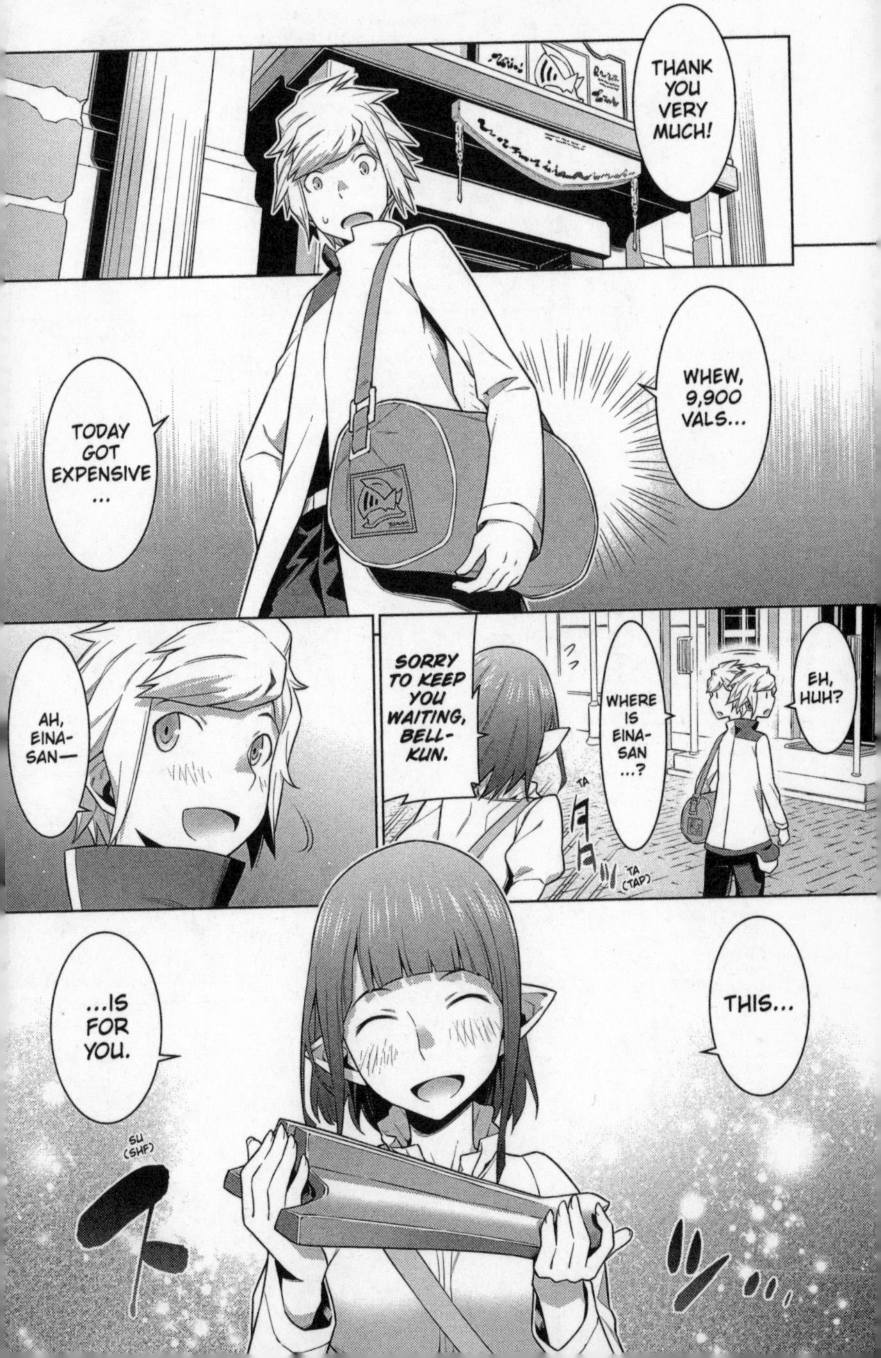
THANK YOU VERY MUCH!
WHEW, 9,900 VALS...
TODAY GOT EXPENSIVE ...
EH, HUH?
WHERE IS EINA-SAN ...?
TA
TA (TAP)
SORRY TO KEEP YOU WAITING, BELL-KUN.
AH, EINA-SAN—
THIS...
...IS FOR YOU.
SU (SHF)

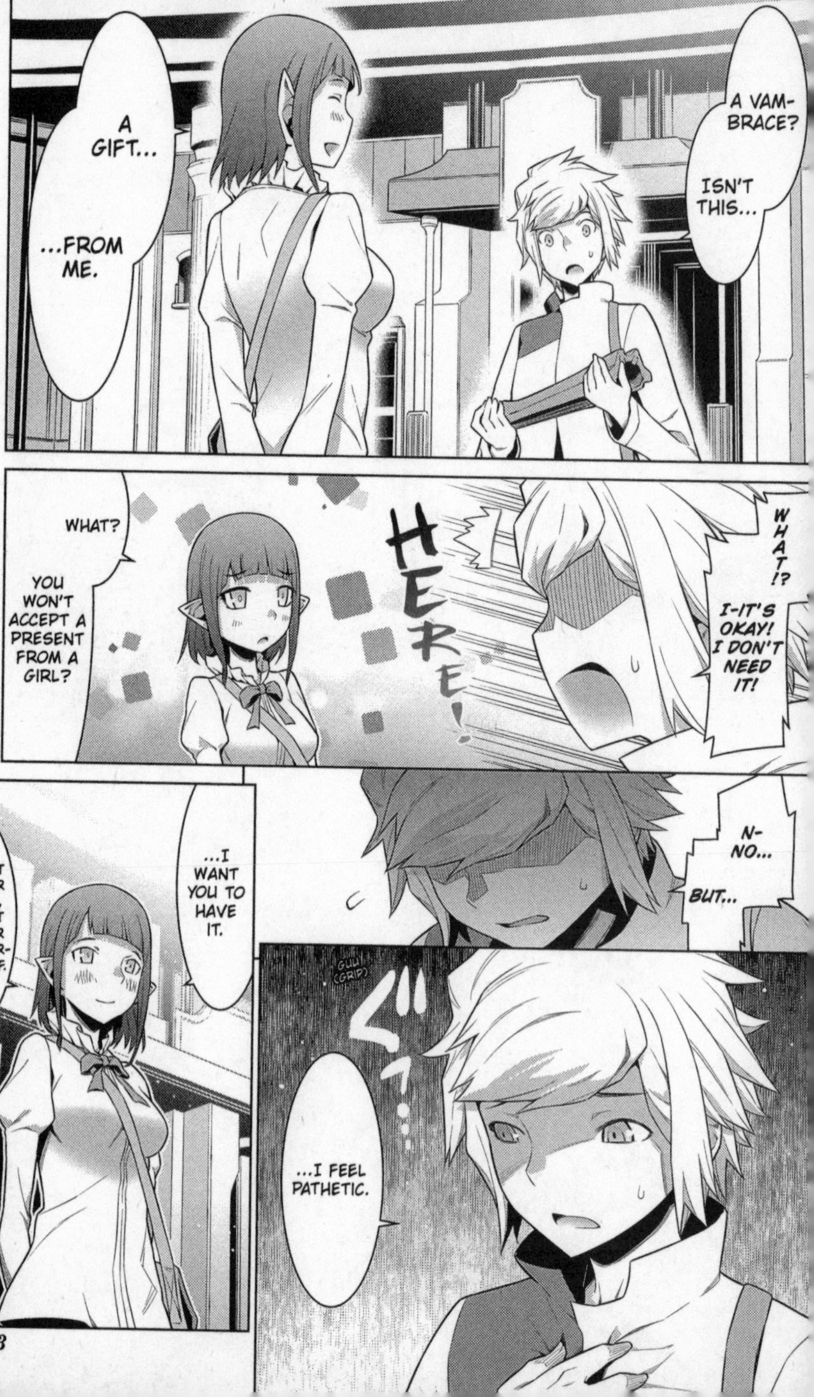
A VAM-BRACE?
ISN'T THIS...
A GIFT...
...FROM ME.
WHAT!?
I-IT'S OKAY! I DON'T NEED IT!
HERE!
WHAT?
YOU WON'T ACCEPT A PRESENT FROM A GIRL?
N-NO...
BUT...
GUU (GRIP)
...I FEEL PATHETIC.
...I WANT YOU TO HAVE IT.
NOT FOR ME, BUT FOR YOUR-SELF.

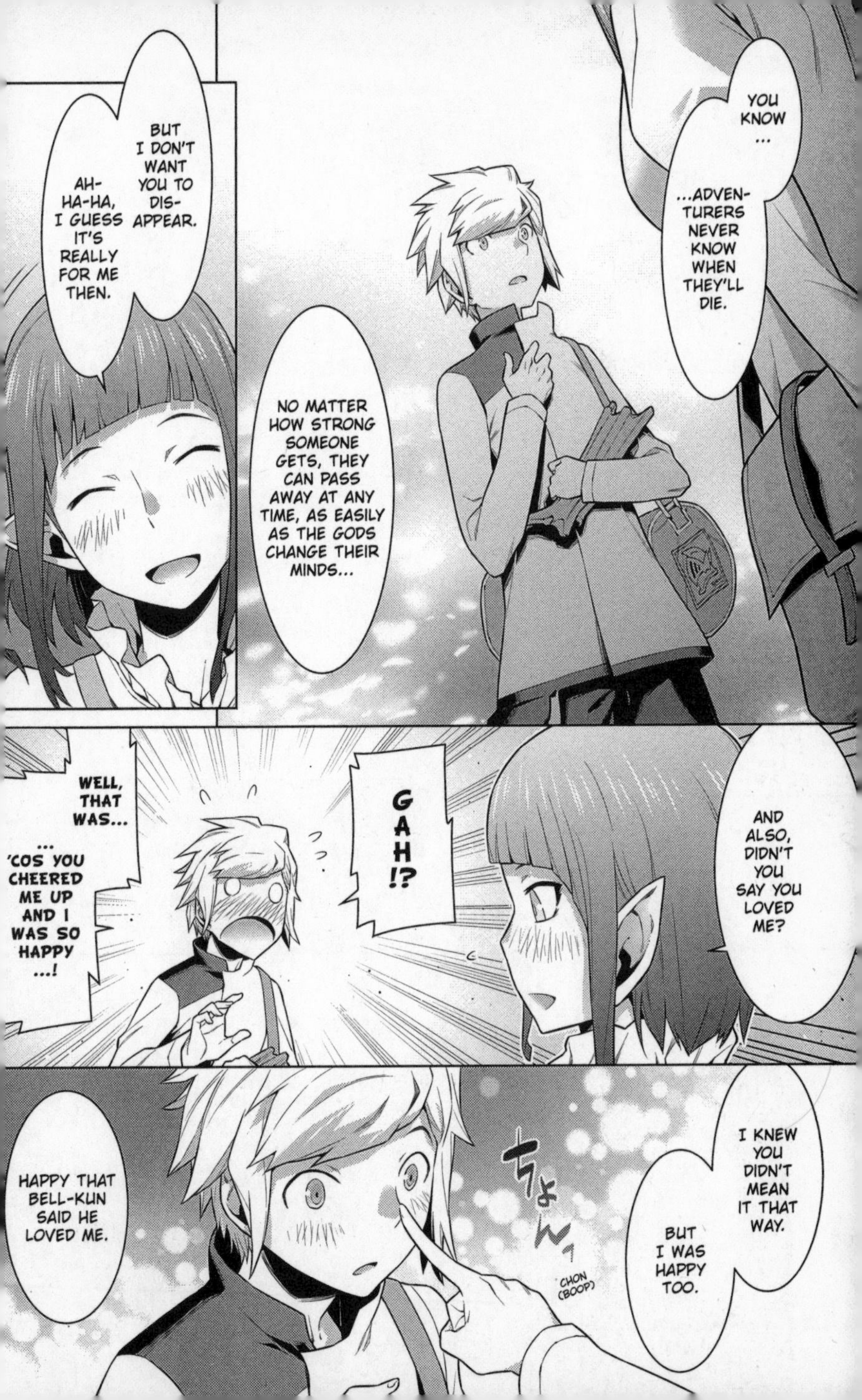
YOU KNOW ...
...ADVENTURERS NEVER KNOW WHEN THEY'LL DIE.
NO MATTER HOW STRONG SOMEONE GETS, THEY CAN PASS AWAY AT ANY TIME, AS EASILY AS THE GODS CHANGE THEIR MINDS...
BUT I DON'T WANT YOU TO DISAPPEAR.
AH-HA-HA, I GUESS IT'S REALLY FOR ME THEN.
AND ALSO, DIDN'T YOU SAY YOU LOVED ME?
GAH!?
WELL, THAT WAS...
...'COS YOU CHEERED ME UP AND I WAS SO HAPPY ...!
I KNEW YOU DIDN'T MEAN IT THAT WAY.
BUT I WAS HAPPY TOO.
ちょん
CHON (BOOP)
HAPPY THAT BELL-KUN SAID HE LOVED ME.

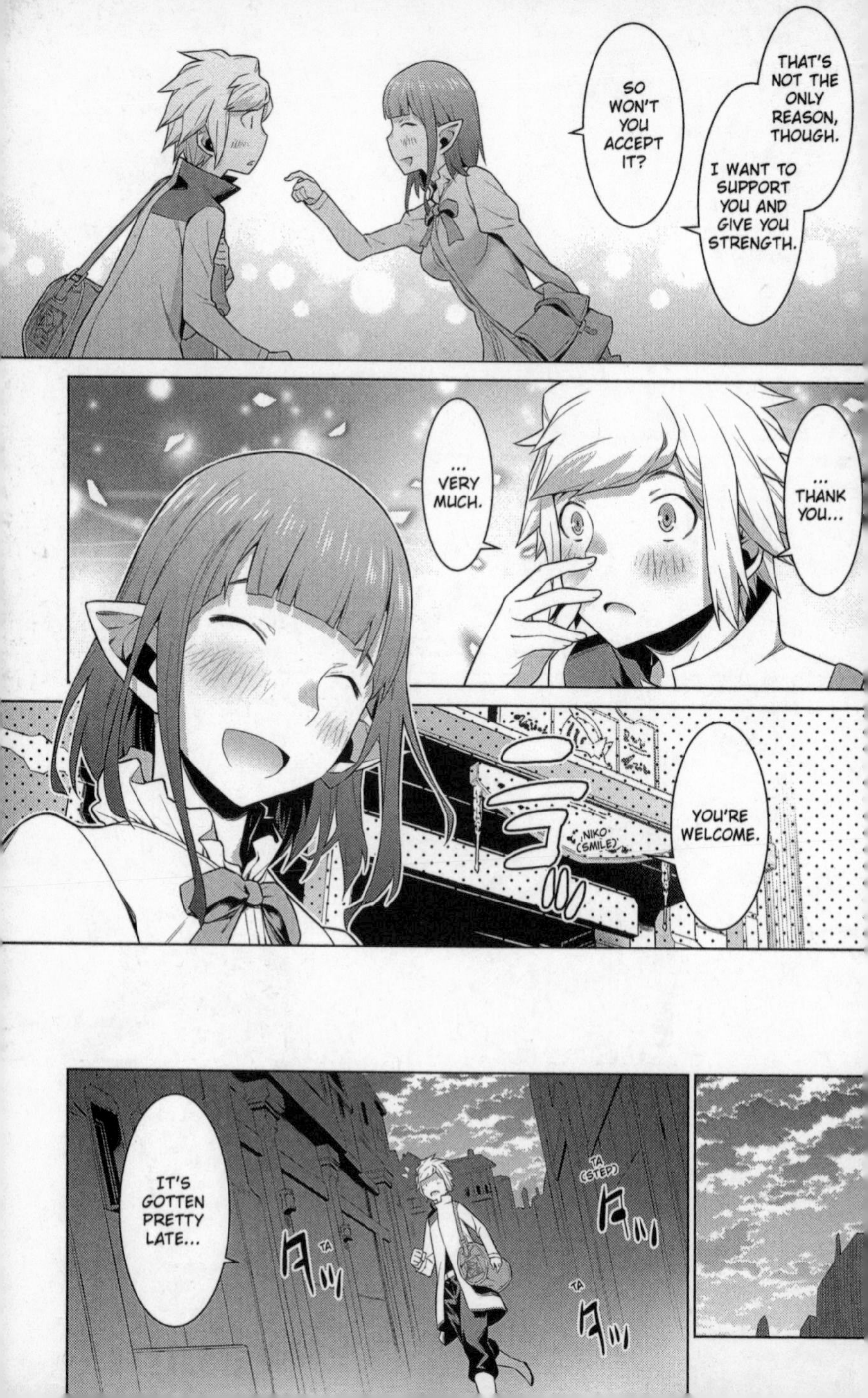
THAT'S NOT THE ONLY REASON, THOUGH.
I WANT TO SUPPORT YOU AND GIVE YOU STRENGTH.
SO WON'T YOU ACCEPT IT?
...THANK YOU...
...VERY MUCH.
YOU'RE WELCOME.
NIKO (SMILE)
TA (STEP)
TA
IT'S GOTTEN PRETTY LATE...
TA

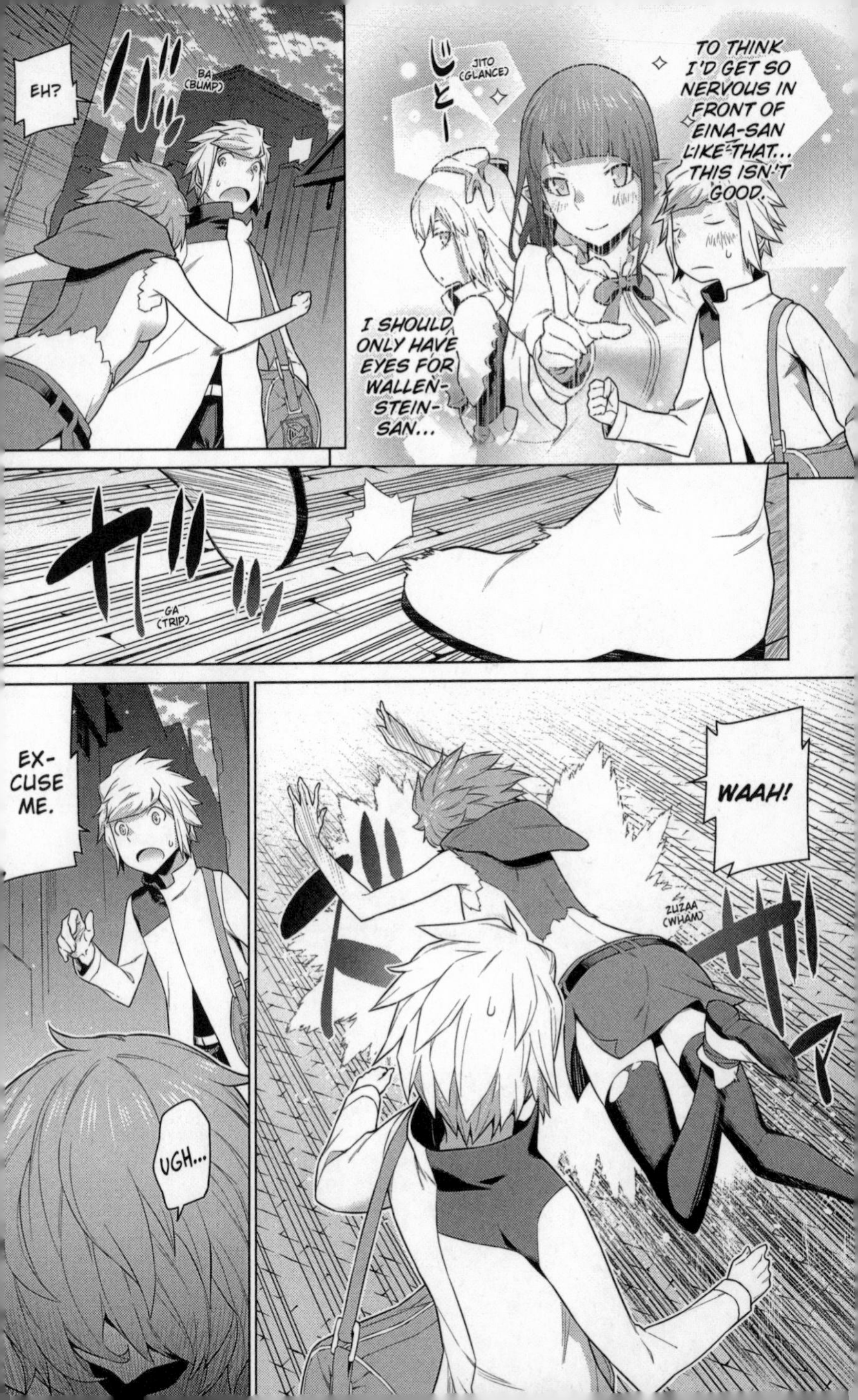

TO THINK I'D GET SO NERVOUS IN FRONT OF EINA-SAN LIKE THAT... THIS ISN'T GOOD.
JITO (GLANCE)
I SHOULD ONLY HAVE EYES FOR WALLEN-STEIN-SAN...
BA (BUMP)
EH?
GA (TRIP)
WAAH!
ZUZAA (WHAM)
EX-CUSE ME.
UGH...

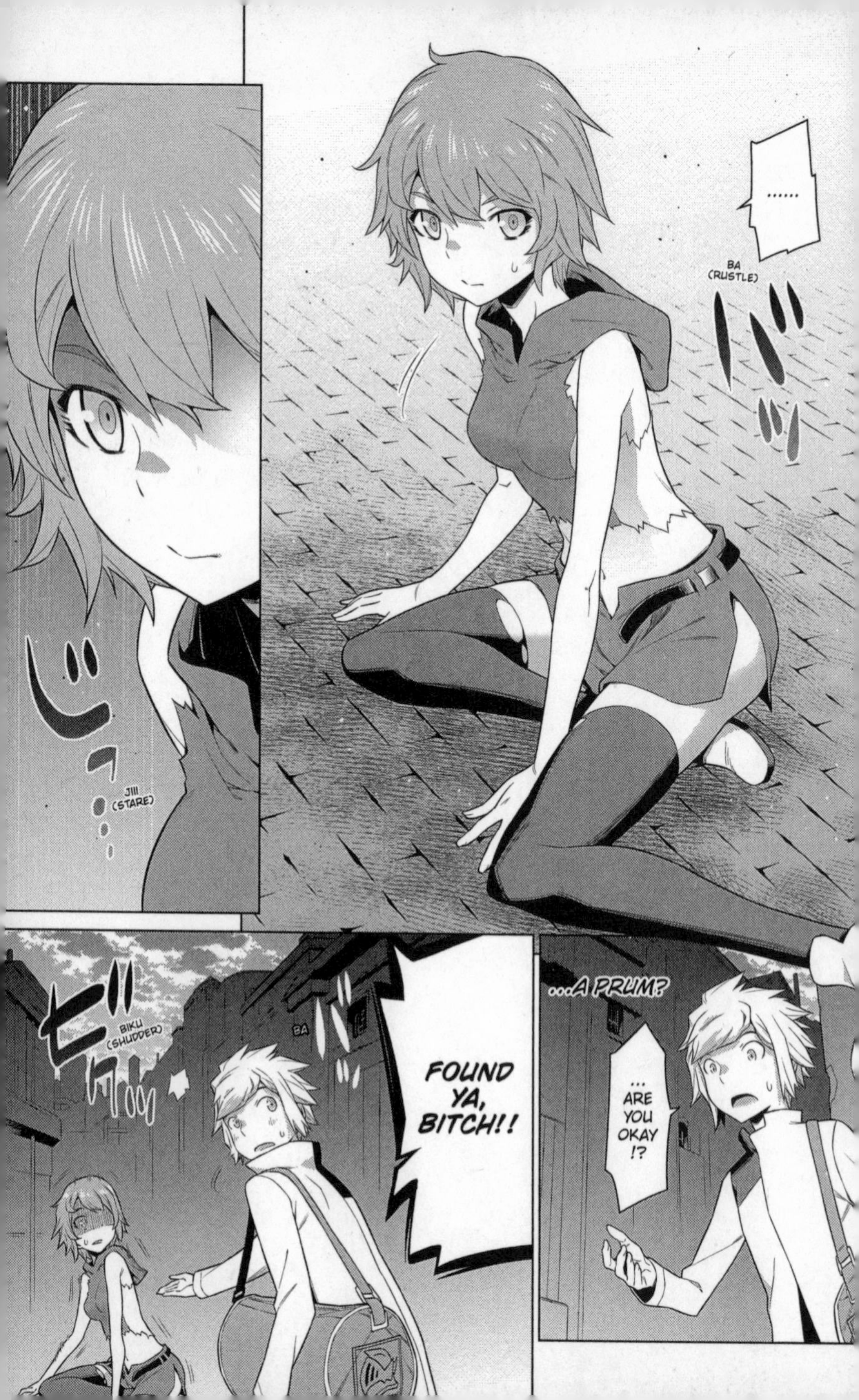
......
BA (RUSTLE)
JIII (STARE)
...A PRUM?
...ARE YOU OKAY!?
FOUND YA, BITCH!!
BA
BIKU (SHUDDER)

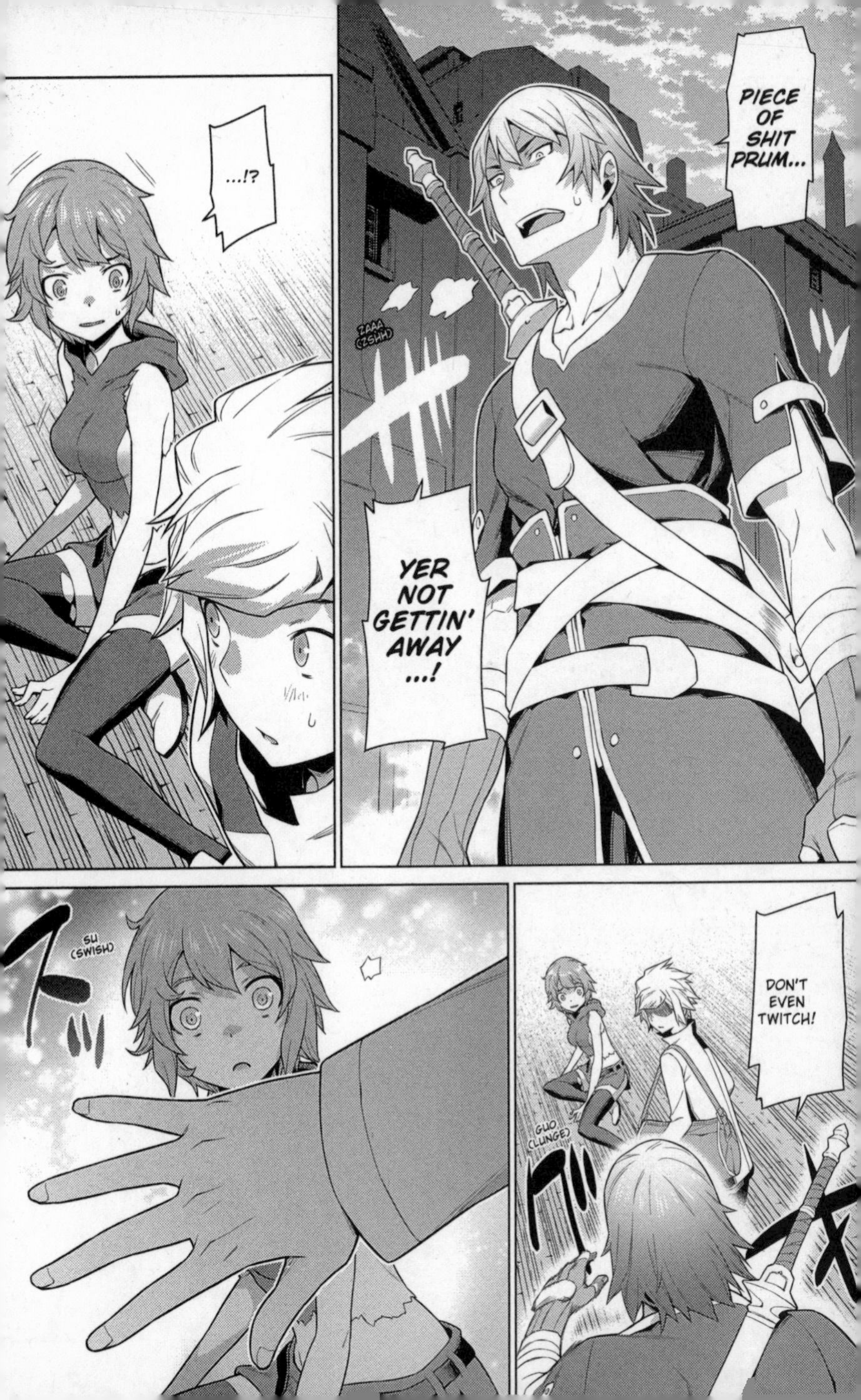
PIECE OF SHIT PRUM...
ZAAA (ZSHH)
YER NOT GETTIN' AWAY ...!
...!?
DON'T EVEN TWITCH!
GUO (LUNGE)
SU (SWISH)

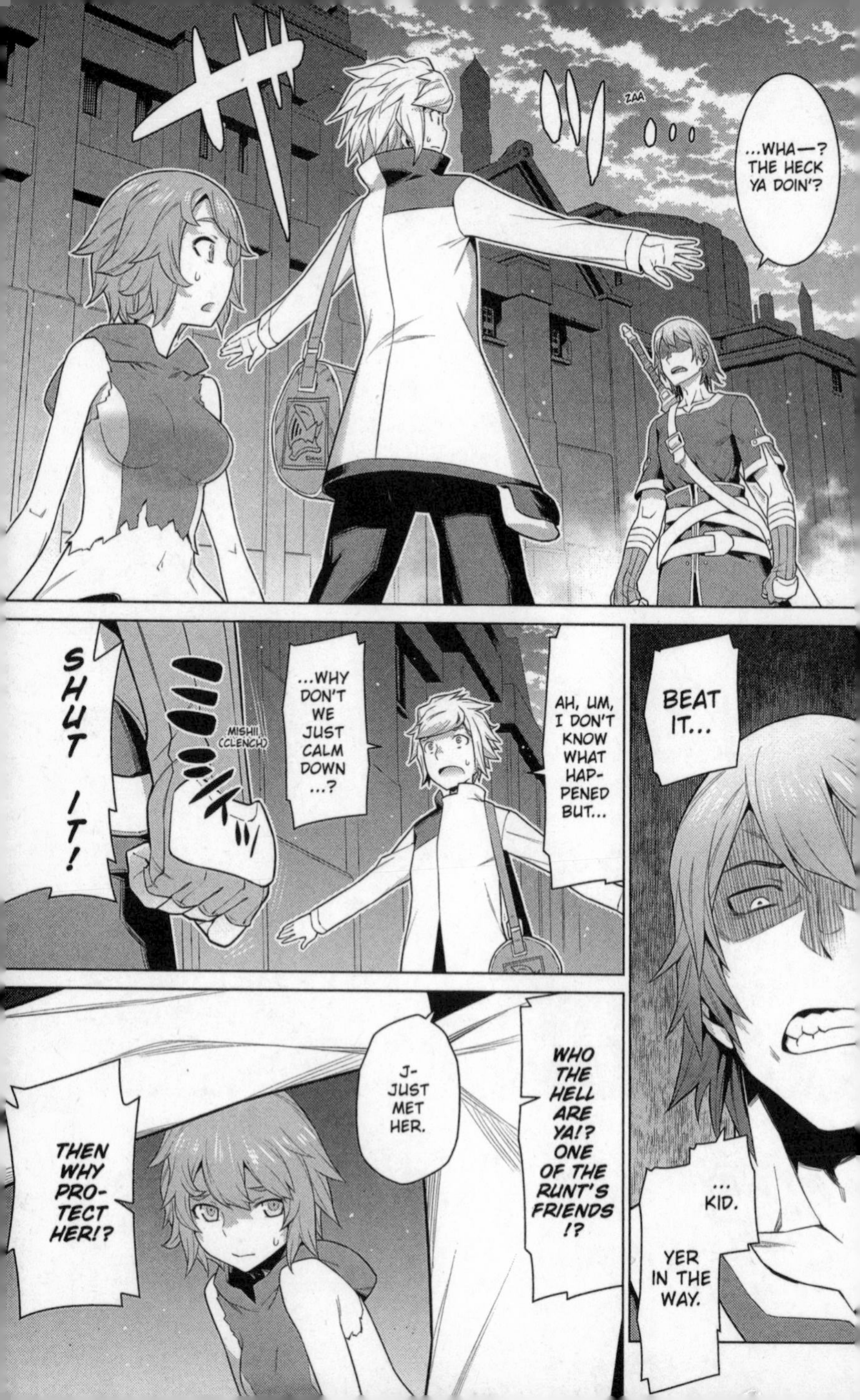
ZAA
...WHA—? THE HECK YA DOIN'?
BEAT IT...
... KID.
YER IN THE WAY.
AH, UM, I DON'T KNOW WHAT HAP-PENED BUT...
...WHY DON'T WE JUST CALM DOWN ...?
MISHI! (CLENCH)
SHUT IT!
WHO THE HELL ARE YA!? ONE OF THE RUNT'S FRIENDS !?
J-JUST MET HER.
THEN WHY PROTECT HER!?

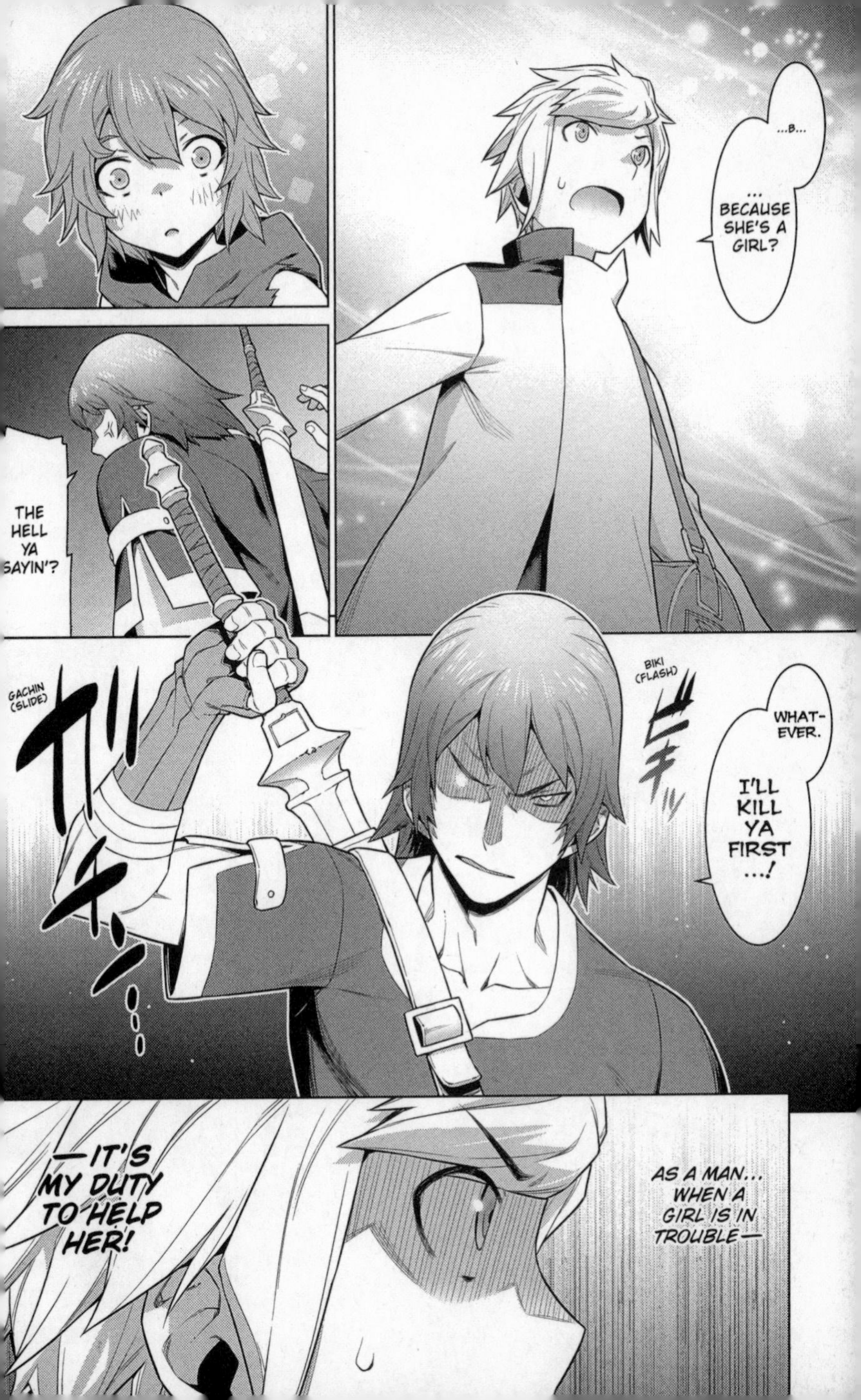
...B...
...BECAUSE SHE'S A GIRL?
THE HELL YA SAYIN'?
WHAT-EVER.
I'LL KILL YA FIRST ...!
BIKI (FLASH)
GACHIN (SLIDE)
AS A MAN... WHEN A GIRL IS IN TROUBLE—
—IT'S MY DUTY TO HELP HER!

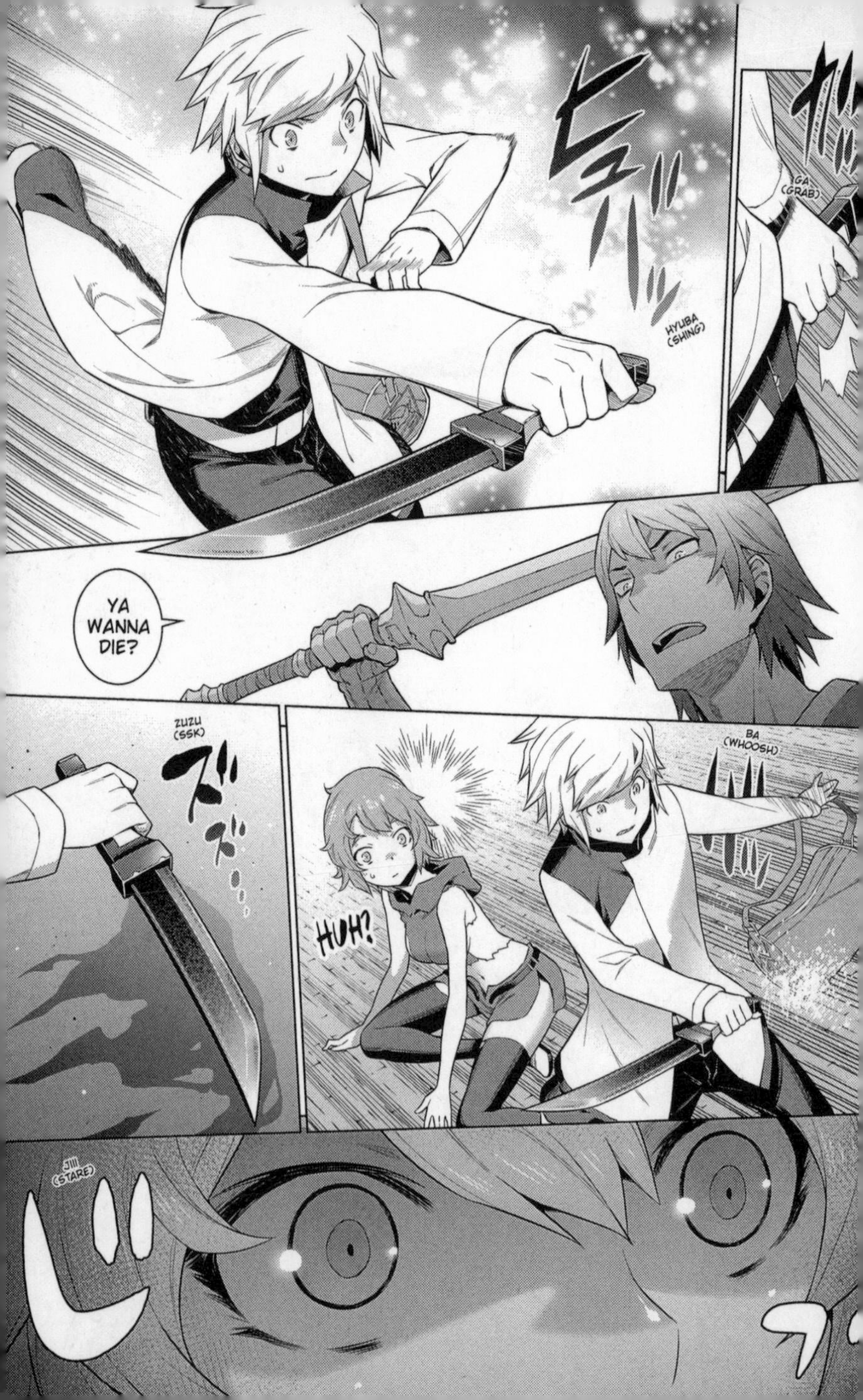
GA
(GRAB)
HYUBA
(SHING)
YA WANNA DIE?
BA
(WHOOSH)
HUH?
ZUZU
(SSK)
JIII
(STARE)

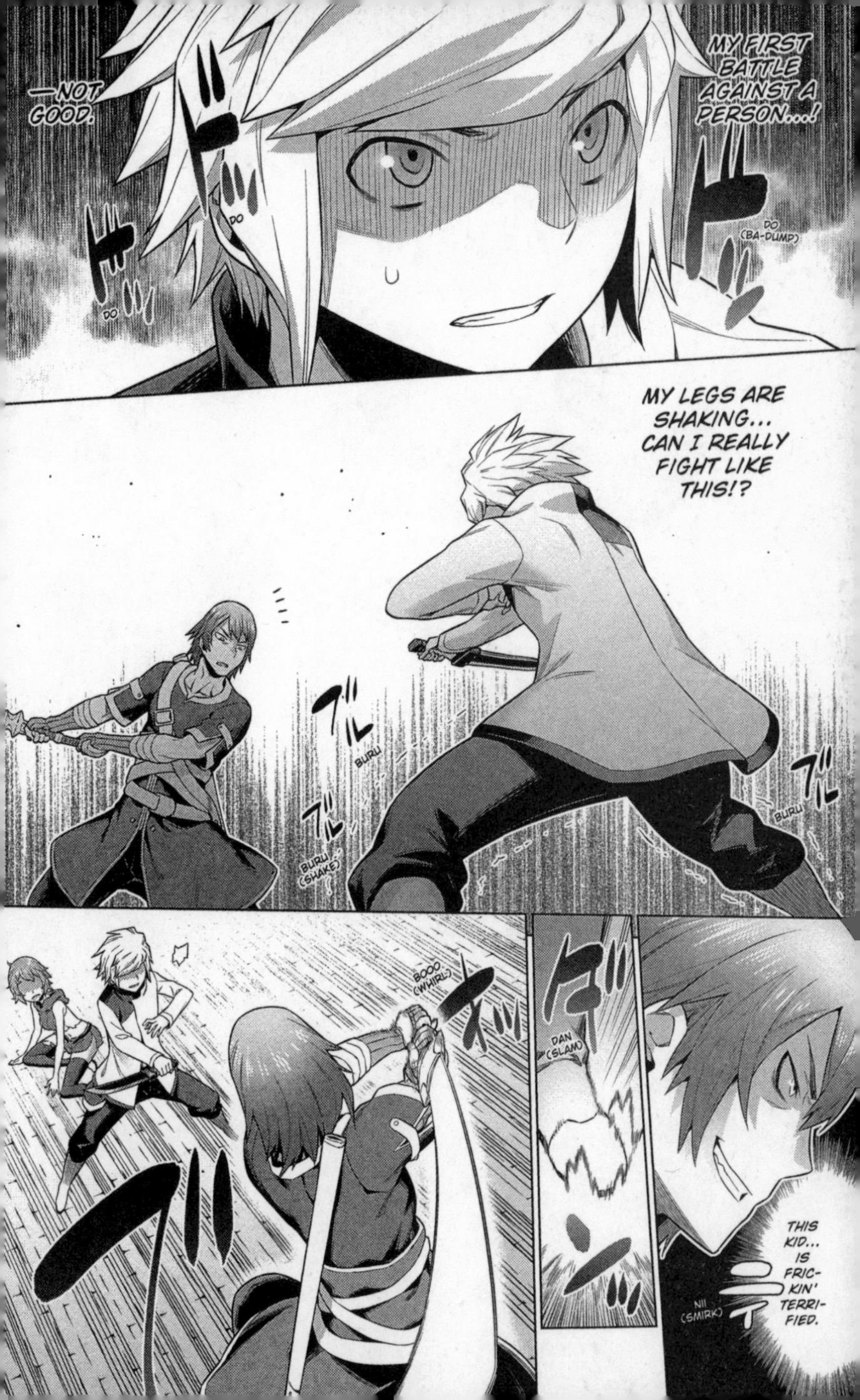
MY FIRST BATTLE AGAINST A PERSON...!
DO (BA-DUMP)
DO
DO
—NOT GOOD.
MY LEGS ARE SHAKING... CAN I REALLY FIGHT LIKE THIS!?
BURU
BURU
BURU (SHAKE)
THIS KID... IS FRIC-KIN' TERRI-FIED.
NII (SMIRK)
DAN (SLAM)
BOOO (WHIRL)

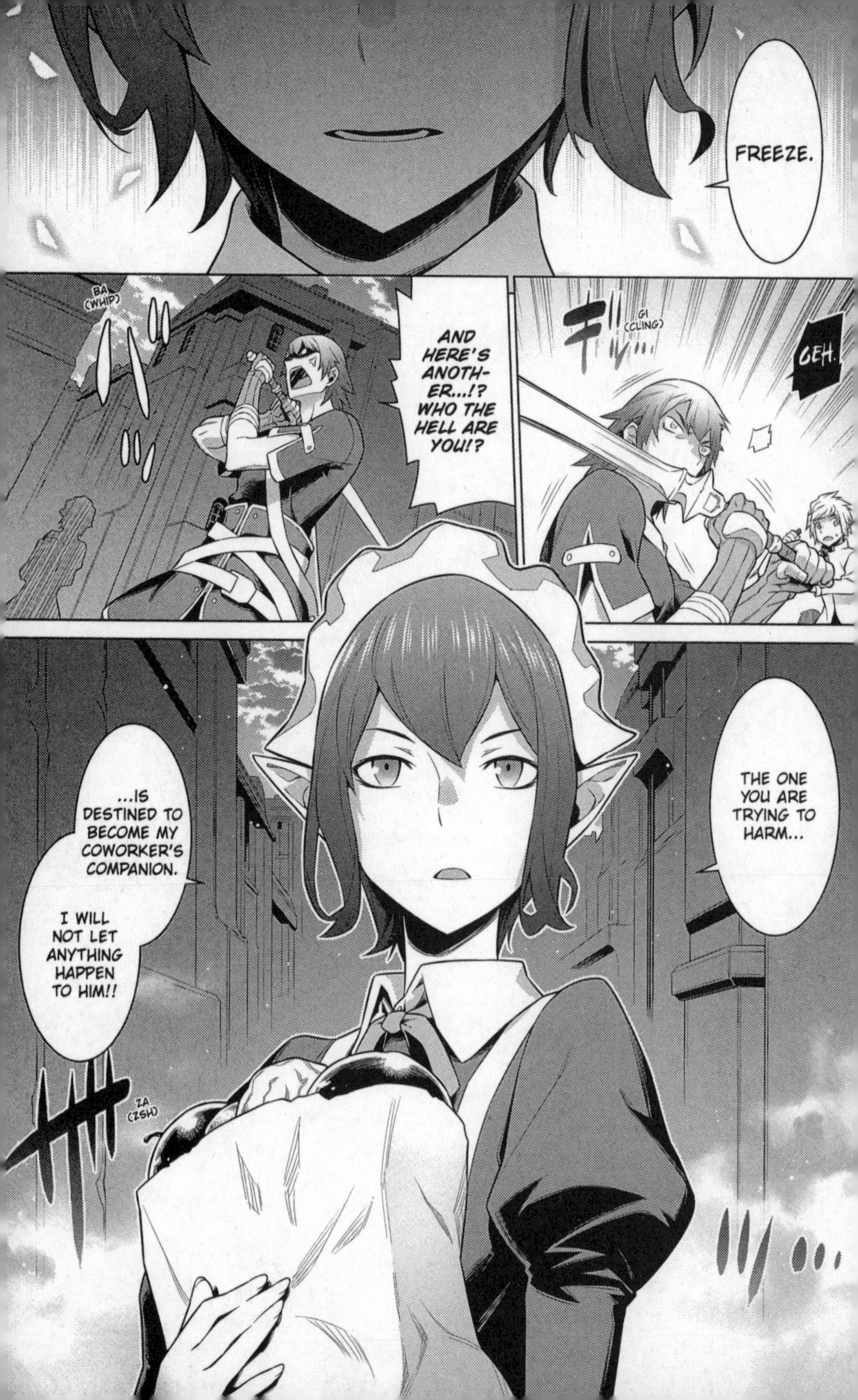
FREEZE.
GI
(CLING)
GEH.
BA
(WHIP)
AND HERE'S ANOTHER...!? WHO THE HELL ARE YOU!?
THE ONE YOU ARE TRYING TO HARM...
...IS DESTINED TO BECOME MY COWORKER'S COMPANION.
I WILL NOT LET ANYTHING HAPPEN TO HIM!!
ZA
(ZSH)

IS it WRONG to TRY to PiCK-UP GIRLS iN A DUNGEON?

STEP 16 ▶▶ THE SUPPORTER'S SITUATION

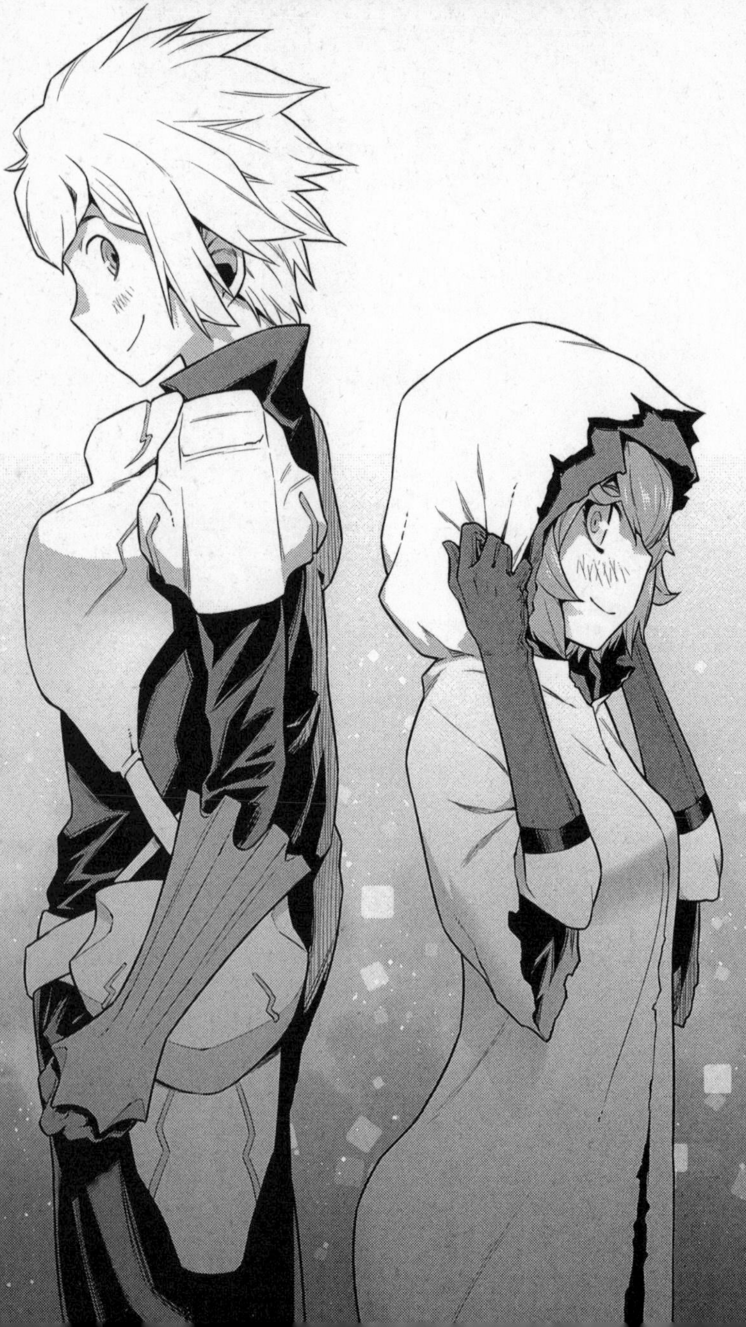

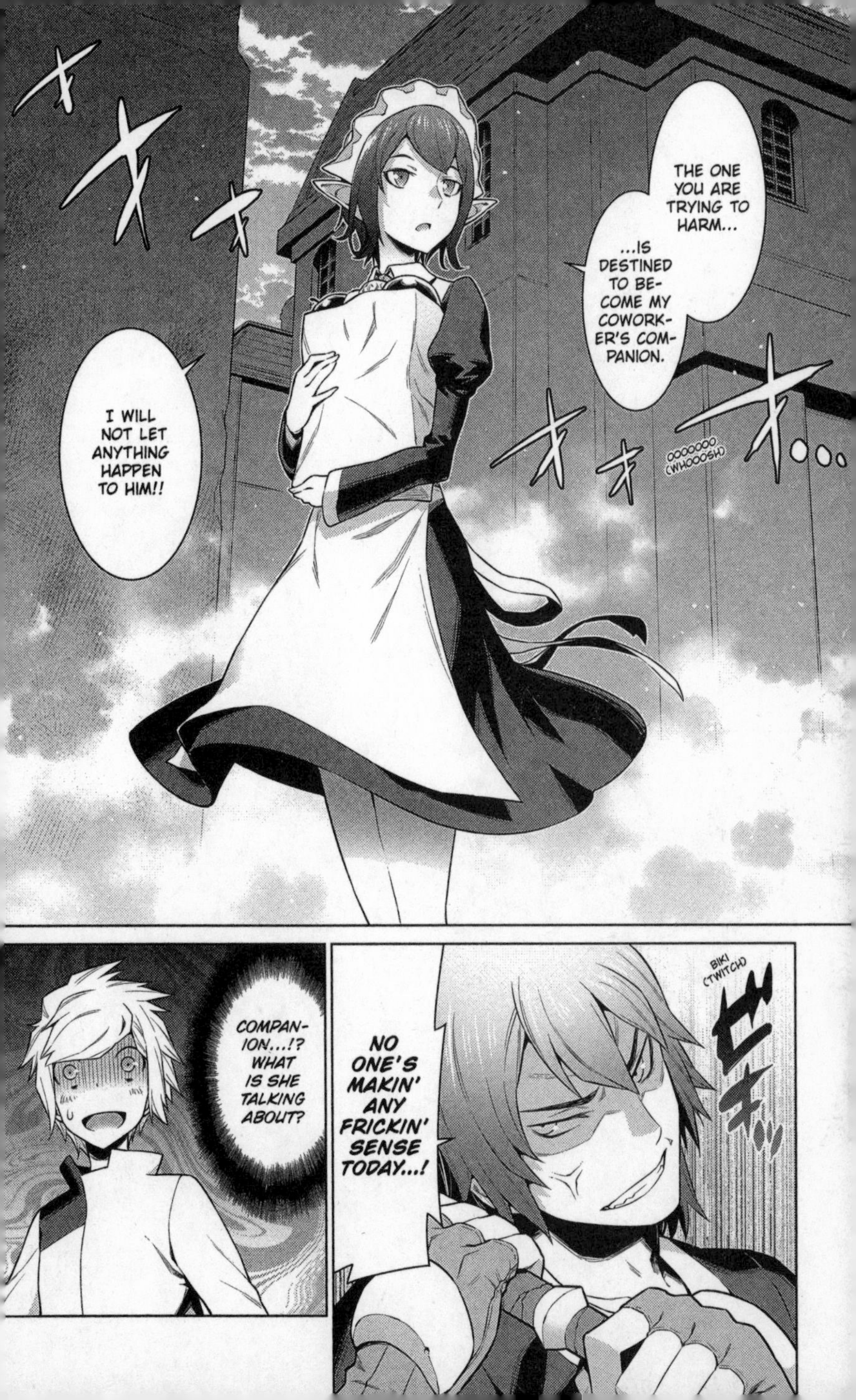
THE ONE YOU ARE TRYING TO HARM...
...IS DESTINED TO BE-COME MY COWORK-ER'S COM-PANION.
OOOOOOO (WHOOOSH)
I WILL NOT LET ANYTHING HAPPEN TO HIM!!
BIKI (TWITCH)
NO ONE'S MAKIN' ANY FRICKIN' SENSE TODAY...!
COMPAN-ION...!? WHAT IS SHE TALKING ABOUT?

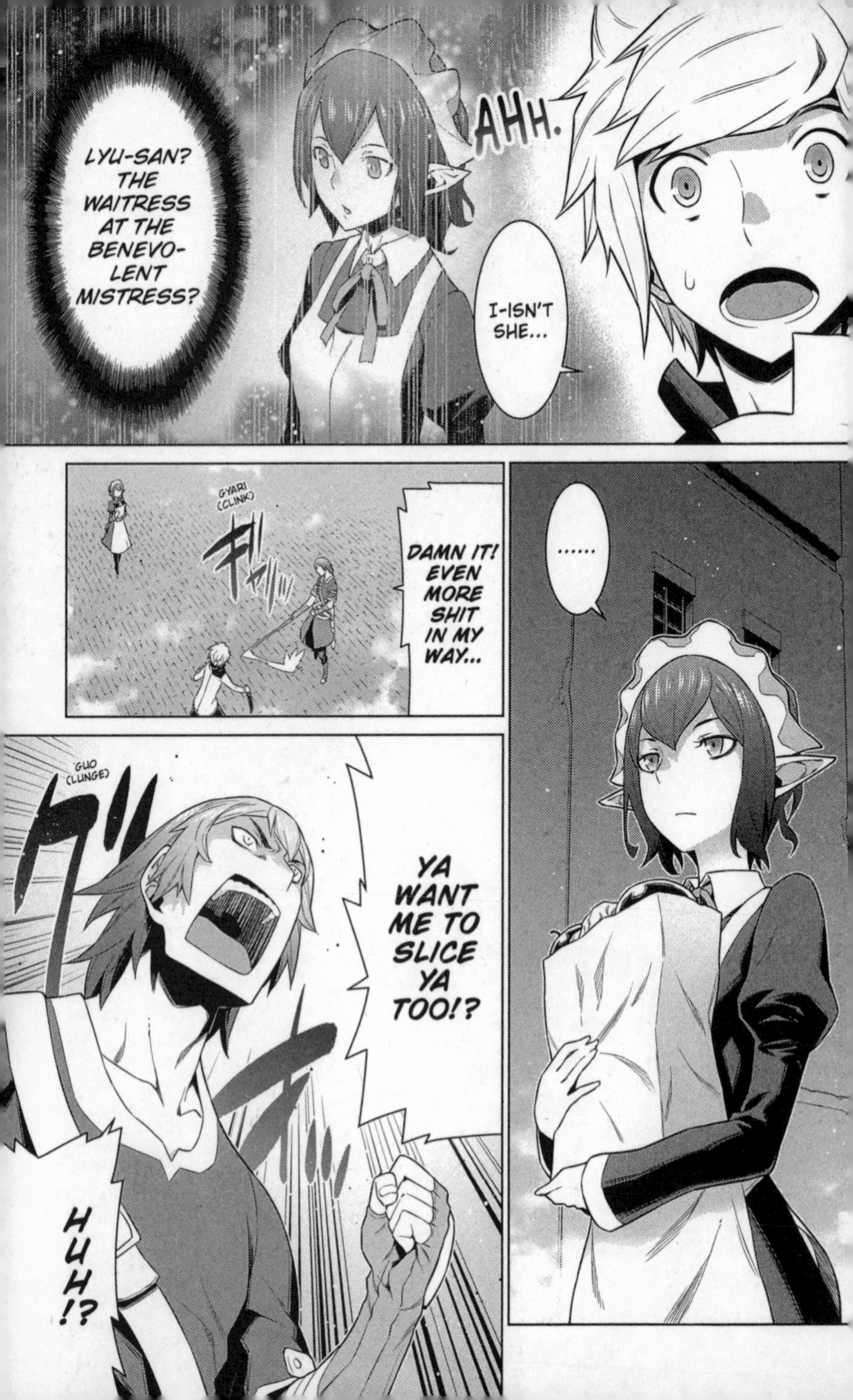
AHH.
I-ISN'T SHE...
LYU-SAN? THE WAITRESS AT THE BENEVOLENT MISTRESS?
......
DAMN IT! EVEN MORE SHIT IN MY WAY...
GYARI (CLINK)
YA WANT ME TO SLICE YA TOO!?
GUO (LUNGE)
HUH!?

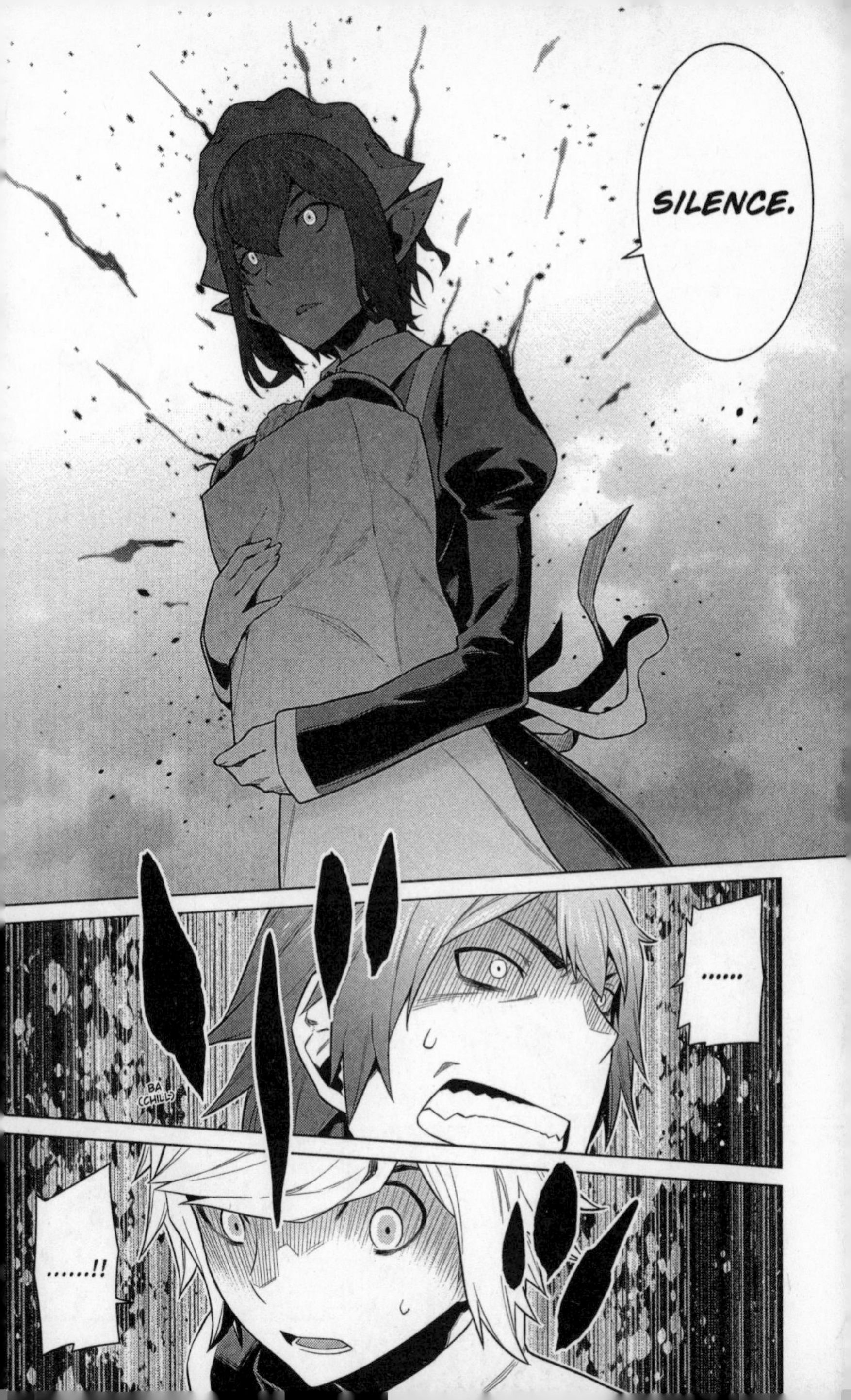
SILENCE.
......
BA (CHILL)
......!!

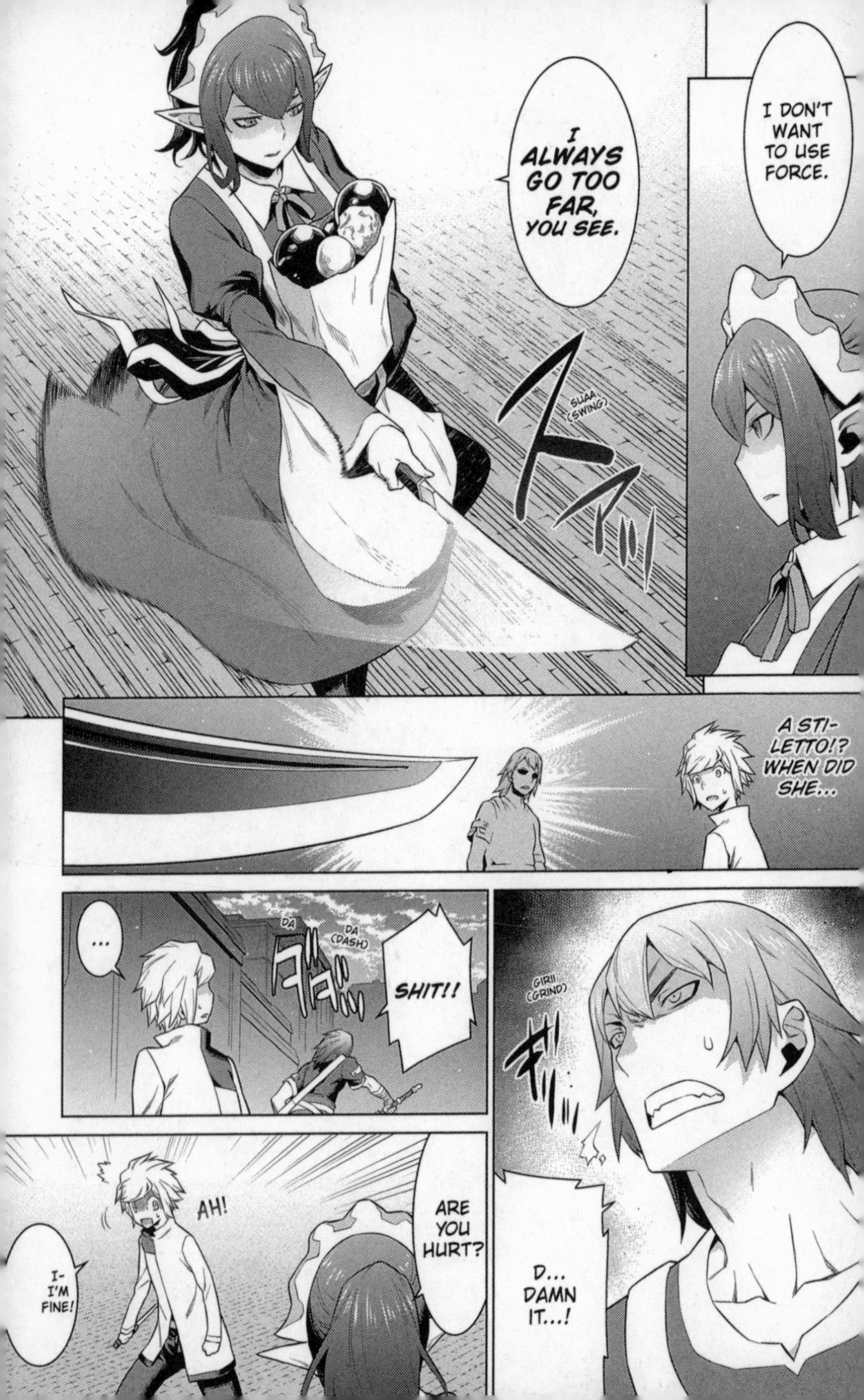
I DON'T WANT TO USE FORCE.
I ALWAYS GO TOO FAR, YOU SEE.
SUAA (SWING)
A STI-LETTO!? WHEN DID SHE...
GIRII (GRIND)
D... DAMN IT...!
...
DA DA (DASH)
SHIT!!
ARE YOU HURT?
AH!
I- I'M FINE!

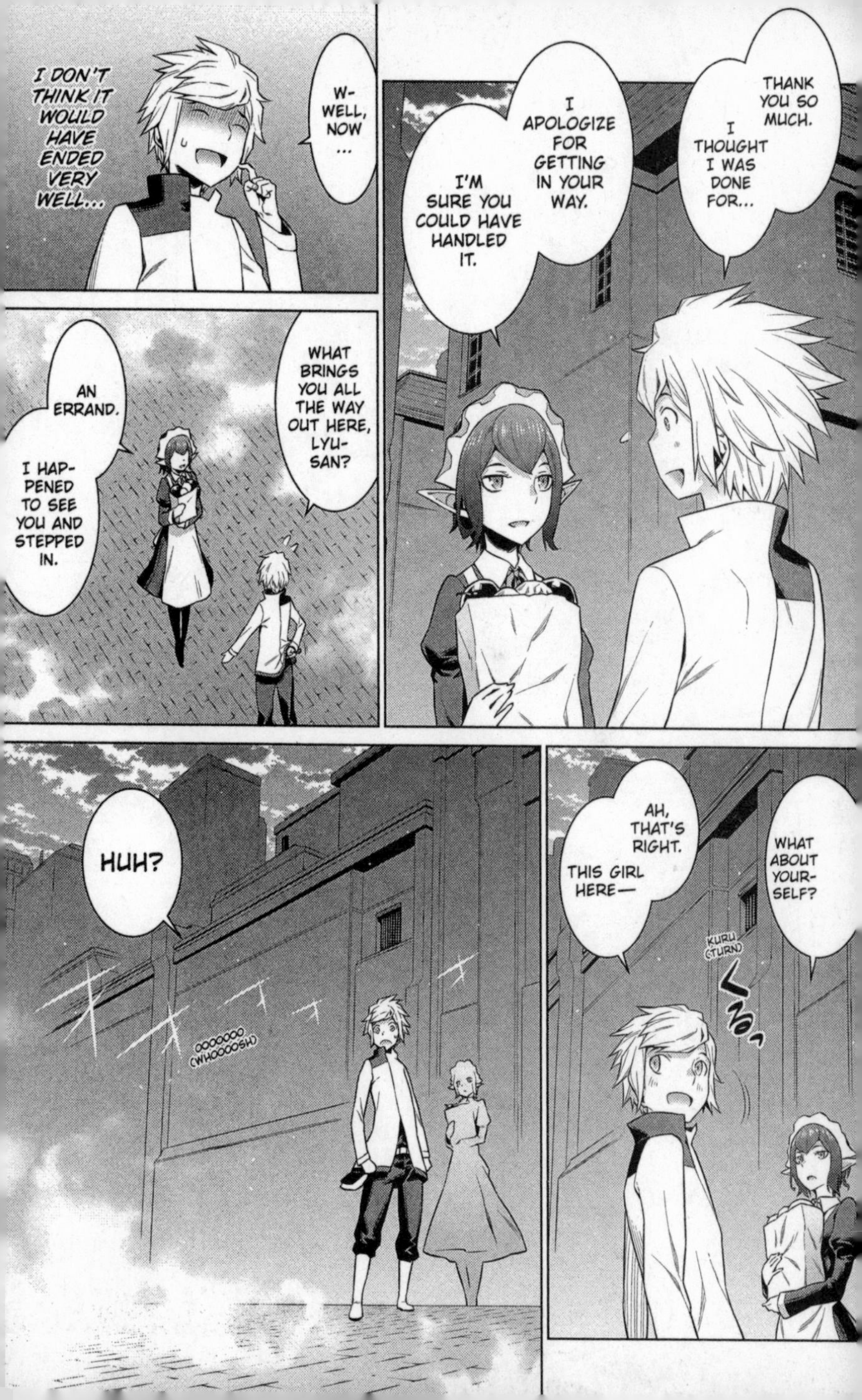
THANK YOU SO MUCH.
I THOUGHT I WAS DONE FOR...
I APOLOGIZE FOR GETTING IN YOUR WAY.
I'M SURE YOU COULD HAVE HANDLED IT.
W-WELL, NOW...
I DON'T THINK IT WOULD HAVE ENDED VERY WELL...
WHAT BRINGS YOU ALL THE WAY OUT HERE, LYU-SAN?
AN ERRAND.
I HAPPENED TO SEE YOU AND STEPPED IN.
WHAT ABOUT YOURSELF?
AH, THAT'S RIGHT.
THIS GIRL HERE—
KURU (TURN)
HUH?
OOOOOOO (WHOOOOSH)

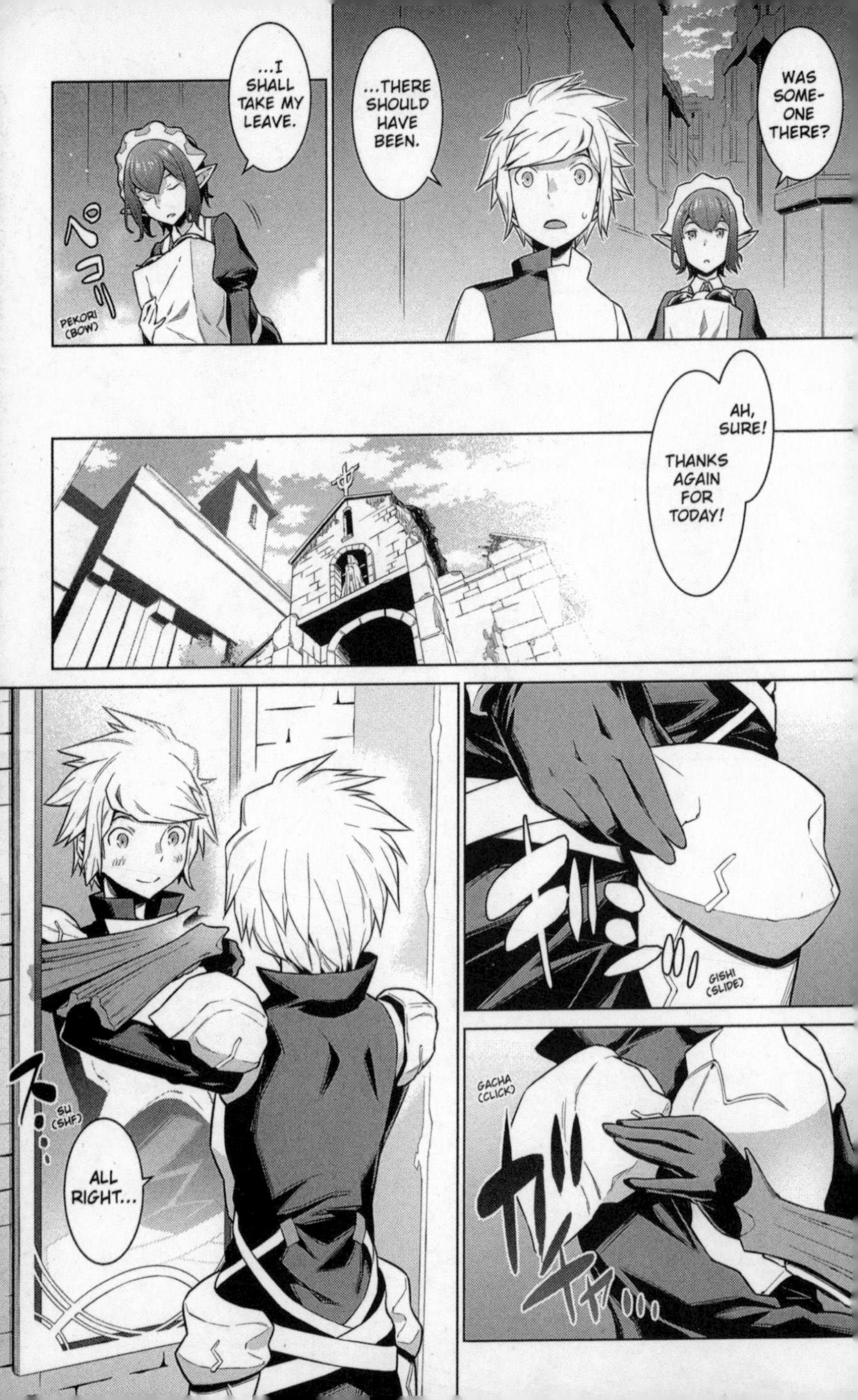
WAS SOME-ONE THERE?
...THERE SHOULD HAVE BEEN.
...I SHALL TAKE MY LEAVE.
PEKORI (BOW)
AH, SURE!
THANKS AGAIN FOR TODAY!
GISHI (SLIDE)
GACHA (CLICK)
SU (SHF)
ALL RIGHT...

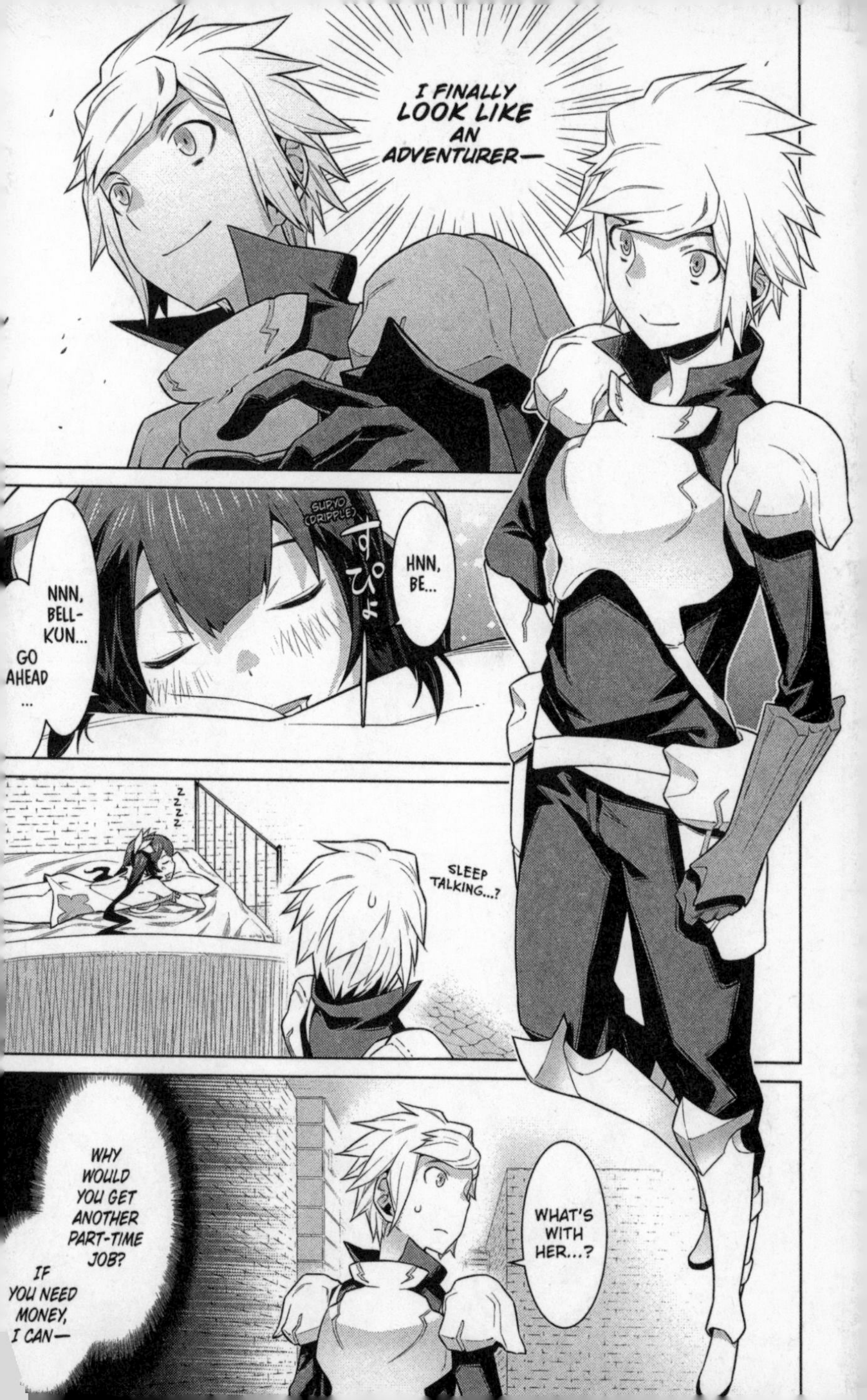

I FINALLY LOOK LIKE AN ADVENTURER—
HNN, BE...
すぴょ
SUPYO (DRIPPLE)
NNN, BELL-KUN... GO AHEAD...
Z Z Z Z
SLEEP TALKING...?
WHAT'S WITH HER...?
WHY WOULD YOU GET ANOTHER PART-TIME JOB?
IF YOU NEED MONEY, I CAN—

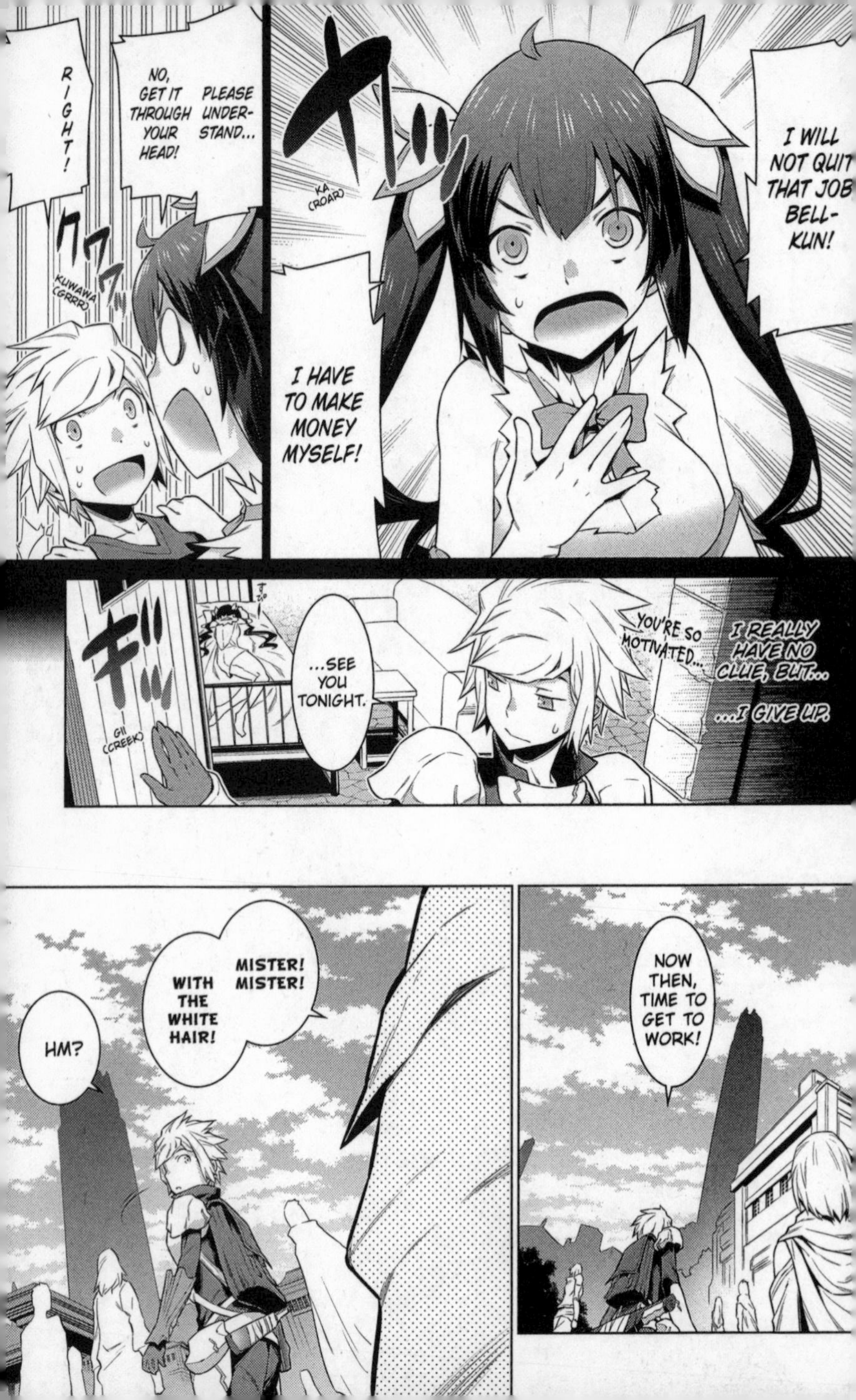
I WILL NOT QUIT THAT JOB BELL-KUN!
KA (ROAR)
I HAVE TO MAKE MONEY MYSELF!
PLEASE UNDERSTAND...
NO, GET IT THROUGH YOUR HEAD!
RIGHT!
KUWAWA (GRRR)
I REALLY HAVE NO CLUE, BUT...
...I GIVE UP.
YOU'RE SO MOTIVATED...
...SEE YOU TONIGHT.
GII (CREEK)
NOW THEN, TIME TO GET TO WORK!
MISTER! MISTER! WITH THE WHITE HAIR!
HM?

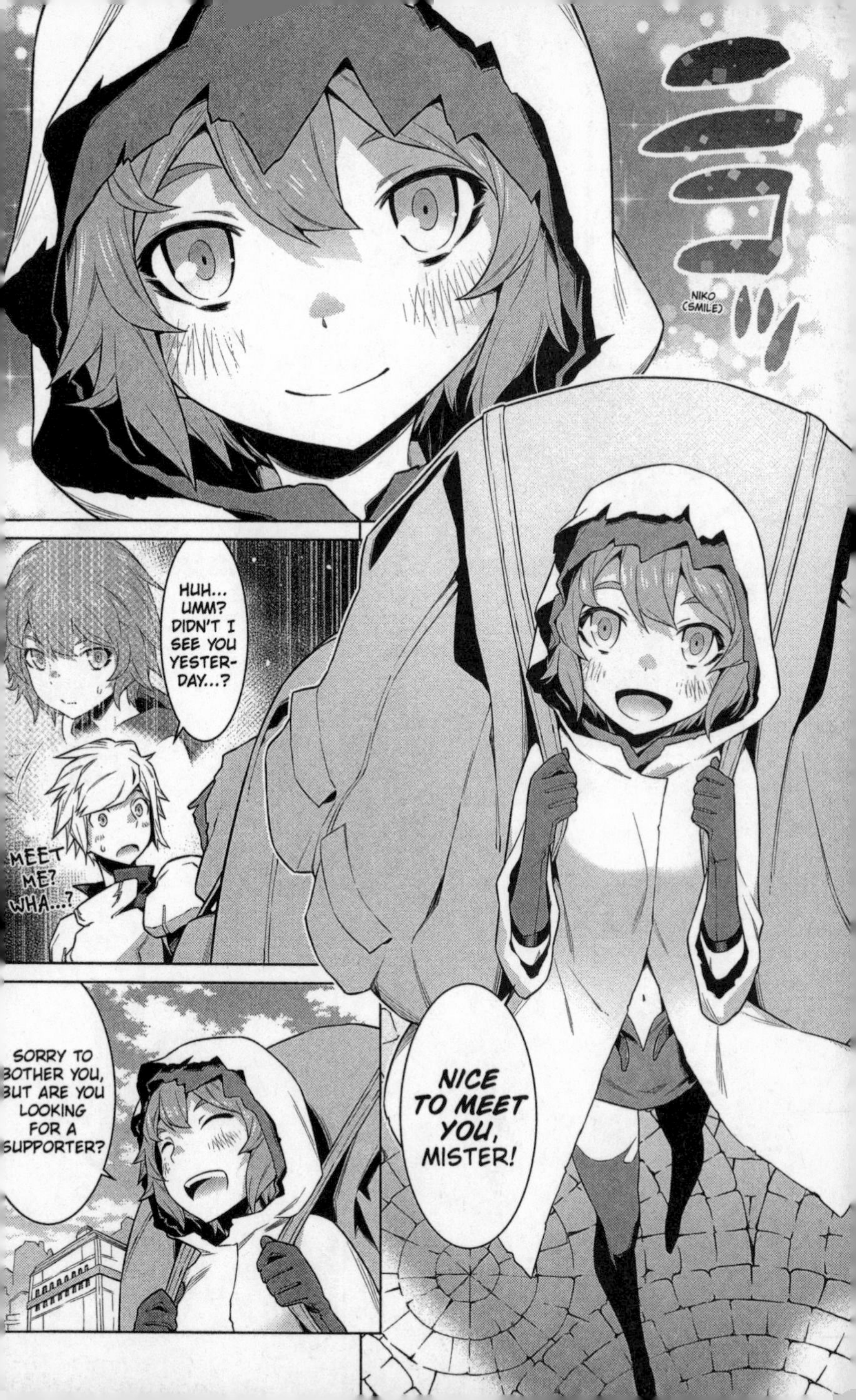
NIKO (SMILE)
NICE TO MEET YOU, MISTER!
HUH... UMM? DIDN'T I SEE YOU YESTER-DAY...?
MEET ME? WHA...?
SORRY TO BOTHER YOU, BUT ARE YOU LOOKING FOR A SUPPORTER?

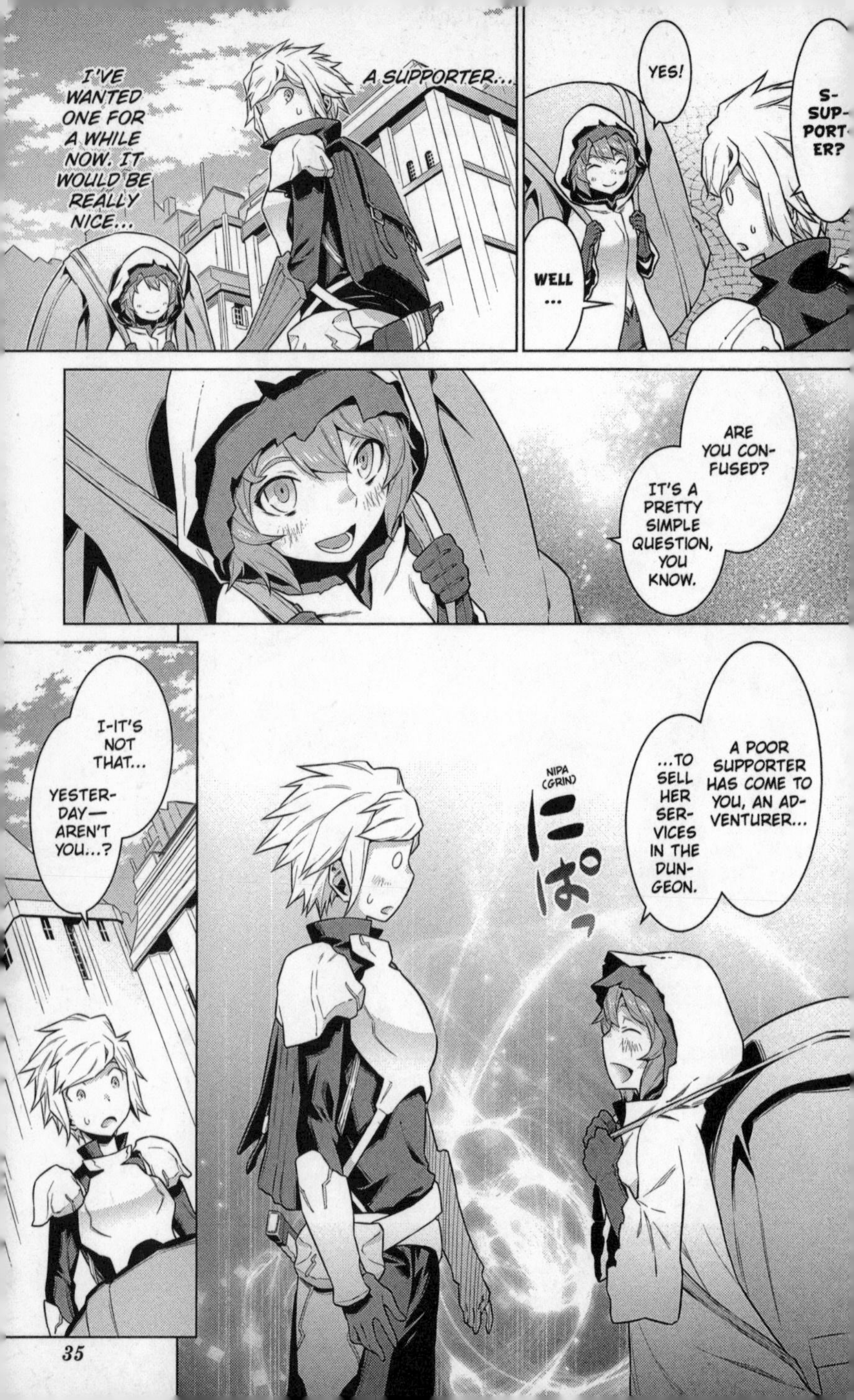
S-SUPPORTER?
YES!
WELL...
A SUPPORTER...
I'VE WANTED ONE FOR A WHILE NOW. IT WOULD BE REALLY NICE...
ARE YOU CONFUSED?
IT'S A PRETTY SIMPLE QUESTION, YOU KNOW.
A POOR SUPPORTER HAS COME TO YOU, AN ADVENTURER...
...TO SELL HER SERVICES IN THE DUNGEON.
NIPA (GRIN)
にぱっ
I-IT'S NOT THAT...
YESTERDAY—AREN'T YOU...?

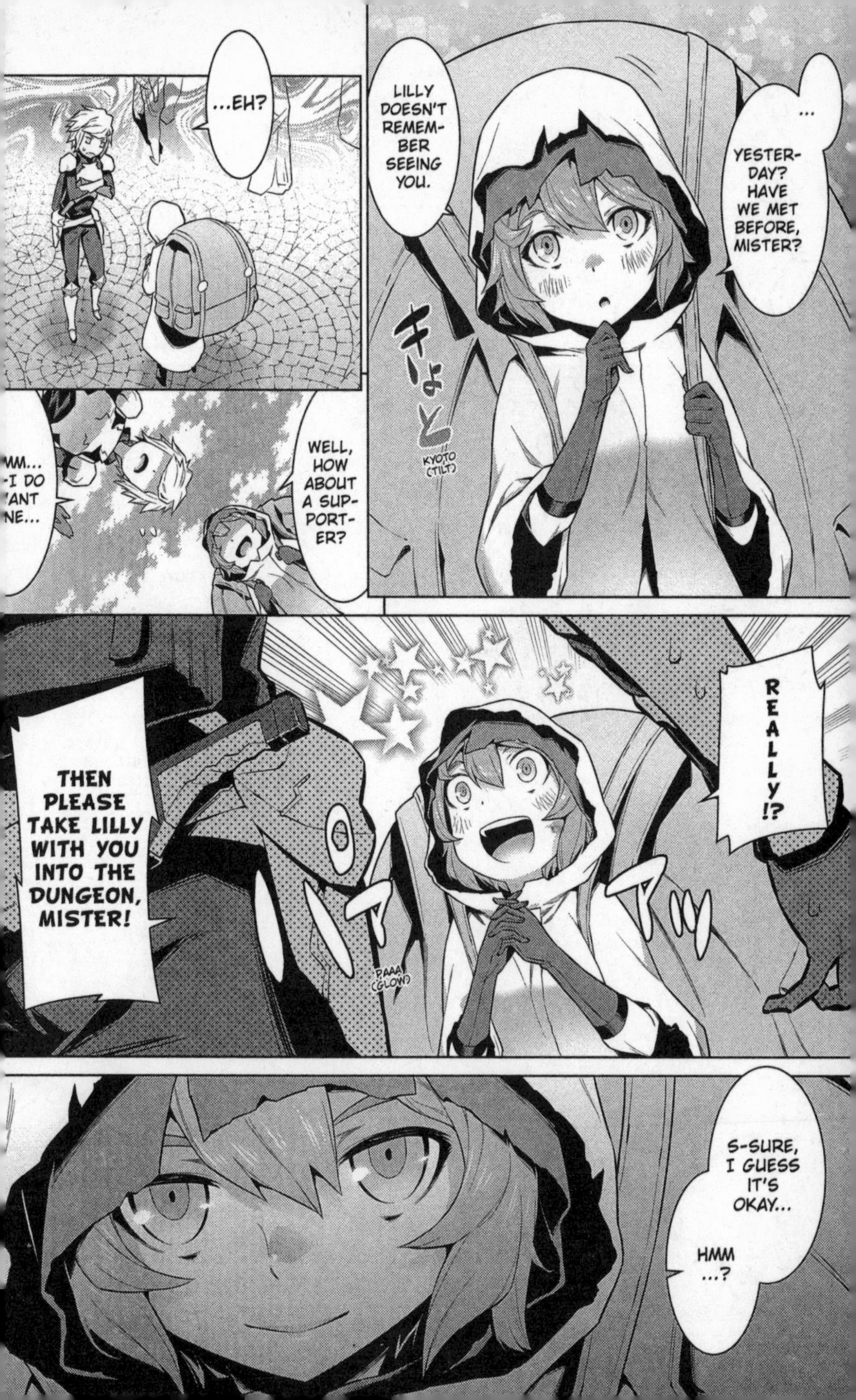
...
YESTERDAY? HAVE WE MET BEFORE, MISTER?
LILLY DOESN'T REMEMBER SEEING YOU.
KYOTO (TILT)
...EH?
WELL, HOW ABOUT A SUPPORTER?
REALLY!?
THEN PLEASE TAKE LILLY WITH YOU INTO THE DUNGEON, MISTER!
PAAA (GLOW)
S-SURE, I GUESS IT'S OKAY...
HMM ...?

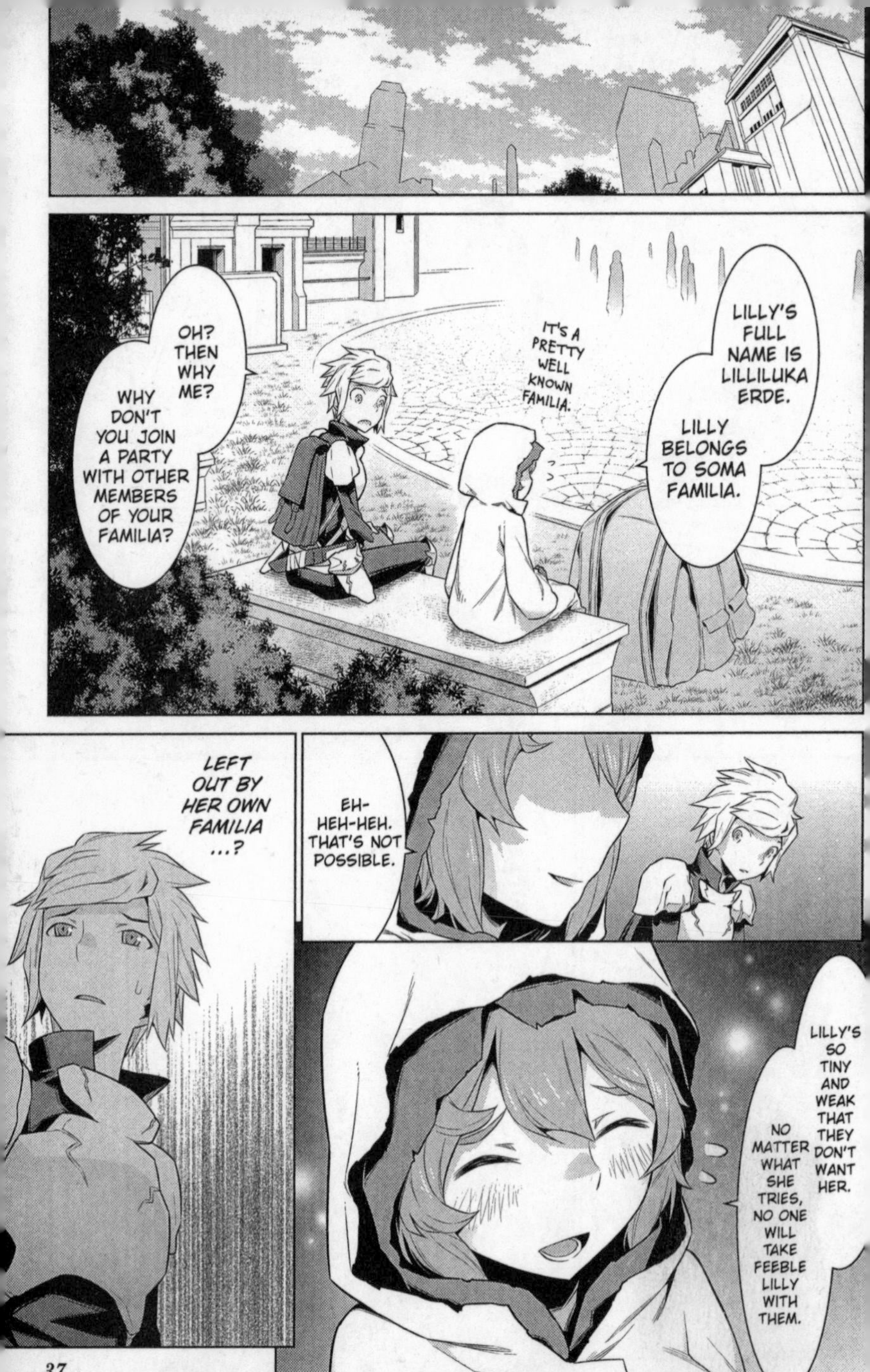
LILLY'S FULL NAME IS LILLILUKA ERDE.
LILLY BELONGS TO SOMA FAMILIA.
IT'S A PRETTY WELL KNOWN FAMILIA.
OH? THEN WHY ME?
WHY DON'T YOU JOIN A PARTY WITH OTHER MEMBERS OF YOUR FAMILIA?
EH-HEH-HEH. THAT'S NOT POSSIBLE.
LILLY'S SO TINY AND WEAK THAT THEY DON'T WANT HER.
NO MATTER WHAT SHE TRIES, NO ONE WILL TAKE FEEBLE LILLY WITH THEM.
LEFT OUT BY HER OWN FAMILIA ...?

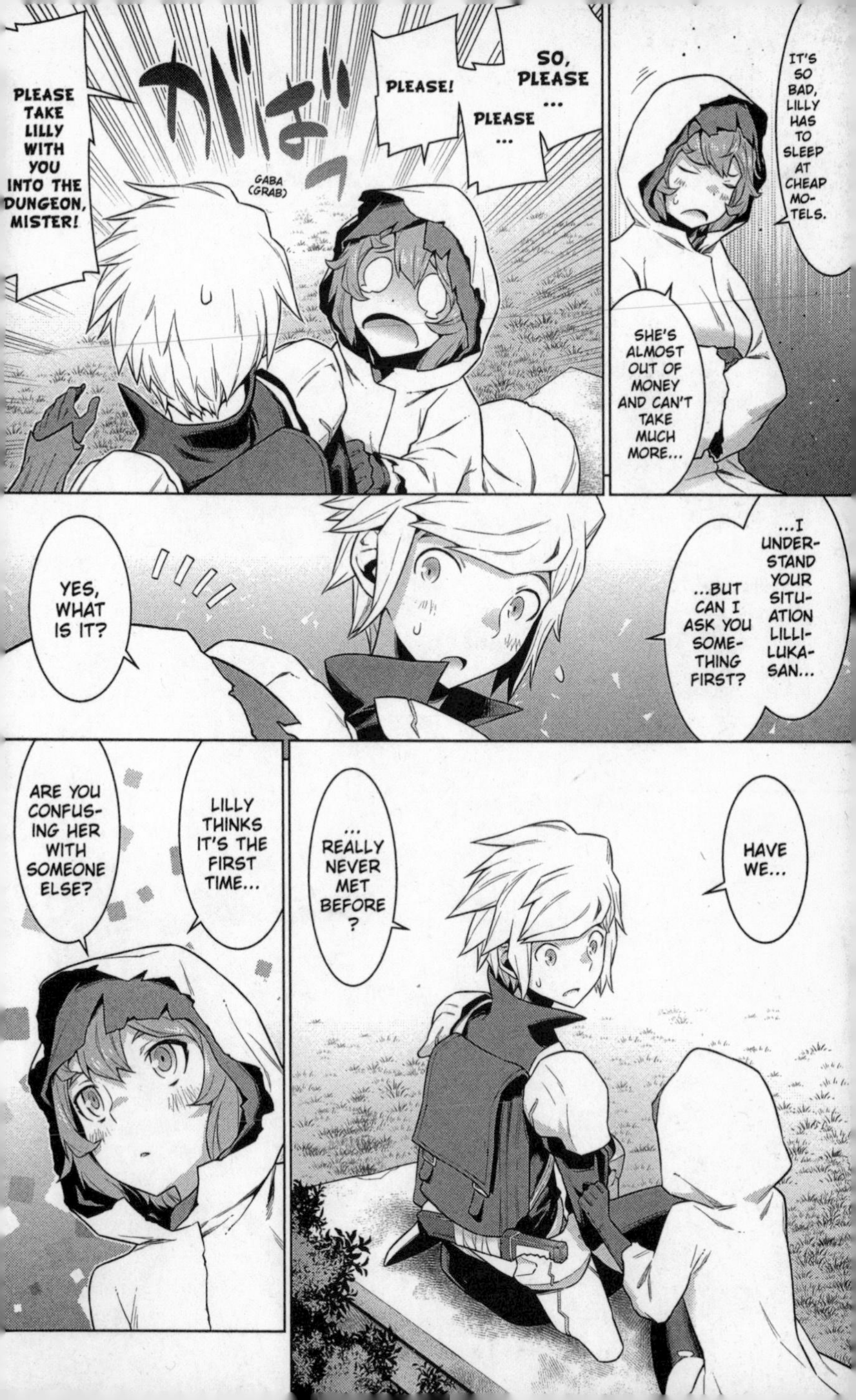
IT'S SO BAD, LILLY HAS TO SLEEP AT CHEAP MO-TELS.
SHE'S ALMOST OUT OF MONEY AND CAN'T TAKE MUCH MORE...
SO, PLEASE ...
PLEASE!
PLEASE ...
がばっ
GABA (GRAB)
PLEASE TAKE LILLY WITH YOU INTO THE DUNGEON, MISTER!
...I UNDER-STAND YOUR SITU-ATION LILLI-LUKA-SAN...
...BUT CAN I ASK YOU SOME-THING FIRST?
YES, WHAT IS IT?
HAVE WE...
... REALLY NEVER MET BEFORE ?
LILLY THINKS IT'S THE FIRST TIME...
ARE YOU CONFUSING HER WITH SOMEONE ELSE?

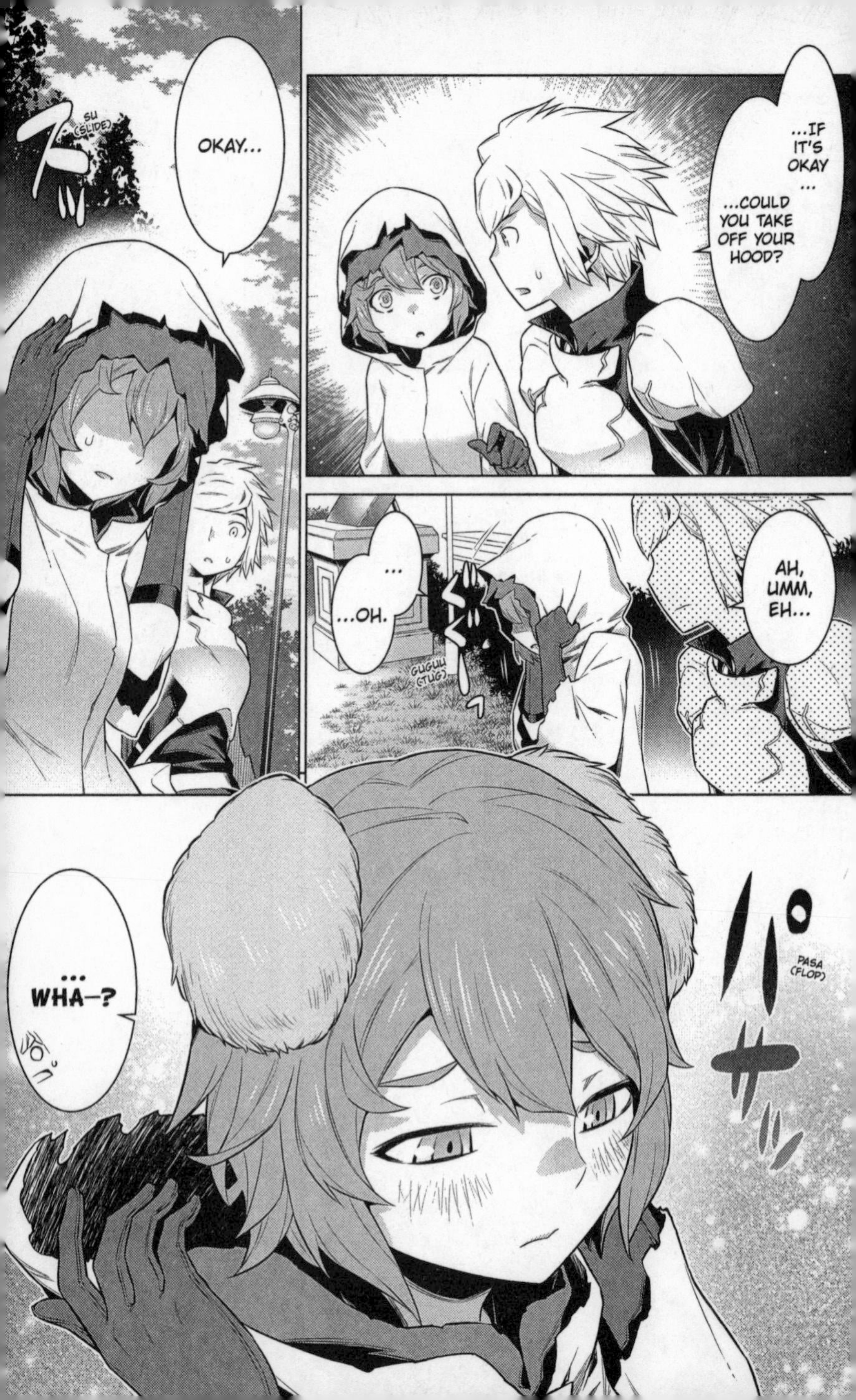

...IF IT'S OKAY ...
...COULD YOU TAKE OFF YOUR HOOD?
AH, UMM, EH...
... ...OH.
GUGUU (TUG)
OKAY...
SU (SLIDE)
PASA (FLOP)
... WHA—?

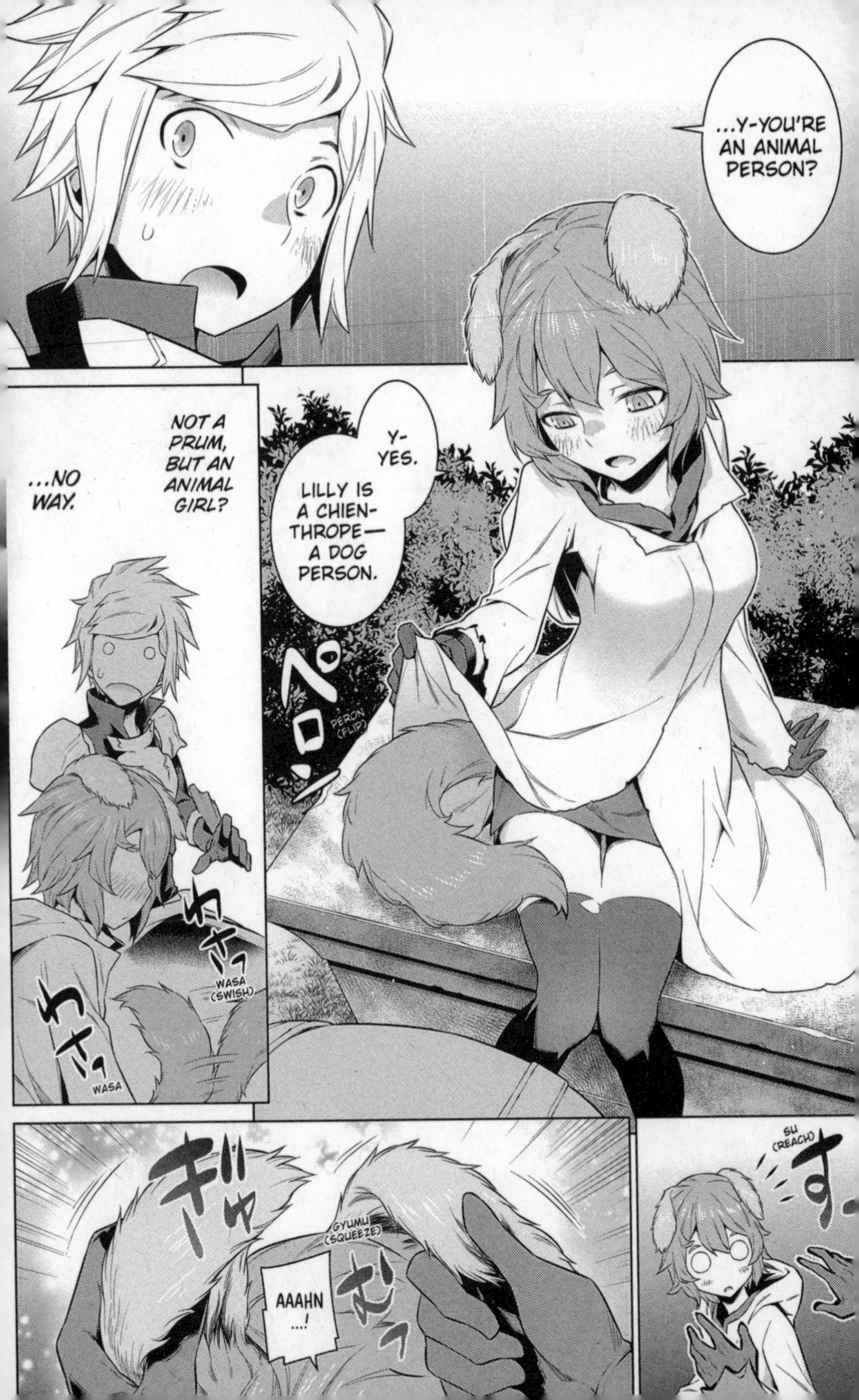
...Y-YOU'RE AN ANIMAL PERSON?
Y- YES.
LILLY IS A CHIEN-THROPE— A DOG PERSON.
PERON (FLIP)
NOT A PRUM, BUT AN ANIMAL GIRL?
...NO WAY.
WASA (SWISH)
WASA
SU (REACH)
GYUMU (SQUEEZE)
AAAHN ...!

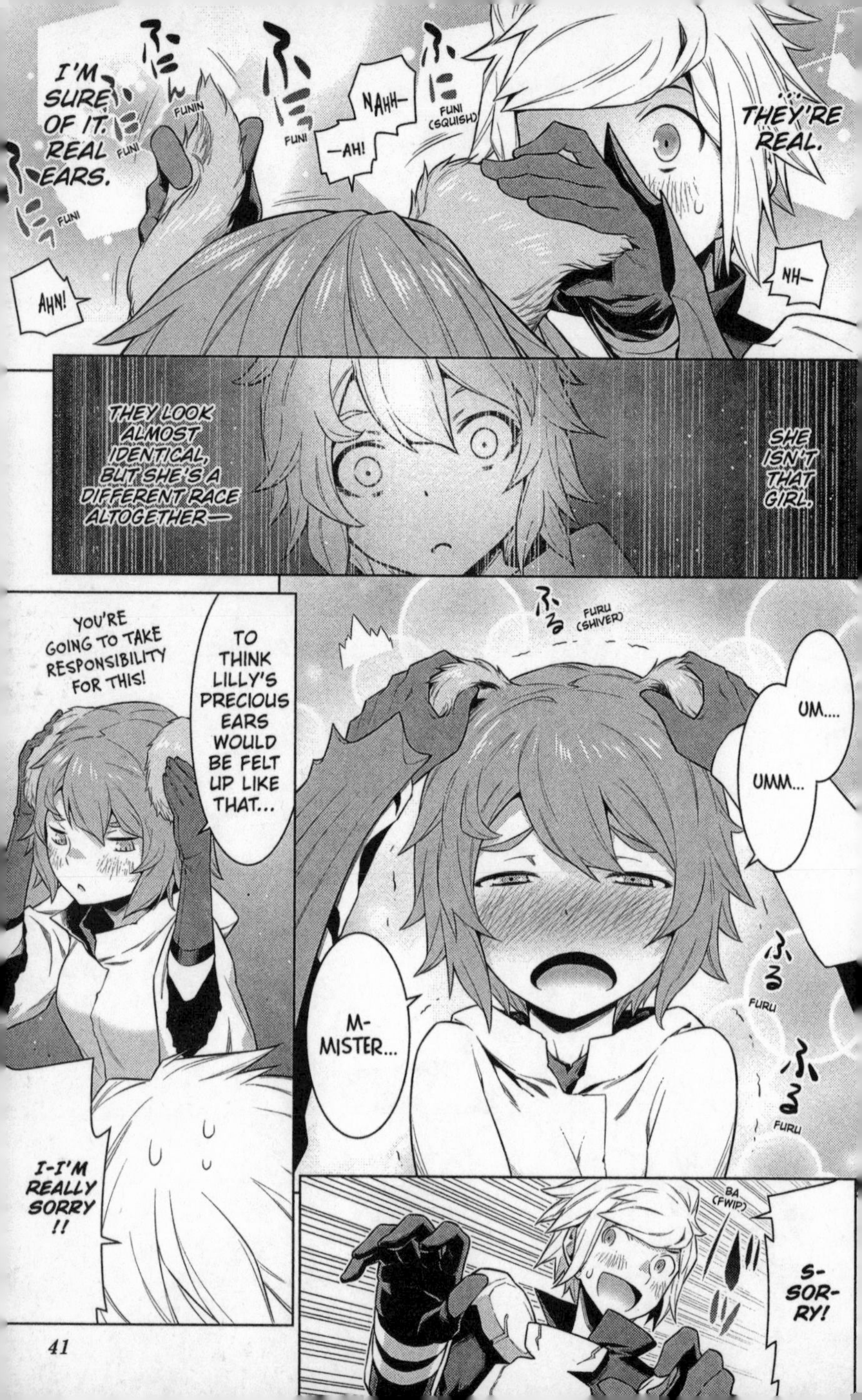
...THEY'RE REAL.
NH—
FUNI (SQUISH)
NAHH—
—AH!
FUNI
FUNIN
I'M SURE OF IT. REAL EARS.
FUNI
FUNI
AHN!
SHE ISN'T THAT GIRL.
THEY LOOK ALMOST IDENTICAL, BUT SHE'S A DIFFERENT RACE ALTOGETHER—
ふる
FURU (SHIVER)
UM....
UMM...
ふる
FURU
ふる
FURU
M-MISTER...
TO THINK LILLY'S PRECIOUS EARS WOULD BE FELT UP LIKE THAT...
YOU'RE GOING TO TAKE RESPONSIBILITY FOR THIS!
BA (FWIP)
S-SORRY!
I-I'M REALLY SORRY!!

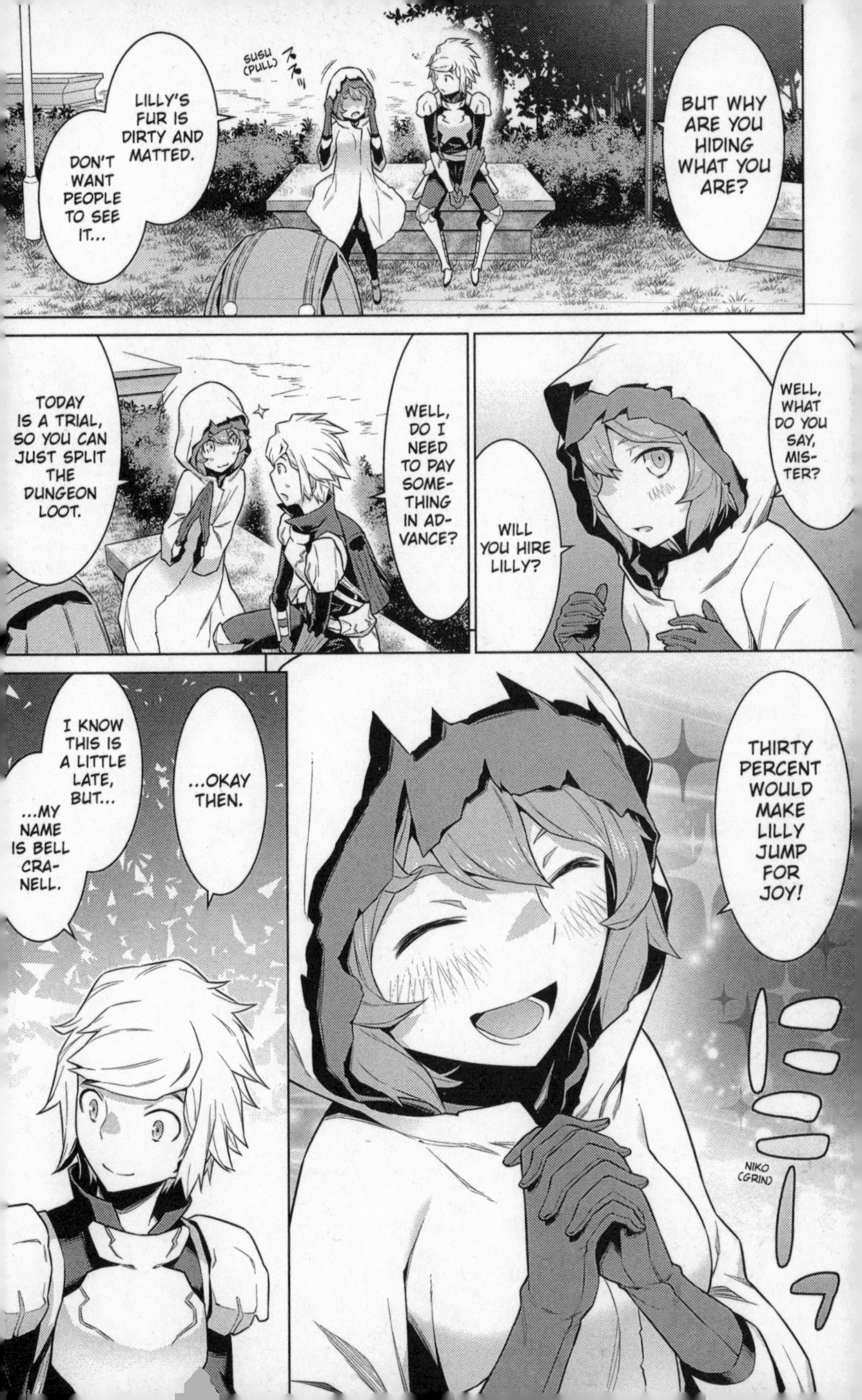
BUT WHY ARE YOU HIDING WHAT YOU ARE?
SUSU (PULL)
LILLY'S FUR IS DIRTY AND MATTED.
DON'T WANT PEOPLE TO SEE IT...
WELL, WHAT DO YOU SAY, MISTER?
WILL YOU HIRE LILLY?
WELL, DO I NEED TO PAY SOMETHING IN ADVANCE?
TODAY IS A TRIAL, SO YOU CAN JUST SPLIT THE DUNGEON LOOT.
THIRTY PERCENT WOULD MAKE LILLY JUMP FOR JOY!
NIKO (GRIN)
...OKAY THEN.
I KNOW THIS IS A LITTLE LATE, BUT...
...MY NAME IS BELL CRANELL.

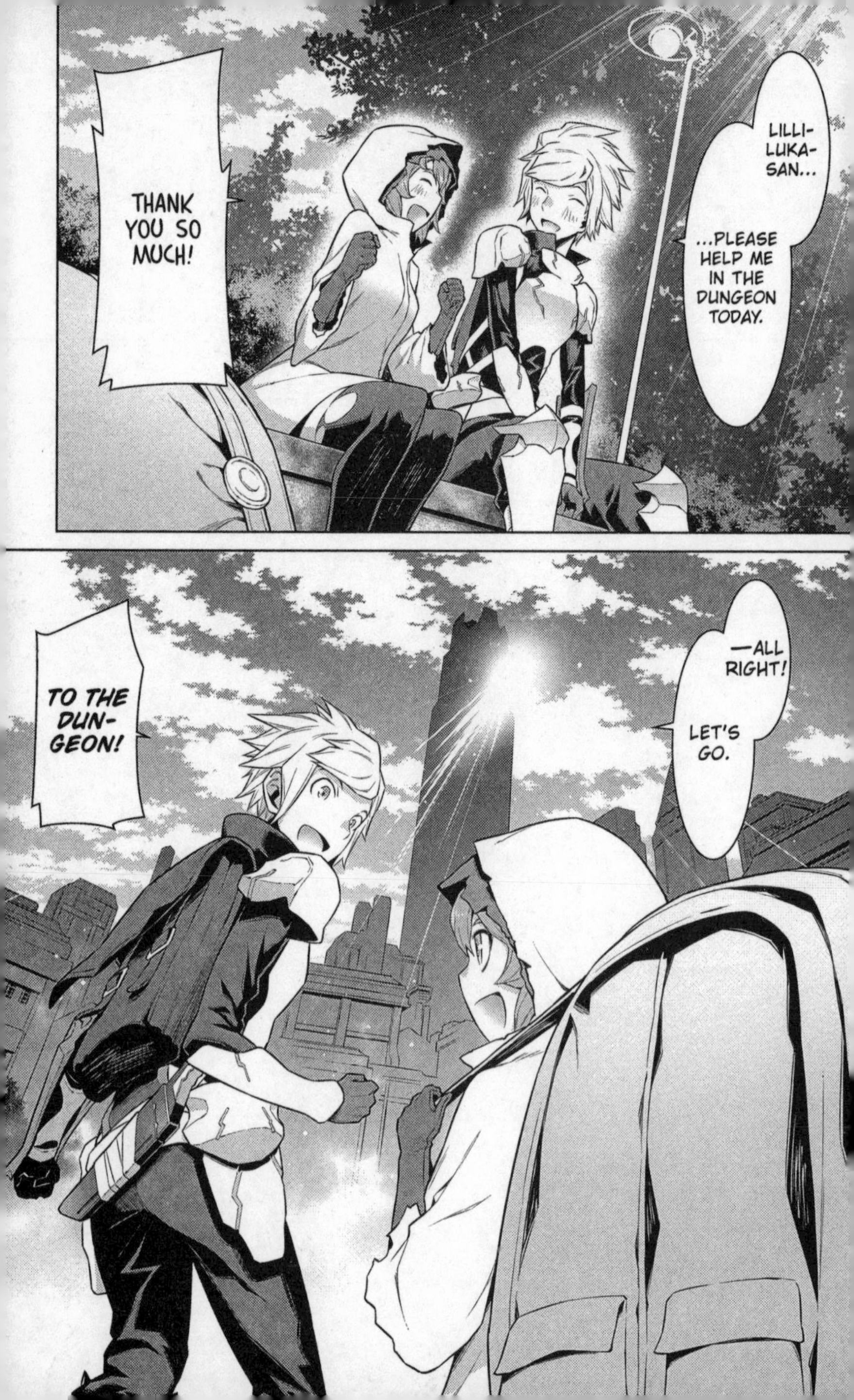
LILLI-LUKA-SAN...
...PLEASE HELP ME IN THE DUNGEON TODAY.
THANK YOU SO MUCH!
—ALL RIGHT!
LET'S GO.
TO THE DUN-GEON!

Is it WRONG to TRY to PiCK-UP GIRLS IN A DUNGEON?

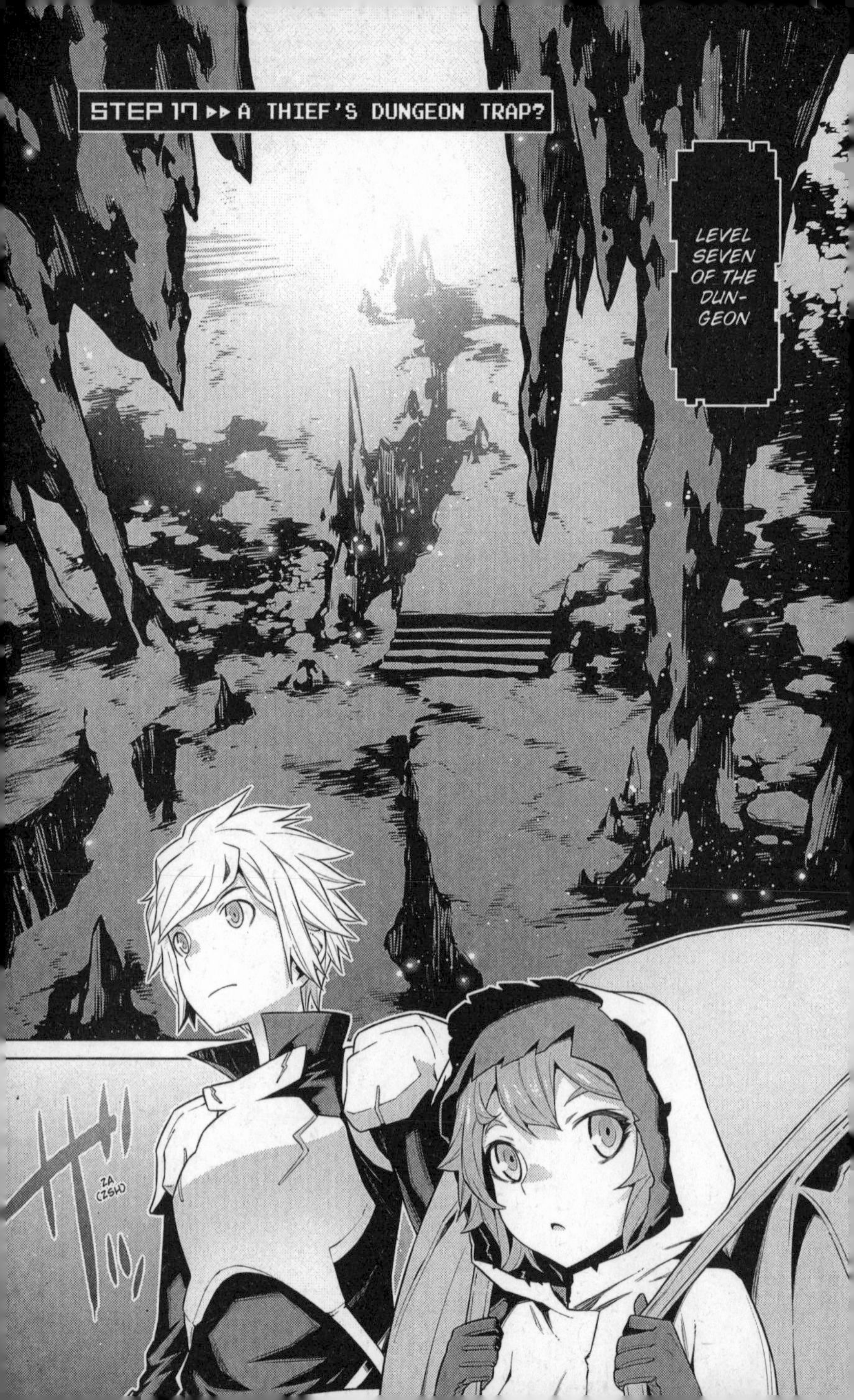
STEP 17 ▸▸ A THIEF'S DUNGEON TRAP?
LEVEL SEVEN OF THE DUN-GEON
ZA (ZSH)

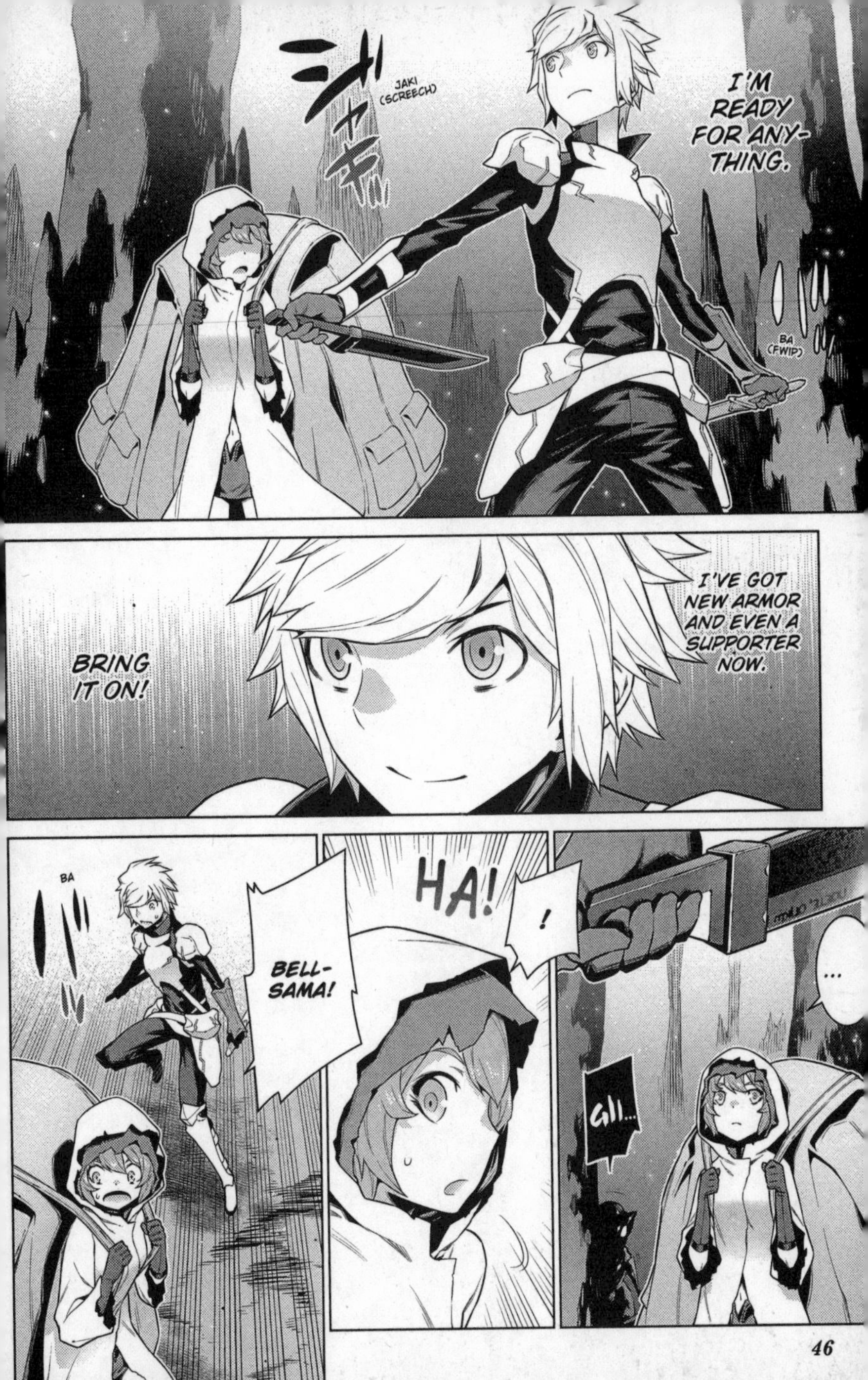

I'M READY FOR ANY-THING.
JAKI (SCREECH)
BA (FWIP)
I'VE GOT NEW ARMOR AND EVEN A SUPPORTER NOW.
BRING IT ON!
...
GII...
HA!
!
BELL-SAMA!
BA

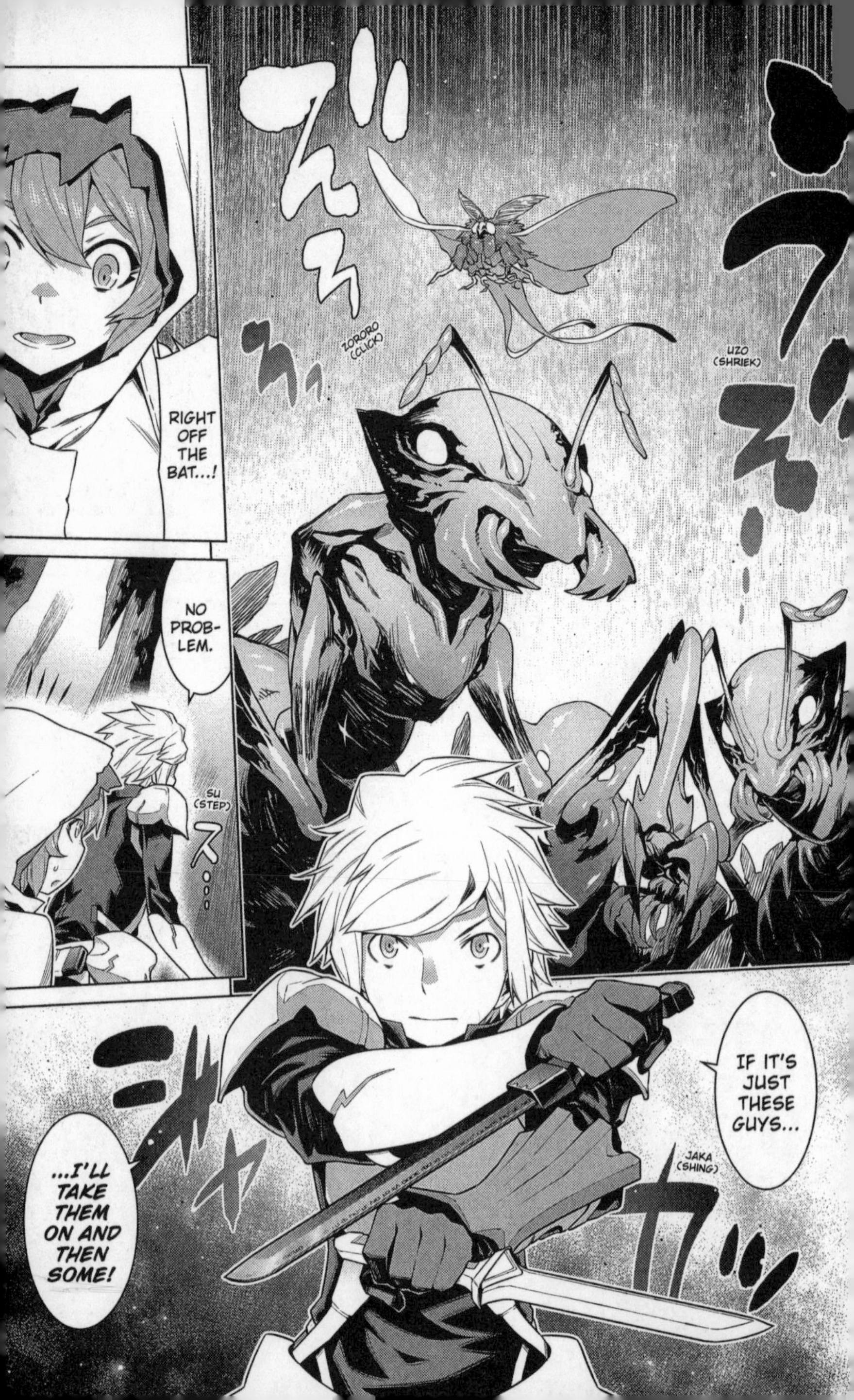
UZO (SHRIEK)
ZORORO (CLICK)
RIGHT OFF THE BAT...!
NO PROBLEM.
SU (STEP)
IF IT'S JUST THESE GUYS...
JAKA (SHING)
...I'LL TAKE THEM ON AND THEN SOME!

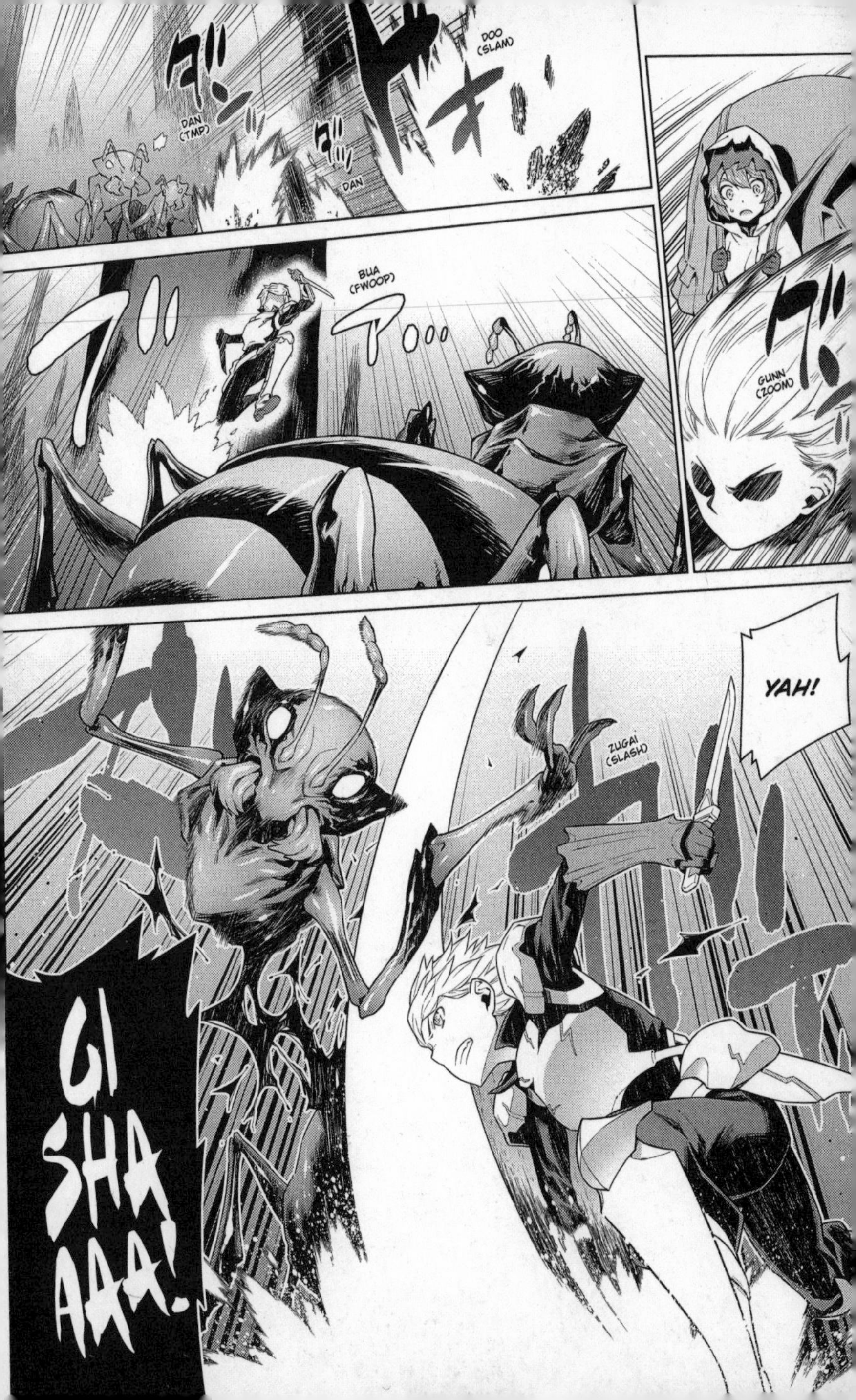
GUNN (ZOOM)
DOO (SLAM)
DAN (TMP)
DAN
BUA (FWOOP)
YAH!
ZUGAI (SLASH)
GI SHA AAA!

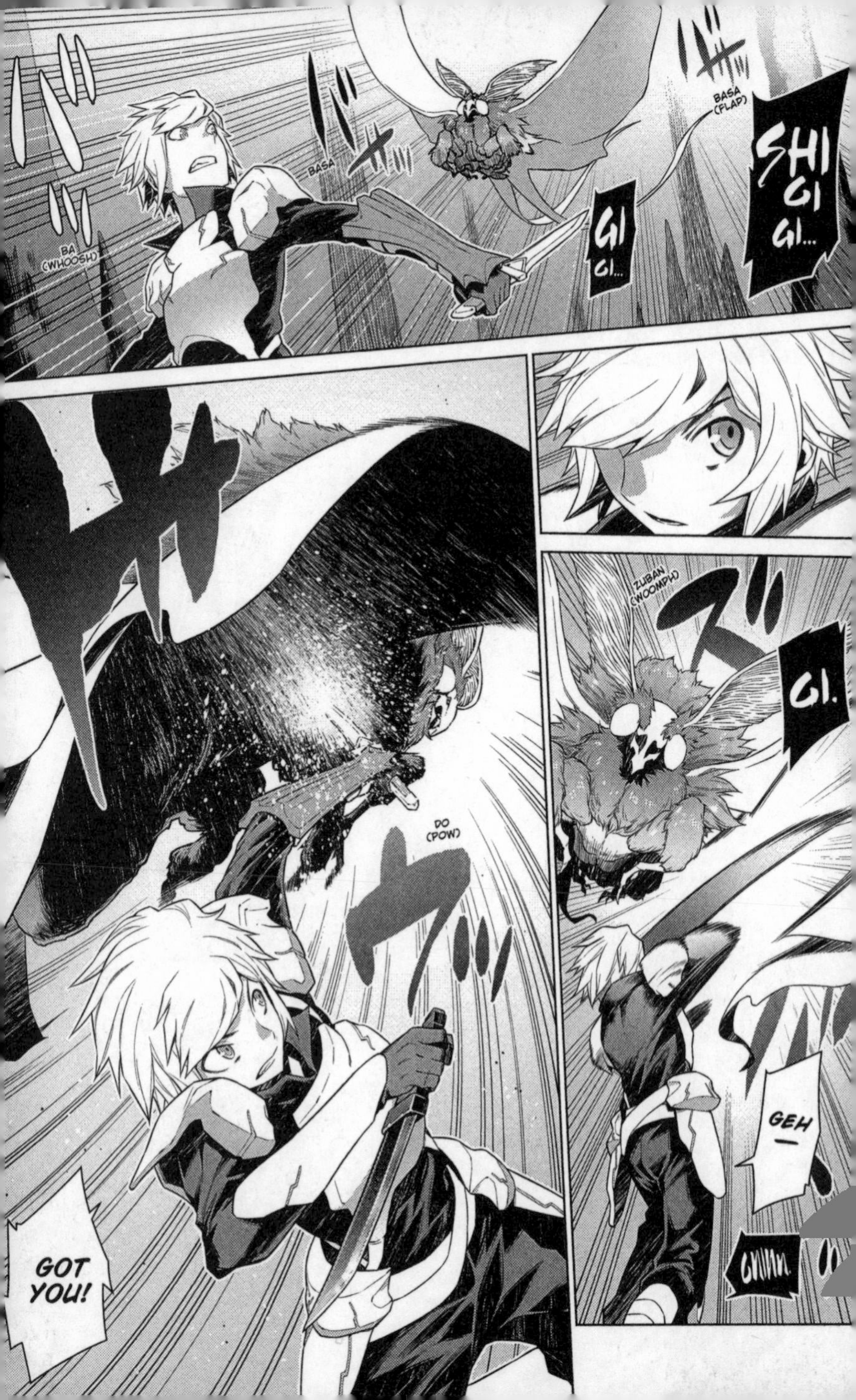
SHI GI GI...
BASA (FLAP)
GI GI...
BASA
BA (WHOOSH)
ZUBAN (WOOMPH)
GI.
GEH—
GNNN.
DO (POW)
GOT YOU!

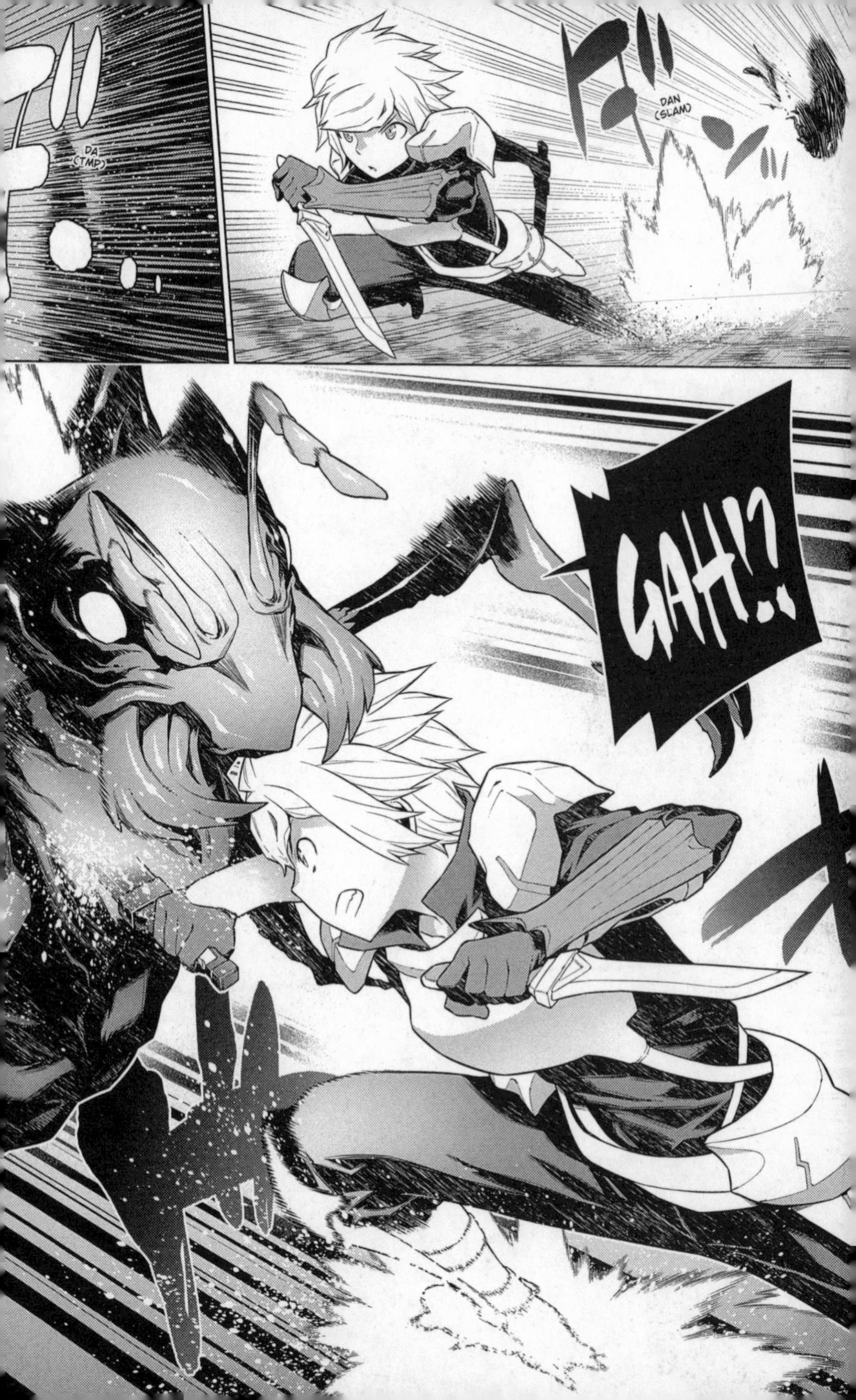
DAN (SLAM)
DA (TMP)
GAH!?

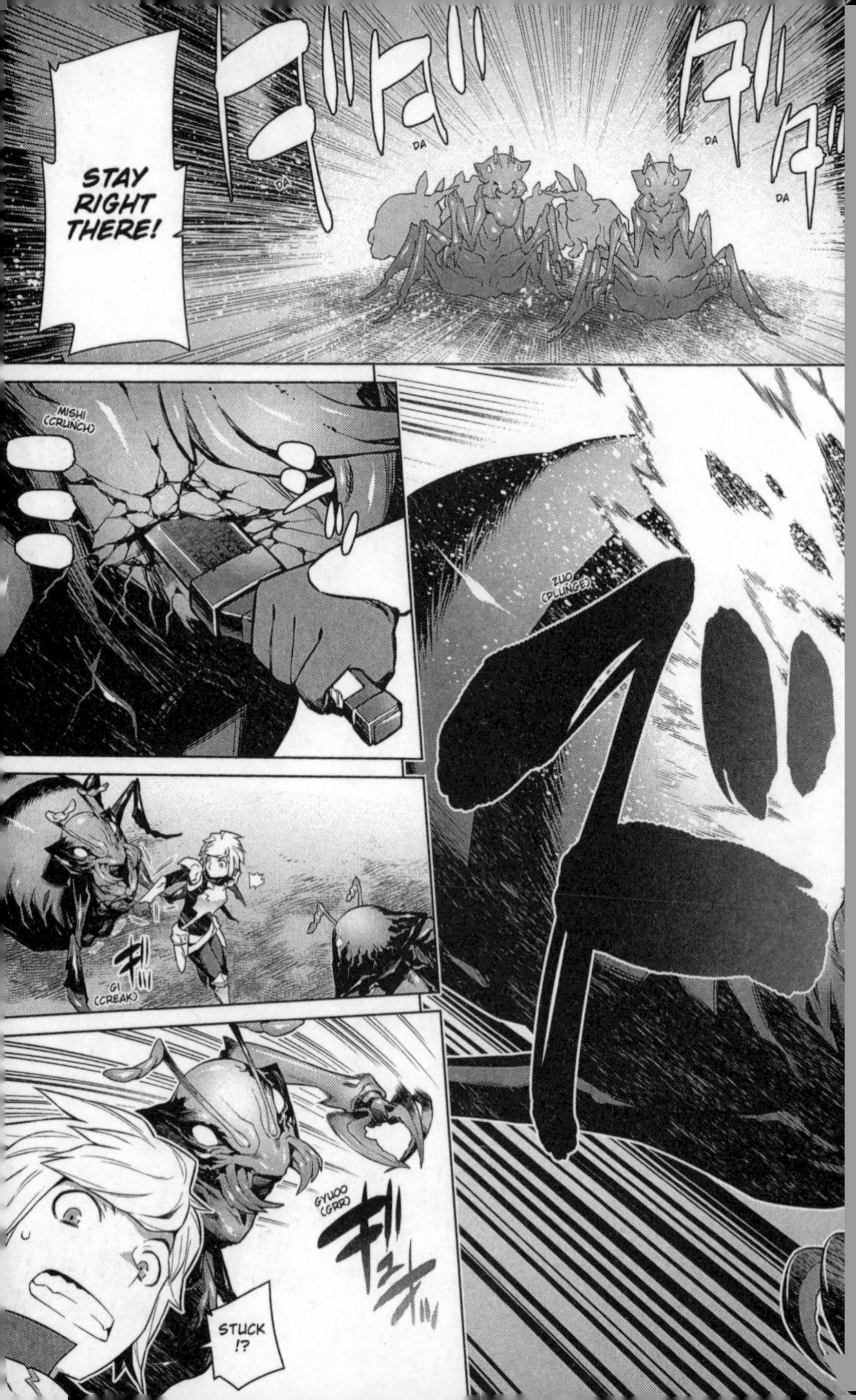
DA
DA
DA
DA
STAY RIGHT THERE!
ZUO (PLUNGE)
MISHI (CRUNCH)
GI (CREAK)
GYUOO (GRR)
STUCK !?

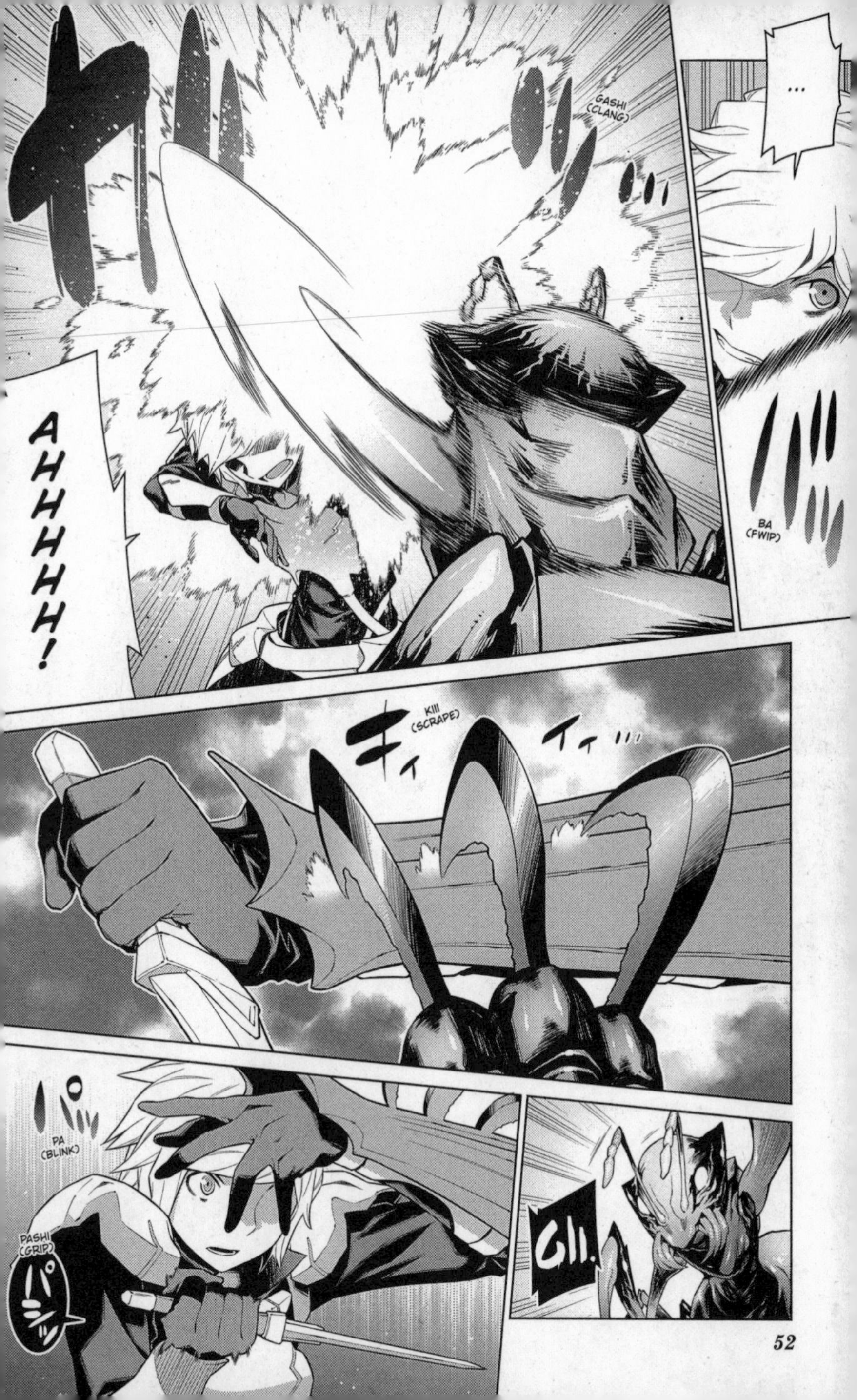
...
BA (FWIP)
GASHI (CLANG)
AHHHHHH!
KIII (SCRAPE)
GII.
PA (BLINK)
PASHI (GRIP)

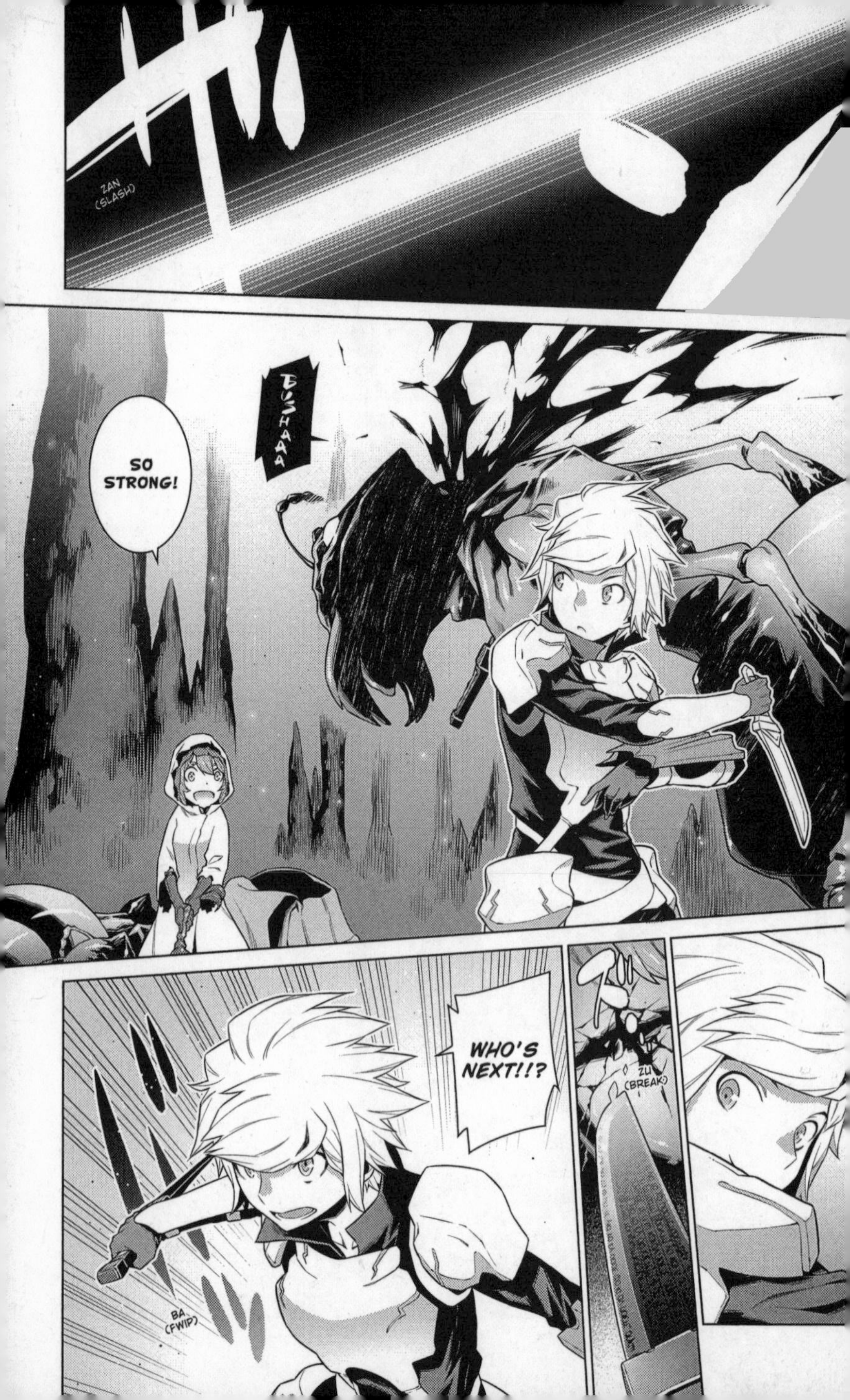
ZAN (SLASH)
BUSHAAA
SO STRONG!
ZU (BREAK)
WHO'S NEXT!!?
BA (FWIP)

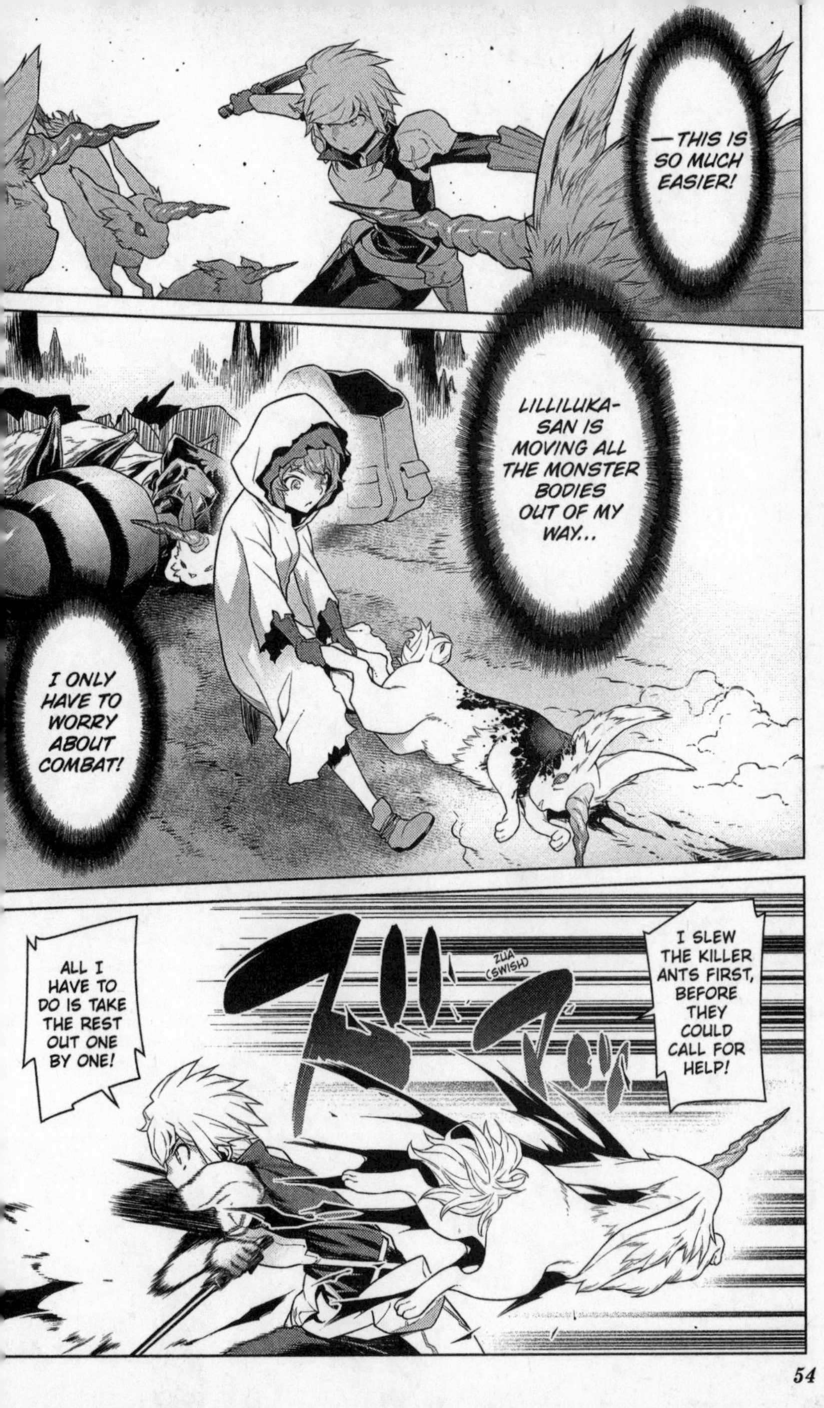
—THIS IS SO MUCH EASIER!
LILLILUKA-SAN IS MOVING ALL THE MONSTER BODIES OUT OF MY WAY...
I ONLY HAVE TO WORRY ABOUT COMBAT!
I SLEW THE KILLER ANTS FIRST, BEFORE THEY COULD CALL FOR HELP!
ZUA (SWISH)
ALL I HAVE TO DO IS TAKE THE REST OUT ONE BY ONE!

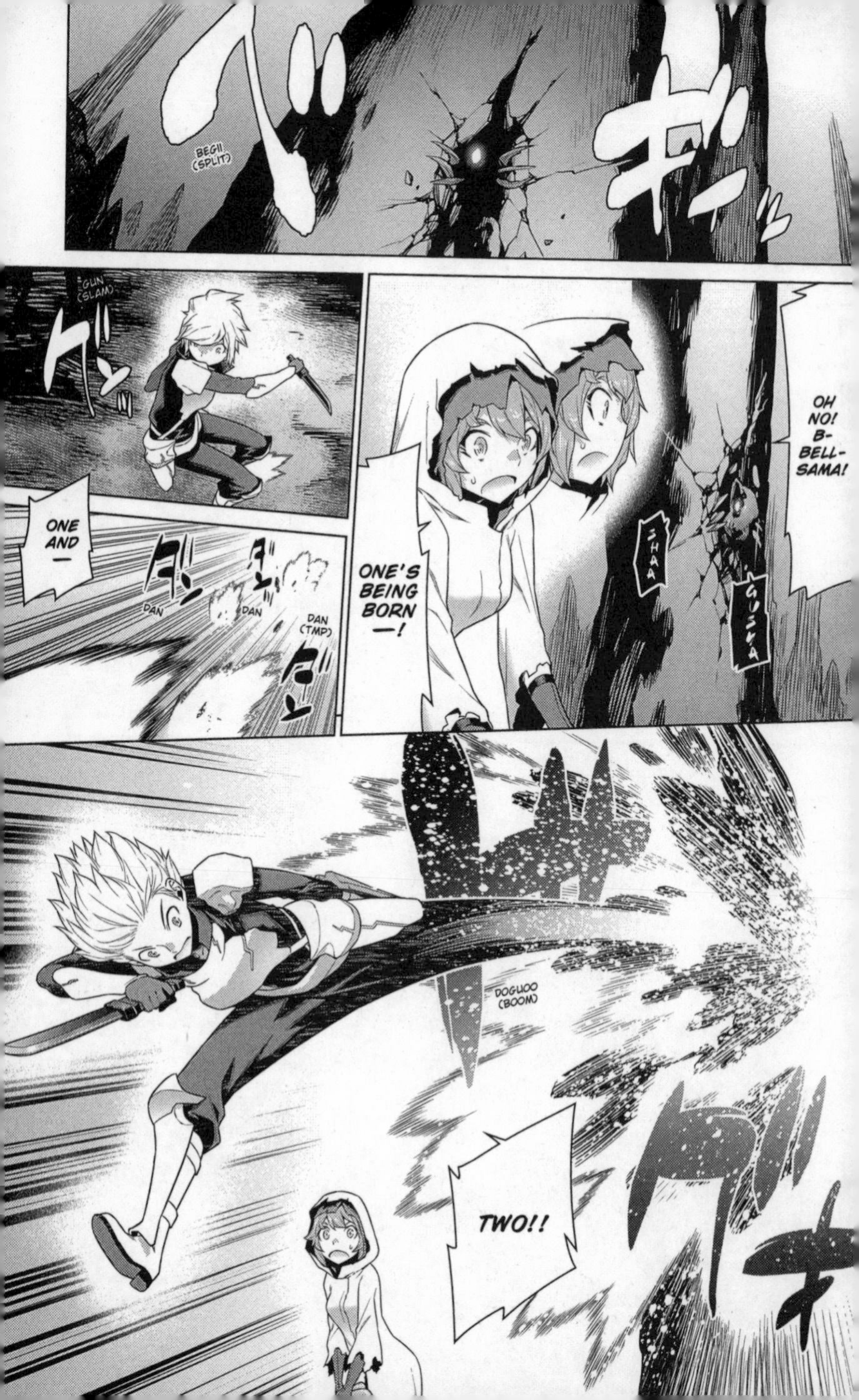
BEGII (SPLIT)
OH NO! B-BELL-SAMA!
GUSHA
SHAA
ONE'S BEING BORN—!
GUN (SLAM)
ONE AND—
DAN
DAN
DAN (TMP)
DOGUOO (BOOM)
TWO!!

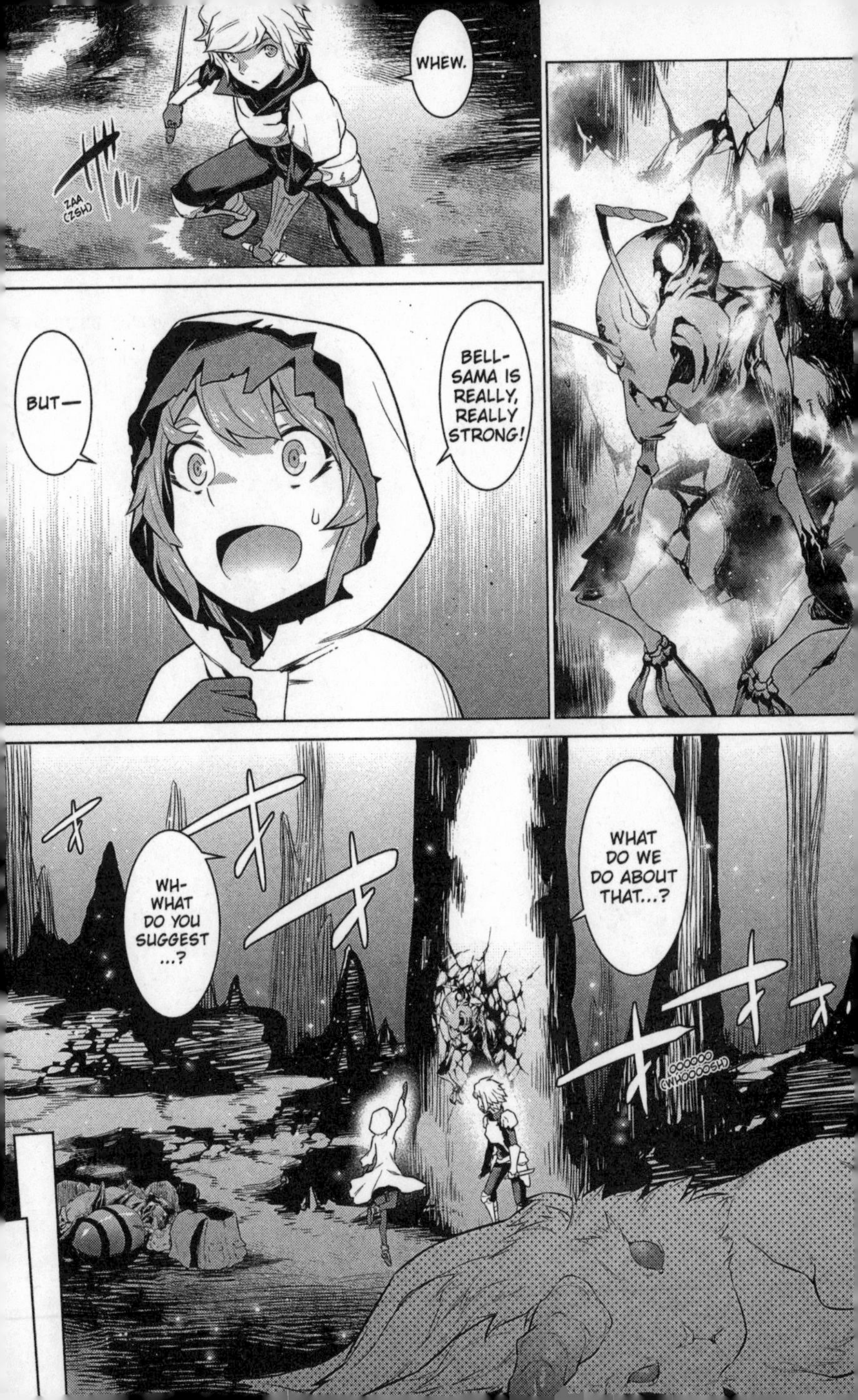

WHEW.
ZAA (ZSH)
BELL-SAMA IS REALLY, REALLY STRONG!
BUT—
WHAT DO WE DO ABOUT THAT...?
WH-WHAT DO YOU SUGGEST ...?
OOOOOO (WHOOOOSH)

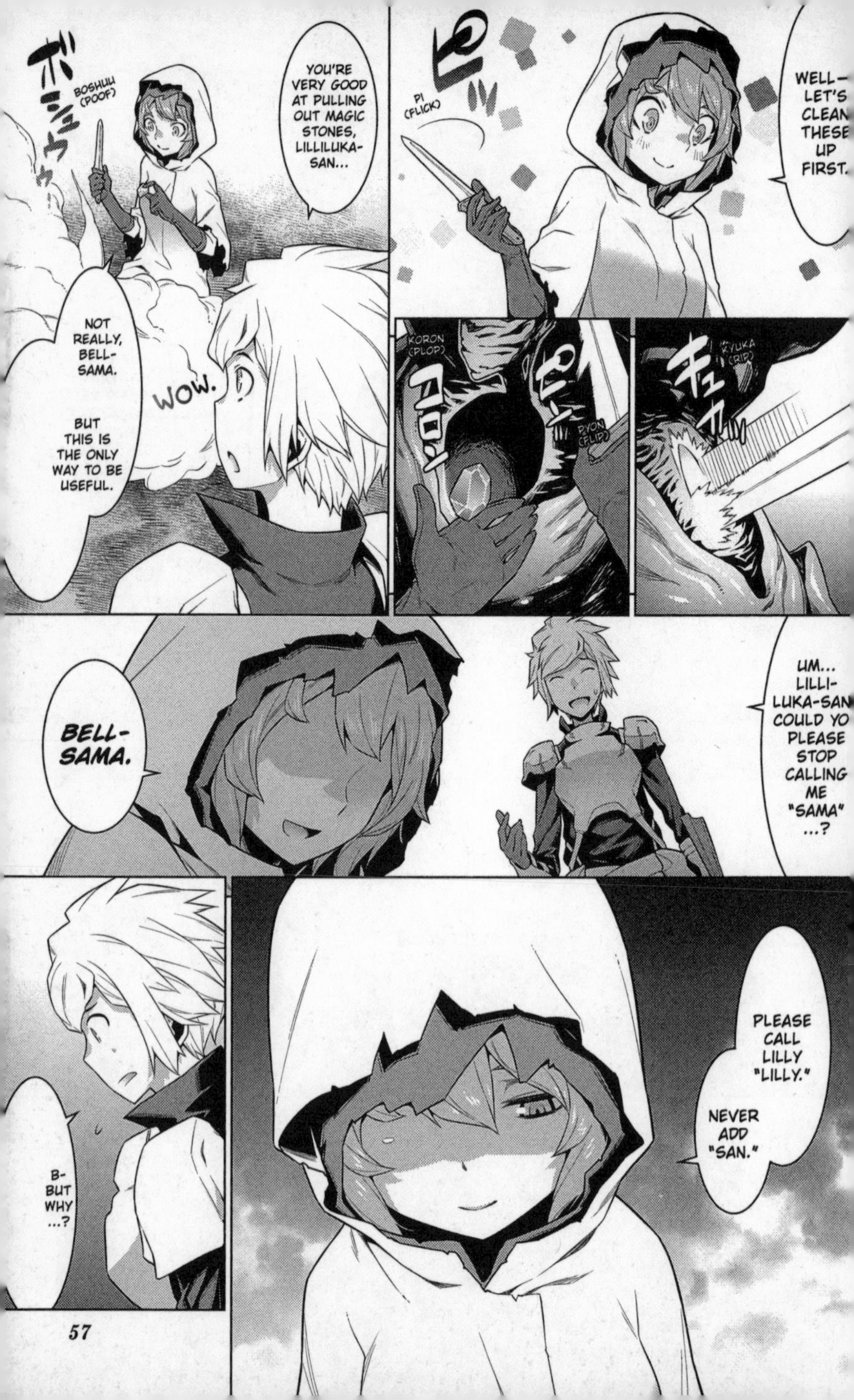
WELL— LET'S CLEAN THESE UP FIRST.
PI (FLICK)
KYUKA (RIP)
PYON (FLIP)
KORON (PLOP)
YOU'RE VERY GOOD AT PULLING OUT MAGIC STONES, LILLILUKA-SAN...
BOSHUU (POOF)
WOW.
NOT REALLY, BELL-SAMA.
BUT THIS IS THE ONLY WAY TO BE USEFUL.
UM... LILLI-LUKA-SAN COULD YO PLEASE STOP CALLING ME "SAMA" ...?
BELL-SAMA.
PLEASE CALL LILLY "LILLY."
NEVER ADD "SAN."
B-BUT WHY ...?

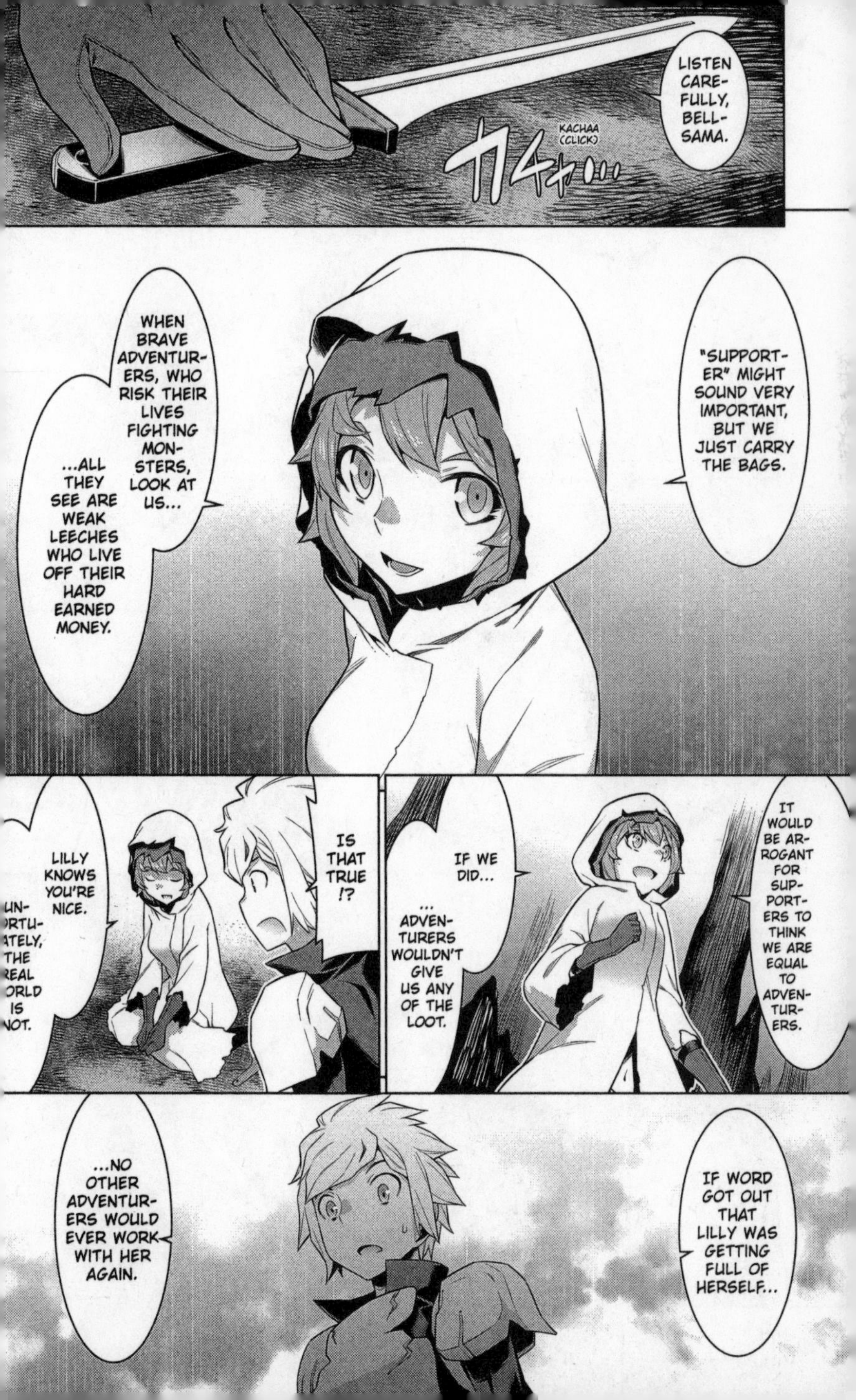
LISTEN CAREFULLY, BELL-SAMA.
KACHAA (CLICK)
"SUPPORTER" MIGHT SOUND VERY IMPORTANT, BUT WE JUST CARRY THE BAGS.
WHEN BRAVE ADVENTURERS, WHO RISK THEIR LIVES FIGHTING MONSTERS, LOOK AT US...
...ALL THEY SEE ARE WEAK LEECHES WHO LIVE OFF THEIR HARD EARNED MONEY.
IT WOULD BE ARROGANT FOR SUPPORTERS TO THINK WE ARE EQUAL TO ADVENTURERS.
IF WE DID...
...ADVENTURERS WOULDN'T GIVE US ANY OF THE LOOT.
IS THAT TRUE!?
LILLY KNOWS YOU'RE NICE.
UN- ORTU- ATELY, THE REAL ORLD IS NOT.
IF WORD GOT OUT THAT LILLY WAS GETTING FULL OF HERSELF...
...NO OTHER ADVENTURERS WOULD EVER WORK WITH HER AGAIN.

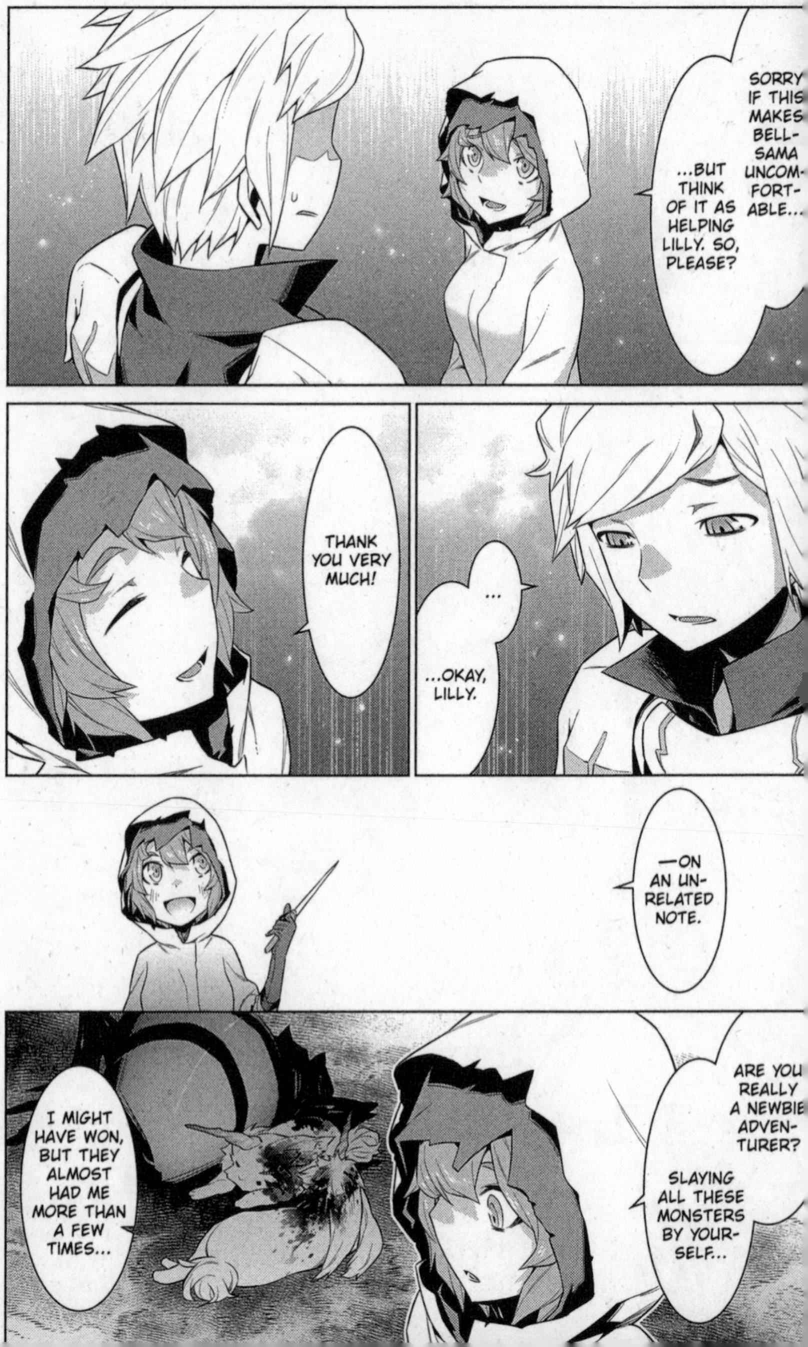
SORRY IF THIS MAKES BELL-SAMA UNCOMFORTABLE...
...BUT THINK OF IT AS HELPING LILLY. SO, PLEASE?
...
...OKAY, LILLY.
THANK YOU VERY MUCH!
—ON AN UNRELATED NOTE.
ARE YOU REALLY A NEWBIE ADVENTURER?
SLAYING ALL THESE MONSTERS BY YOURSELF...
I MIGHT HAVE WON, BUT THEY ALMOST HAD ME MORE THAN A FEW TIMES...

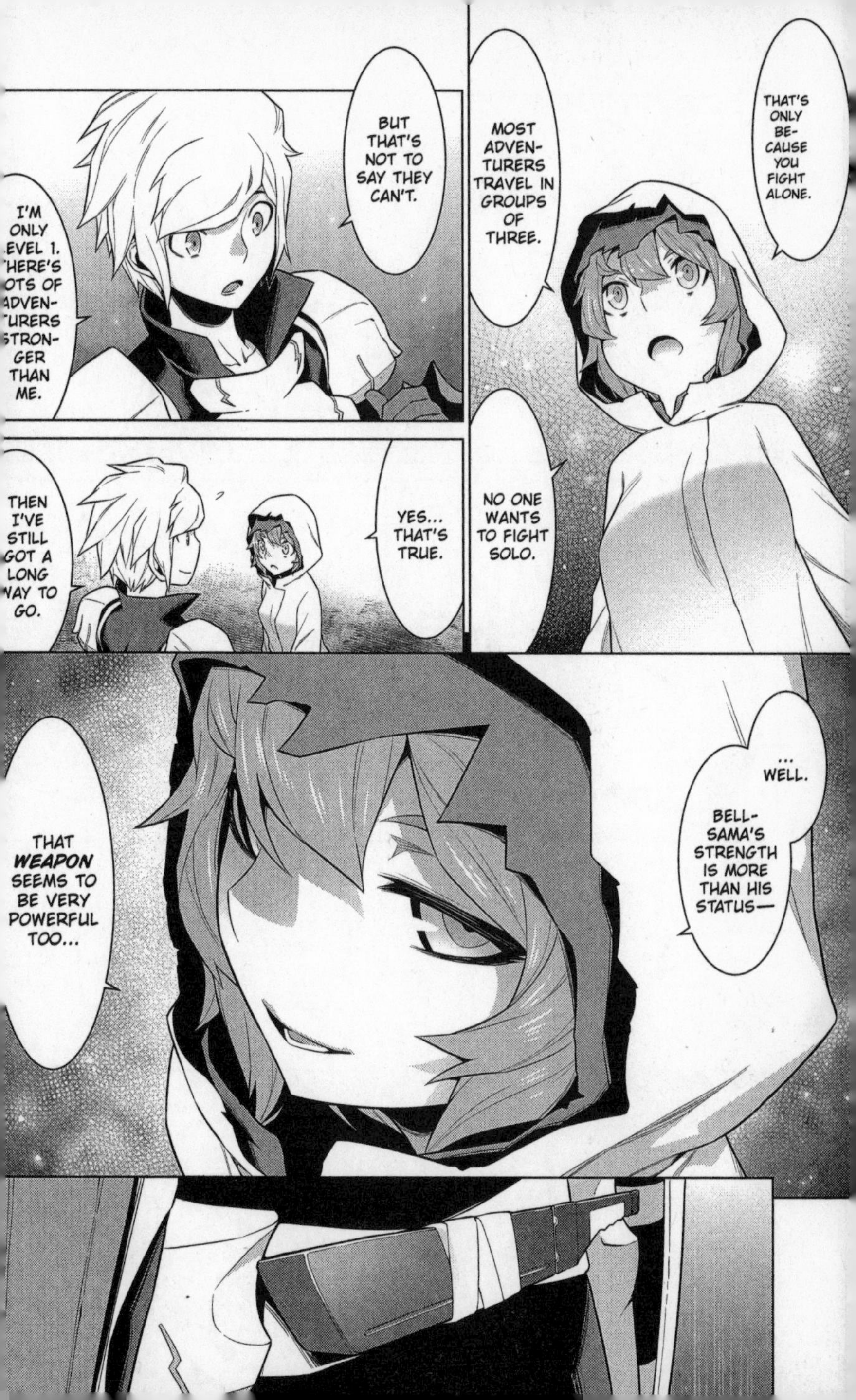

THAT'S ONLY BECAUSE YOU FIGHT ALONE.
MOST ADVENTURERS TRAVEL IN GROUPS OF THREE.
NO ONE WANTS TO FIGHT SOLO.
BUT THAT'S NOT TO SAY THEY CAN'T.
I'M ONLY EVEL 1. HERE'S OTS OF DVENTURERS TRONGER THAN ME.
YES... THAT'S TRUE.
THEN I'VE STILL GOT A LONG AY TO GO.
... WELL.
BELL-SAMA'S STRENGTH IS MORE THAN HIS STATUS—
THAT *WEAPON* SEEMS TO BE VERY POWERFUL TOO...

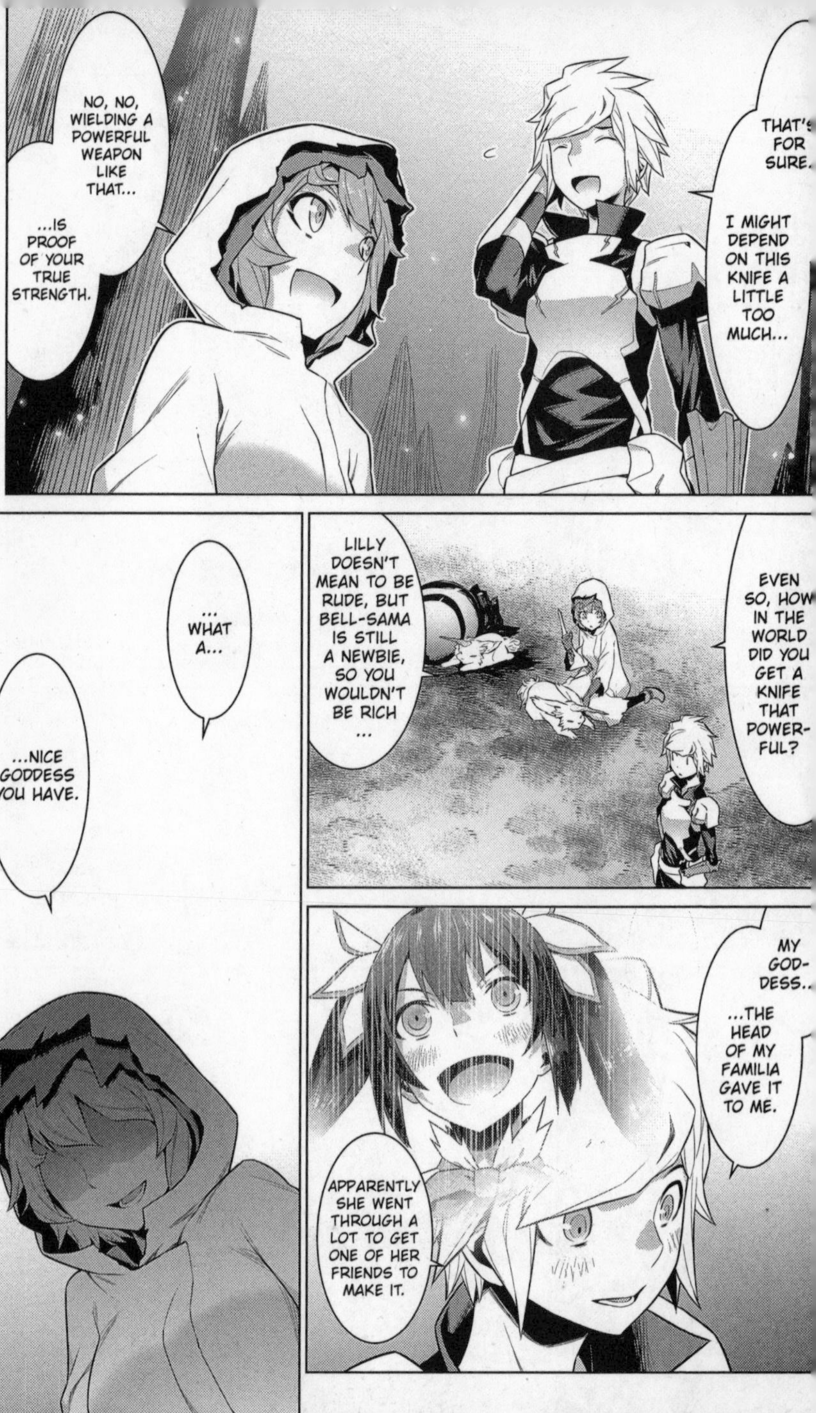
THAT'S FOR SURE.
I MIGHT DEPEND ON THIS KNIFE A LITTLE TOO MUCH...
NO, NO, WIELDING A POWERFUL WEAPON LIKE THAT...
...IS PROOF OF YOUR TRUE STRENGTH.
EVEN SO, HOW IN THE WORLD DID YOU GET A KNIFE THAT POWERFUL?
LILLY DOESN'T MEAN TO BE RUDE, BUT BELL-SAMA IS STILL A NEWBIE, SO YOU WOULDN'T BE RICH...
MY GODDESS...
...THE HEAD OF MY FAMILIA GAVE IT TO ME.
APPARENTLY SHE WENT THROUGH A LOT TO GET ONE OF HER FRIENDS TO MAKE IT.
...WHAT A...
...NICE GODDESS YOU HAVE.

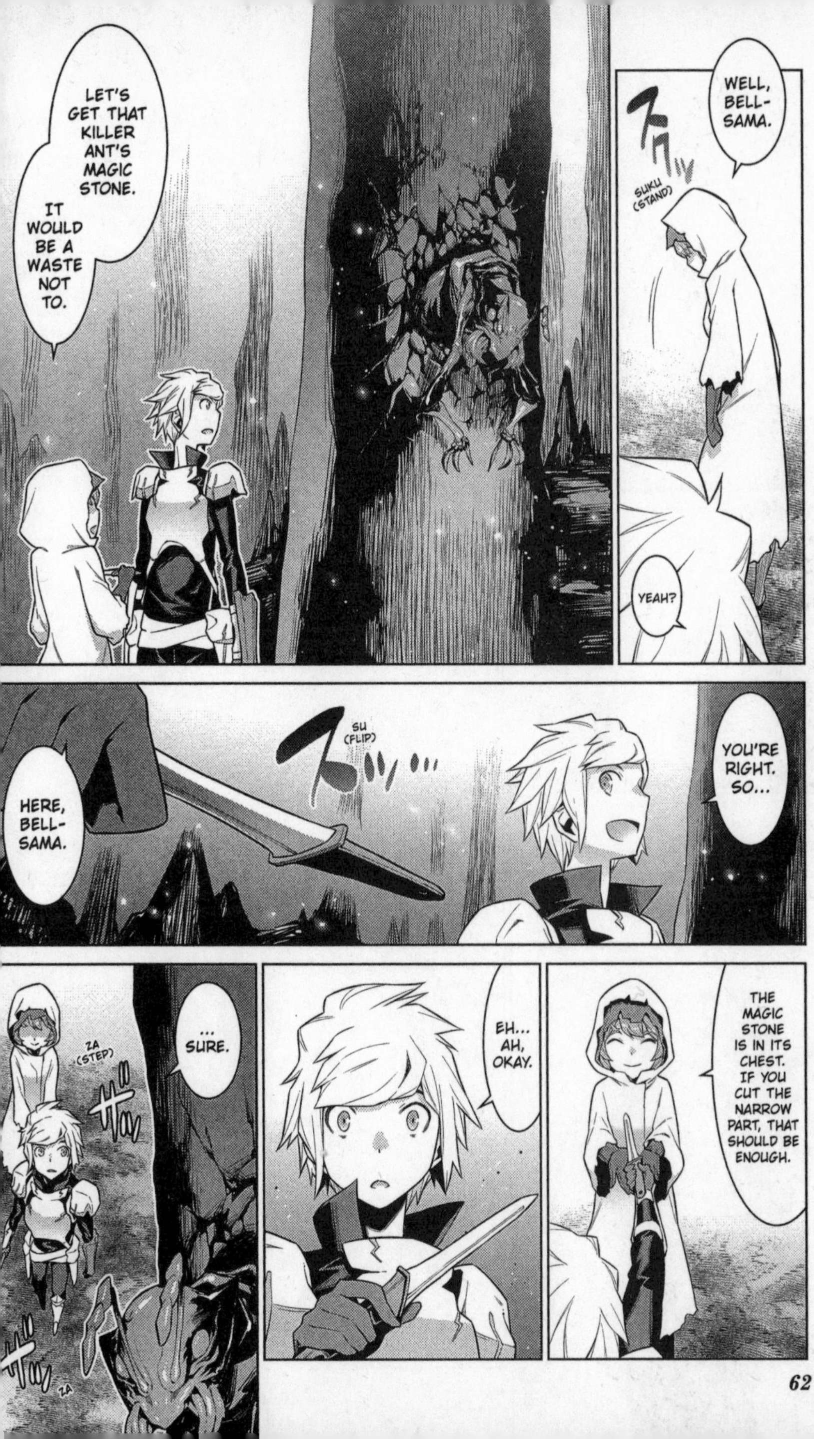
WELL, BELL-SAMA.
SUKU (STAND)
YEAH?
LET'S GET THAT KILLER ANT'S MAGIC STONE.
IT WOULD BE A WASTE NOT TO.
YOU'RE RIGHT. SO...
SU (FLIP)
HERE, BELL-SAMA.
THE MAGIC STONE IS IN ITS CHEST. IF YOU CUT THE NARROW PART, THAT SHOULD BE ENOUGH.
EH... AH, OKAY.
... SURE.
ZA (STEP)
ZA

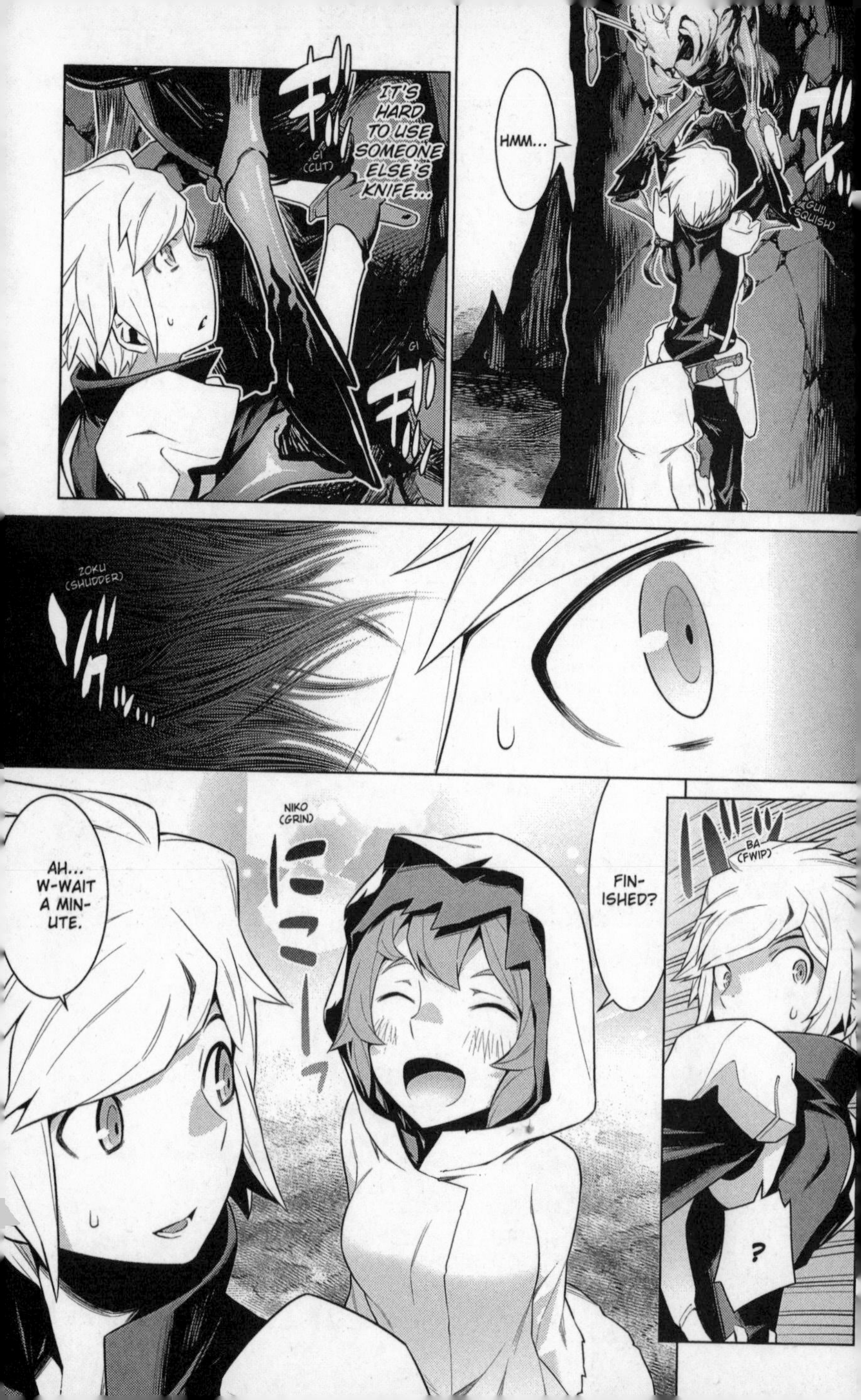
HMM...
GUII (SQUISH)
IT'S HARD TO USE SOMEONE ELSE'S KNIFE...
GI (CUT)
GI
ZOKU (SHUDDER)
BA (FWIP)
?
FIN-ISHED?
NIKO (GRIN)
AH... W-WAIT A MIN-UTE.

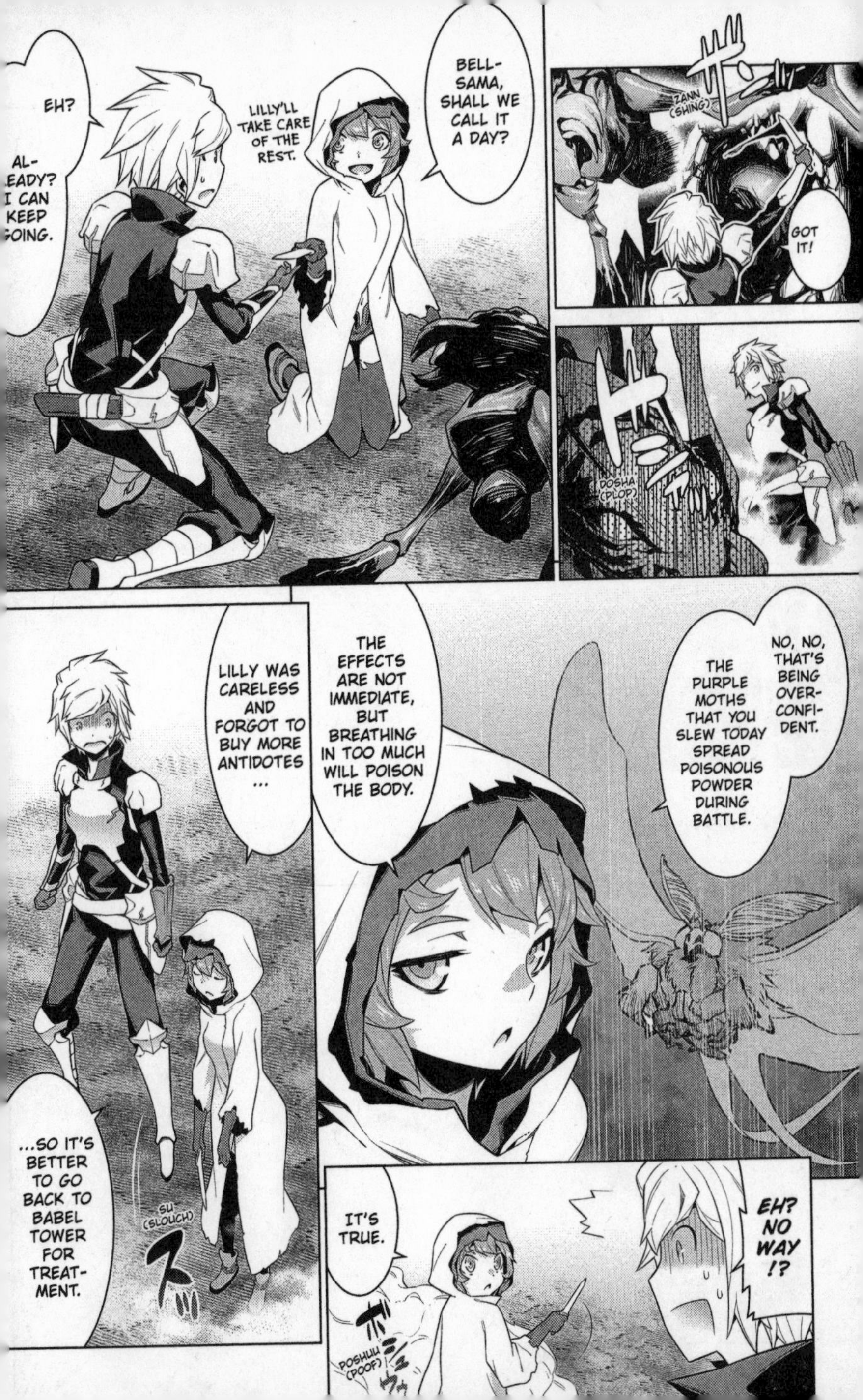
ZANN (SHING)
GOT IT!
DOSHA (PLOP)
BELL-SAMA, SHALL WE CALL IT A DAY?
LILLY'LL TAKE CARE OF THE REST.
EH?
AL-EADY? I CAN KEEP GOING.
NO, NO, THAT'S BEING OVER-CONFI-DENT.
THE PURPLE MOTHS THAT YOU SLEW TODAY SPREAD POISONOUS POWDER DURING BATTLE.
THE EFFECTS ARE NOT IMMEDIATE, BUT BREATHING IN TOO MUCH WILL POISON THE BODY.
EH? NO WAY!?
IT'S TRUE.
POSHUU (POOF)
LILLY WAS CARELESS AND FORGOT TO BUY MORE ANTIDOTES ...
...SO IT'S BETTER TO GO BACK TO BABEL TOWER FOR TREAT-MENT.
SU (SLOUCH)

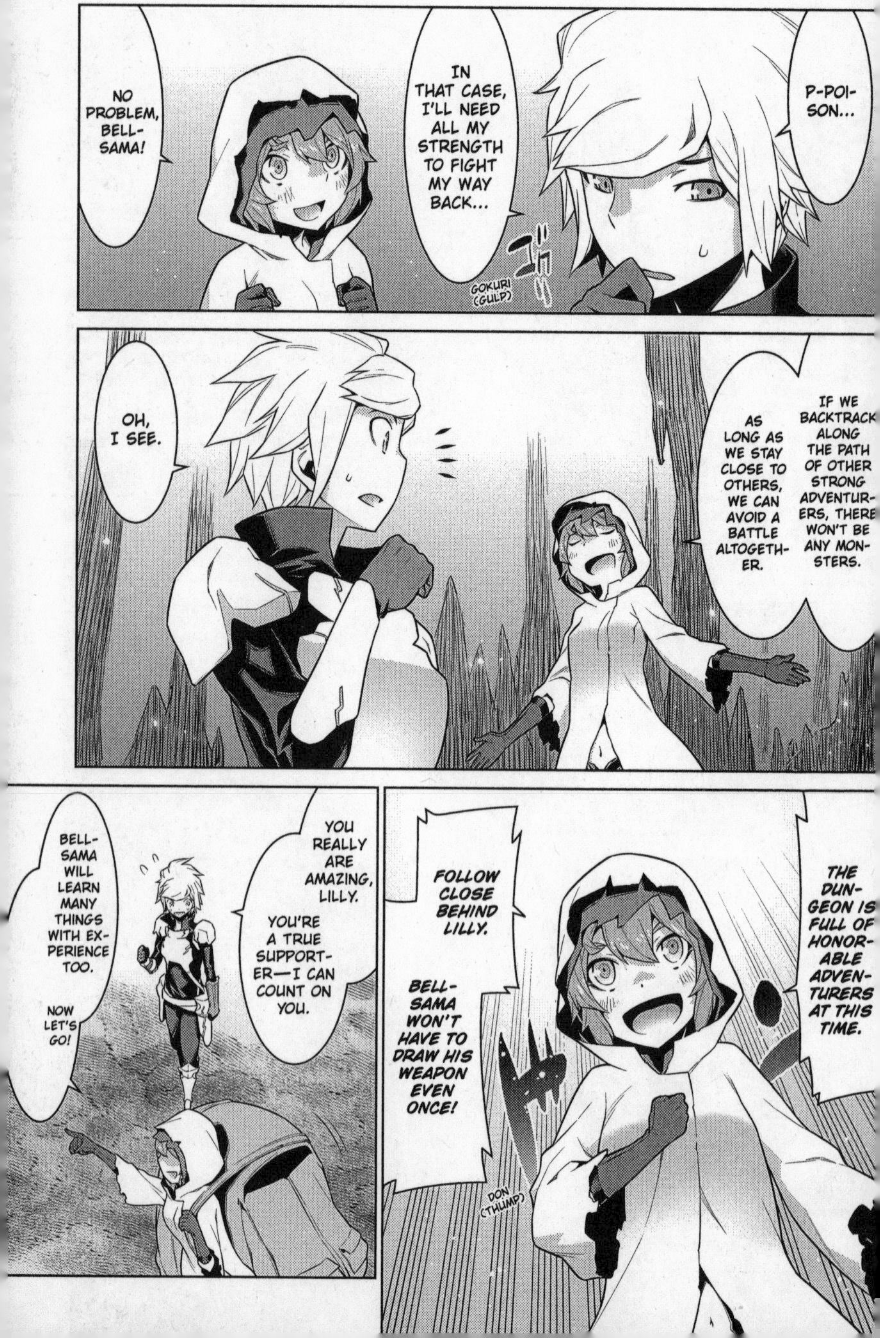
P-POISON...
IN THAT CASE, I'LL NEED ALL MY STRENGTH TO FIGHT MY WAY BACK...
GOKURI (GULP)
NO PROBLEM, BELL-SAMA!
IF WE BACKTRACK ALONG THE PATH OF OTHER STRONG ADVENTURERS, THERE WON'T BE ANY MONSTERS.
AS LONG AS WE STAY CLOSE TO OTHERS, WE CAN AVOID A BATTLE ALTOGETHER.
OH, I SEE.
THE DUNGEON IS FULL OF HONORABLE ADVENTURERS AT THIS TIME.
FOLLOW CLOSE BEHIND LILLY.
BELL-SAMA WON'T HAVE TO DRAW HIS WEAPON EVEN ONCE!
DON (THUMP)
YOU REALLY ARE AMAZING, LILLY.
YOU'RE A TRUE SUPPORTER—I CAN COUNT ON YOU.
BELL-SAMA WILL LEARN MANY THINGS WITH EXPERIENCE TOO.
NOW LET'S GO!

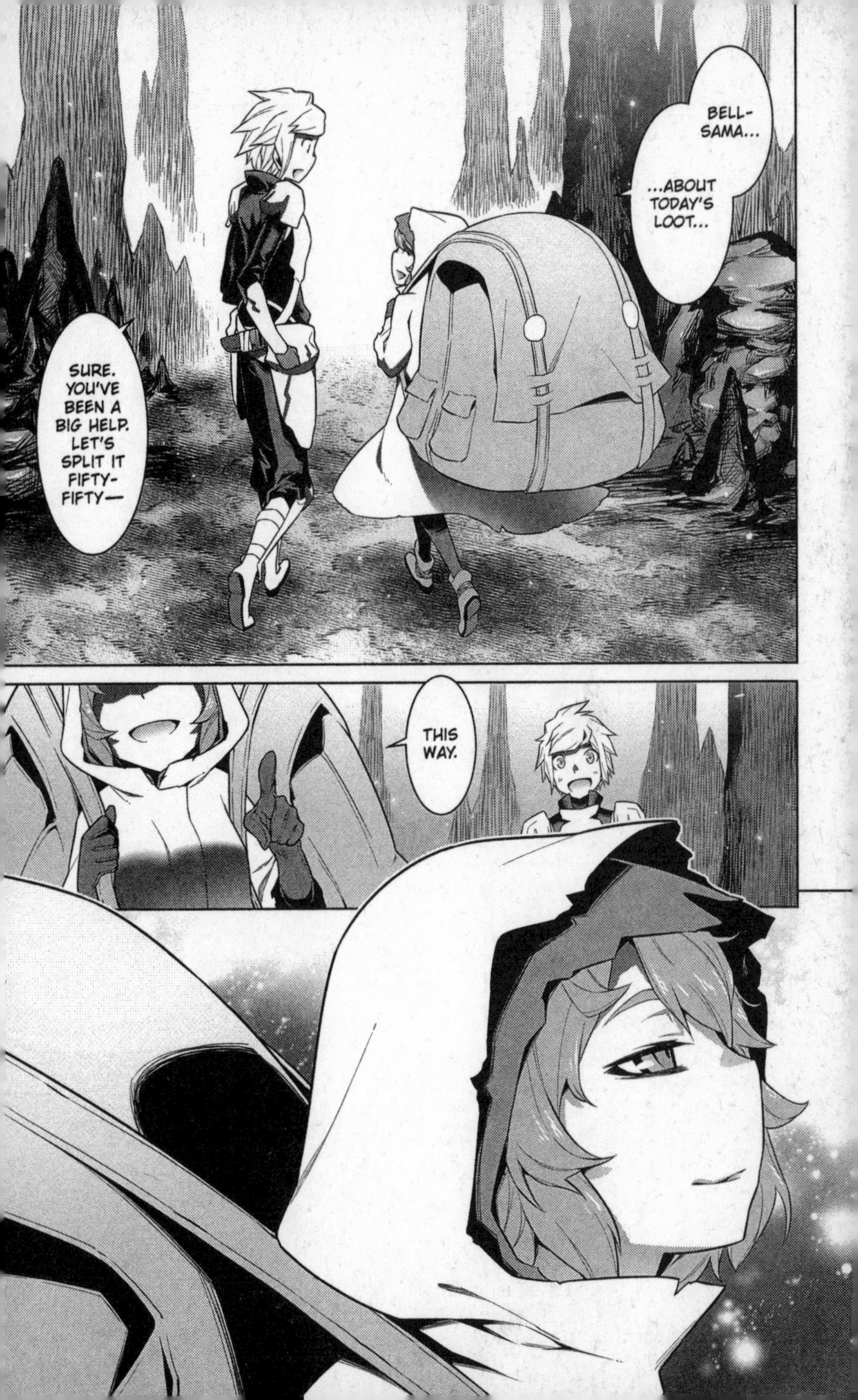
BELL-SAMA... ...ABOUT TODAY'S LOOT...
SURE. YOU'VE BEEN A BIG HELP. LET'S SPLIT IT FIFTY-FIFTY—
THIS WAY.

Is it WRONG to TRY to PiCK UP GiRLS iN A DUNGEON?

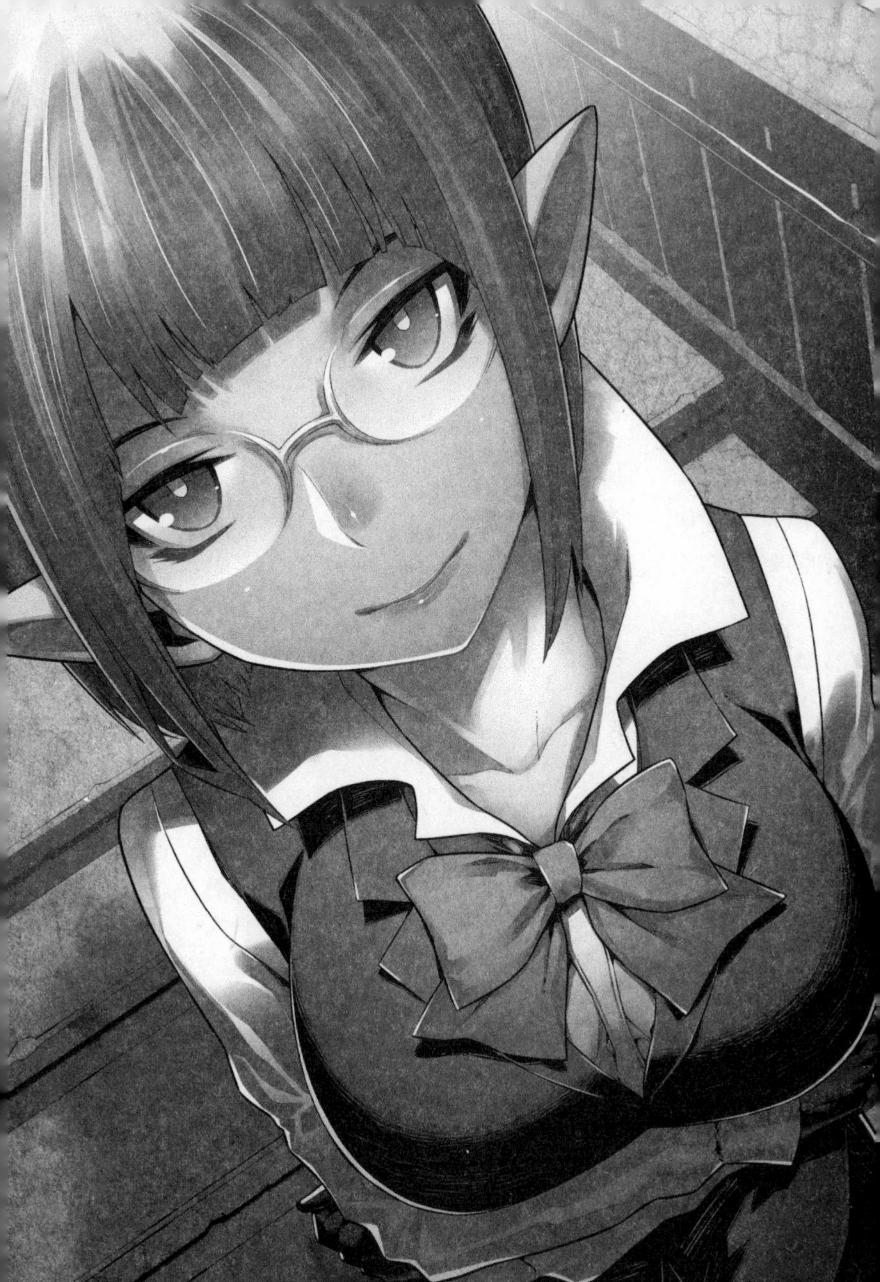

STEP 18 ▸▸ FIASCO AND MISCALCULATION

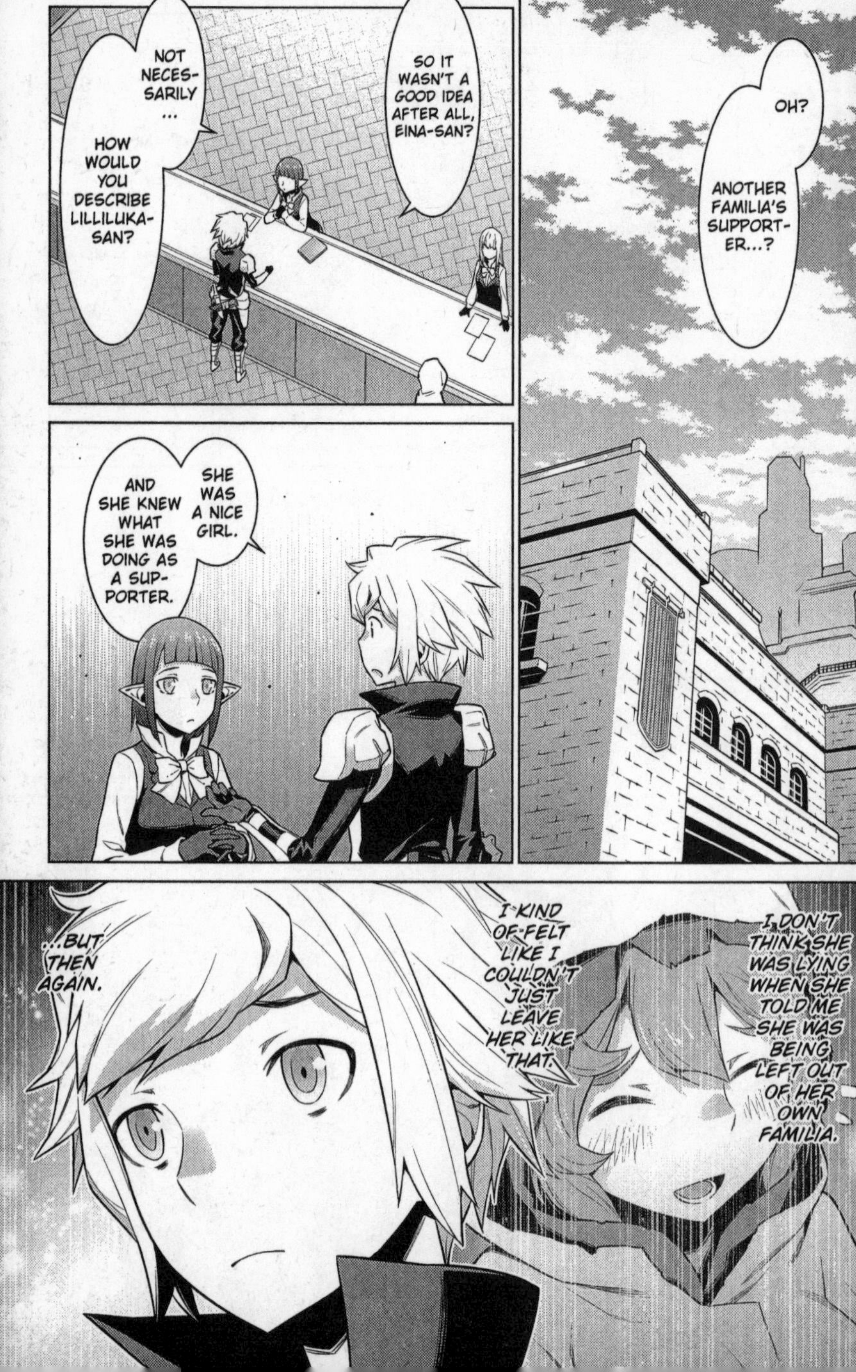
OH?
ANOTHER FAMILIA'S SUPPORTER...?
SO IT WASN'T A GOOD IDEA AFTER ALL, EINA-SAN?
NOT NECESSARILY...
HOW WOULD YOU DESCRIBE LILLILUKA-SAN?
SHE WAS A NICE GIRL.
AND SHE KNEW WHAT SHE WAS DOING AS A SUPPORTER.
I DON'T THINK SHE WAS LYING WHEN SHE TOLD ME SHE WAS BEING LEFT OUT OF HER OWN FAMILIA.
I KIND OF FELT LIKE I COULDN'T JUST LEAVE HER LIKE THAT.
...BUT THEN AGAIN.

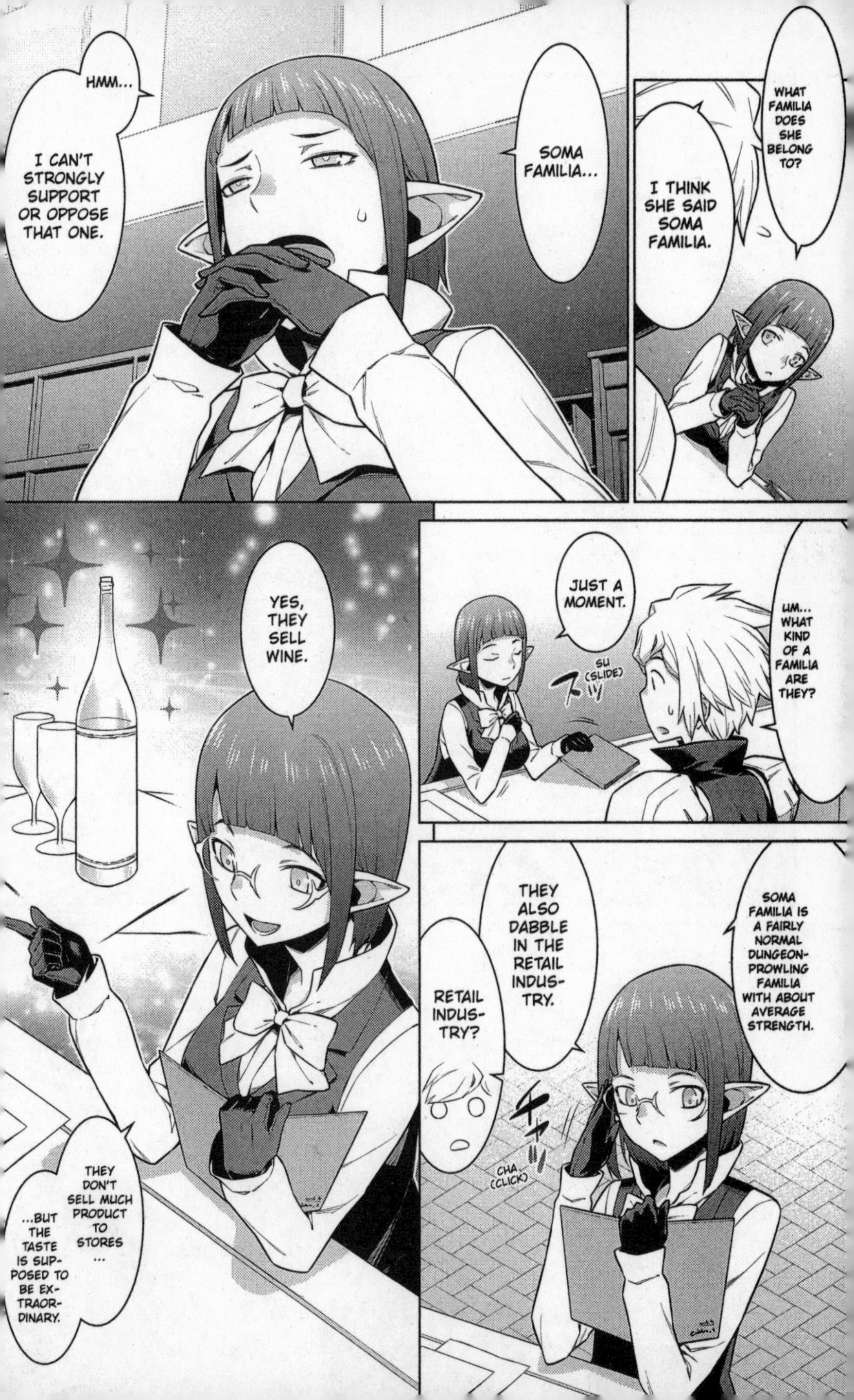
WHAT FAMILIA DOES SHE BELONG TO?
I THINK SHE SAID SOMA FAMILIA.
SOMA FAMILIA...
HMM...
I CAN'T STRONGLY SUPPORT OR OPPOSE THAT ONE.
UM... WHAT KIND OF A FAMILIA ARE THEY?
JUST A MOMENT.
SU (SLIDE)
SOMA FAMILIA IS A FAIRLY NORMAL DUNGEON-PROWLING FAMILIA WITH ABOUT AVERAGE STRENGTH.
THEY ALSO DABBLE IN THE RETAIL INDUSTRY.
RETAIL INDUSTRY?
CHA (CLICK)
YES, THEY SELL WINE.
THEY DON'T SELL MUCH PRODUCT TO STORES...
...BUT THE TASTE IS SUPPOSED TO BE EXTRAORDINARY.

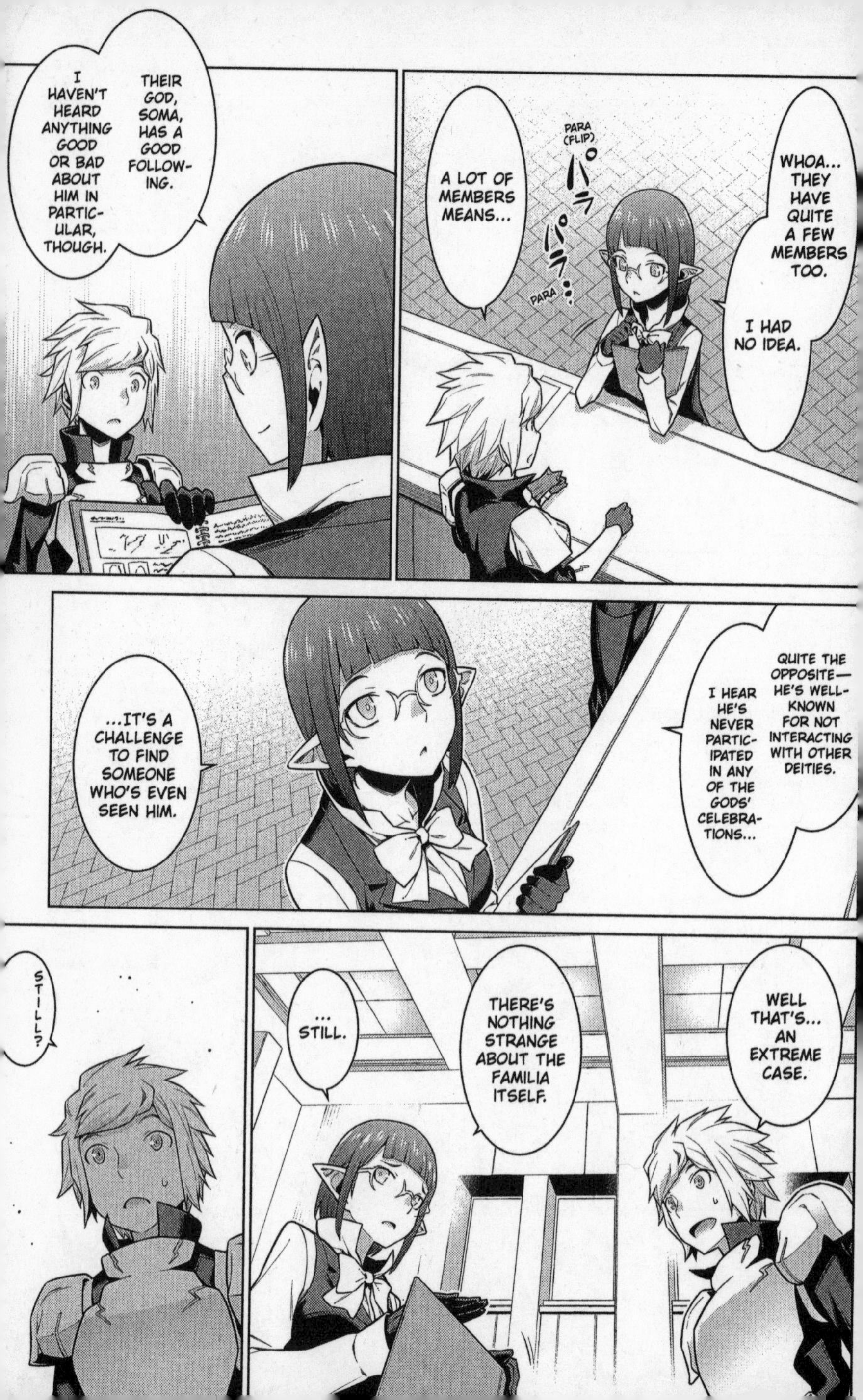
WHOA... THEY HAVE QUITE A FEW MEMBERS TOO.
I HAD NO IDEA.
PARA (FLIP)
パラ
パラ…
PARA
A LOT OF MEMBERS MEANS...
THEIR GOD, SOMA, HAS A GOOD FOLLOWING.
I HAVEN'T HEARD ANYTHING GOOD OR BAD ABOUT HIM IN PARTICULAR, THOUGH.
QUITE THE OPPOSITE—HE'S WELL-KNOWN FOR NOT INTERACTING WITH OTHER DEITIES.
I HEAR HE'S NEVER PARTICIPATED IN ANY OF THE GODS' CELEBRATIONS...
...IT'S A CHALLENGE TO FIND SOMEONE WHO'S EVEN SEEN HIM.
WELL THAT'S... AN EXTREME CASE.
THERE'S NOTHING STRANGE ABOUT THE FAMILIA ITSELF.
... STILL.
STILL?

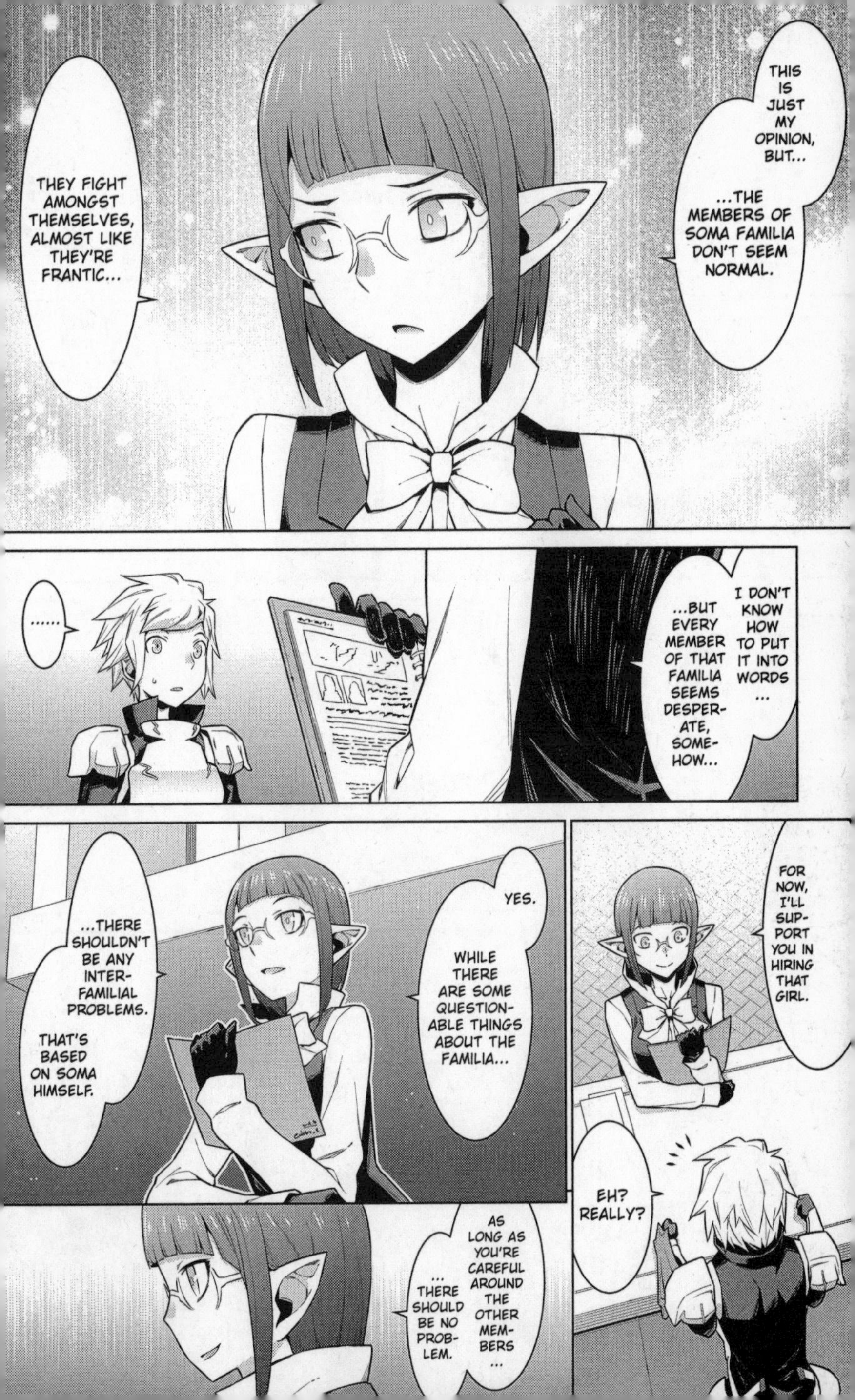
THIS IS JUST MY OPINION, BUT...
...THE MEMBERS OF SOMA FAMILIA DON'T SEEM NORMAL.
THEY FIGHT AMONGST THEMSELVES, ALMOST LIKE THEY'RE FRANTIC...
I DON'T KNOW HOW TO PUT IT INTO WORDS...
...BUT EVERY MEMBER OF THAT FAMILIA SEEMS DESPERATE, SOMEHOW...
......
FOR NOW, I'LL SUPPORT YOU IN HIRING THAT GIRL.
EH? REALLY?
YES.
WHILE THERE ARE SOME QUESTIONABLE THINGS ABOUT THE FAMILIA...
...THERE SHOULDN'T BE ANY INTER-FAMILIAL PROBLEMS.
THAT'S BASED ON SOMA HIMSELF.
AS LONG AS YOU'RE CAREFUL AROUND THE OTHER MEMBERS...
...THERE SHOULD BE NO PROBLEM.

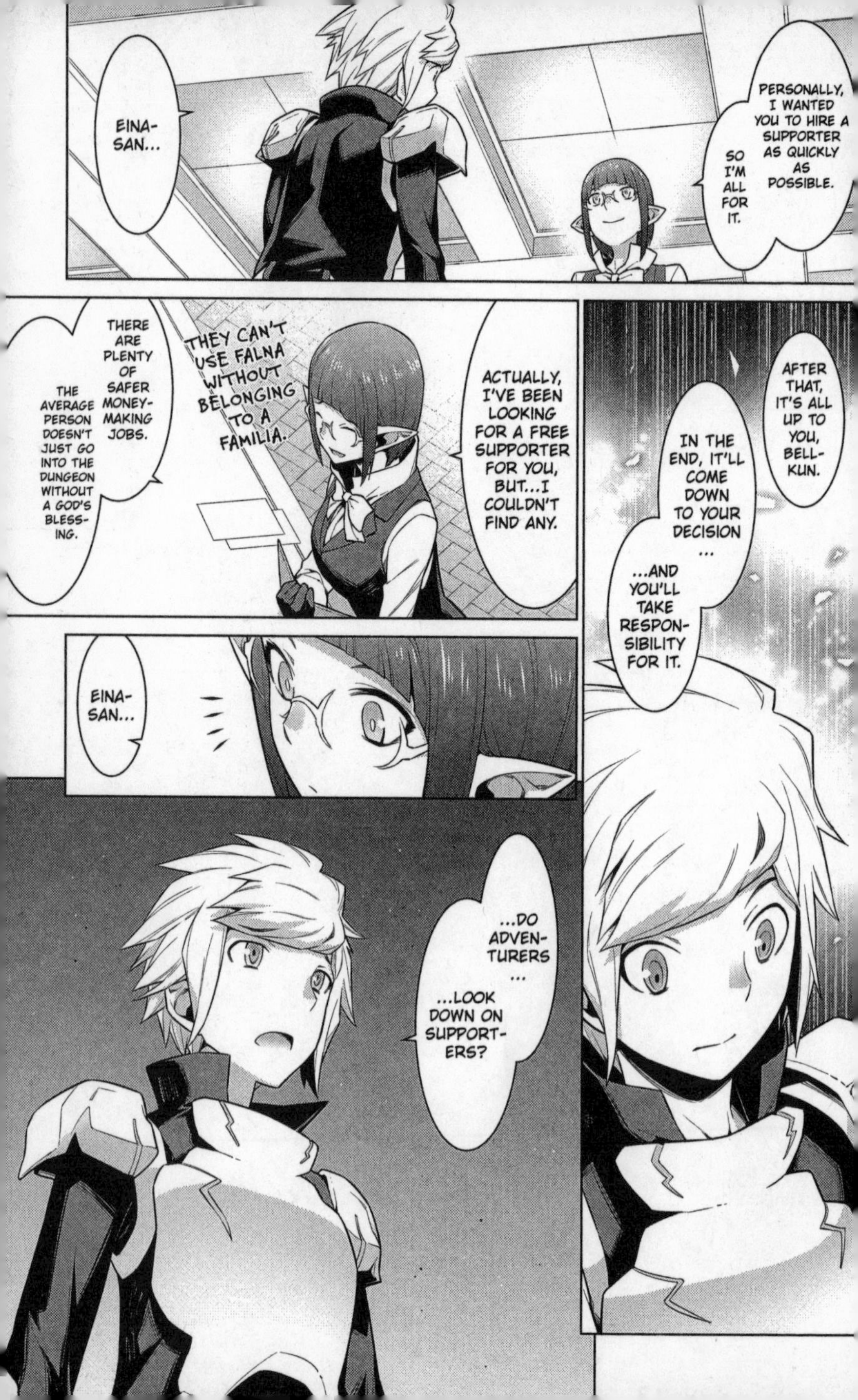
PERSONALLY, I WANTED YOU TO HIRE A SUPPORTER AS QUICKLY AS POSSIBLE.
SO I'M ALL FOR IT.
EINA-SAN...
AFTER THAT, IT'S ALL UP TO YOU, BELL-KUN.
IN THE END, IT'LL COME DOWN TO YOUR DECISION...
...AND YOU'LL TAKE RESPONSIBILITY FOR IT.
ACTUALLY, I'VE BEEN LOOKING FOR A FREE SUPPORTER FOR YOU, BUT...I COULDN'T FIND ANY.
THEY CAN'T USE FALNA WITHOUT BELONGING TO A FAMILIA.
THERE ARE PLENTY OF SAFER MONEY-MAKING JOBS.
THE AVERAGE PERSON DOESN'T JUST GO INTO THE DUNGEON WITHOUT A GOD'S BLESS-ING.
EINA-SAN...
...DO ADVENTURERS...
...LOOK DOWN ON SUPPORTERS?

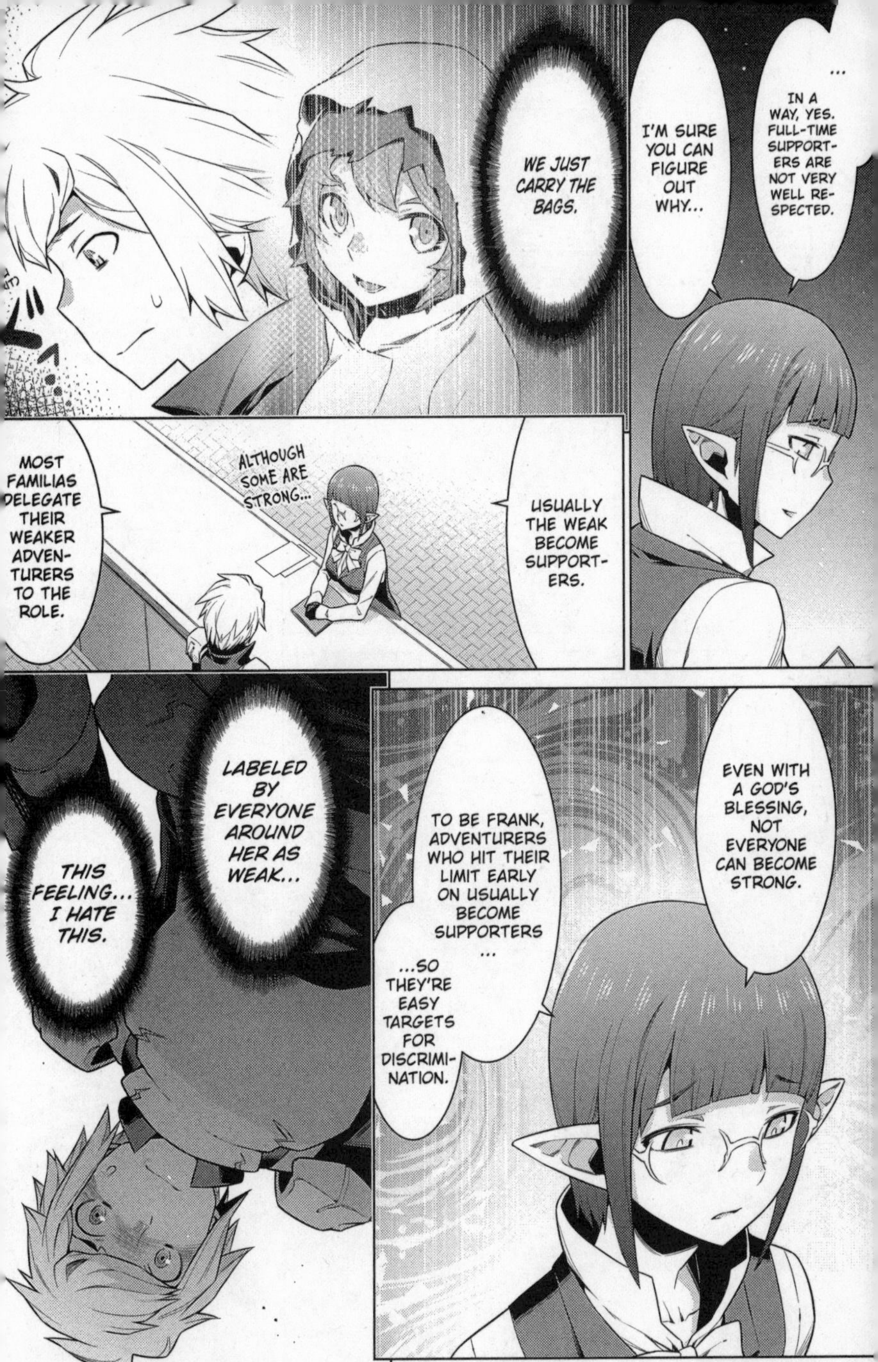
...
IN A WAY, YES. FULL-TIME SUPPORTERS ARE NOT VERY WELL RESPECTED.
I'M SURE YOU CAN FIGURE OUT WHY...
WE JUST CARRY THE BAGS.
USUALLY THE WEAK BECOME SUPPORTERS.
ALTHOUGH SOME ARE STRONG...
MOST FAMILIAS DELEGATE THEIR WEAKER ADVENTURERS TO THE ROLE.
EVEN WITH A GOD'S BLESSING, NOT EVERYONE CAN BECOME STRONG.
TO BE FRANK, ADVENTURERS WHO HIT THEIR LIMIT EARLY ON USUALLY BECOME SUPPORTERS...
...SO THEY'RE EASY TARGETS FOR DISCRIMINATION.
LABELED BY EVERYONE AROUND HER AS WEAK...
THIS FEELING... I HATE THIS.

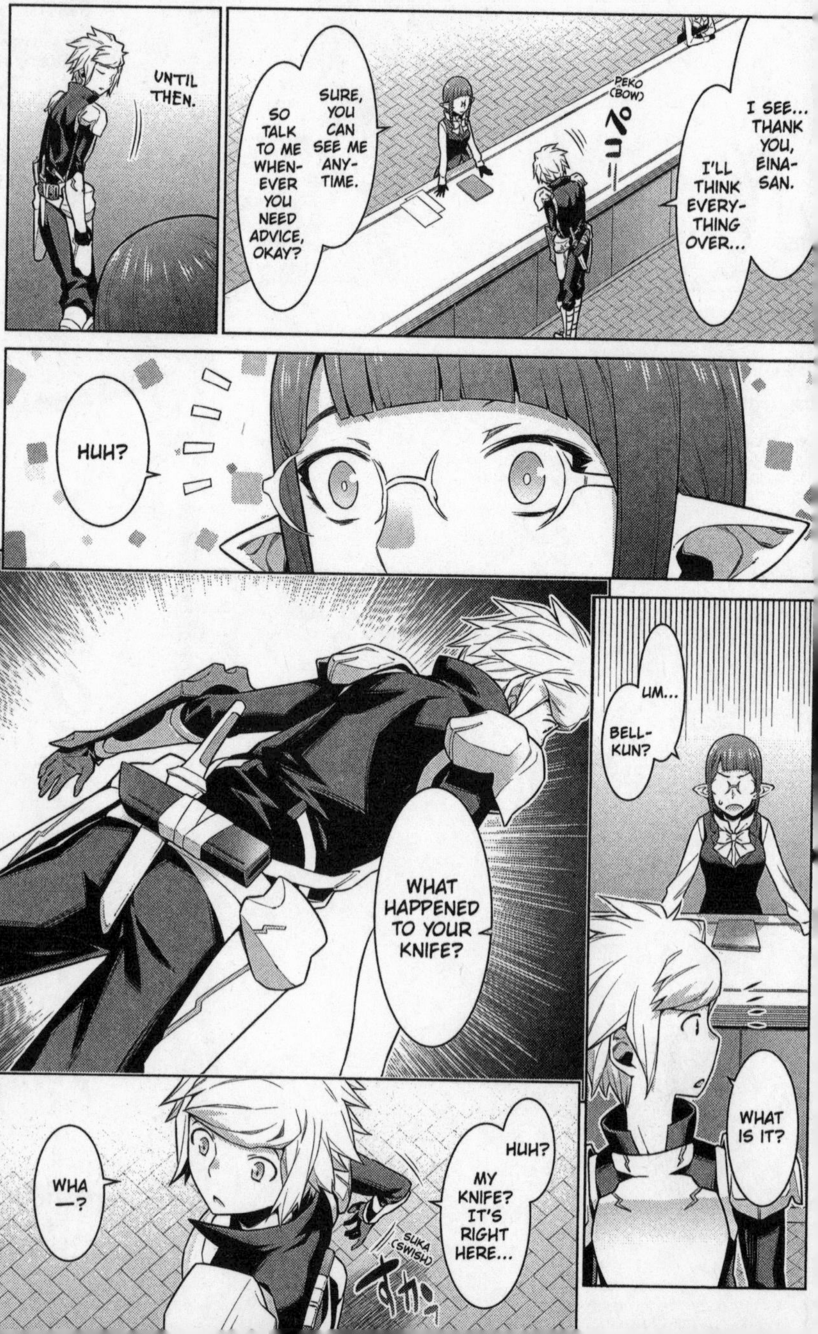
I SEE... THANK YOU, EINA-SAN.
I'LL THINK EVERYTHING OVER...
PEKO (BOW)
SURE, YOU CAN SEE ME ANYTIME.
SO TALK TO ME WHENEVER YOU NEED ADVICE, OKAY?
UNTIL THEN.
HUH?
UM...
BELL-KUN?
WHAT IS IT?
WHAT HAPPENED TO YOUR KNIFE?
HUH?
MY KNIFE? IT'S RIGHT HERE...
SUKA (SWISH)
WHA—?

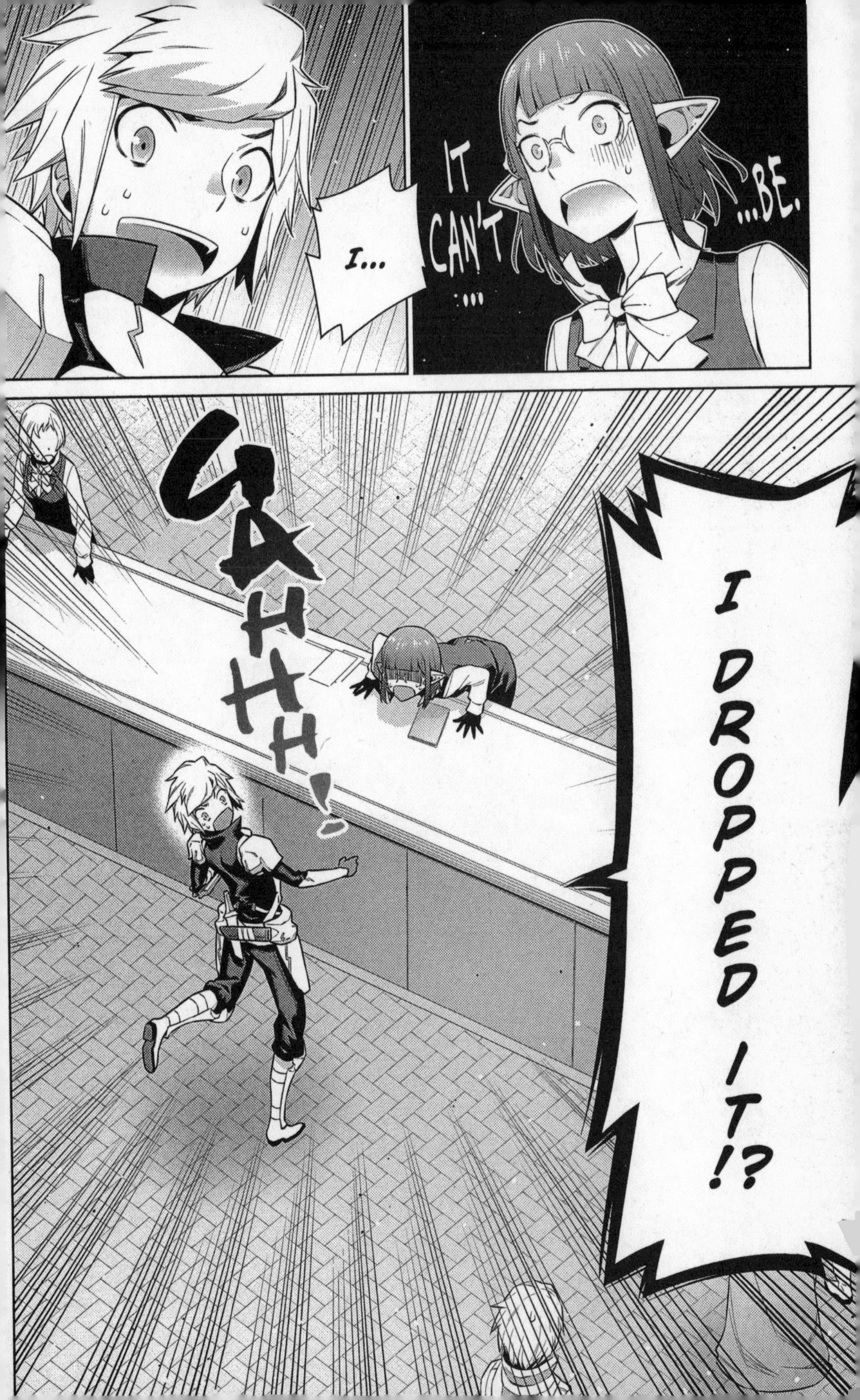
IT CAN'T
...BE.
I...
I DROPPED IT!?
UAHHH!

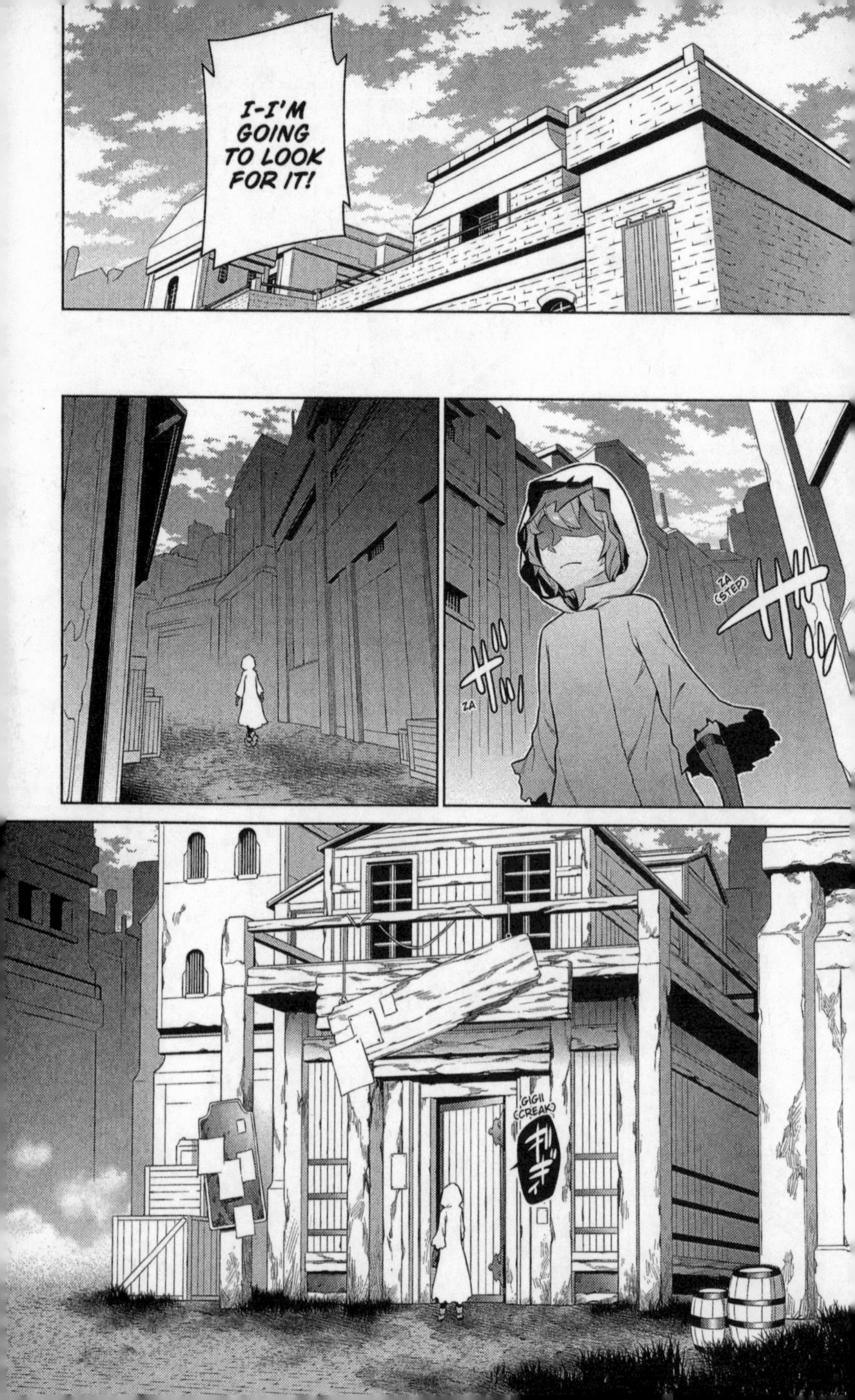
I-I'M GOING TO LOOK FOR IT!
ZA (STEP)
ZA
GIGII (CREAK)

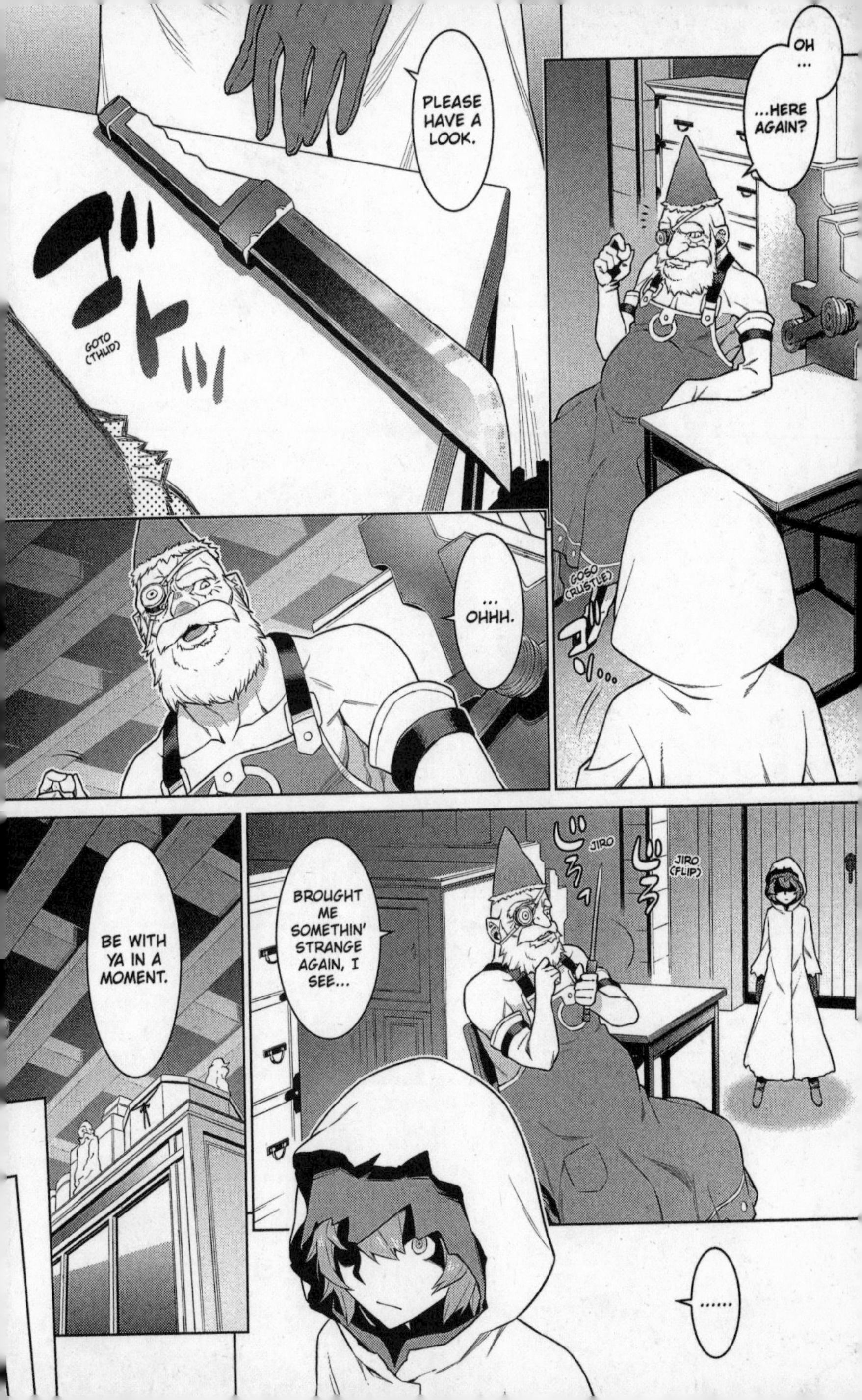
OH ... ...HERE AGAIN?
GOSO (RUSTLE)
PLEASE HAVE A LOOK.
GOTO (THUD)
... OHHH.
JIRO (FLIP)
JIRO
BROUGHT ME SOMETHIN' STRANGE AGAIN, I SEE...
......
BE WITH YA IN A MOMENT.

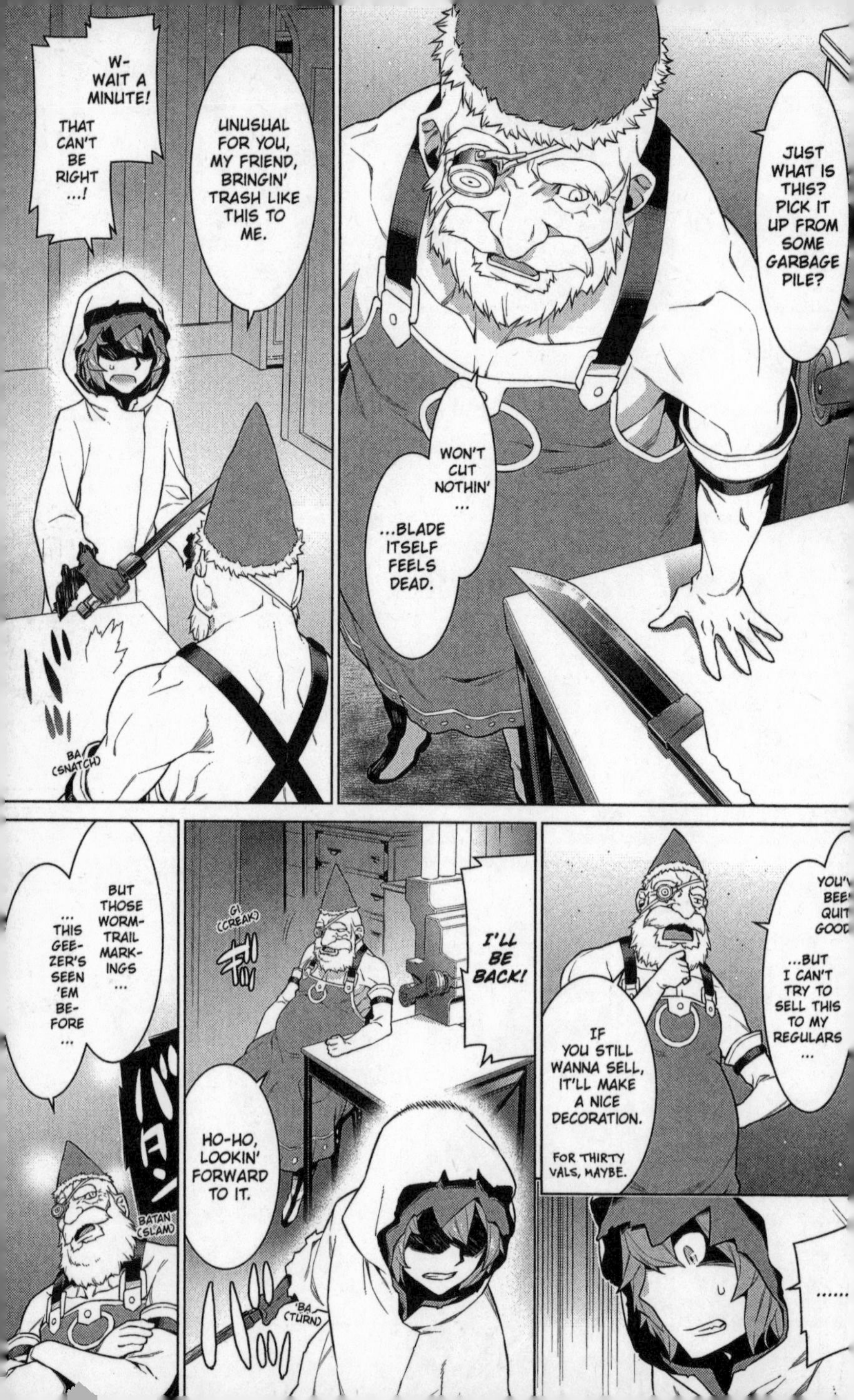

JUST WHAT IS THIS? PICK IT UP FROM SOME GARBAGE PILE?
WON'T CUT NOTHIN' ...
...BLADE ITSELF FEELS DEAD.
UNUSUAL FOR YOU, MY FRIEND, BRINGIN' TRASH LIKE THIS TO ME.
W- WAIT A MINUTE!
THAT CAN'T BE RIGHT ...!
BA (SNATCH)
YOU'V BEE QUIT GOOD
...BUT I CAN'T TRY TO SELL THIS TO MY REGULARS ...
IF YOU STILL WANNA SELL, IT'LL MAKE A NICE DECORATION.
FOR THIRTY VALS, MAYBE.
......
I'LL BE BACK!
GI (CREAK)
HO-HO, LOOKIN' FORWARD TO IT.
BA (TURN)
BUT THOSE WORM-TRAIL MARKINGS ...
... THIS GEEZER'S SEEN 'EM BEFORE ...
BATAN (SLAM)

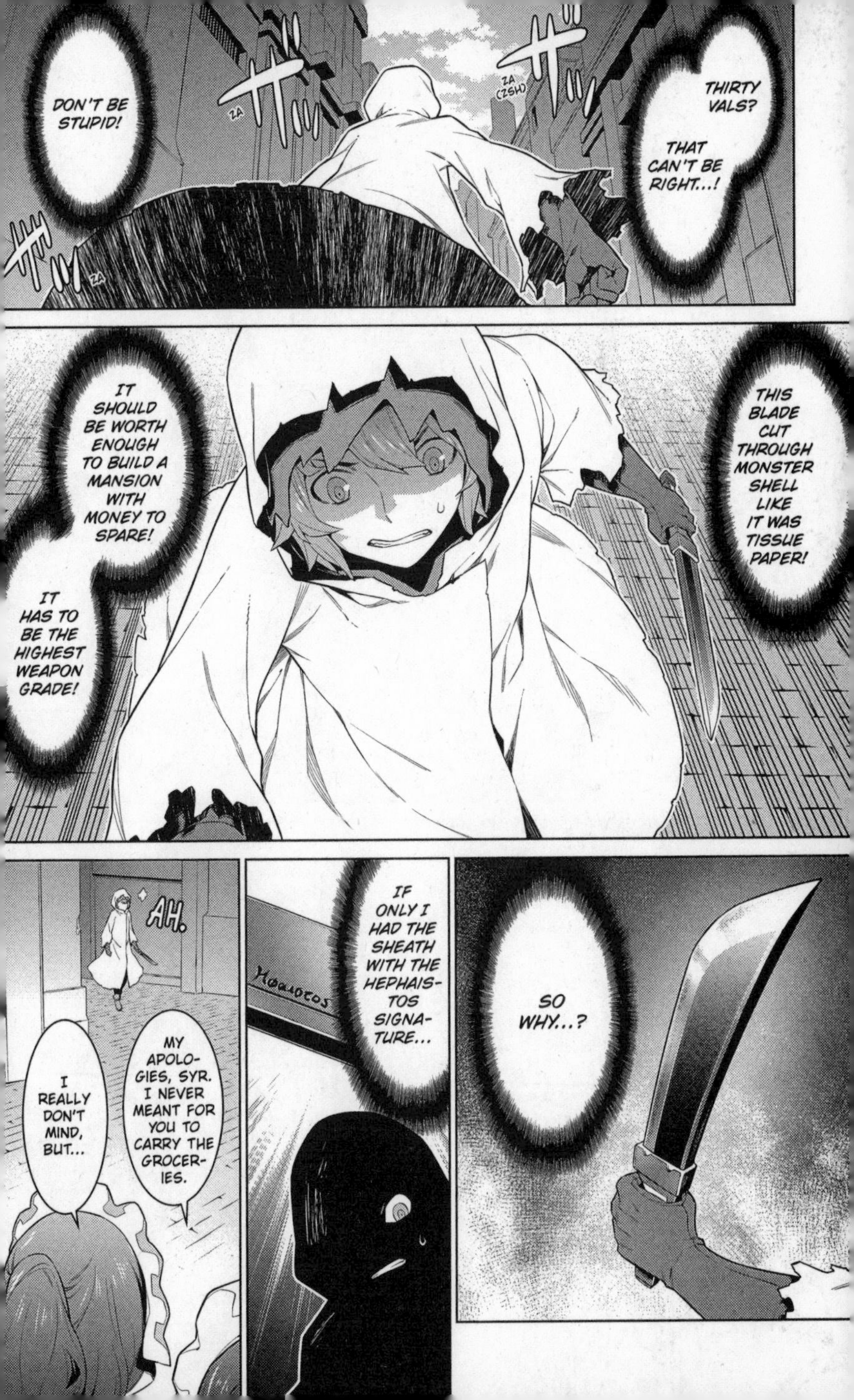
THIRTY VALS?
THAT CAN'T BE RIGHT...!
ZA (ZSH)
ZA
DON'T BE STUPID!
ZA
THIS BLADE CUT THROUGH MONSTER SHELL LIKE IT WAS TISSUE PAPER!
IT SHOULD BE WORTH ENOUGH TO BUILD A MANSION WITH MONEY TO SPARE!
IT HAS TO BE THE HIGHEST WEAPON GRADE!
SO WHY...?
IF ONLY I HAD THE SHEATH WITH THE HEPHAISTOS SIGNATURE...
Ηφαιστος
AH.
MY APOLOGIES, SYR. I NEVER MEANT FOR YOU TO CARRY THE GROCERIES.
I REALLY DON'T MIND, BUT...

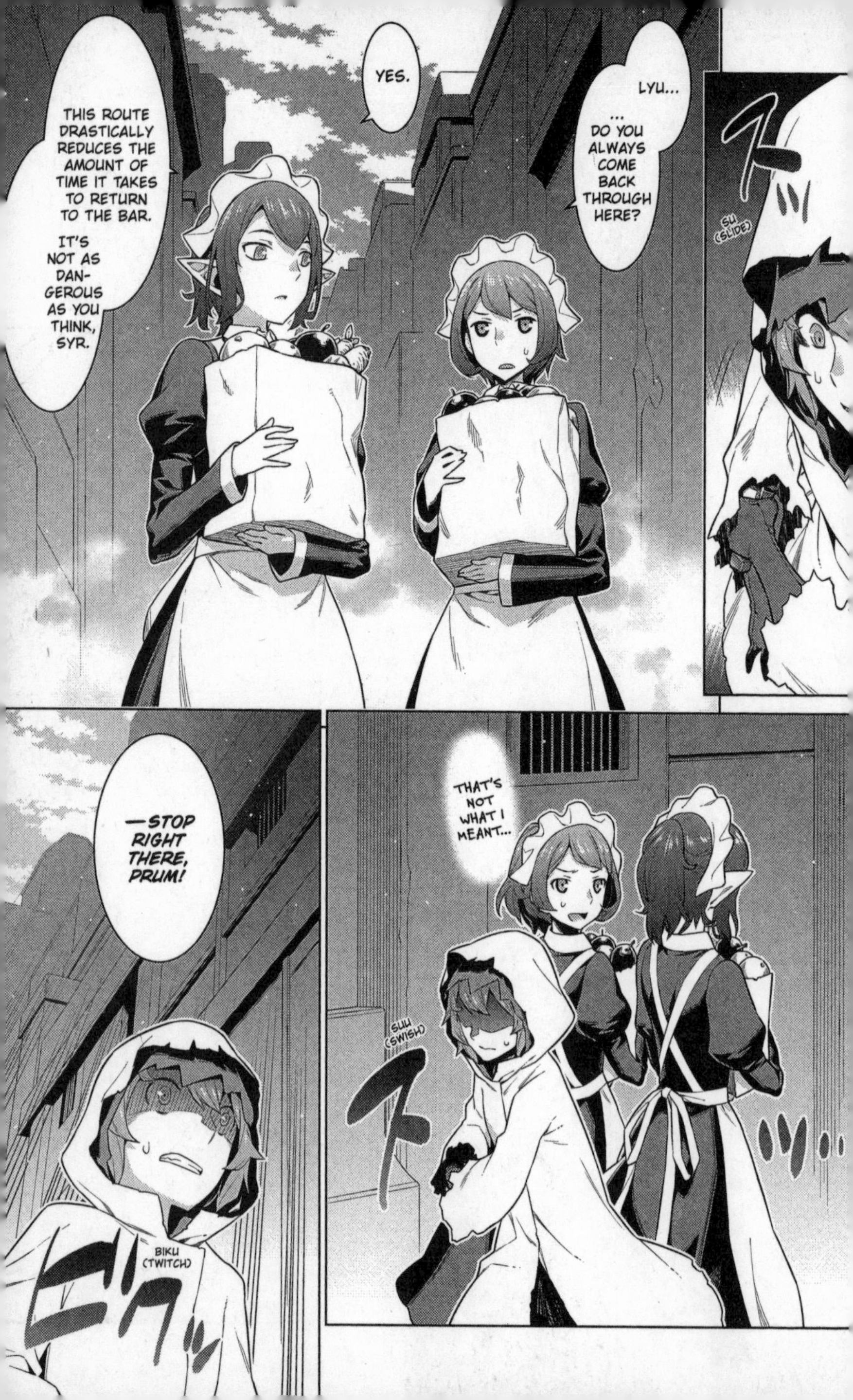
SU (SLIDE)
LYU... ...DO YOU ALWAYS COME BACK THROUGH HERE?
YES.
THIS ROUTE DRASTICALLY REDUCES THE AMOUNT OF TIME IT TAKES TO RETURN TO THE BAR.
IT'S NOT AS DAN-GEROUS AS YOU THINK, SYR.
THAT'S NOT WHAT I MEANT...
SUU (SWISH)
—STOP RIGHT THERE, PRUM!
BIKU (TWITCH)

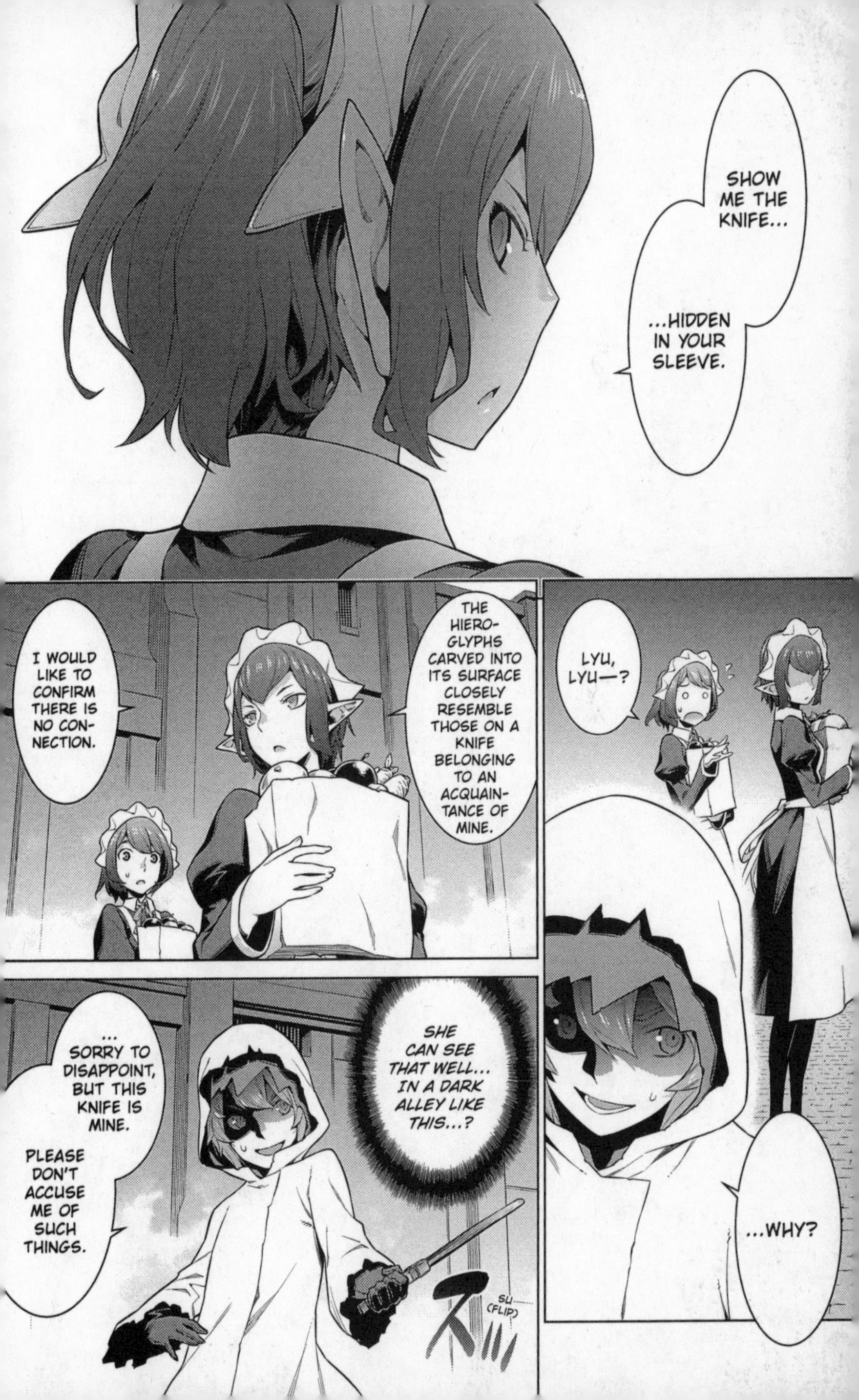
SHOW ME THE KNIFE...
...HIDDEN IN YOUR SLEEVE.
LYU, LYU—?
...WHY?
THE HIERO-GLYPHS CARVED INTO ITS SURFACE CLOSELY RESEMBLE THOSE ON A KNIFE BELONGING TO AN ACQUAIN-TANCE OF MINE.
I WOULD LIKE TO CONFIRM THERE IS NO CON-NECTION.
SHE CAN SEE THAT WELL... IN A DARK ALLEY LIKE THIS...?
... SORRY TO DISAPPOINT, BUT THIS KNIFE IS MINE.
PLEASE DON'T ACCUSE ME OF SUCH THINGS.
SU— (FLIP)

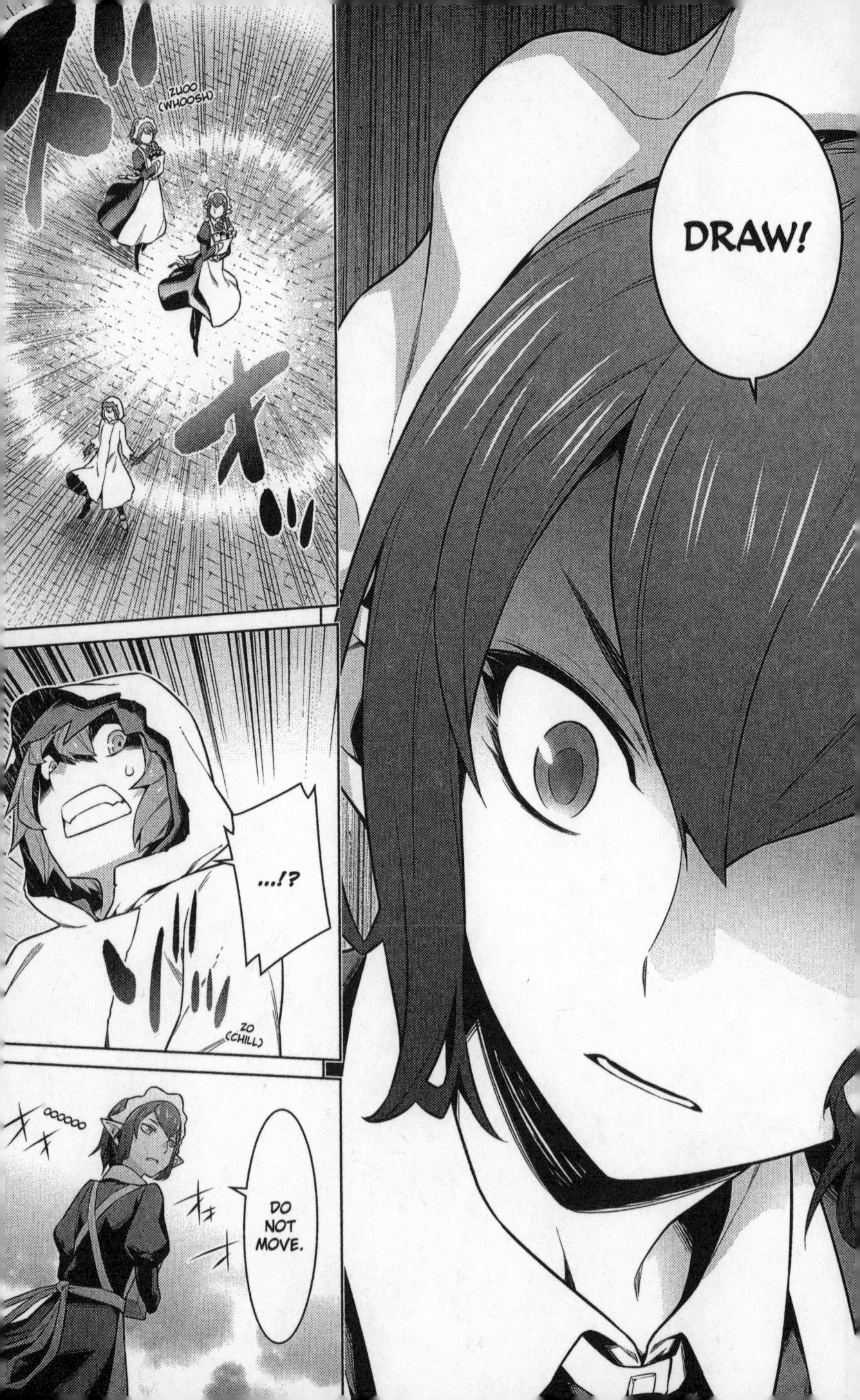
DRAW!
ZUOO (WHOOSH)
...!?
ZO (CHILL)
OOOOOO
DO NOT MOVE.

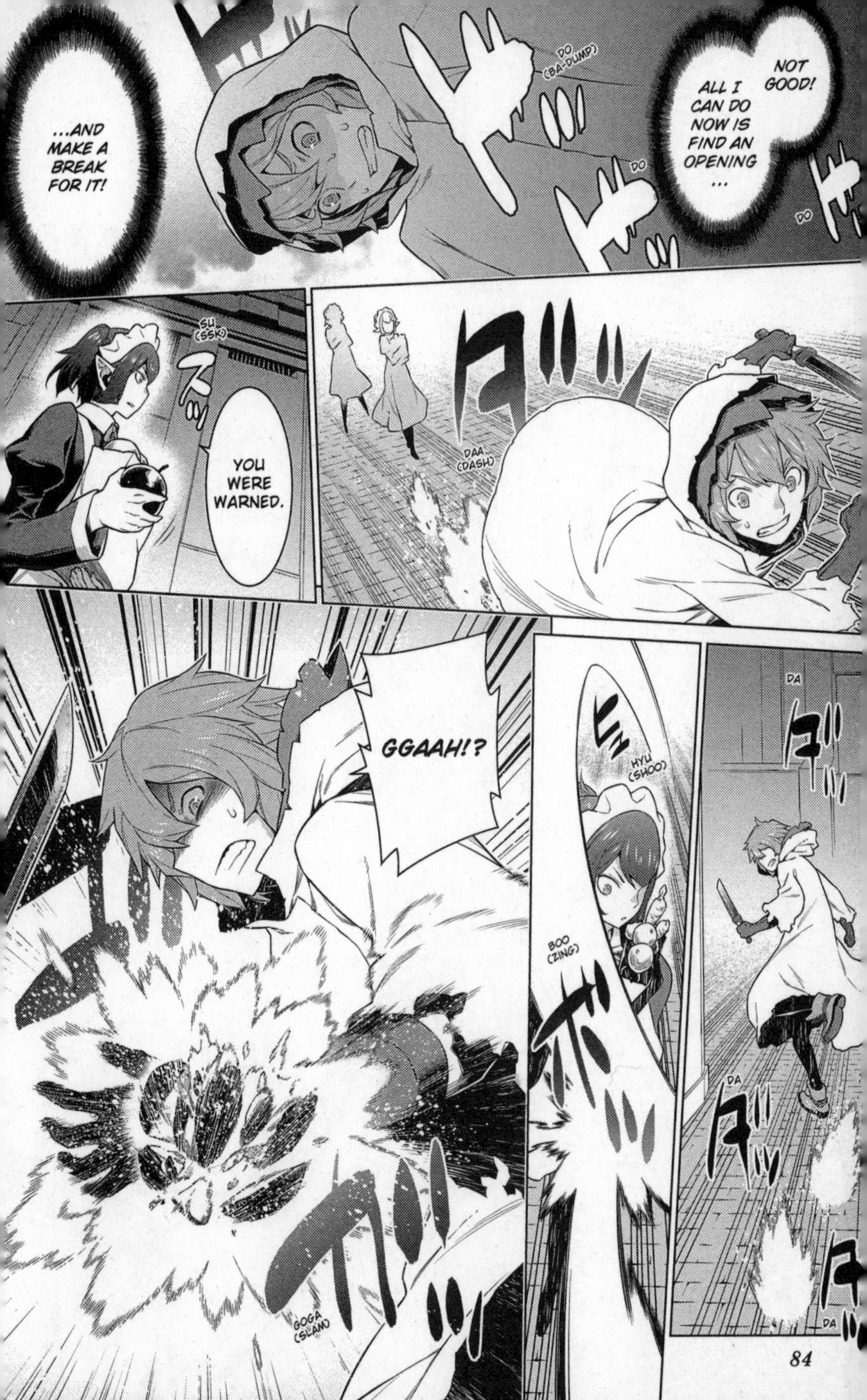
NOT GOOD! ALL I CAN DO NOW IS FIND AN OPENING ...
DO (BA-DUMP)
DO
DO
...AND MAKE A BREAK FOR IT!
DAA (DASH)
SU (SSK)
YOU WERE WARNED.
DA
DA
DA
HYU (SHOO)
BOO (ZING)
GGAAH!?
GOGA (SLAM)

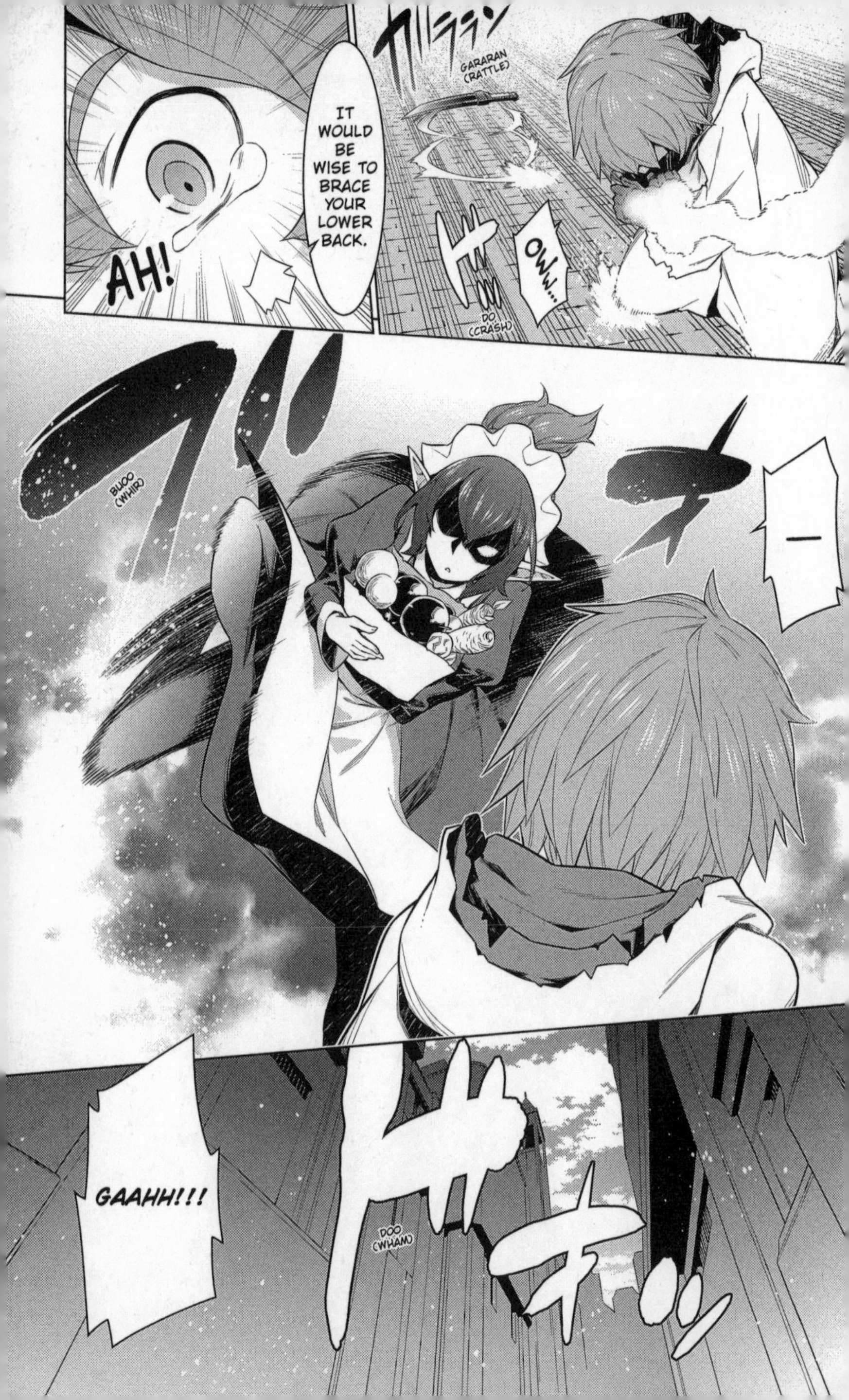
GARARAN (RATTLE)
OWW...
DO (CRASH)
IT WOULD BE WISE TO BRACE YOUR LOWER BACK.
AH!
—
BUOO (WHIR)
GAAHH!!!
DOO (WHAM)

STEP 19 ▸▸ A BIG MISUNDERSTANDING!?

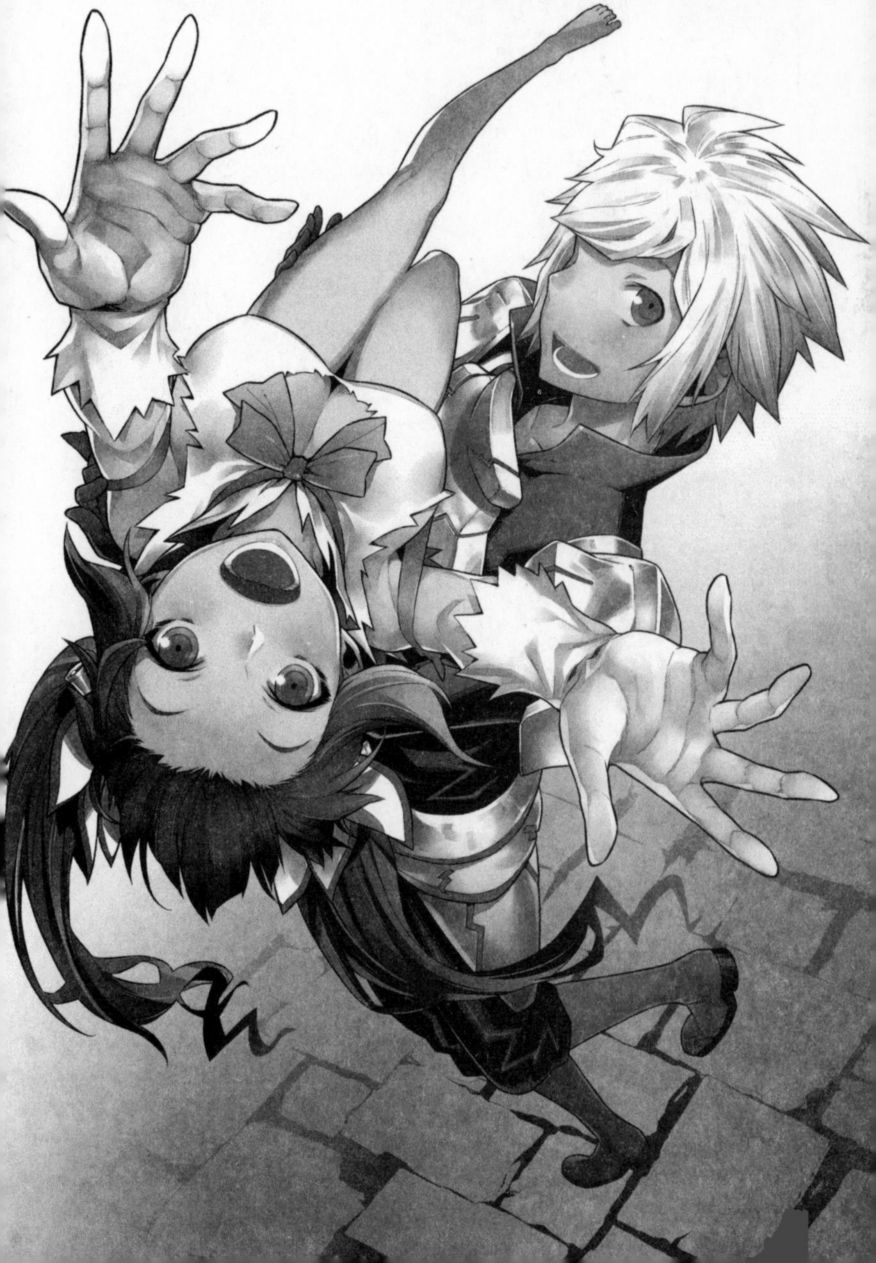

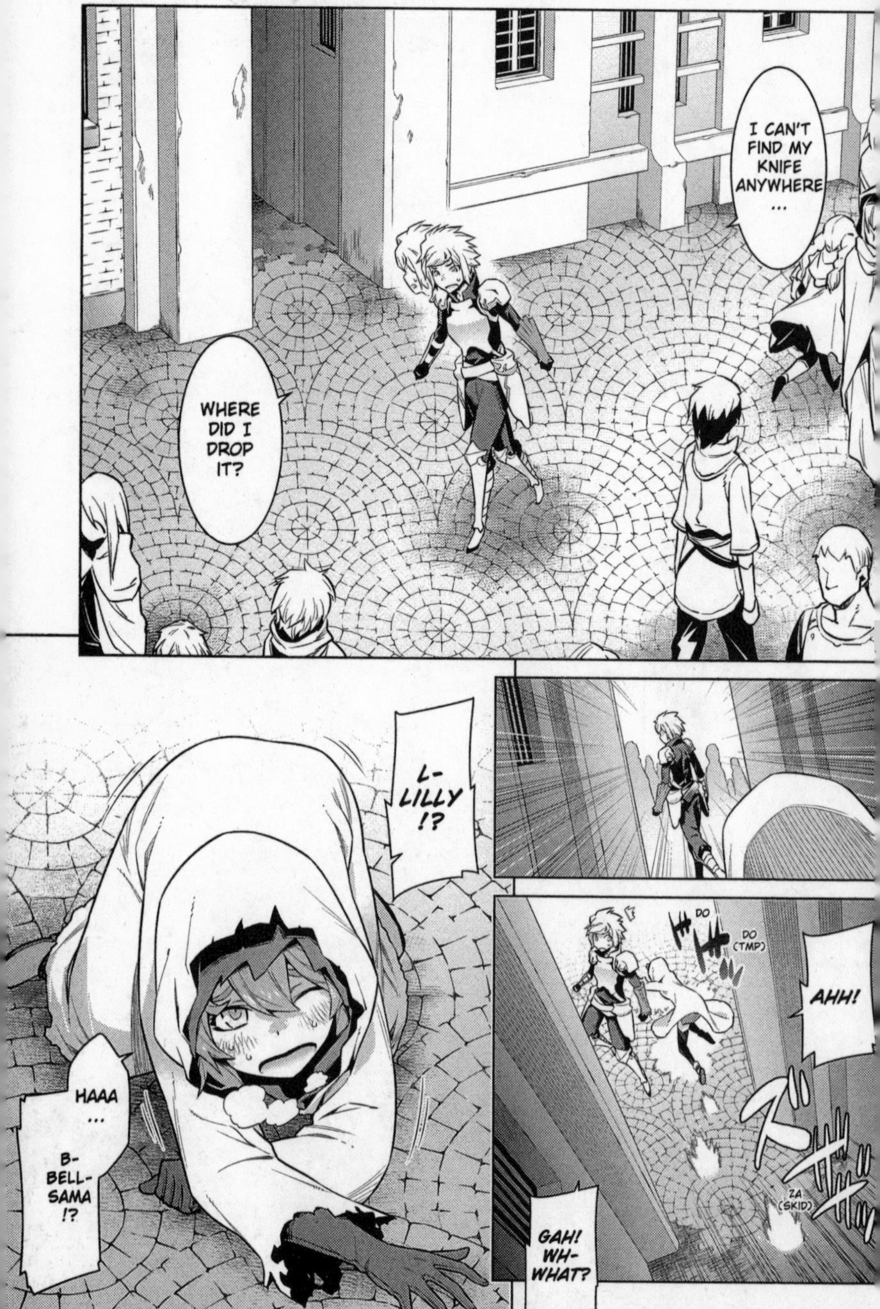
I CAN'T FIND MY KNIFE ANYWHERE...
WHERE DID I DROP IT?
DO
DO (TMP)
AHH!
ZA (SKID)
GAH! WH-WHAT?
L-LILLY!?
HAAA... B-BELL-SAMA!?

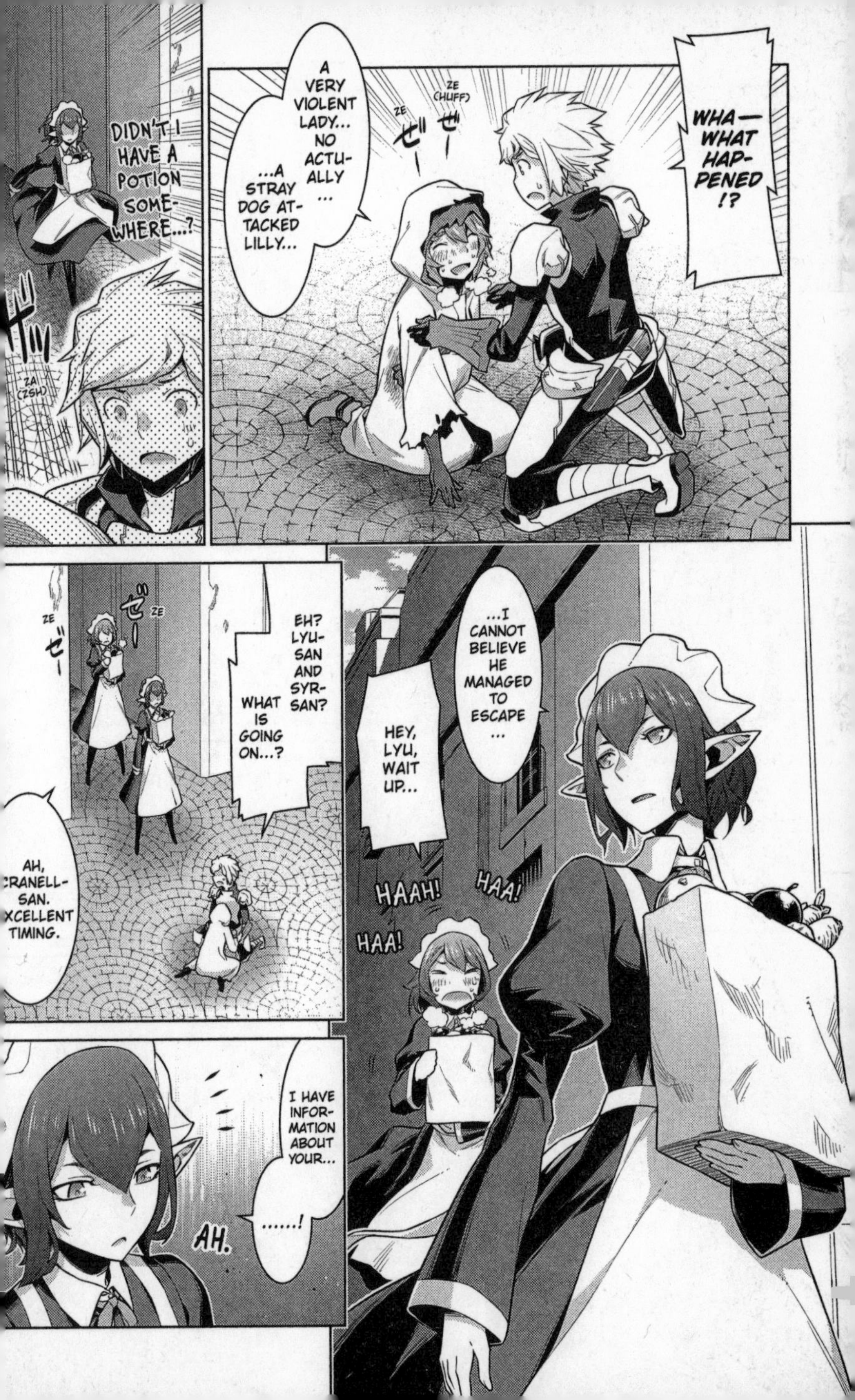

WHA—WHAT HAPPENED!?
ZE (HUFF) ゼ ゼ
A VERY VIOLENT LADY... NO ACTUALLY...
...A STRAY DOG ATTACKED LILLY...
DIDN'T I HAVE A POTION SOMEWHERE...?
ZA (ZSH)
...I CANNOT BELIEVE HE MANAGED TO ESCAPE...
HEY, LYU, WAIT UP...
HAAH! HAA!
HAA!
EH? LYU-SAN AND SYR-SAN?
WHAT IS GOING ON...?
ZE ゼ ZE ゼ
AH, CRANELL-SAN. XCELLENT TIMING.
I HAVE INFORMATION ABOUT YOUR...
......!
AH.

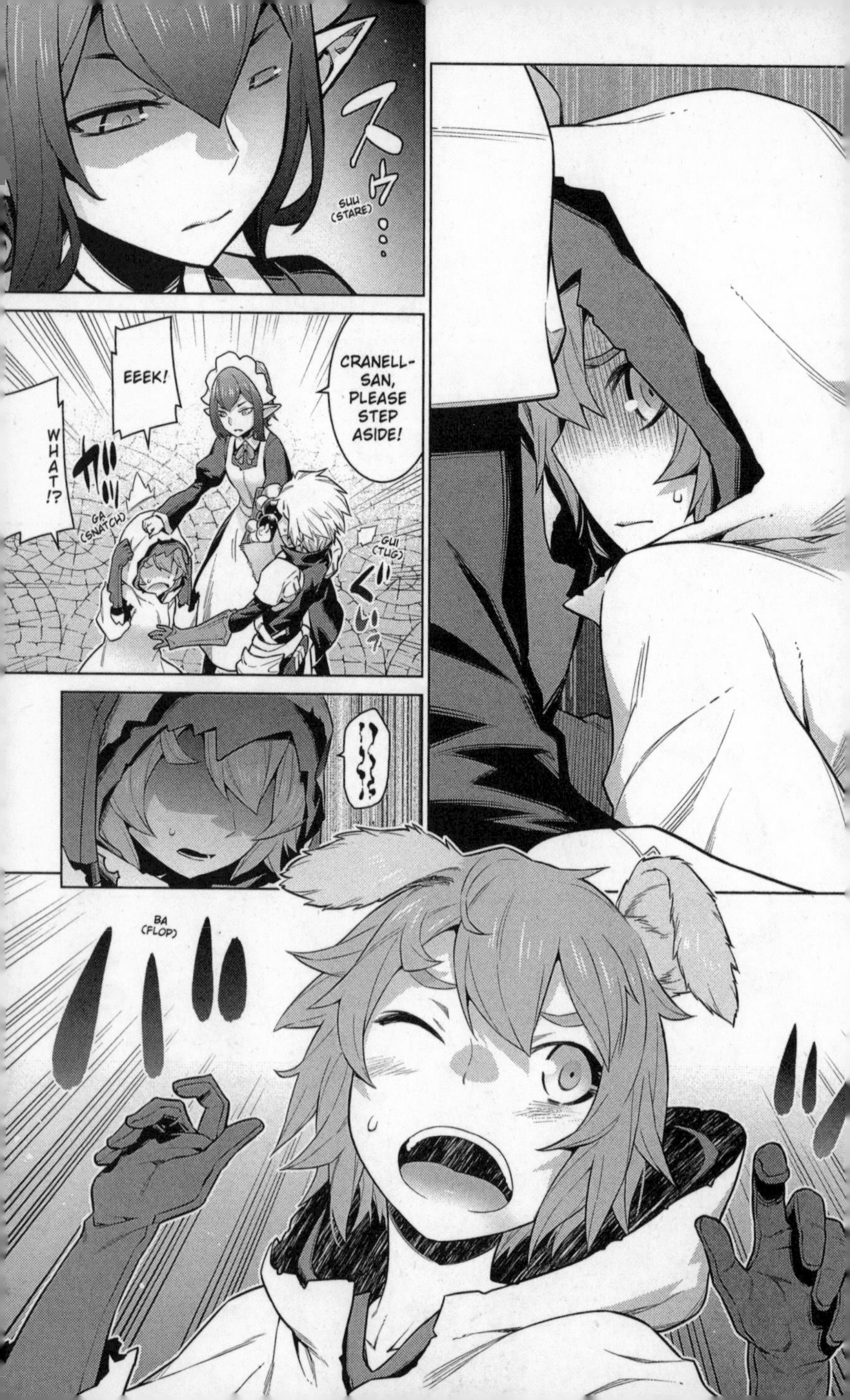
SUU (STARE)
CRANELL-SAN, PLEASE STEP ASIDE!
GUI (TUG)
EEEK!
WHAT!?
GA (SNATCH)
BA (FLOP)

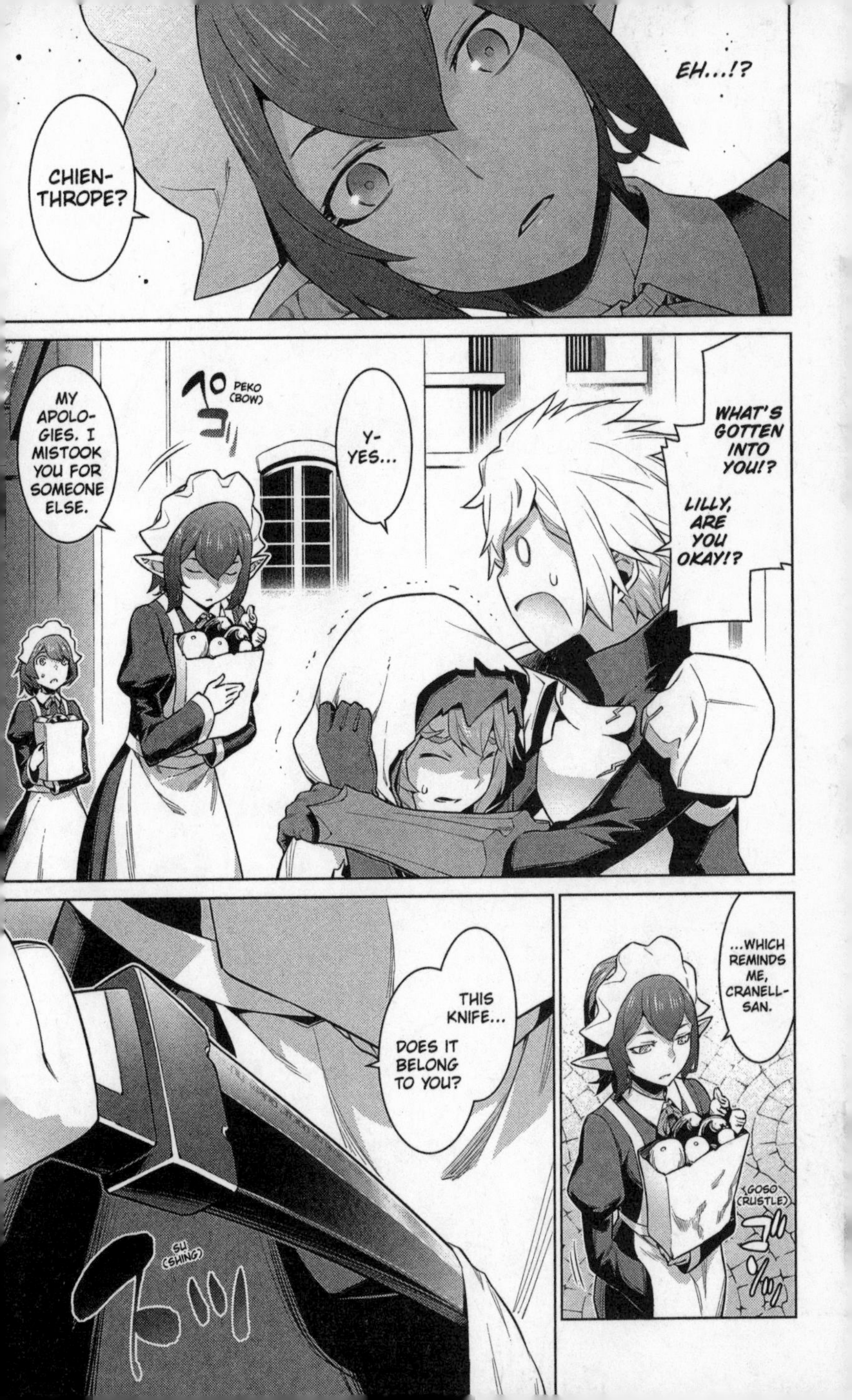
EH...!?
CHIEN-THROPE?
WHAT'S GOTTEN INTO YOU!?
LILLY, ARE YOU OKAY!?
Y-YES...
PEKO (BOW)
MY APOLOGIES. I MISTOOK YOU FOR SOMEONE ELSE.
...WHICH REMINDS ME, CRANELL-SAN.
GOSO (RUSTLE)
THIS KNIFE...
DOES IT BELONG TO YOU?
SU (SHING)

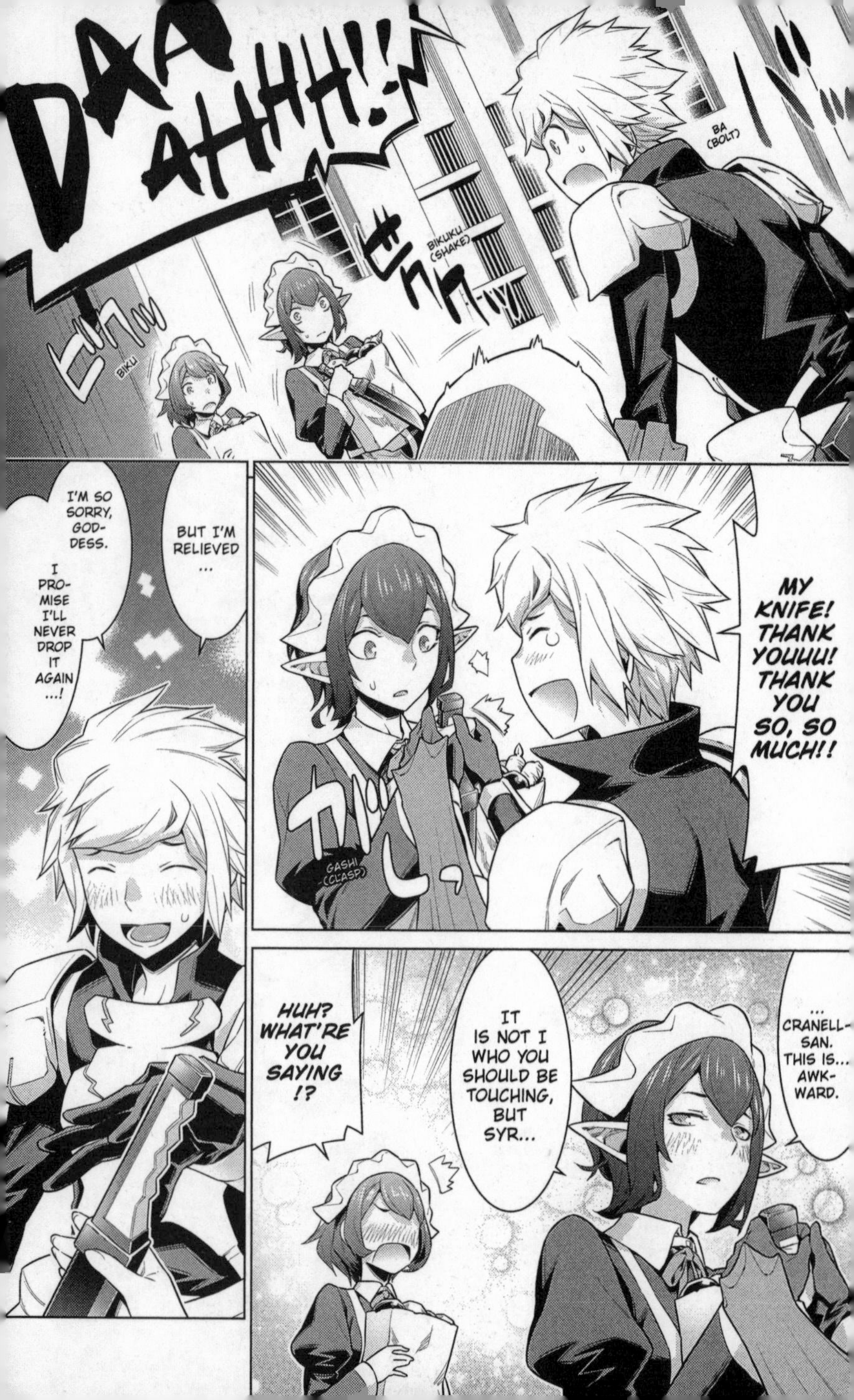
DAA AHHH!!
BA (BOLT)
BIKUKU (SHAKE)
BIKU
MY KNIFE! THANK YOUUU! THANK YOU SO, SO MUCH!!
GASHI (CLASP)
... CRANELL-SAN. THIS IS... AWK-WARD.
IT IS NOT I WHO YOU SHOULD BE TOUCHING, BUT SYR...
HUH? WHAT'RE YOU SAYING !?
BUT I'M RELIEVED ...
I'M SO SORRY, GOD-DESS.
I PRO-MISE I'LL NEVER DROP IT AGAIN ...!

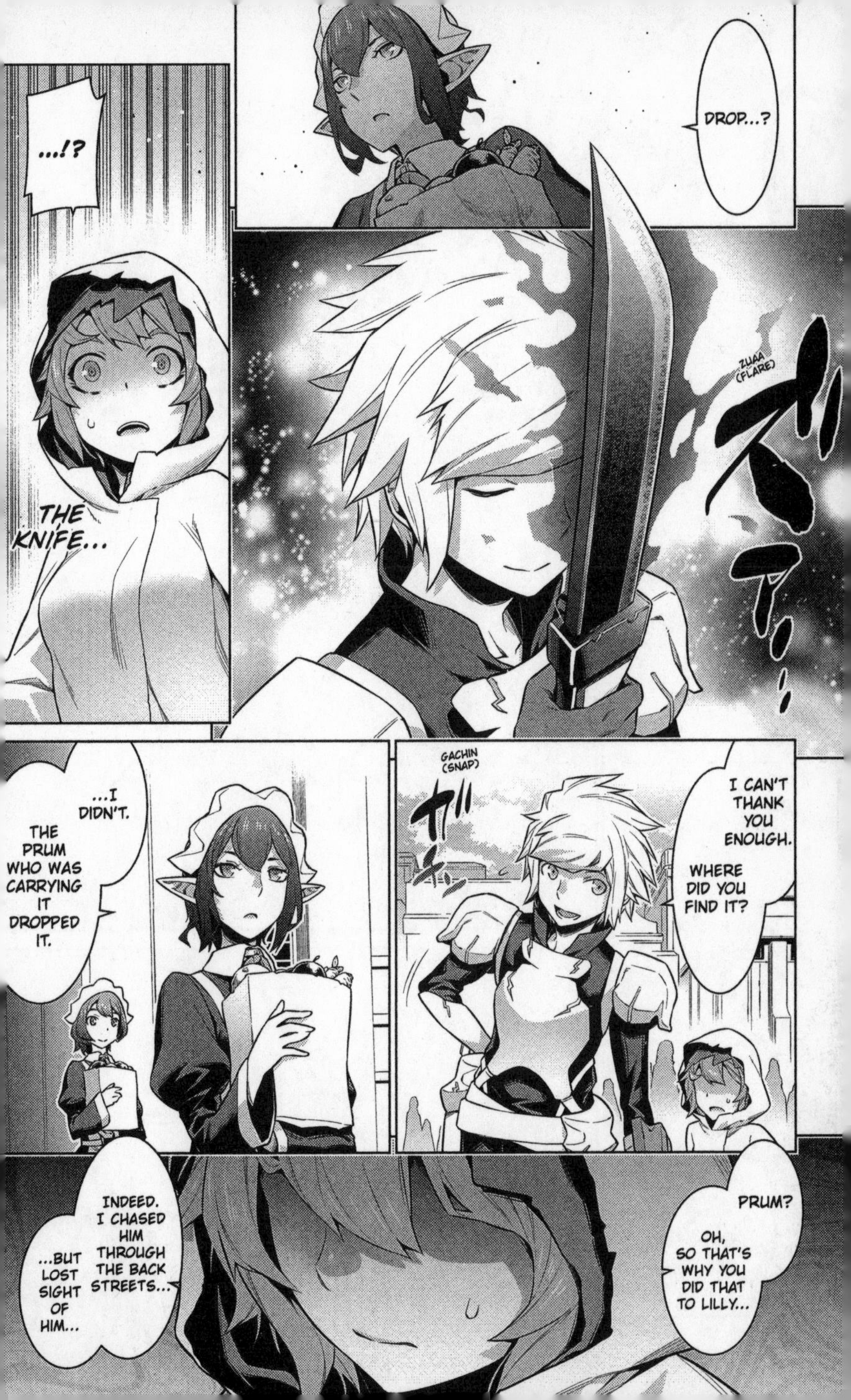
DROP...?
ZUAA (FLARE)
...!?
THE KNIFE...
GACHIN (SNAP)
I CAN'T THANK YOU ENOUGH.
WHERE DID YOU FIND IT?
...I DIDN'T.
THE PRUM WHO WAS CARRYING IT DROPPED IT.
PRUM?
OH, SO THAT'S WHY YOU DID THAT TO LILLY...
INDEED. I CHASED HIM THROUGH THE BACK STREETS...
...BUT LOST SIGHT OF HIM...

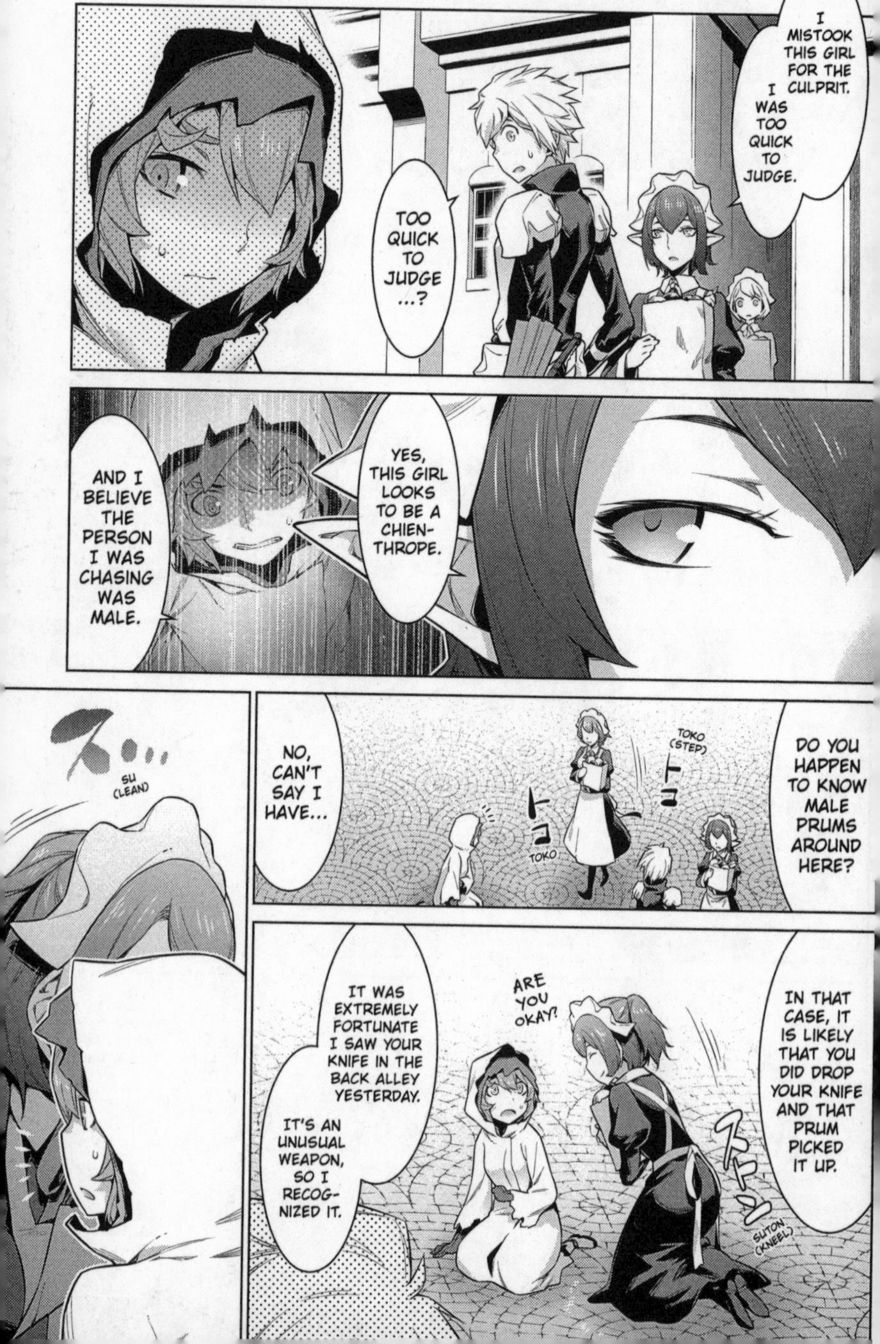
I MISTOOK THIS GIRL FOR THE CULPRIT. I WAS TOO QUICK TO JUDGE.
TOO QUICK TO JUDGE ...?
YES, THIS GIRL LOOKS TO BE A CHIEN-THROPE.
AND I BELIEVE THE PERSON I WAS CHASING WAS MALE.
DO YOU HAPPEN TO KNOW MALE PRUMS AROUND HERE?
TOKO (STEP)
TOKO
NO, CAN'T SAY I HAVE...
IN THAT CASE, IT IS LIKELY THAT YOU DID DROP YOUR KNIFE AND THAT PRUM PICKED IT UP.
SUTON (KNEEL)
ARE YOU OKAY?
IT WAS EXTREMELY FORTUNATE I SAW YOUR KNIFE IN THE BACK ALLEY YESTERDAY.
IT'S AN UNUSUAL WEAPON, SO I RECOG-NIZED IT.
SU (LEAN)

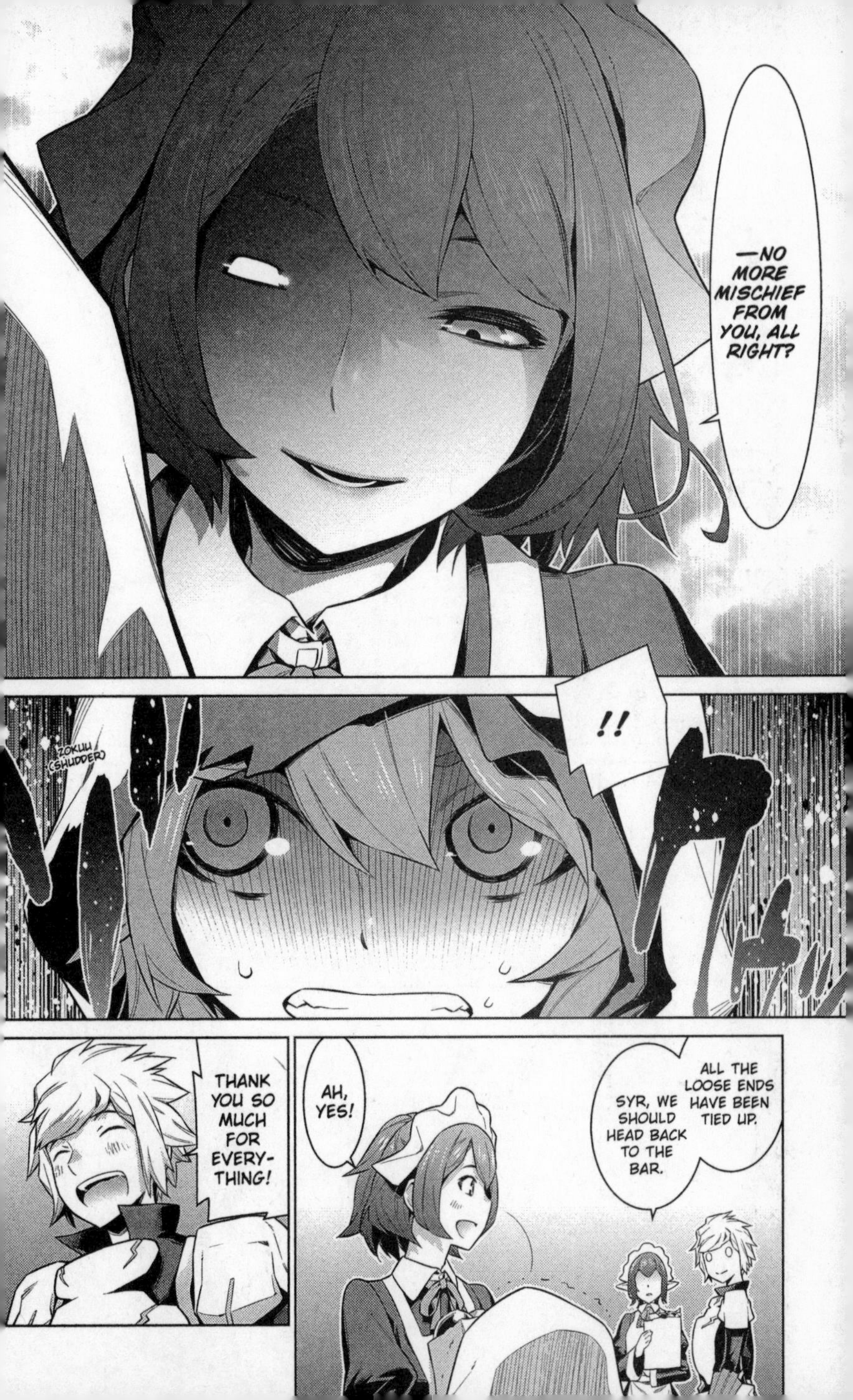
—NO MORE MISCHIEF FROM YOU, ALL RIGHT?
!!
ZOKUU (SHUDDER)
ALL THE LOOSE ENDS HAVE BEEN TIED UP.
SYR, WE SHOULD HEAD BACK TO THE BAR.
AH, YES!
THANK YOU SO MUCH FOR EVERY-THING!

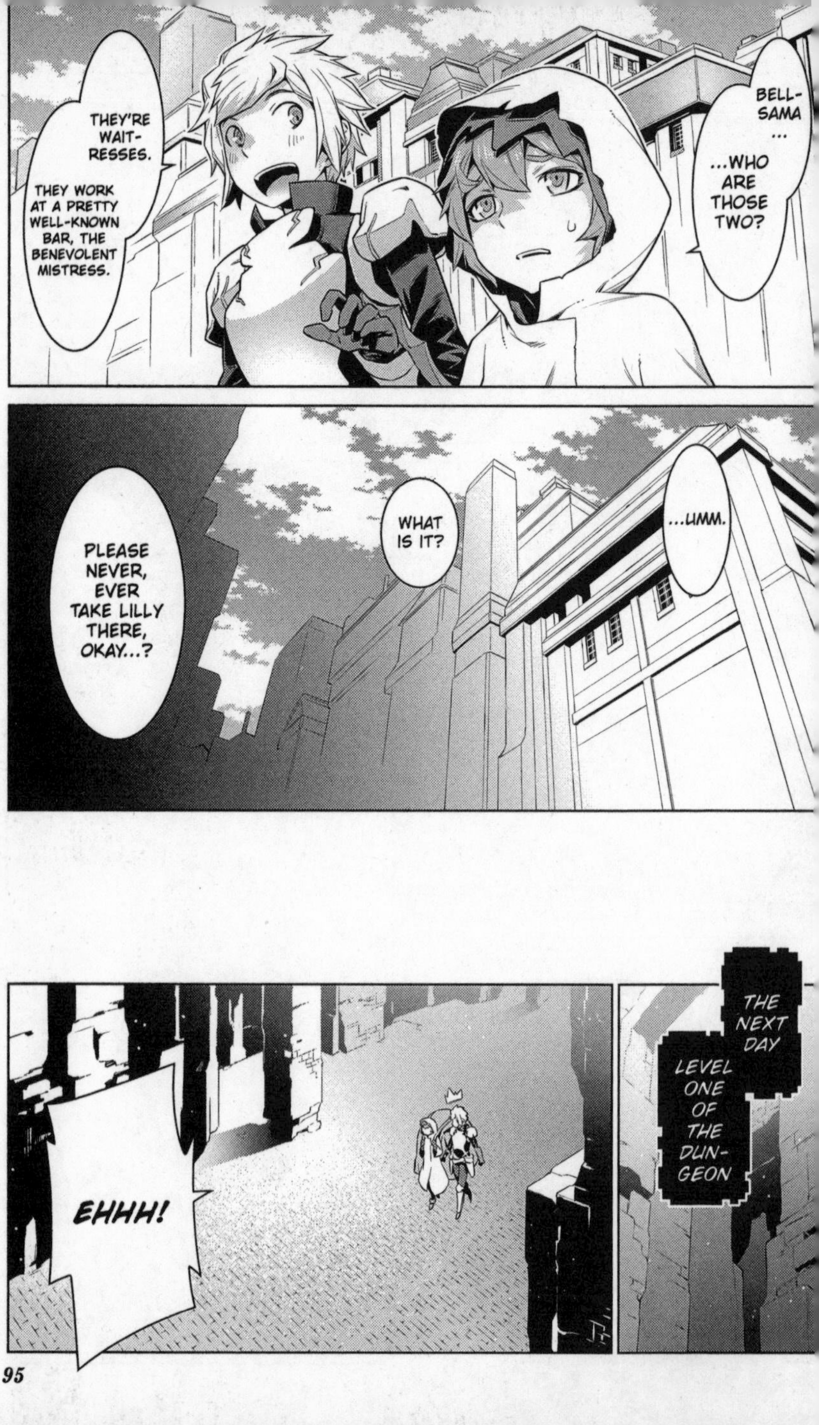
BELL-SAMA ... ...WHO ARE THOSE TWO?
THEY'RE WAIT-RESSES.
THEY WORK AT A PRETTY WELL-KNOWN BAR, THE BENEVOLENT MISTRESS.
...UMM.
WHAT IS IT?
PLEASE NEVER, EVER TAKE LILLY THERE, OKAY...?
THE NEXT DAY
LEVEL ONE OF THE DUN-GEON
EHHH!

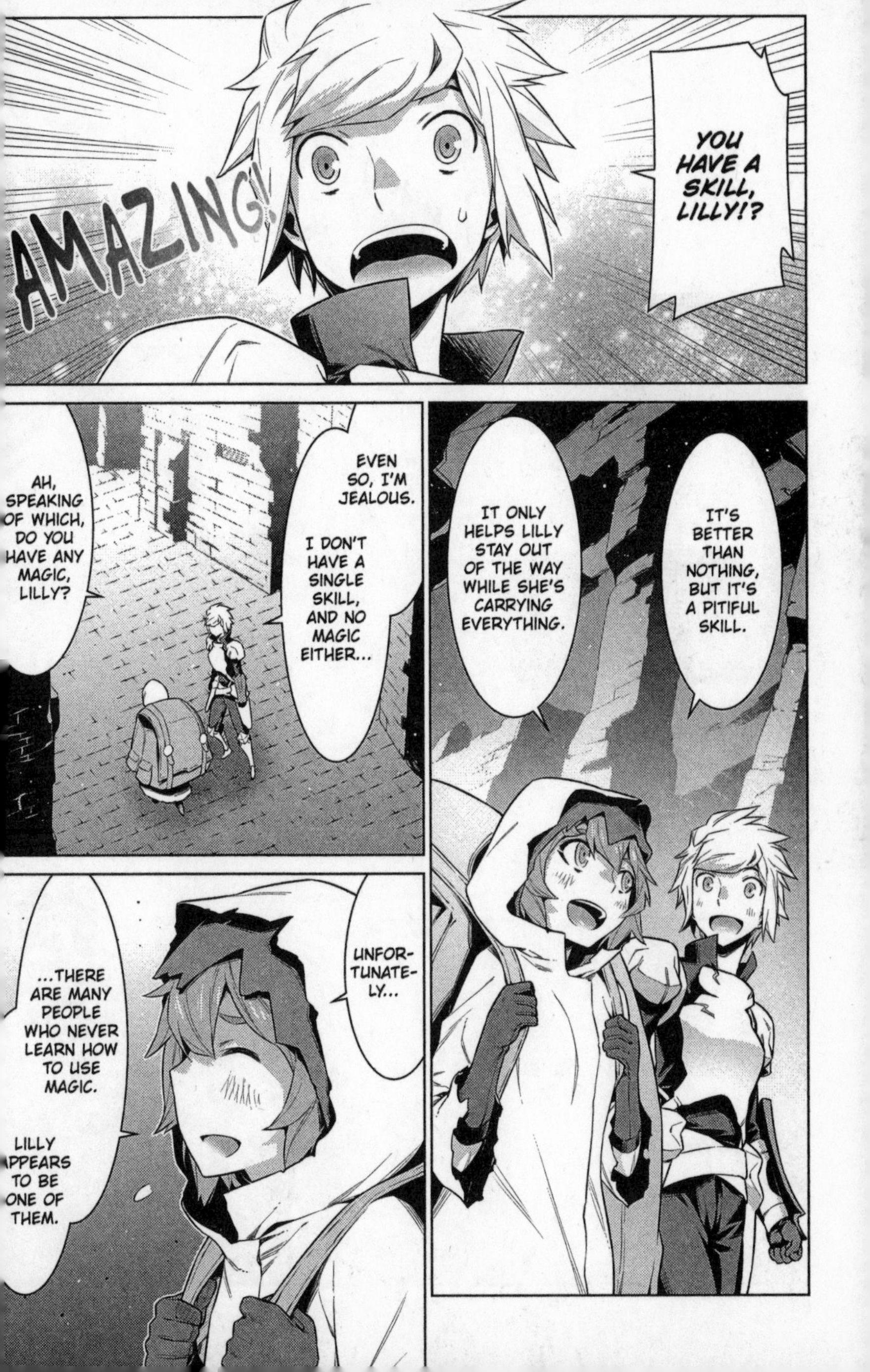
YOU HAVE A SKILL, LILLY!?
AMAZING!!
IT'S BETTER THAN NOTHING, BUT IT'S A PITIFUL SKILL.
IT ONLY HELPS LILLY STAY OUT OF THE WAY WHILE SHE'S CARRYING EVERYTHING.
EVEN SO, I'M JEALOUS.
I DON'T HAVE A SINGLE SKILL, AND NO MAGIC EITHER...
AH, SPEAKING OF WHICH, DO YOU HAVE ANY MAGIC, LILLY?
UNFOR-TUNATE-LY...
...THERE ARE MANY PEOPLE WHO NEVER LEARN HOW TO USE MAGIC.
LILLY APPEARS TO BE ONE OF THEM.

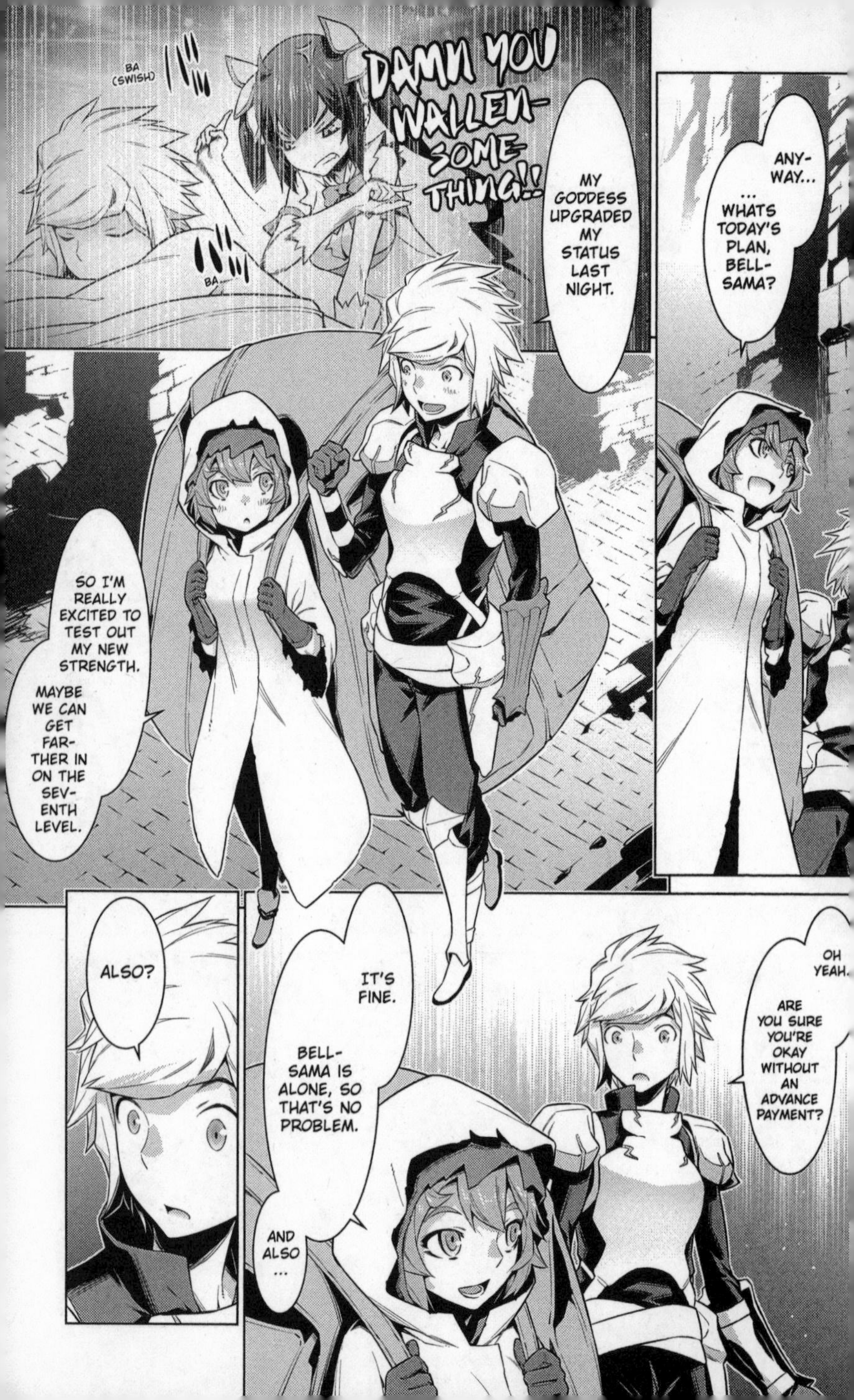
BA (SWISH)
BA
DAMN YOU WALLEN-SOME-THING!!
MY GODDESS UPGRADED MY STATUS LAST NIGHT.
SO I'M REALLY EXCITED TO TEST OUT MY NEW STRENGTH.
MAYBE WE CAN GET FARTHER IN ON THE SEVENTH LEVEL.
ANYWAY... ...WHATS TODAY'S PLAN, BELL-SAMA?
OH YEAH.
ARE YOU SURE YOU'RE OKAY WITHOUT AN ADVANCE PAYMENT?
IT'S FINE.
BELL-SAMA IS ALONE, SO THAT'S NO PROBLEM.
AND ALSO ...
ALSO?

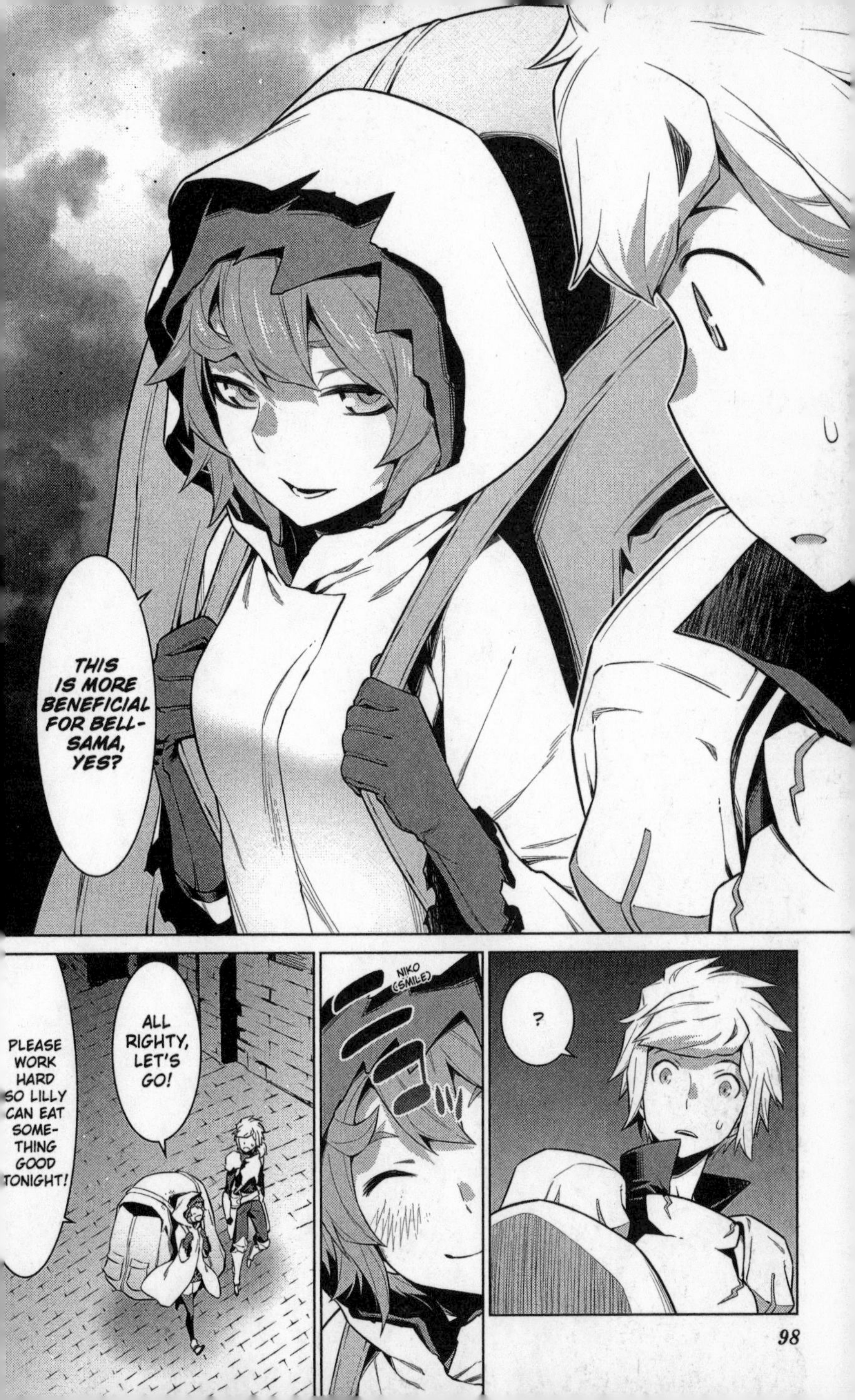
THIS IS MORE BENEFICIAL FOR BELL-SAMA, YES?
?
NIKO (SMILE)
ALL RIGHTY, LET'S GO!
PLEASE WORK HARD SO LILLY CAN EAT SOME-THING GOOD TONIGHT!

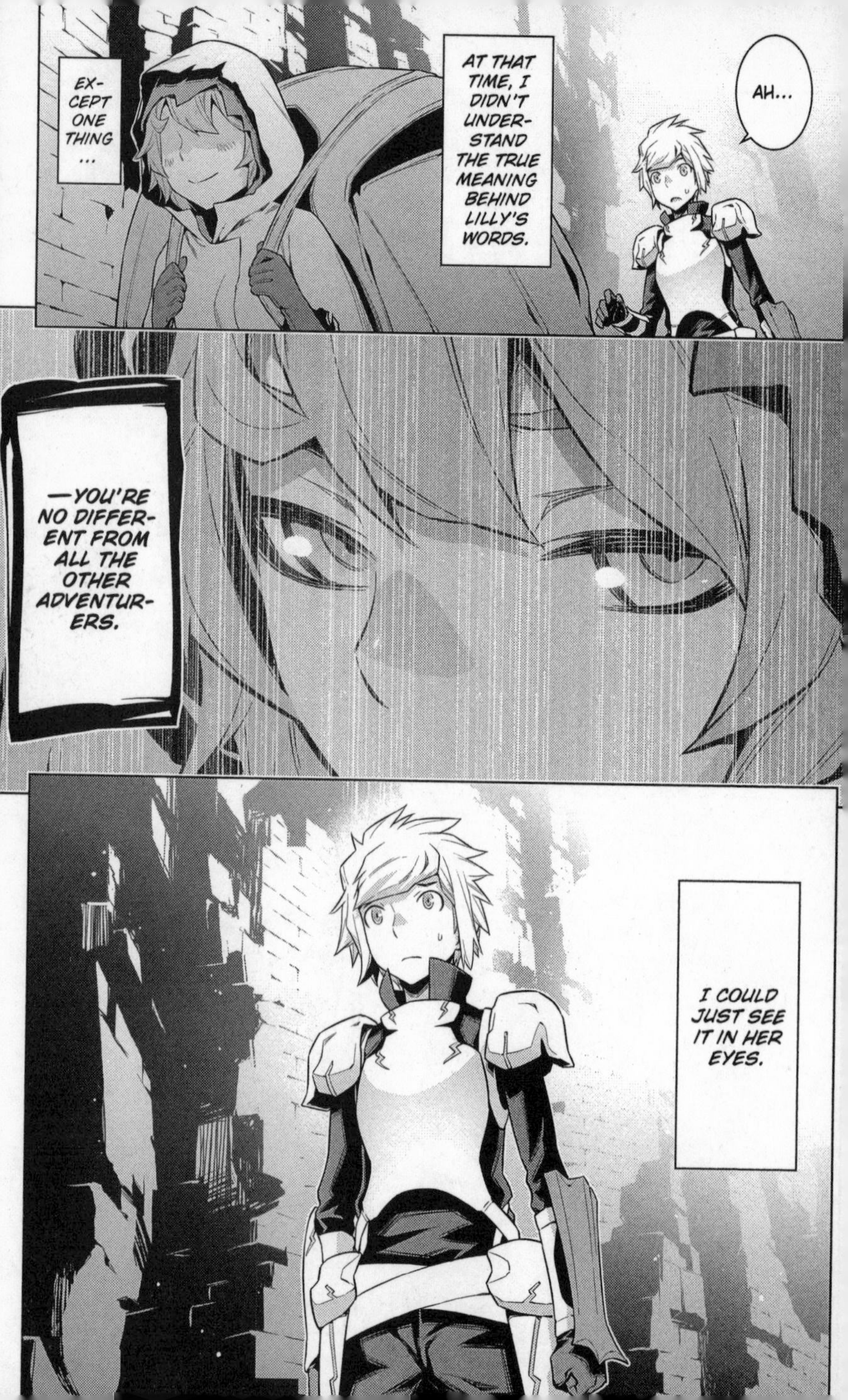
AH...
AT THAT TIME, I DIDN'T UNDER-STAND THE TRUE MEANING BEHIND LILLY'S WORDS.
EX-CEPT ONE THING...
—YOU'RE NO DIFFER-ENT FROM ALL THE OTHER ADVENTUR-ERS.
I COULD JUST SEE IT IN HER EYES.

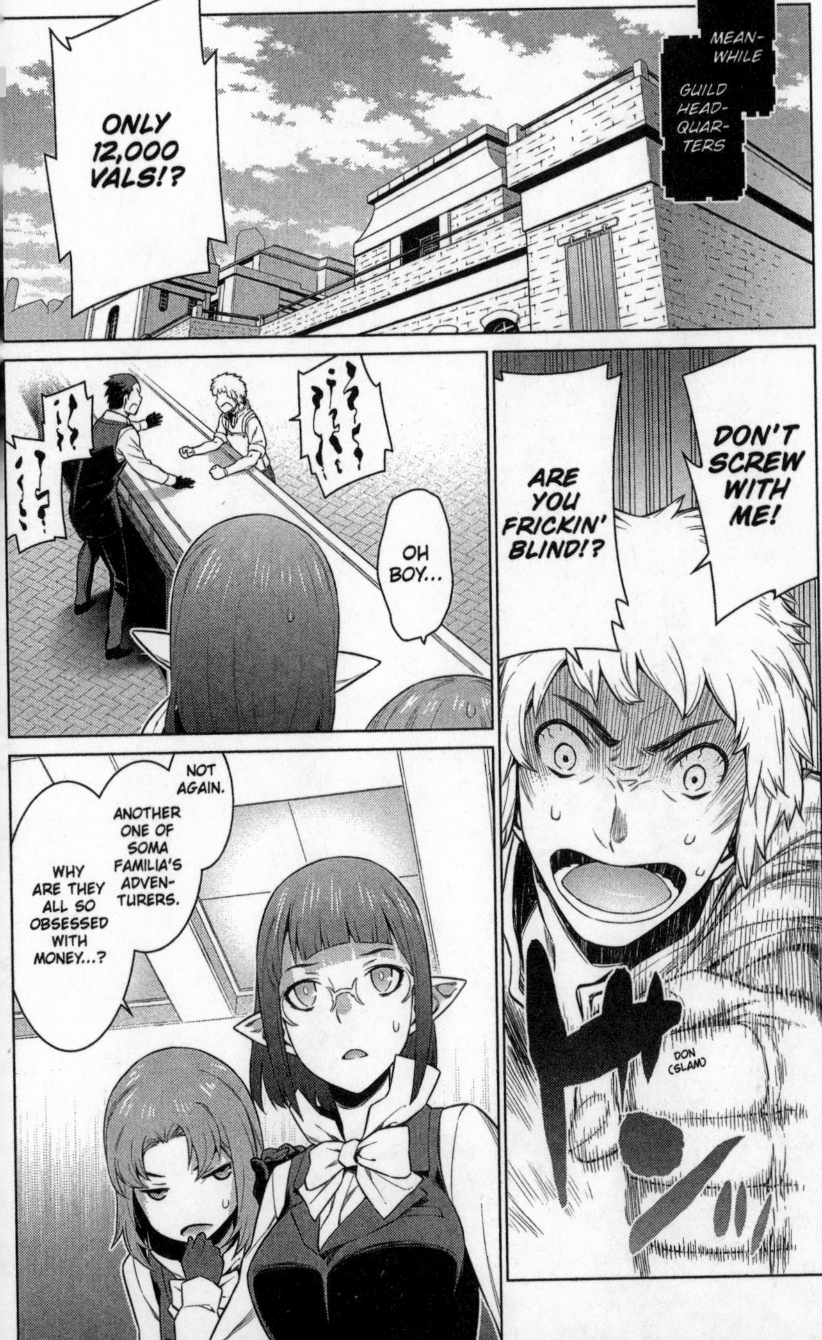
MEAN-WHILE
GUILD HEAD-QUARTERS
ONLY 12,000 VALS!?
DON'T SCREW WITH ME!
ARE YOU FRICKIN' BLIND!?
DON (SLAM)
OH BOY...
NOT AGAIN.
ANOTHER ONE OF SOMA FAMILIA'S ADVENTURERS.
WHY ARE THEY ALL SO OBSESSED WITH MONEY...?

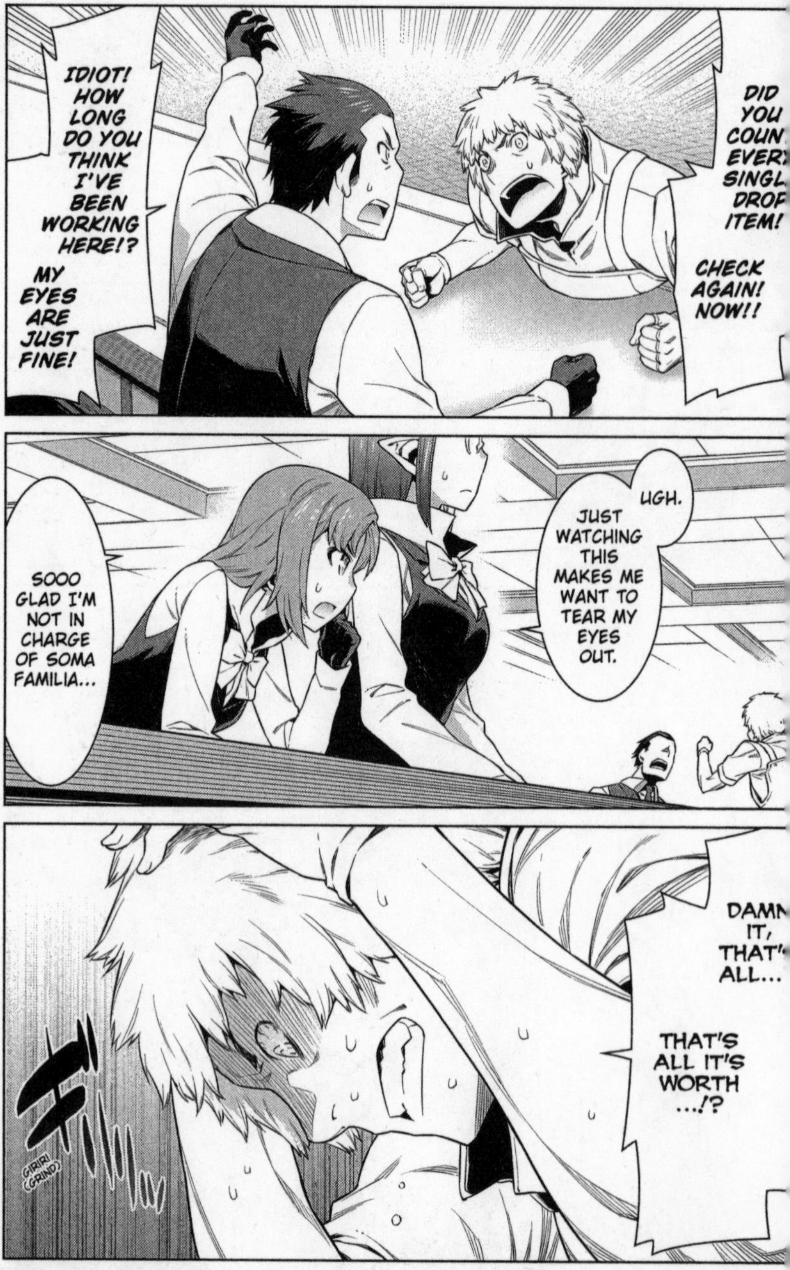
DID YOU COUN EVER SINGL DROF ITEM!
CHECK AGAIN! NOW!!
IDIOT! HOW LONG DO YOU THINK I'VE BEEN WORKING HERE!?
MY EYES ARE JUST FINE!
UGH.
JUST WATCHING THIS MAKES ME WANT TO TEAR MY EYES OUT.
SOOO GLAD I'M NOT IN CHARGE OF SOMA FAMILIA...
DAMN IT, THAT'S ALL...
THAT'S ALL IT'S WORTH ...!?
GIRIRI (GRIND)

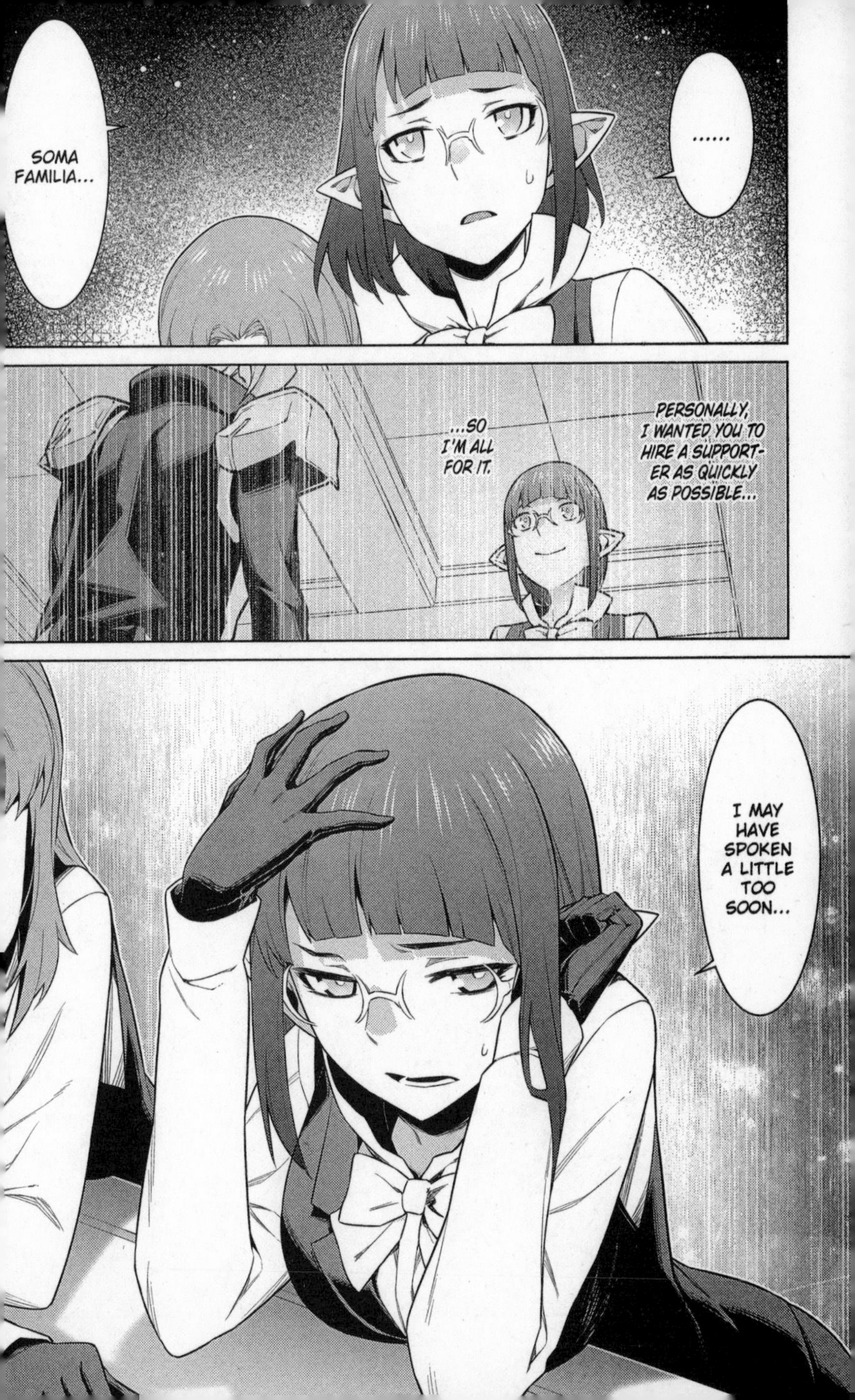
......
SOMA FAMILIA...
PERSONALLY, I WANTED YOU TO HIRE A SUPPORT-ER AS QUICKLY AS POSSIBLE...
...SO I'M ALL FOR IT.
I MAY HAVE SPOKEN A LITTLE TOO SOON...

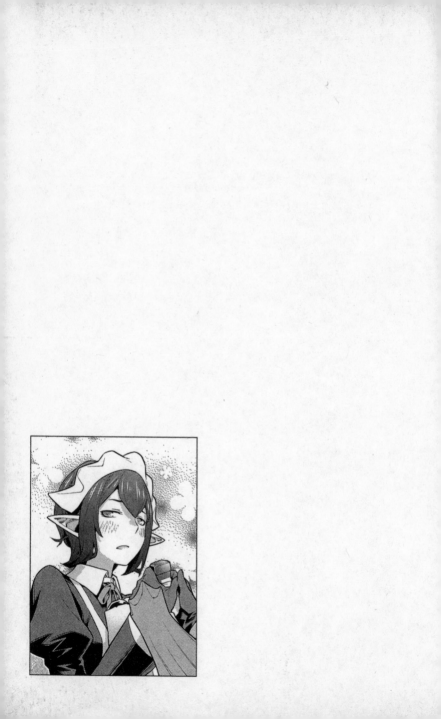

Is it WRONG to TRY to PiCK-UP GIRLS iN A DUNGEON?

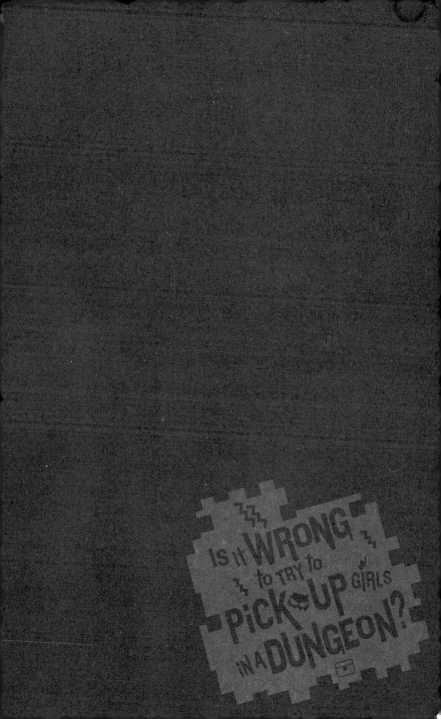

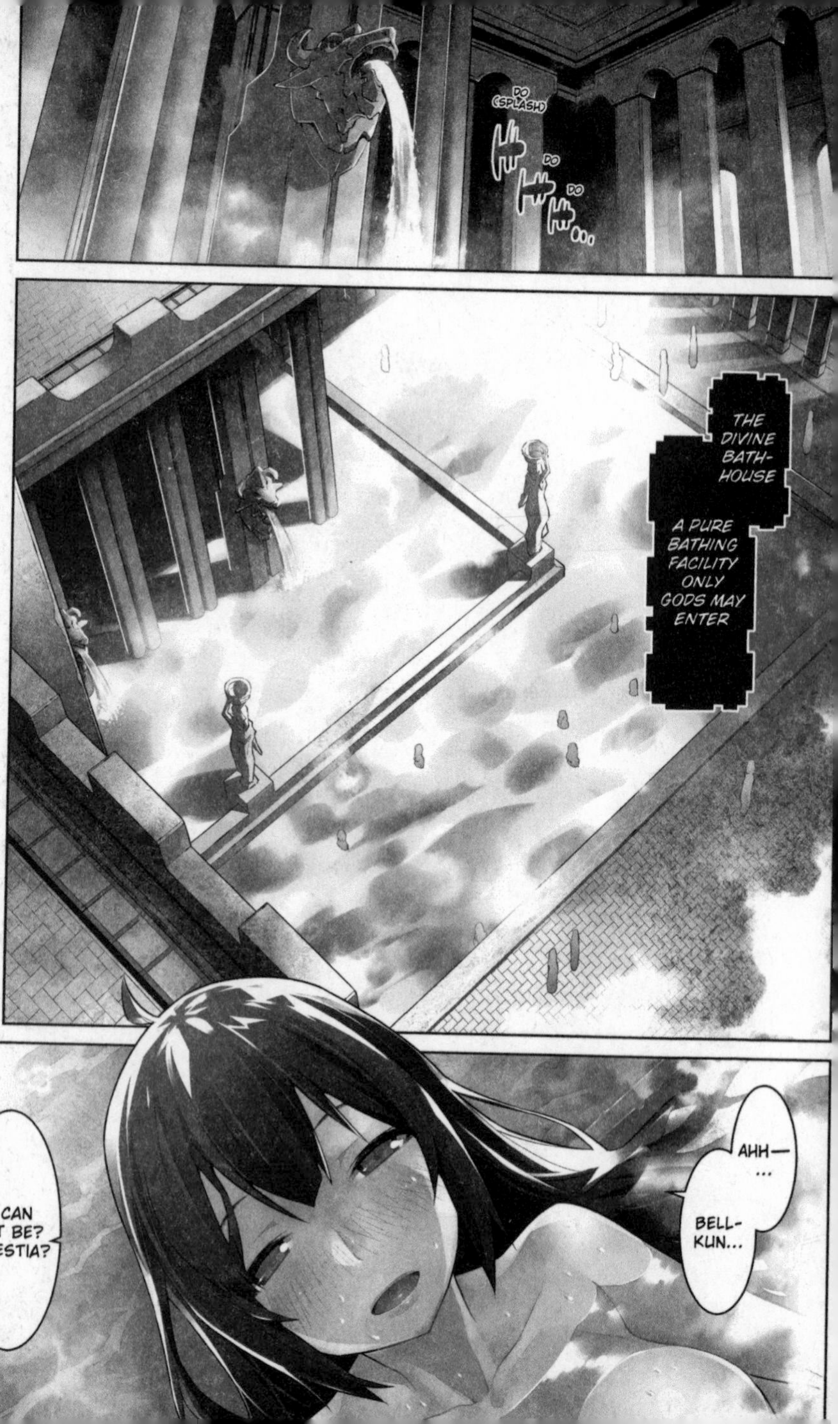
DO (SPLASH)
ドド
DO
ドド
DO
ド...
THE DIVINE BATH-HOUSE
A PURE BATHING FACILITY ONLY GODS MAY ENTER
AHH—...
BELL-KUN...
CAN IT BE? HESTIA?

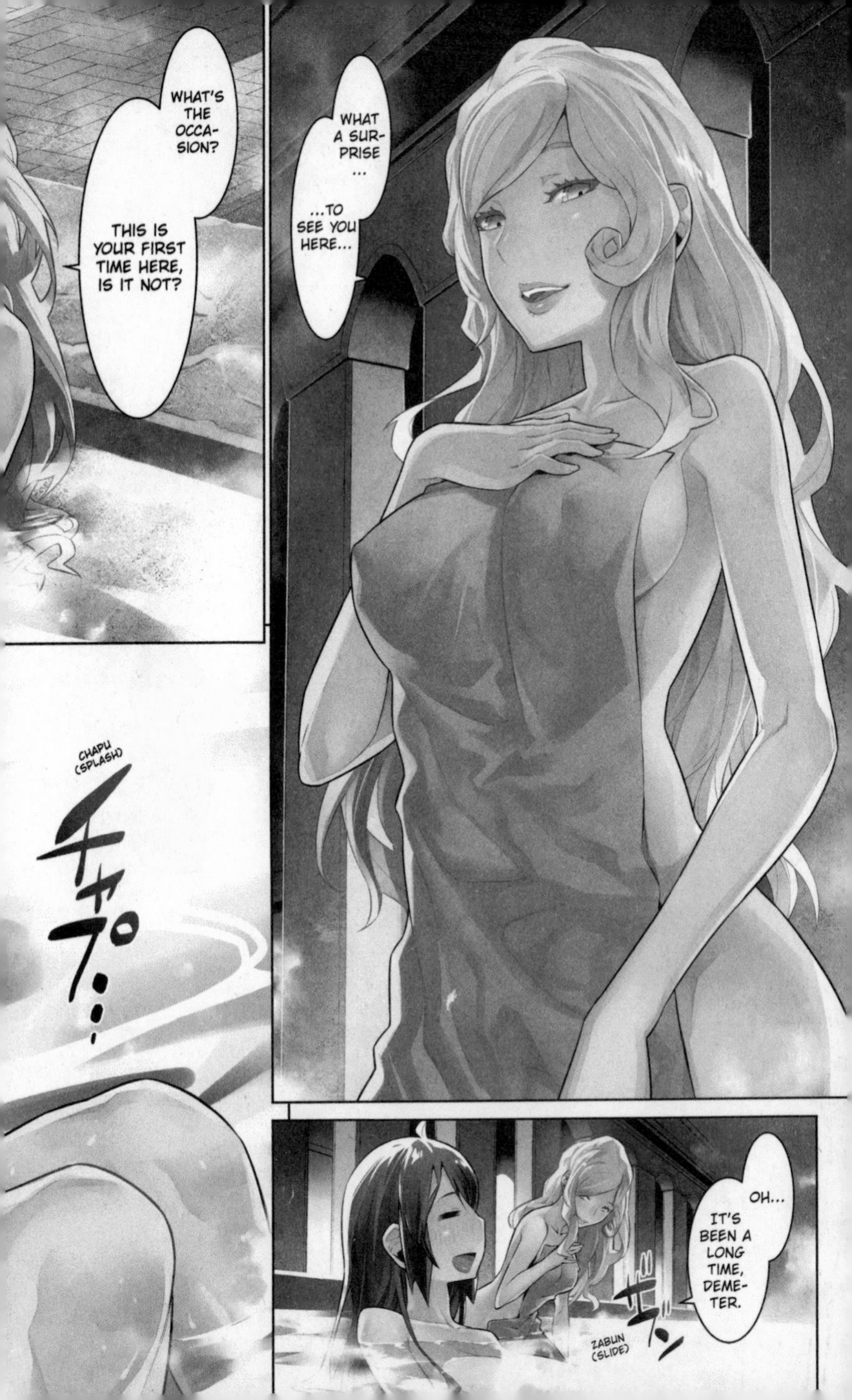
WHAT A SUR-PRISE...
...TO SEE YOU HERE...
WHAT'S THE OCCA-SION?
THIS IS YOUR FIRST TIME HERE, IS IT NOT?
CHAPU (SPLASH)
チャプ…
OH...
IT'S BEEN A LONG TIME, DEMETER.
ZABUN (SLIDE)

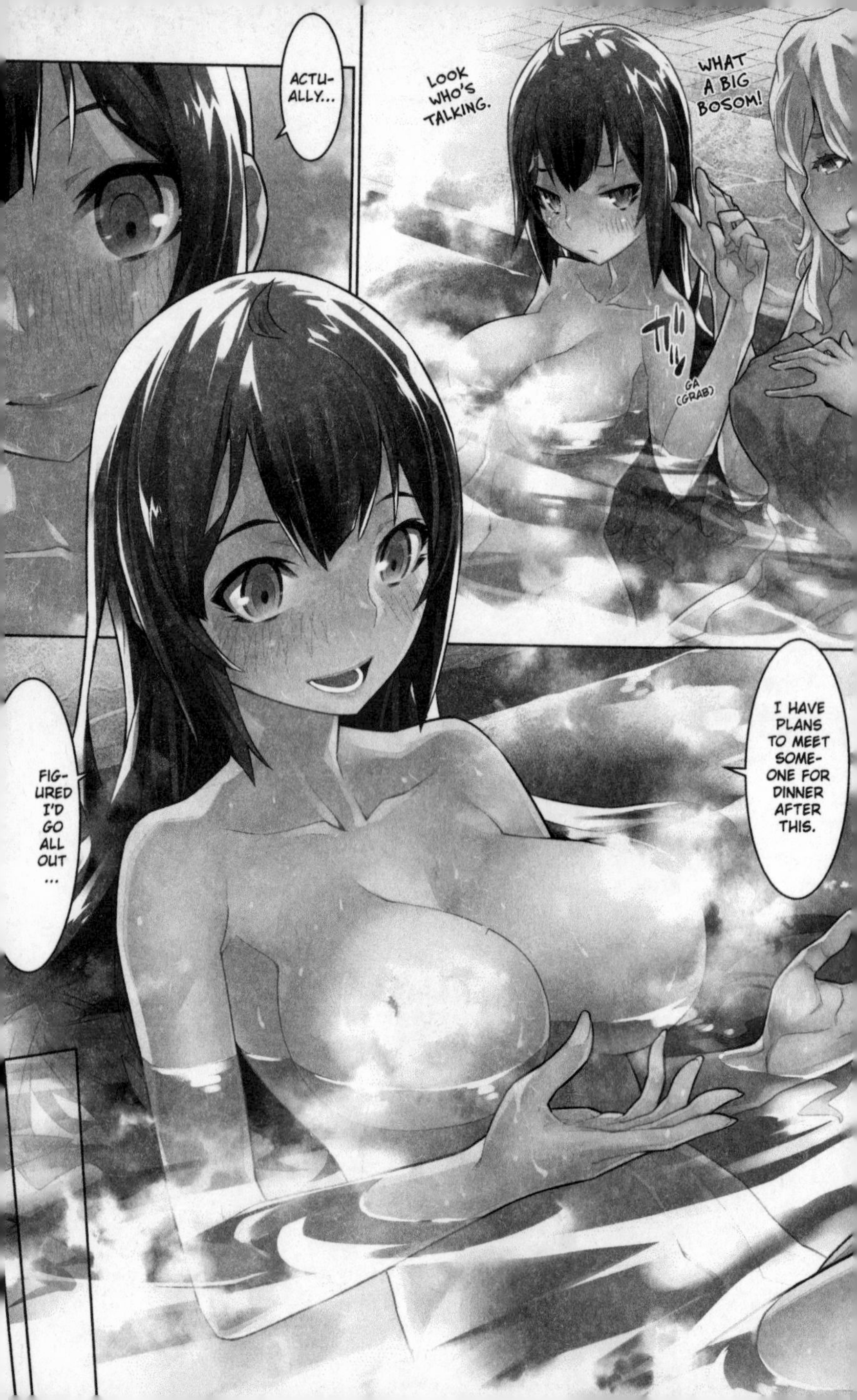
WHAT A BIG BOSOM!
LOOK WHO'S TALKING.
GA (GRAB)
ACTU-ALLY...
I HAVE PLANS TO MEET SOME-ONE FOR DINNER AFTER THIS.
FIG-URED I'D GO ALL OUT...

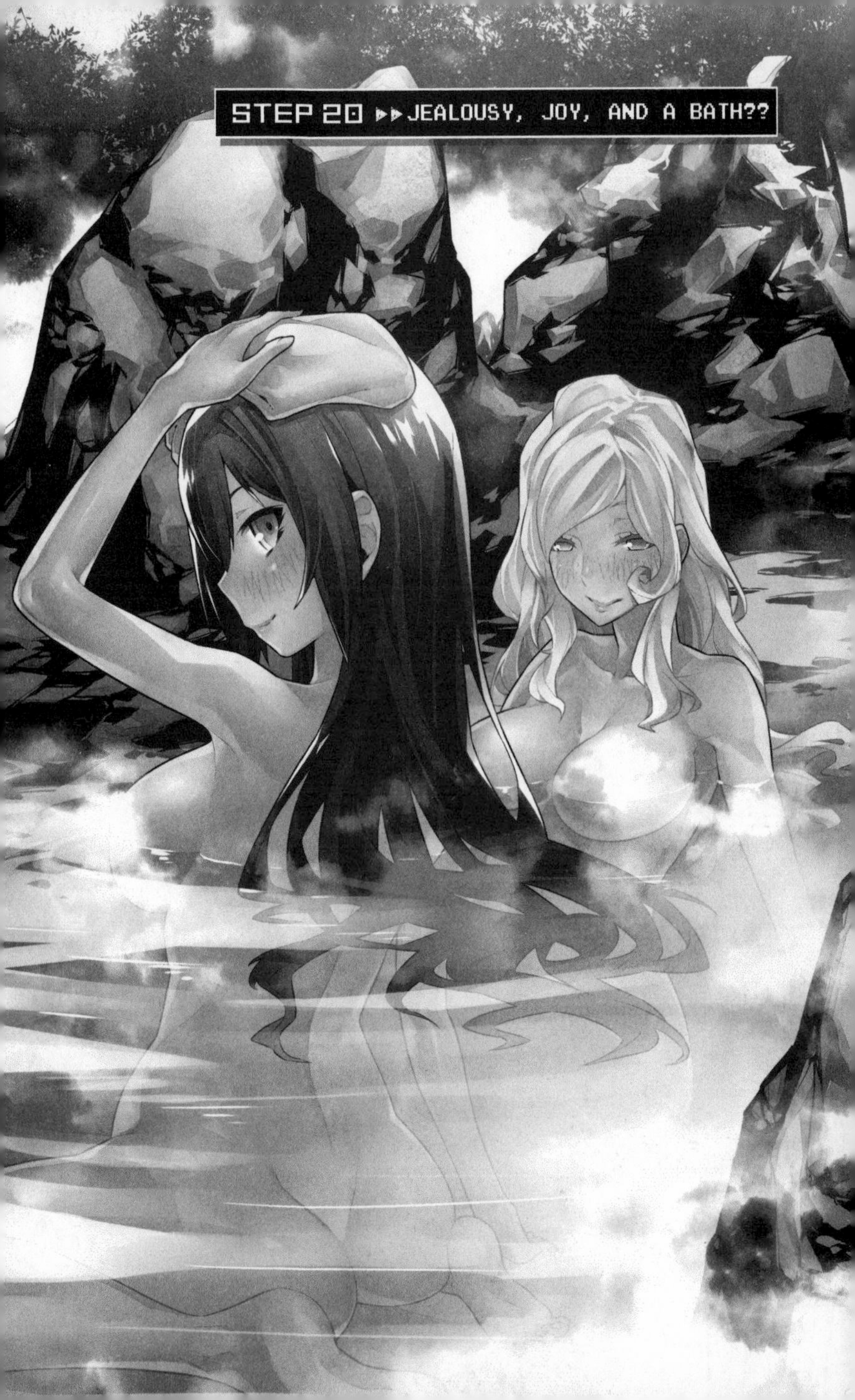
STEP 20 ▸▸ JEALOUSY, JOY, AND A BATH??

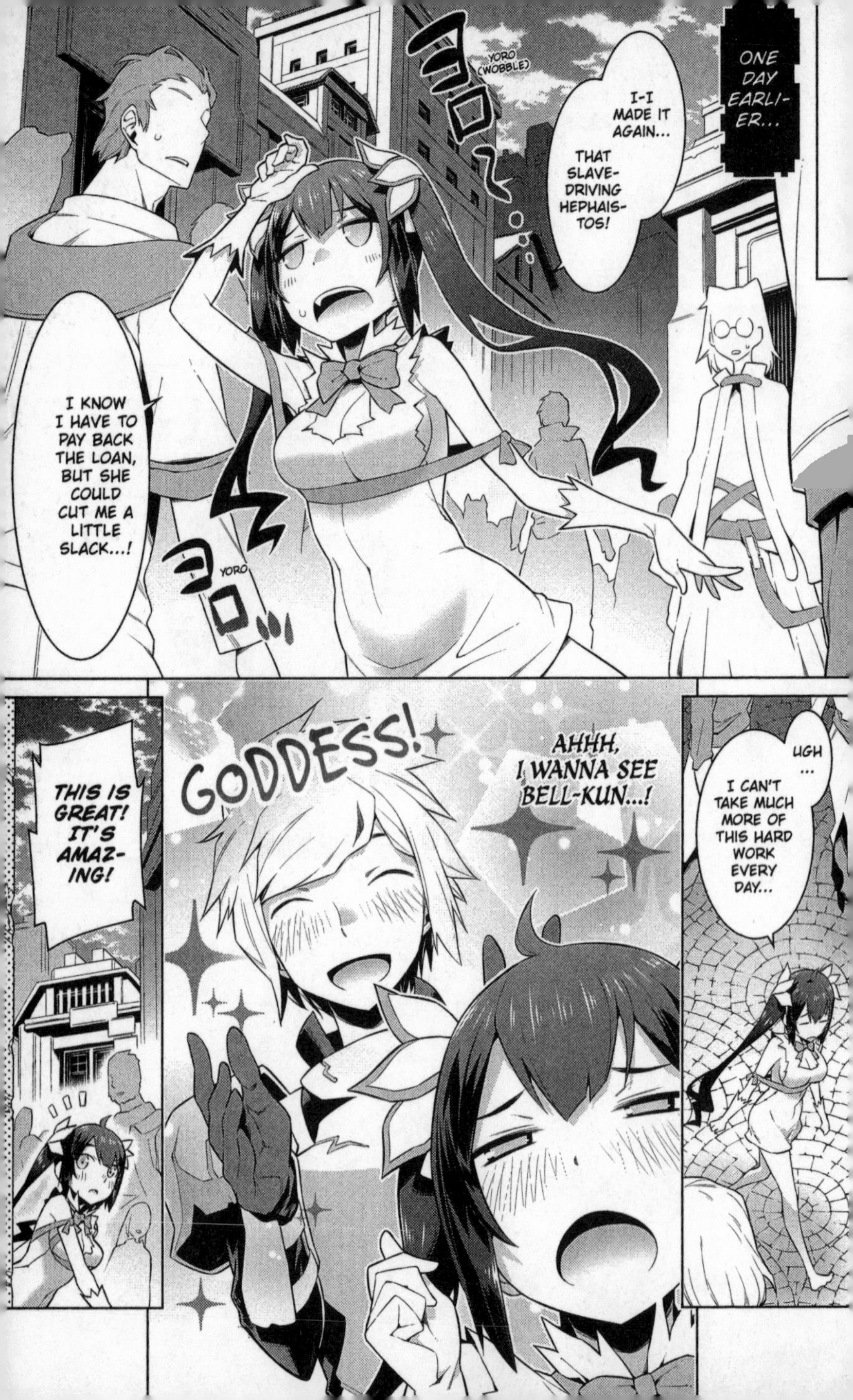
ONE DAY EARLIER...
YORO (WOBBLE)
I-I MADE IT AGAIN... THAT SLAVE-DRIVING HEPHAISTOS!
I KNOW I HAVE TO PAY BACK THE LOAN, BUT SHE COULD CUT ME A LITTLE SLACK...!
YORO
UGH... I CAN'T TAKE MUCH MORE OF THIS HARD WORK EVERY DAY...
AHHH, I WANNA SEE BELL-KUN...!
GODDESS!
THIS IS GREAT! IT'S AMAZING!

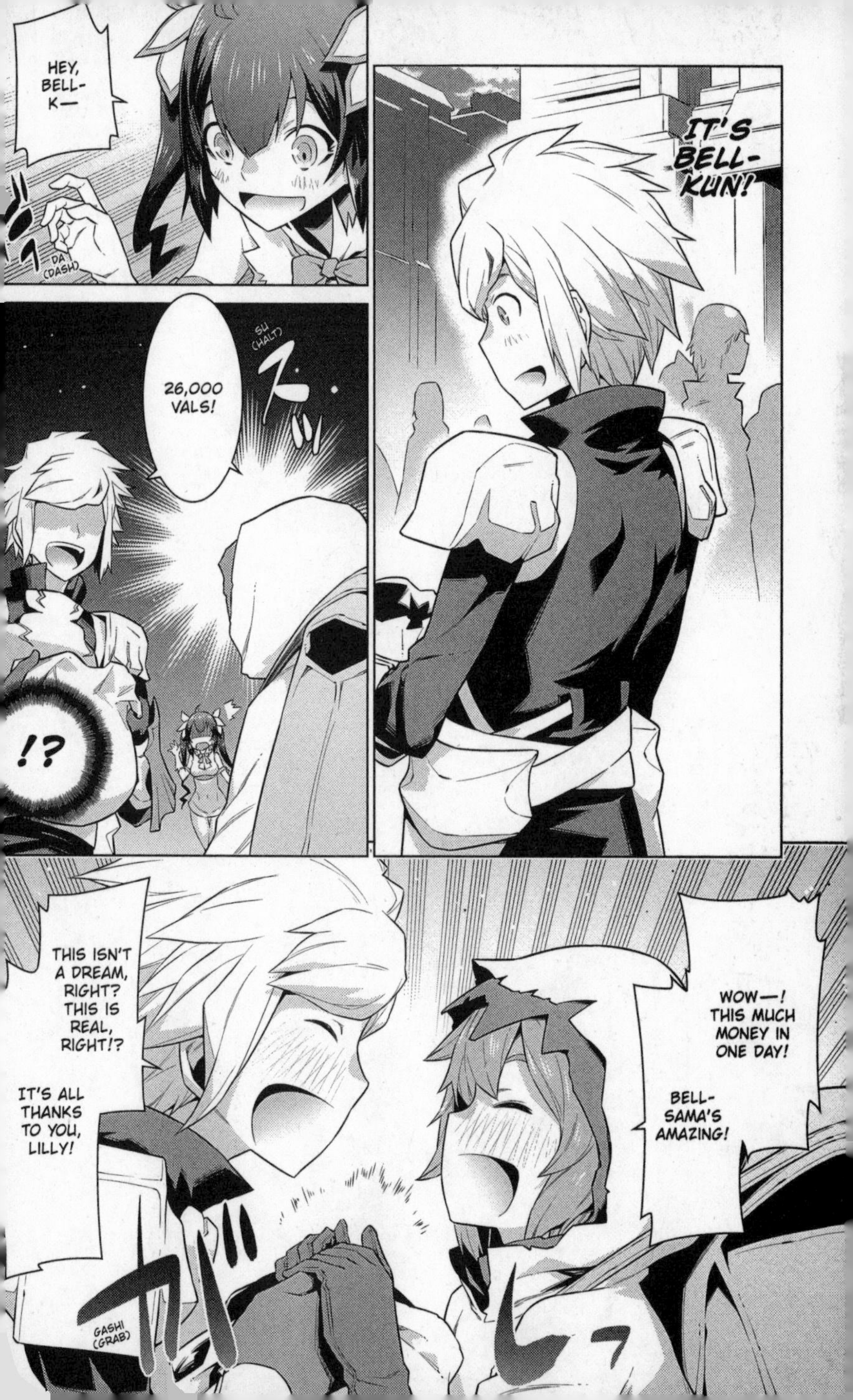
IT'S BELL-KUN!
HEY, BELL-K—
DA (DASH)
26,000 VALS!
SU (HALT)
!?
WOW—! THIS MUCH MONEY IN ONE DAY!
BELL-SAMA'S AMAZING!
THIS ISN'T A DREAM, RIGHT? THIS IS REAL, RIGHT!?
IT'S ALL THANKS TO YOU, LILLY!
GASHI (GRAB)

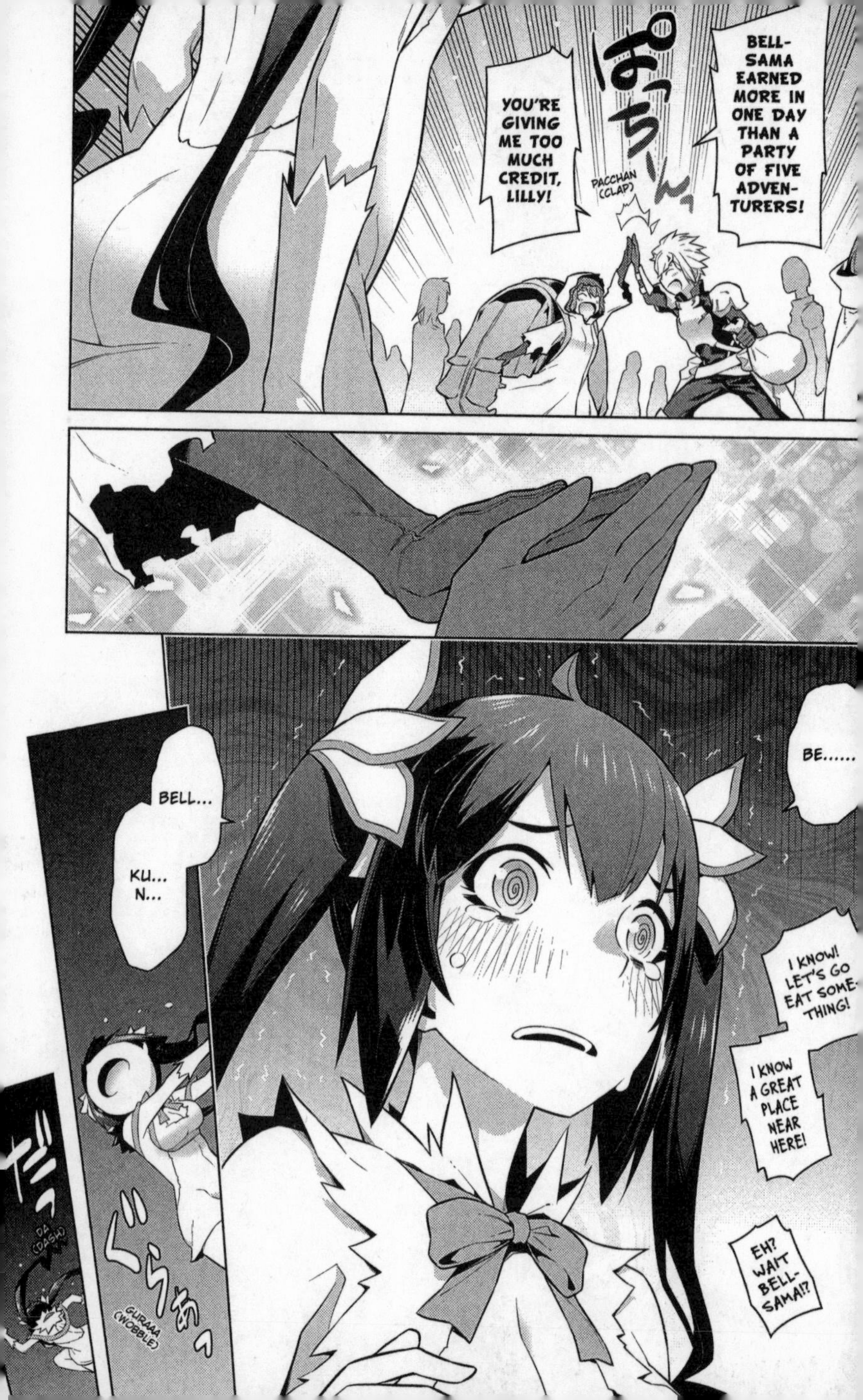
BELL-SAMA EARNED MORE IN ONE DAY THAN A PARTY OF FIVE ADVENTURERS!
ぱっちーん
PACCHAN (CLAP)
YOU'RE GIVING ME TOO MUCH CREDIT, LILLY!
BE......
I KNOW! LET'S GO EAT SOME-THING!
I KNOW A GREAT PLACE NEAR HERE!
EH? WAIT BELL-SAMA!?
BELL...
KU... N...
ぐらぁっ
GURAAA (WOBBLE)
ダッ
DA (DASH)

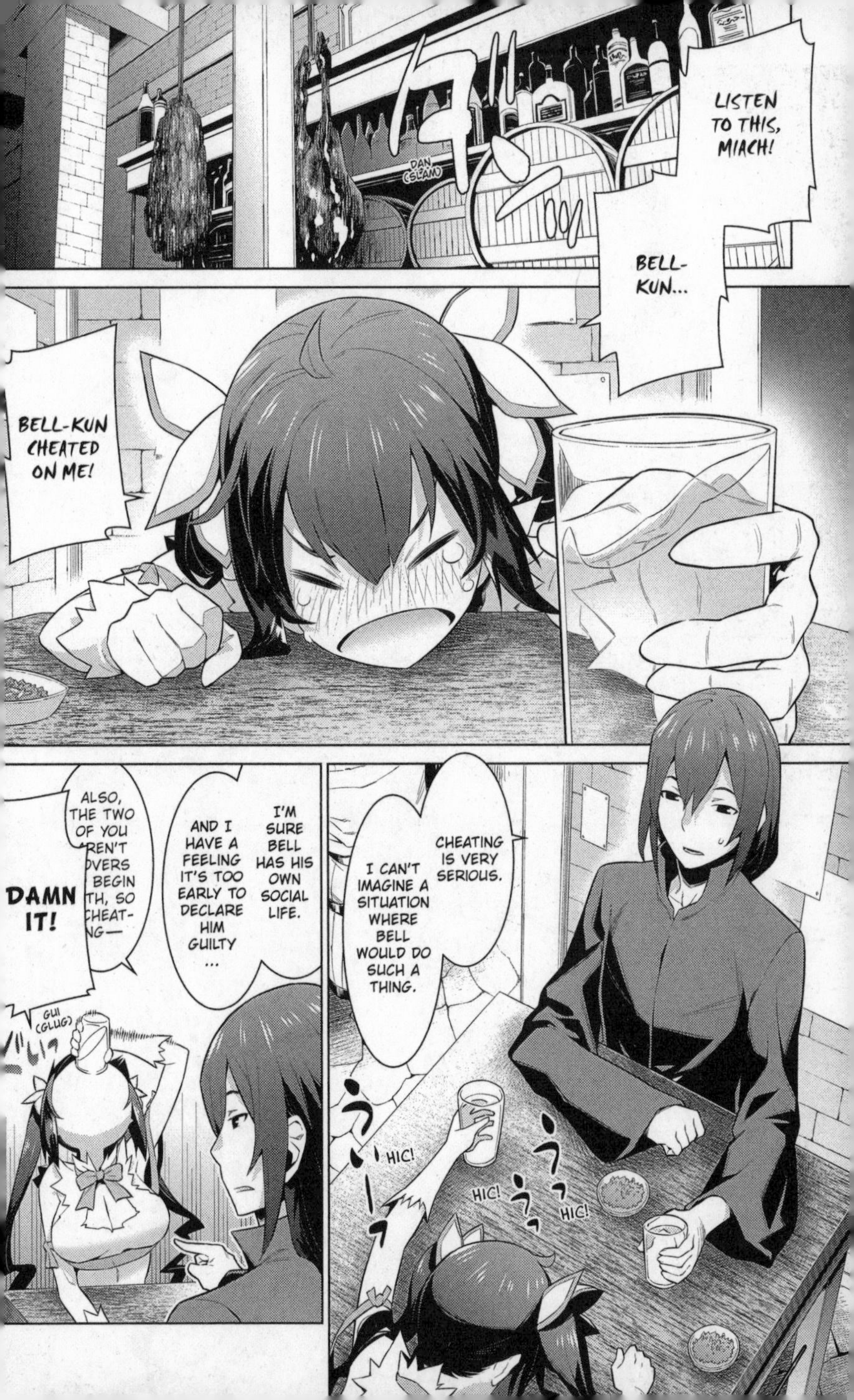
DAN (SLAM)
LISTEN TO THIS, MIACH!
BELL-KUN...
BELL-KUN CHEATED ON ME!
CHEATING IS VERY SERIOUS.
I CAN'T IMAGINE A SITUATION WHERE BELL WOULD DO SUCH A THING.
HIC!
HIC!
HIC!
I'M SURE BELL HAS HIS OWN SOCIAL LIFE.
AND I HAVE A FEELING IT'S TOO EARLY TO DECLARE HIM GUILTY...
ALSO, THE TWO OF YOU RENT'T OVERS BEGIN TH, SO CHEAT-NG—
DAMN IT!
GUI (GLUG)

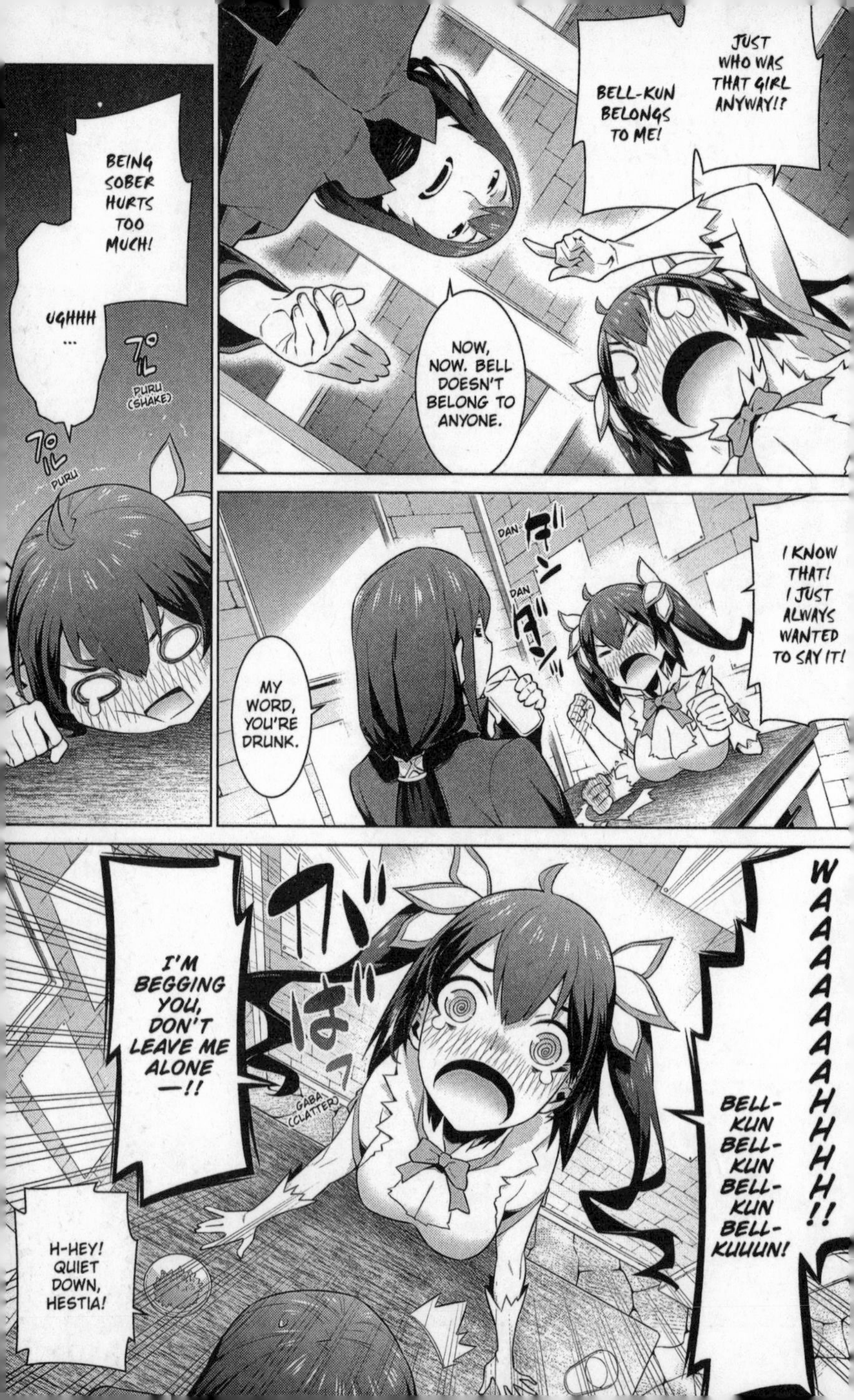
JUST WHO WAS THAT GIRL ANYWAY!?
BELL-KUN BELONGS TO ME!
NOW, NOW. BELL DOESN'T BELONG TO ANYONE.
I KNOW THAT! I JUST ALWAYS WANTED TO SAY IT!
DAN
DAN
MY WORD, YOU'RE DRUNK.
BEING SOBER HURTS TOO MUCH!
UGHHH ...
PURU (SHAKE)
PURU
WAAAAAAAAAHHHHH!!
BELL-KUN BELL-KUN BELL-KUN BELL-KUUUN!
I'M BEGGING YOU, DON'T LEAVE ME ALONE—!!
GABA (CLATTER)
H-HEY! QUIET DOWN, HESTIA!

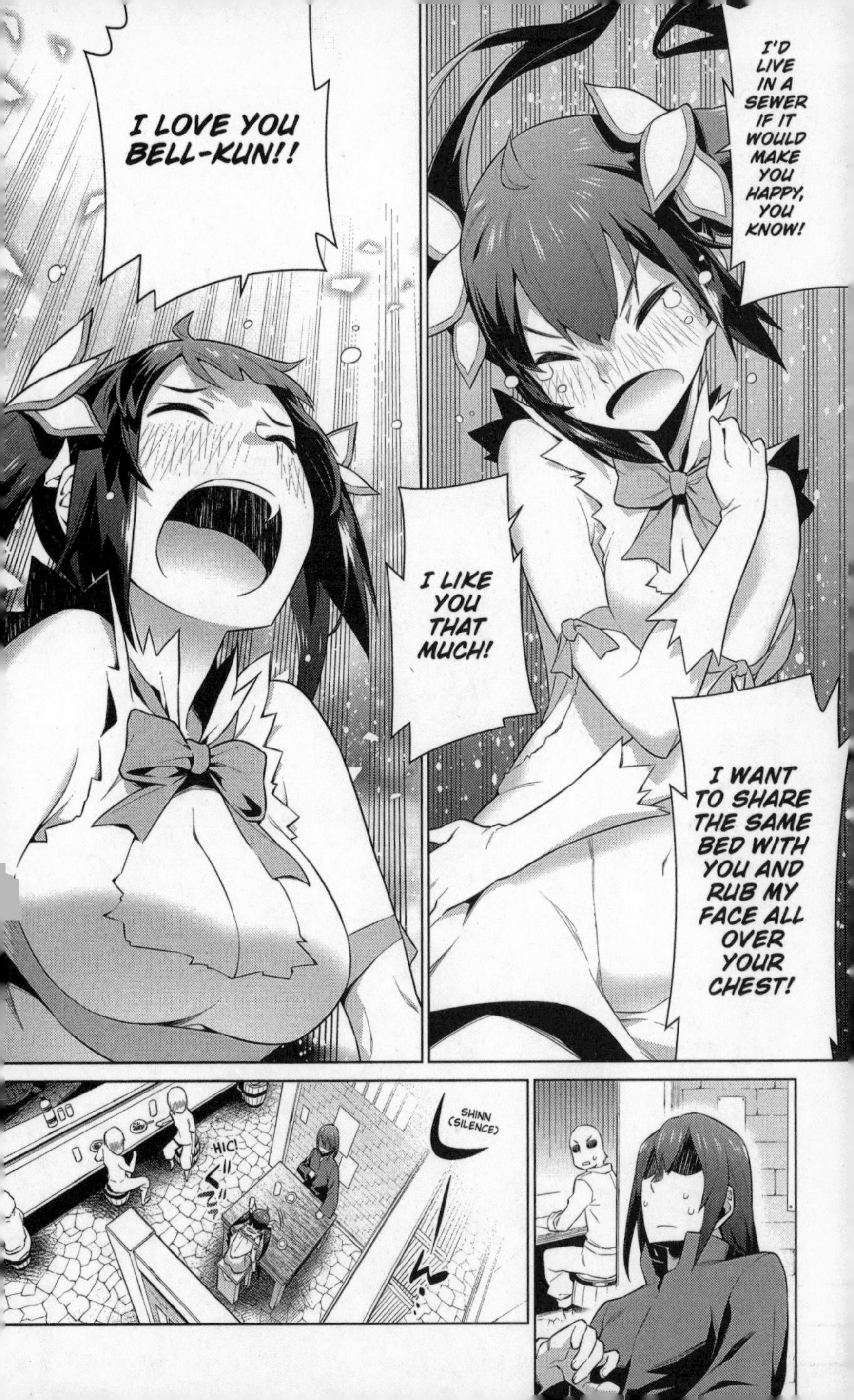
I'D LIVE IN A SEWER IF IT WOULD MAKE YOU HAPPY, YOU KNOW!
I LIKE YOU THAT MUCH!
I WANT TO SHARE THE SAME BED WITH YOU AND RUB MY FACE ALL OVER YOUR CHEST!
I LOVE YOU BELL-KUN!!
SHINN (SILENCE)
HIC!

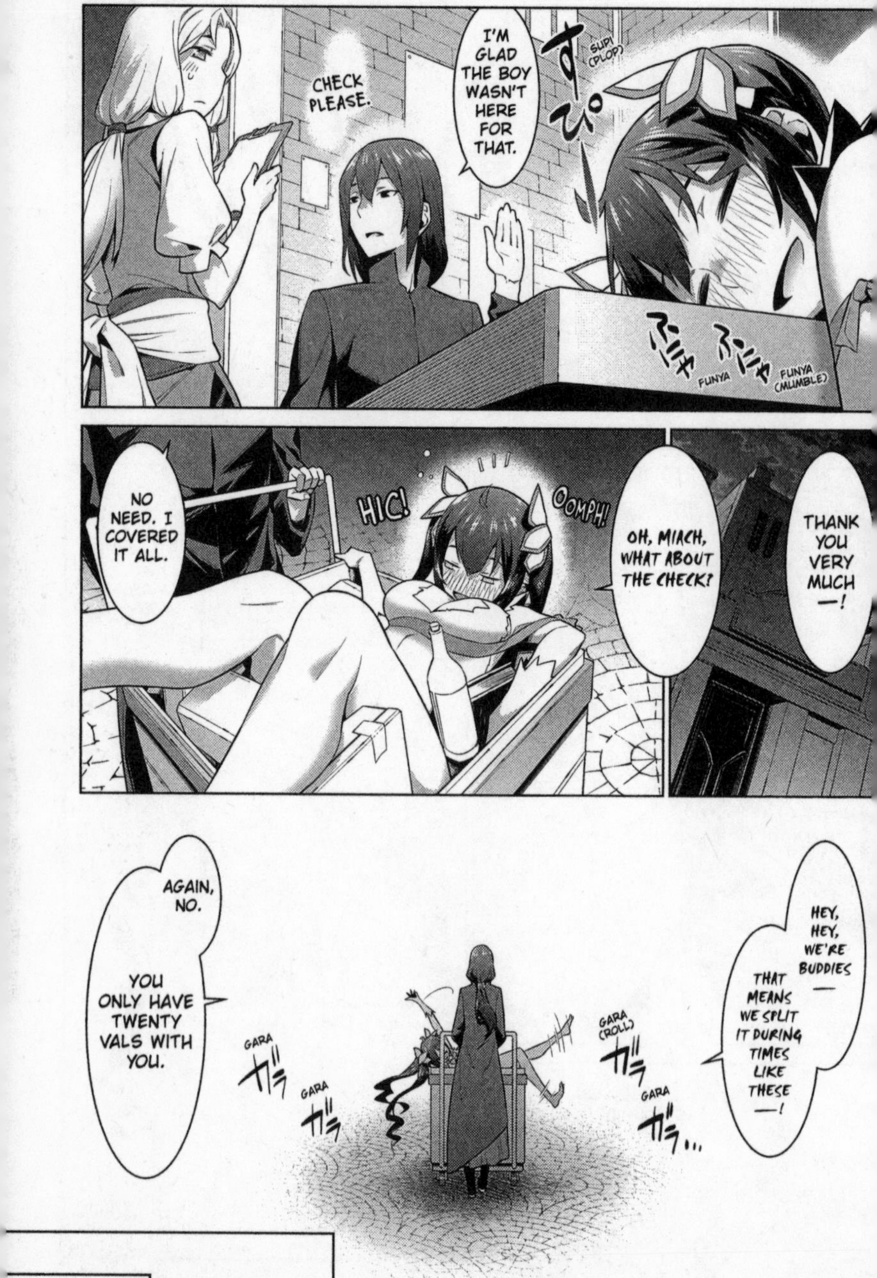
すぴ
SUPI (PLOP)
I'M GLAD THE BOY WASN'T HERE FOR THAT.
CHECK PLEASE.
ふにゃ ふにゃ
FUNYA FUNYA (MUMBLE)
THANK YOU VERY MUCH—!
OH, MIACH, WHAT ABOUT THE CHECK?
OOMPH!
HIC!
NO NEED. I COVERED IT ALL.
HEY, HEY, WE'RE BUDDIES—
THAT MEANS WE SPLIT IT DURING TIMES LIKE THESE—!
GARA (ROLL) ガラ
GARA ガラ...
GARA ガラ
GARA ガラ
AGAIN, NO.
YOU ONLY HAVE TWENTY VALS WITH YOU.

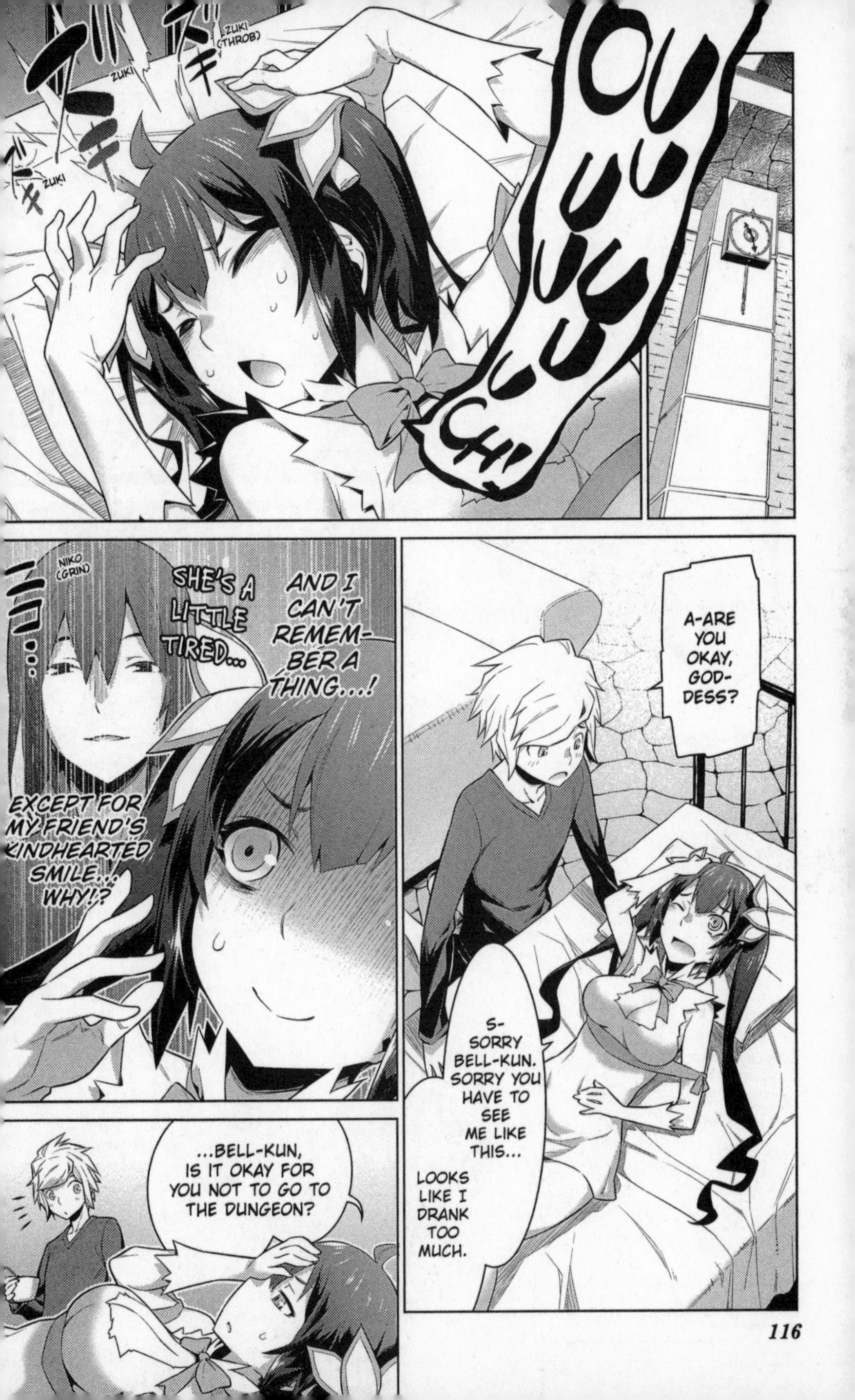
ZUKI (THROB)
ZUKI
ZUKI
OUUUUUUUCH!
A-ARE YOU OKAY, GOD-DESS?
S-SORRY BELL-KUN. SORRY YOU HAVE TO SEE ME LIKE THIS...
LOOKS LIKE I DRANK TOO MUCH.
AND I CAN'T REMEM-BER A THING...!
SHE'S A LITTLE TIRED...
NIKO (GRIN)
EXCEPT FOR MY FRIEND'S KINDHEARTED SMILE... WHY!?
...BELL-KUN, IS IT OKAY FOR YOU NOT TO GO TO THE DUNGEON?

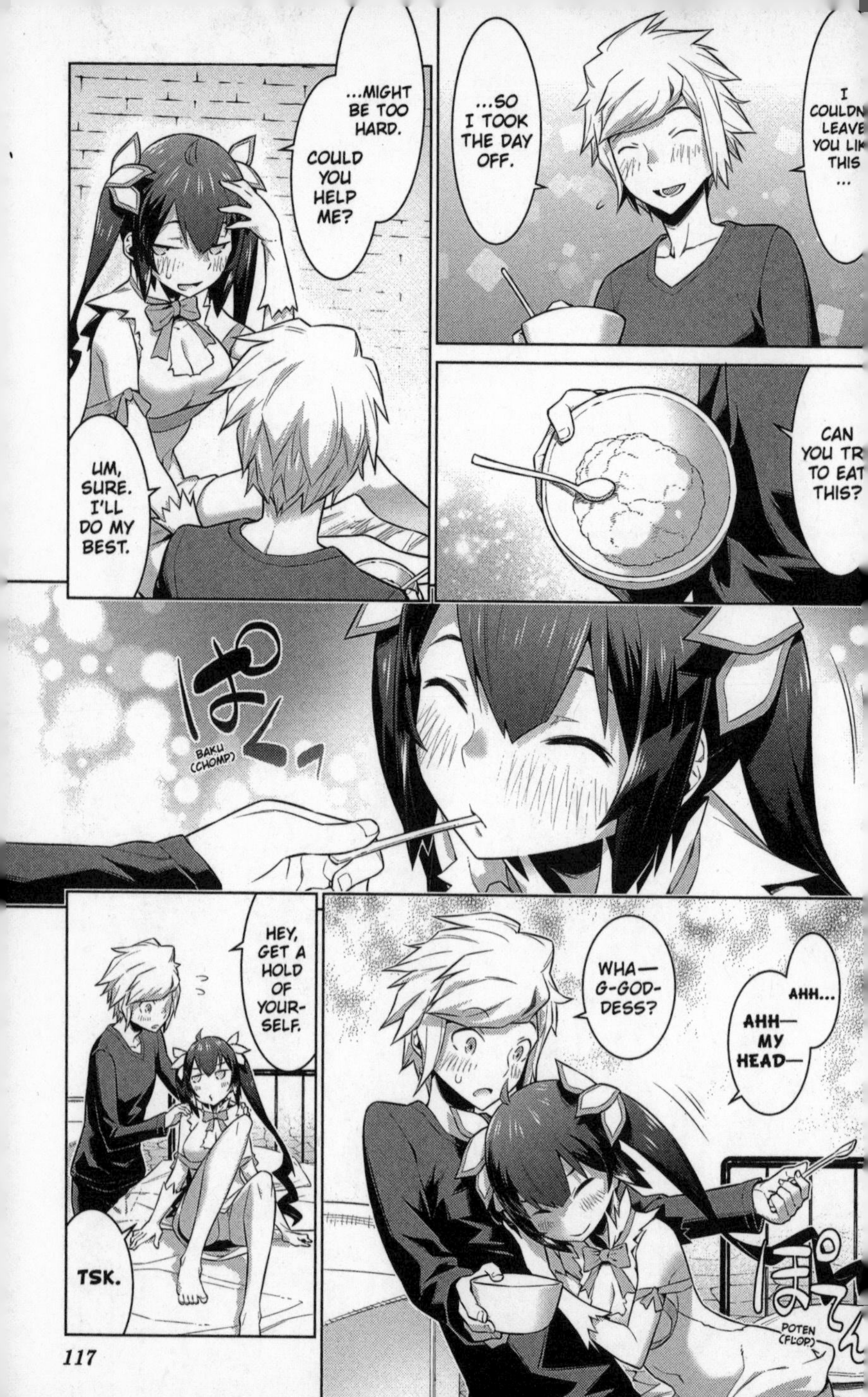

I COULDN LEAVE YOU LIK THIS ...
...SO I TOOK THE DAY OFF.
CAN YOU TR TO EAT THIS?
...MIGHT BE TOO HARD.
COULD YOU HELP ME?
UM, SURE. I'LL DO MY BEST.
BAKU (CHOMP)
AHH...
AHH— MY HEAD—
WHA— G-GOD-DESS?
POTEN (FLOP)
HEY, GET A HOLD OF YOUR-SELF.
TSK.

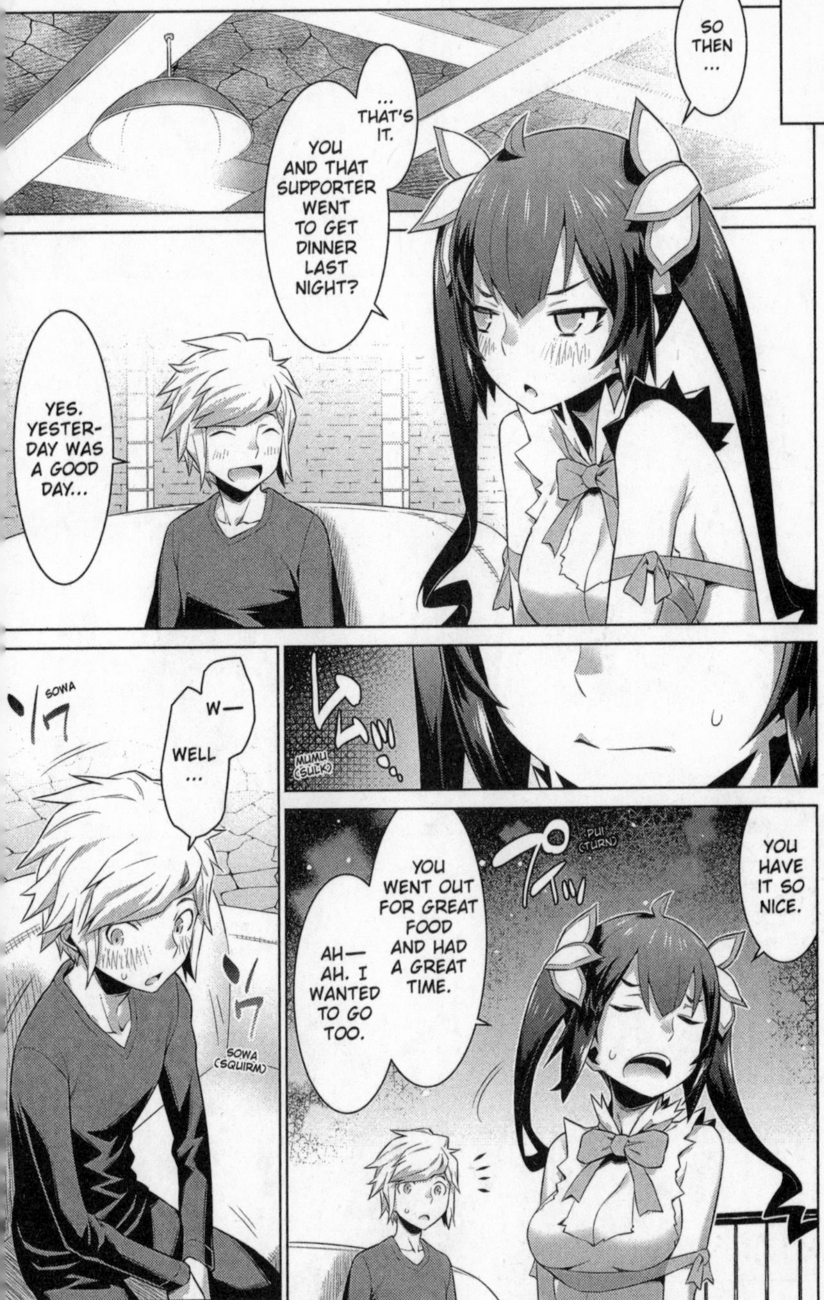
SO THEN ...
... THAT'S IT.
YOU AND THAT SUPPORTER WENT TO GET DINNER LAST NIGHT?
YES. YESTER-DAY WAS A GOOD DAY...
MUMU (SULK)
YOU HAVE IT SO NICE.
PUI (TURN)
YOU WENT OUT FOR GREAT FOOD AND HAD A GREAT TIME.
AH—AH. I WANTED TO GO TOO.
SOWA
W— WELL ...
SOWA (SQUIRM)

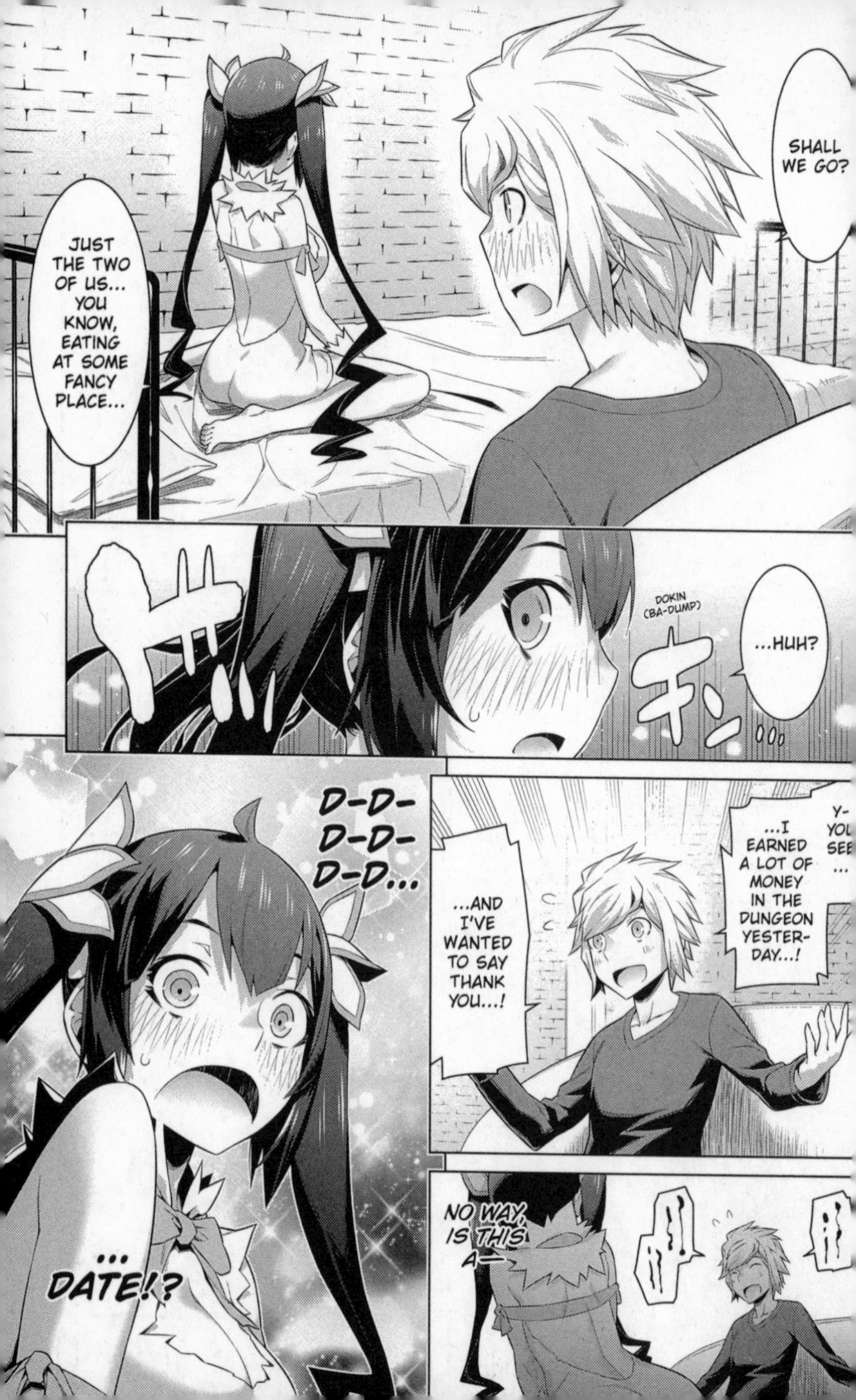
SHALL WE GO?
JUST THE TWO OF US... YOU KNOW, EATING AT SOME FANCY PLACE...
...HUH?
DOKIN (BA-DUMP)
Y-YOU SEE...
...I EARNED A LOT OF MONEY IN THE DUNGEON YESTER-DAY...!
...AND I'VE WANTED TO SAY THANK YOU...!
NO WAY, IS THIS A—
D-D-D-D-D-D...
...DATE!?

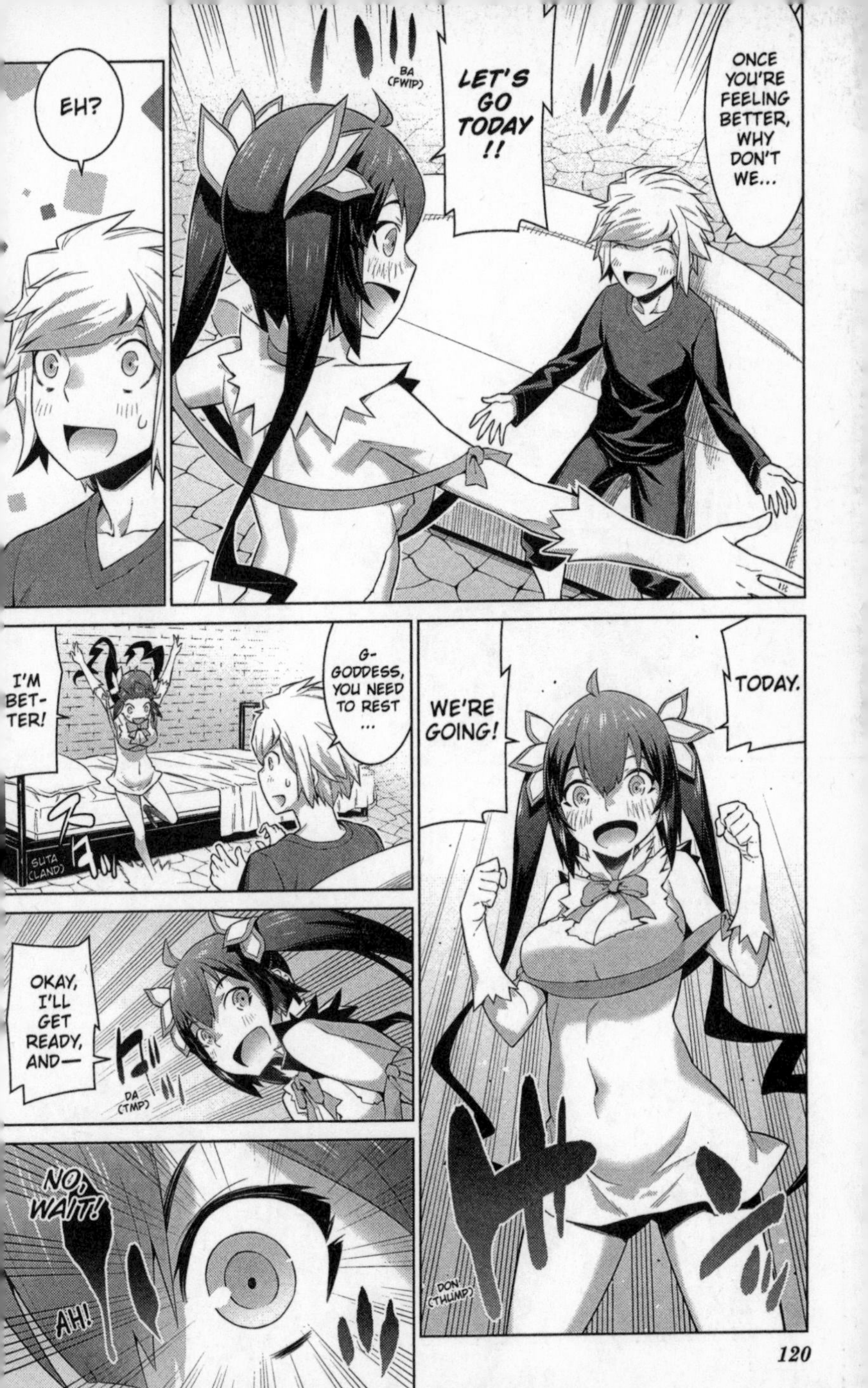
ONCE YOU'RE FEELING BETTER, WHY DON'T WE...
BA (FWIP)
LET'S GO TODAY!!
EH?
TODAY.
WE'RE GOING!
DON (THUMP)
G-GODDESS, YOU NEED TO REST ...
I'M BET-TER!
SUTA (LAND)
OKAY, I'LL GET READY, AND—
DA (TMP)
NO, WAIT!
AH!

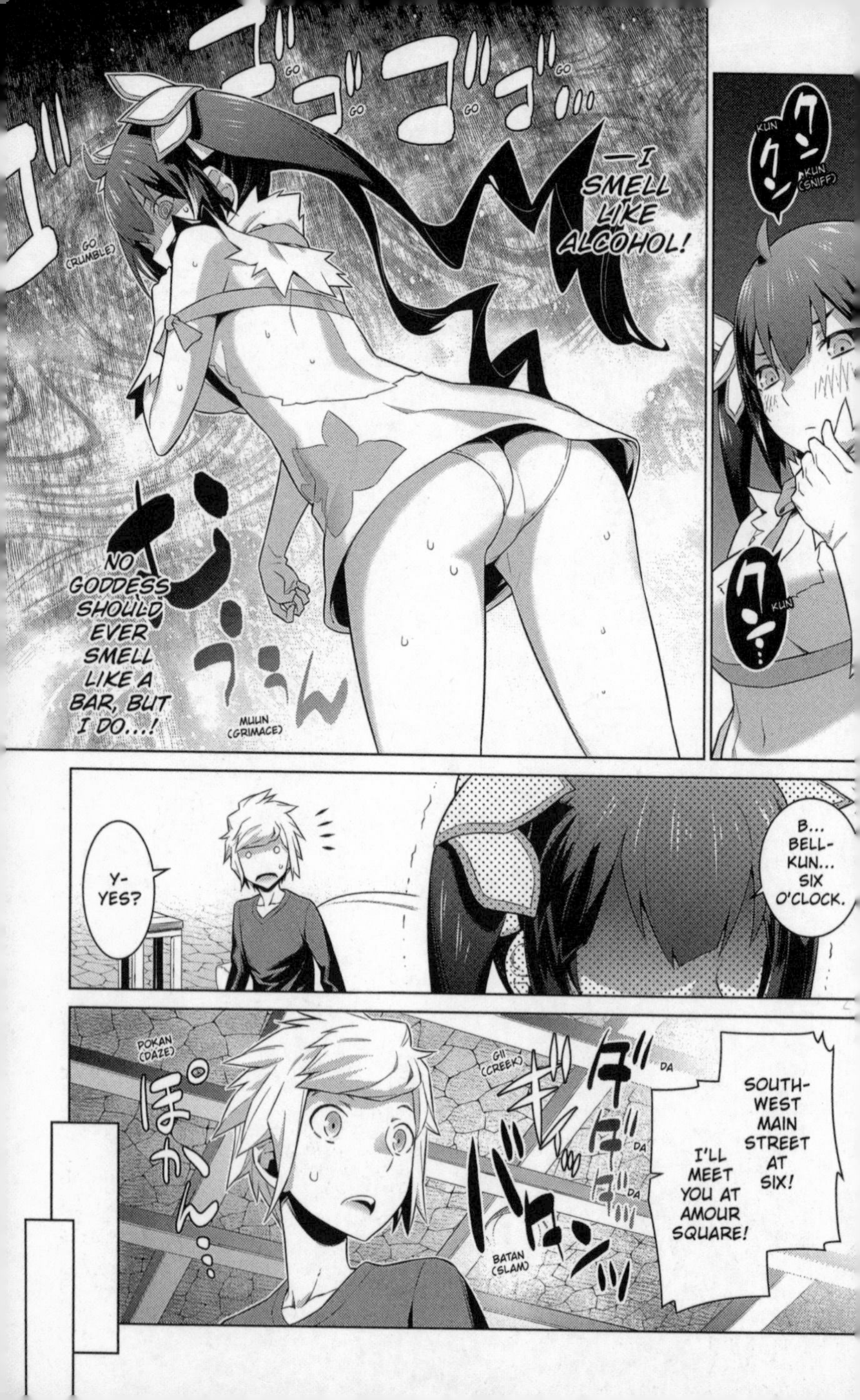
KUN
KUN (SNIFF)
KUN
GO
GO
GO
GO
GO
—I SMELL LIKE ALCOHOL!
GO (RUMBLE)
NO GODDESS SHOULD EVER SMELL LIKE A BAR, BUT I DO...!
MUUN (GRIMACE)
B... BELL-KUN... SIX O'CLOCK.
Y-YES?
SOUTH-WEST MAIN STREET AT SIX!
I'LL MEET YOU AT AMOUR SQUARE!
DA
DA
DA
GII (CREEK)
BATAN (SLAM)
POKAN (DAZE)

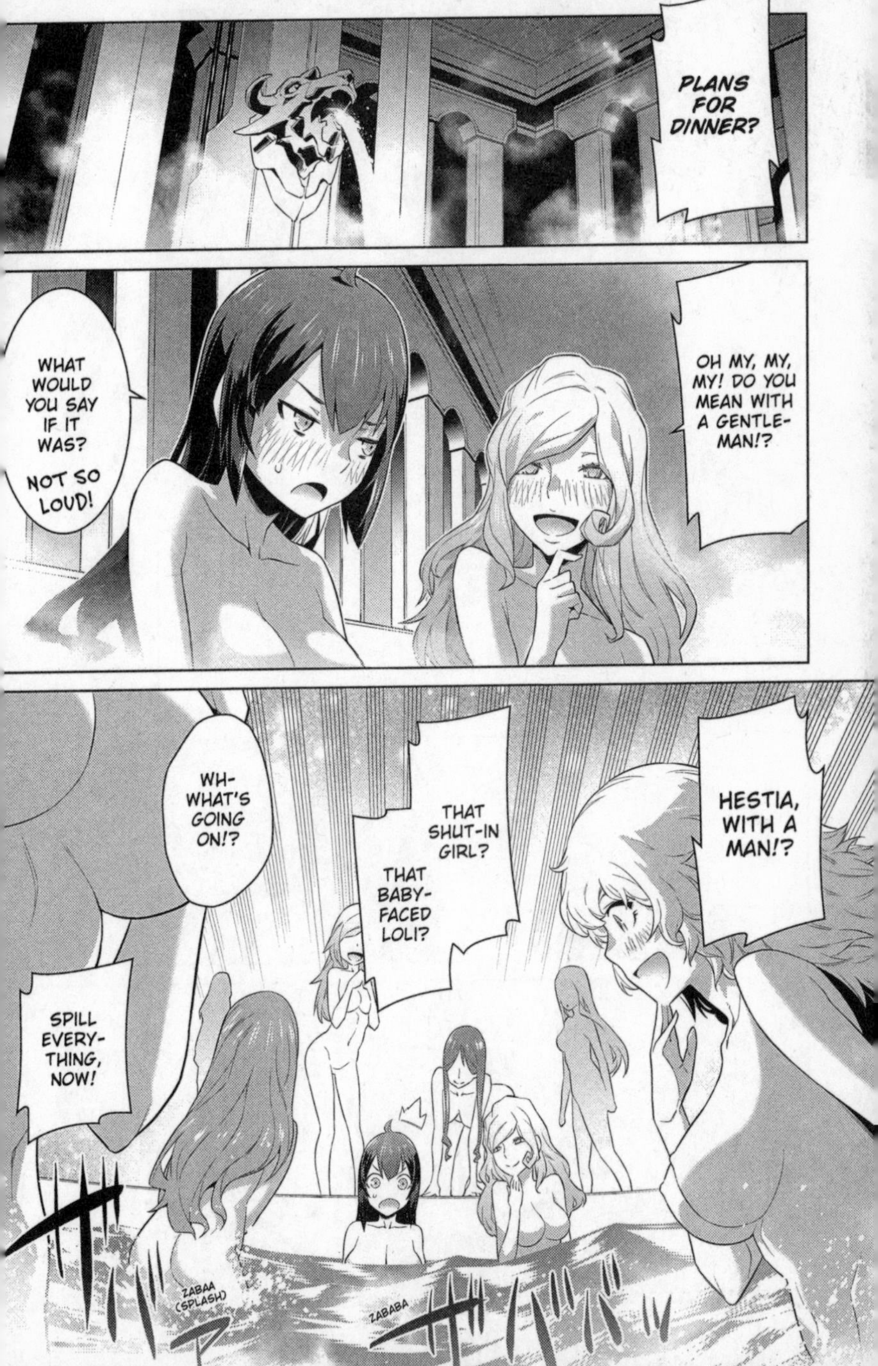
PLANS FOR DINNER?
OH MY, MY, MY! DO YOU MEAN WITH A GENTLEMAN!?
WHAT WOULD YOU SAY IF IT WAS?
NOT SO LOUD!
HESTIA, WITH A MAN!?
THAT SHUT-IN GIRL?
THAT BABY-FACED LOLI?
WH-WHAT'S GOING ON!?
SPILL EVERYTHING, NOW!
ZABAA (SPLASH)
ZABABA

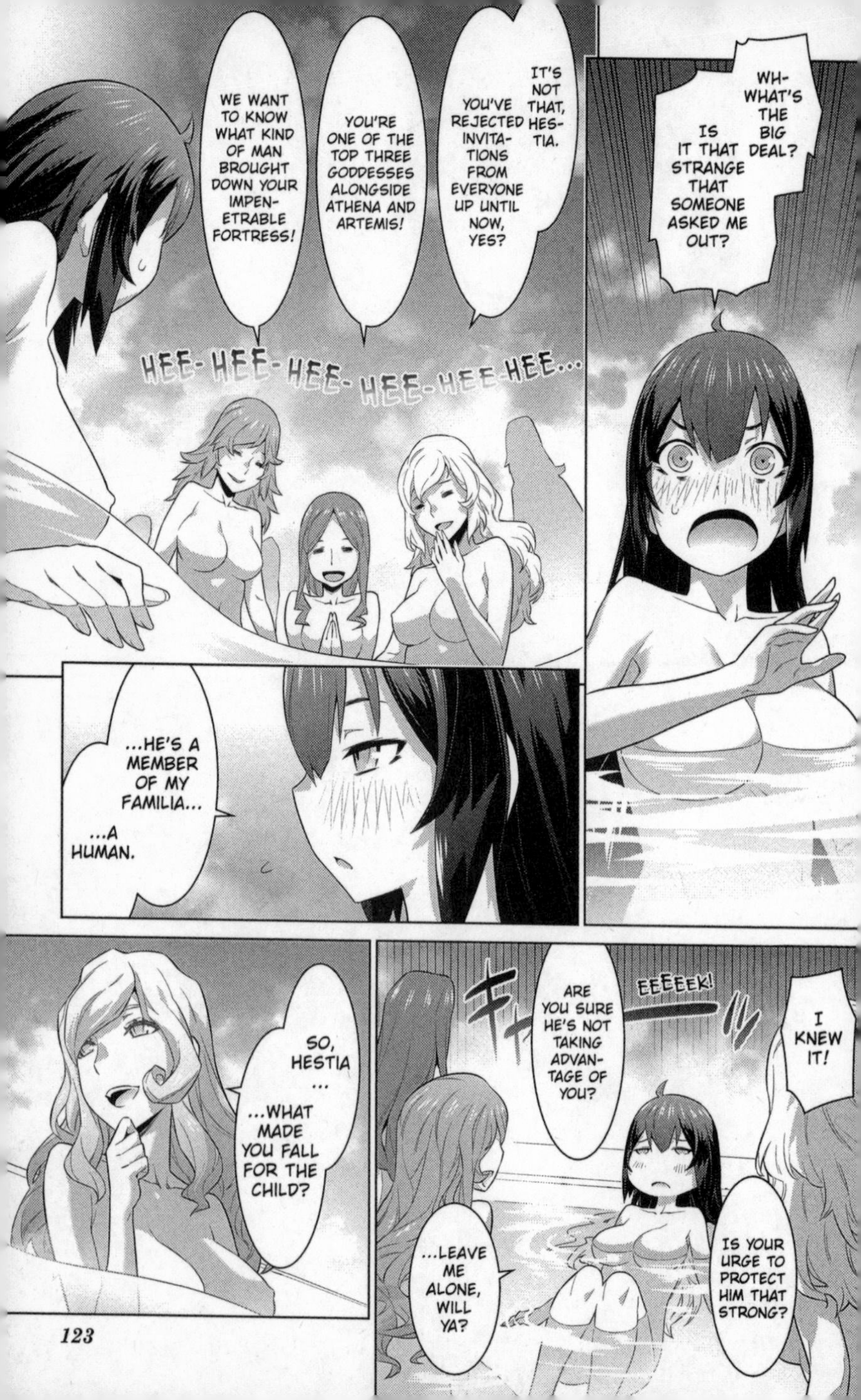
WH-WHAT'S THE BIG DEAL? IS IT THAT STRANGE THAT SOMEONE ASKED ME OUT?
IT'S NOT THAT, HESTIA. YOU'VE REJECTED INVITATIONS FROM EVERYONE UP UNTIL NOW, YES?
YOU'RE ONE OF THE TOP THREE GODDESSES ALONGSIDE ATHENA AND ARTEMIS!
WE WANT TO KNOW WHAT KIND OF MAN BROUGHT DOWN YOUR IMPENETRABLE FORTRESS!
HEE-HEE-HEE-HEE-HEE-HEE...
...HE'S A MEMBER OF MY FAMILIA...
...A HUMAN.
I KNEW IT!
EEEEEK!
ARE YOU SURE HE'S NOT TAKING ADVANTAGE OF YOU?
IS YOUR URGE TO PROTECT HIM THAT STRONG?
...LEAVE ME ALONE, WILL YA?
SO, HESTIA...
...WHAT MADE YOU FALL FOR THE CHILD?

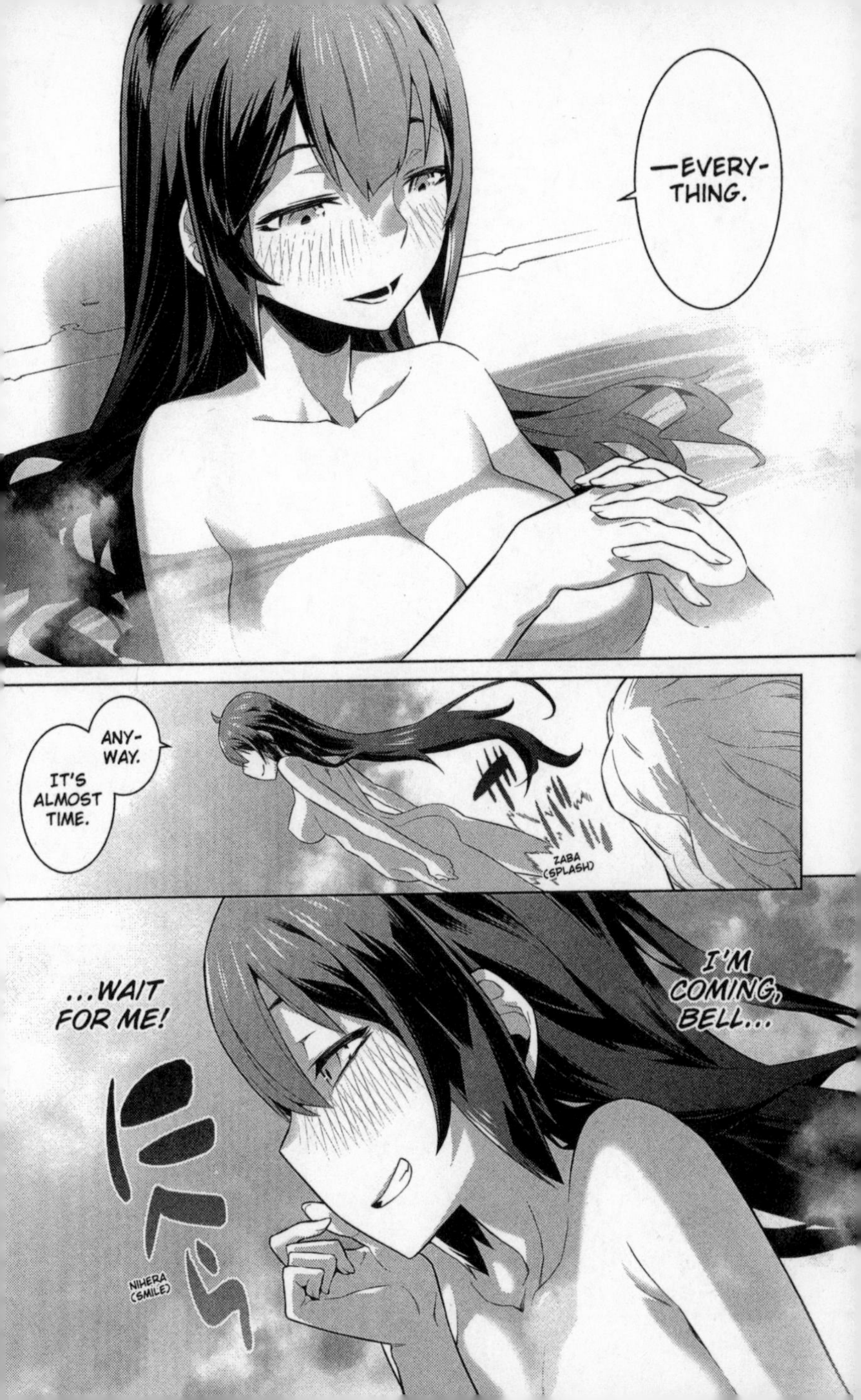
—EVERY-
THING.
ANY-
WAY.
IT'S
ALMOST
TIME.
ZABA
(SPLASH)
I'M
COMING,
BELL...
...WAIT
FOR ME!
NIHERA
(SMILE)

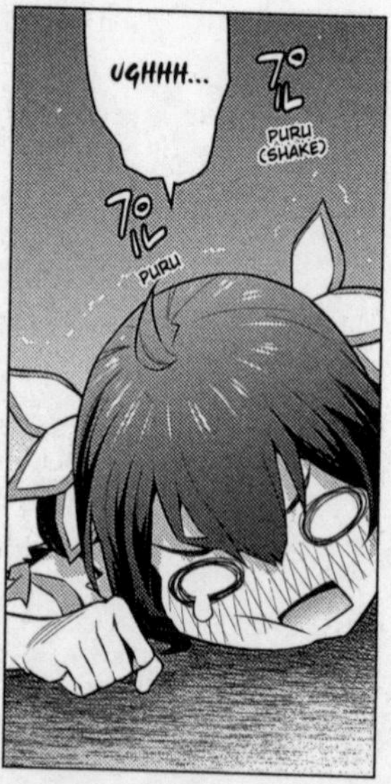
UGHHH...
プル
PURU (SHAKE)
プル
PURU

Is it WRONG to TRY to PiCK UP GiRLS iN A DUNGEON?

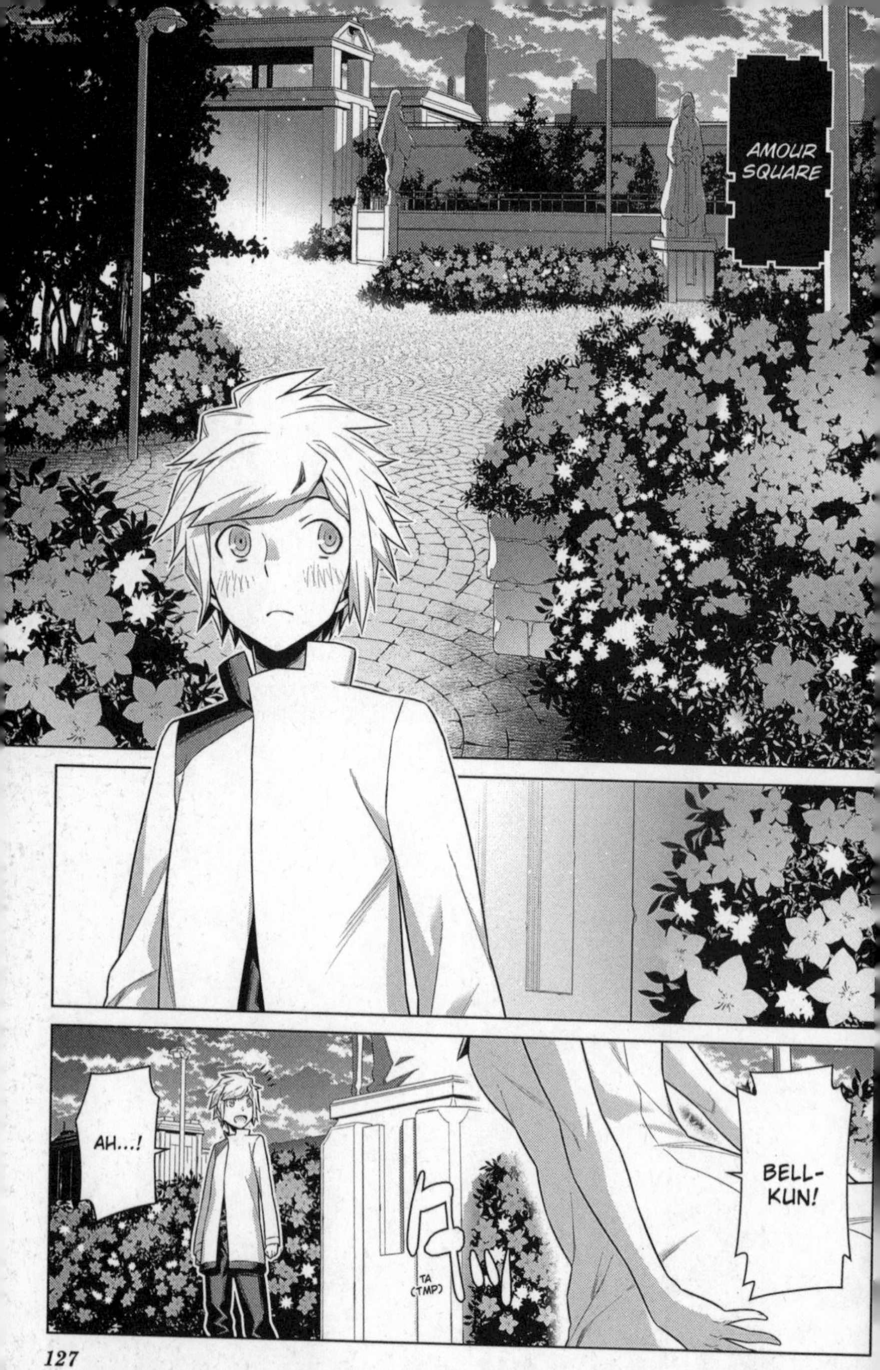
AMOUR SQUARE
BELL-KUN!
TA (TMP)
AH...!

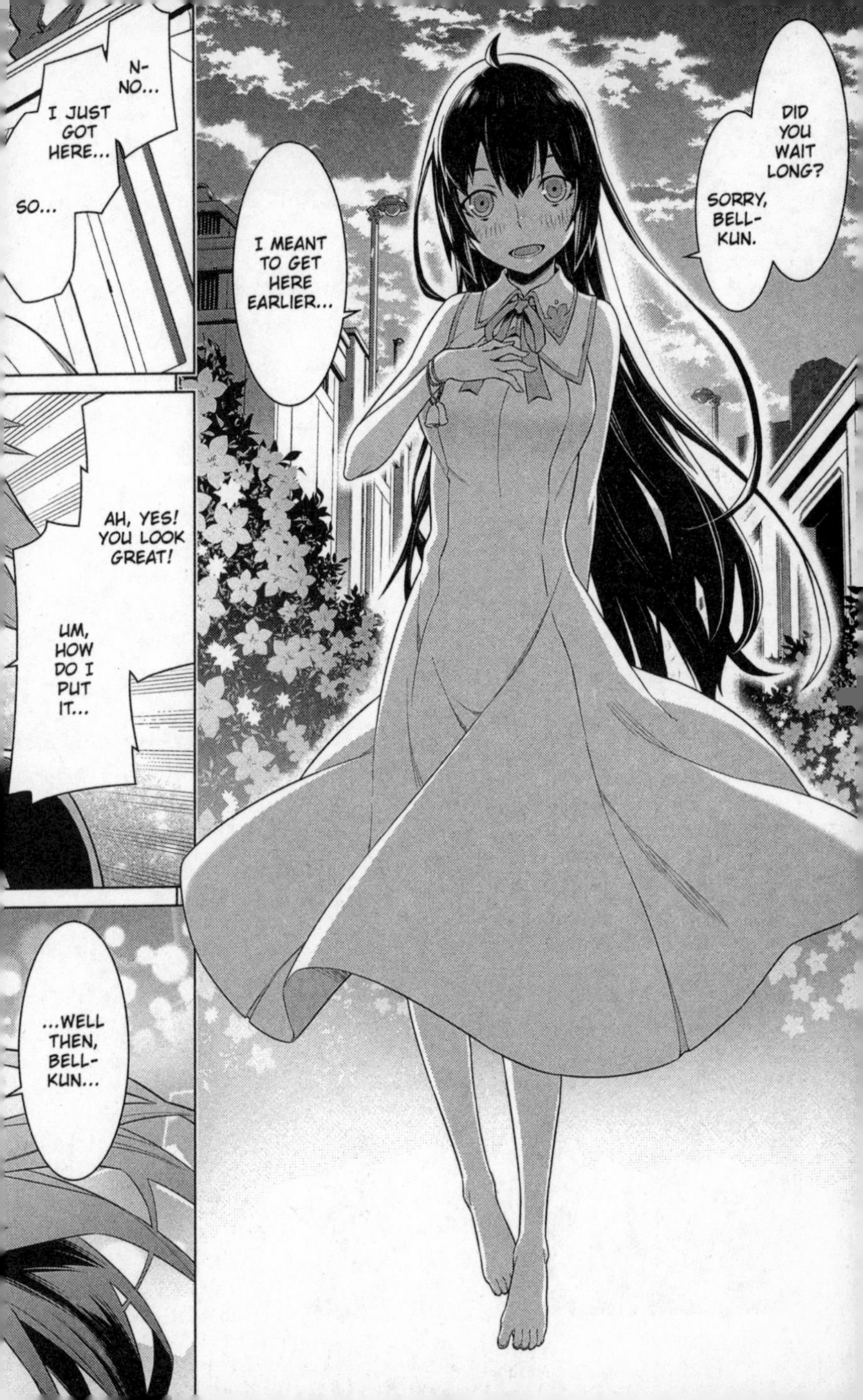
DID YOU WAIT LONG?
SORRY, BELL-KUN.
I MEANT TO GET HERE EARLIER...
N-NO...
I JUST GOT HERE...
SO...
AH, YES! YOU LOOK GREAT!
UM, HOW DO I PUT IT...
...WELL THEN, BELL-KUN...

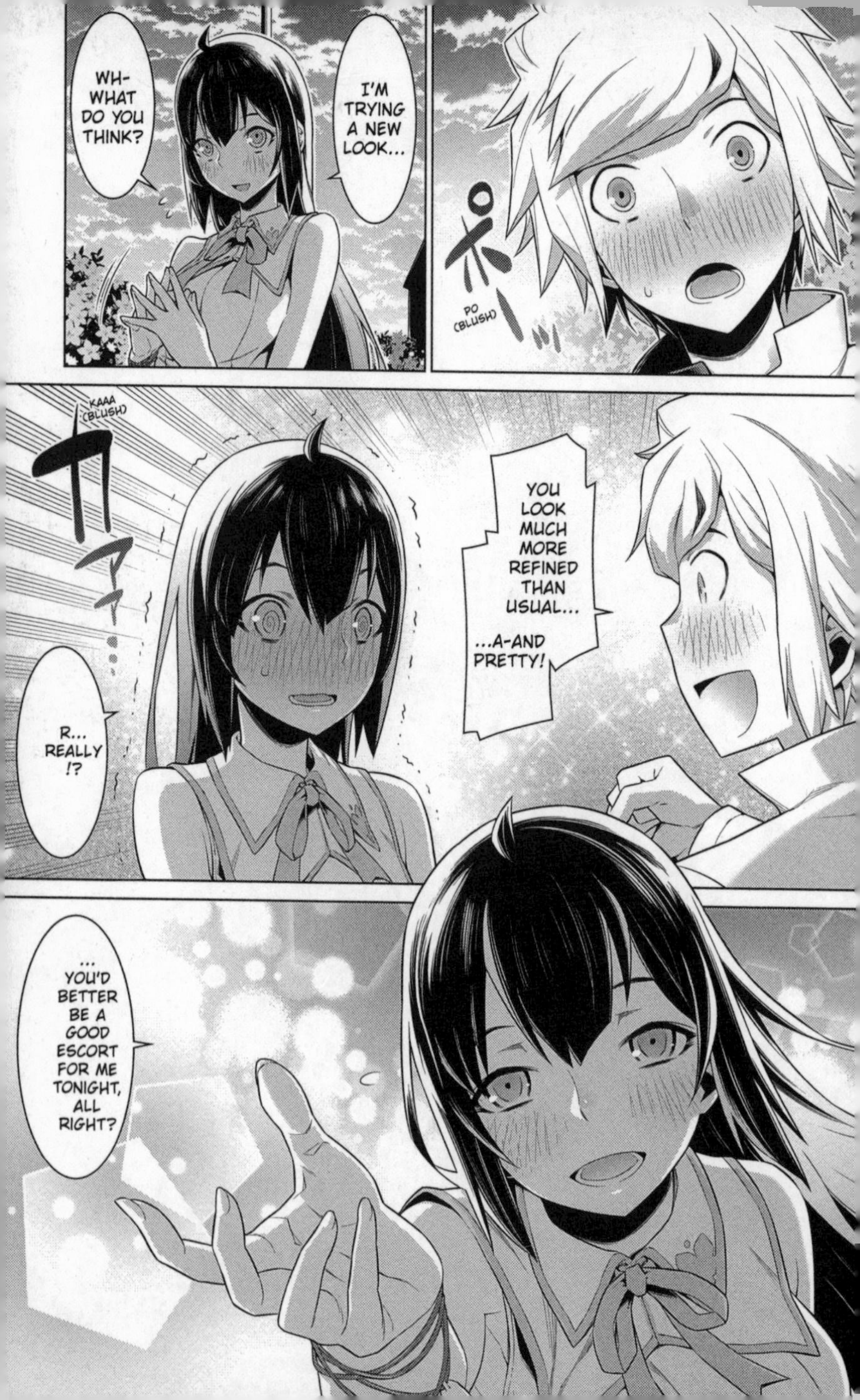
PO (BLUSH)
I'M TRYING A NEW LOOK...
WH-WHAT DO YOU THINK?
YOU LOOK MUCH MORE REFINED THAN USUAL...
...A-AND PRETTY!
KAAA (BLUSH)
R... REALLY!?
...YOU'D BETTER BE A GOOD ESCORT FOR ME TONIGHT, ALL RIGHT?

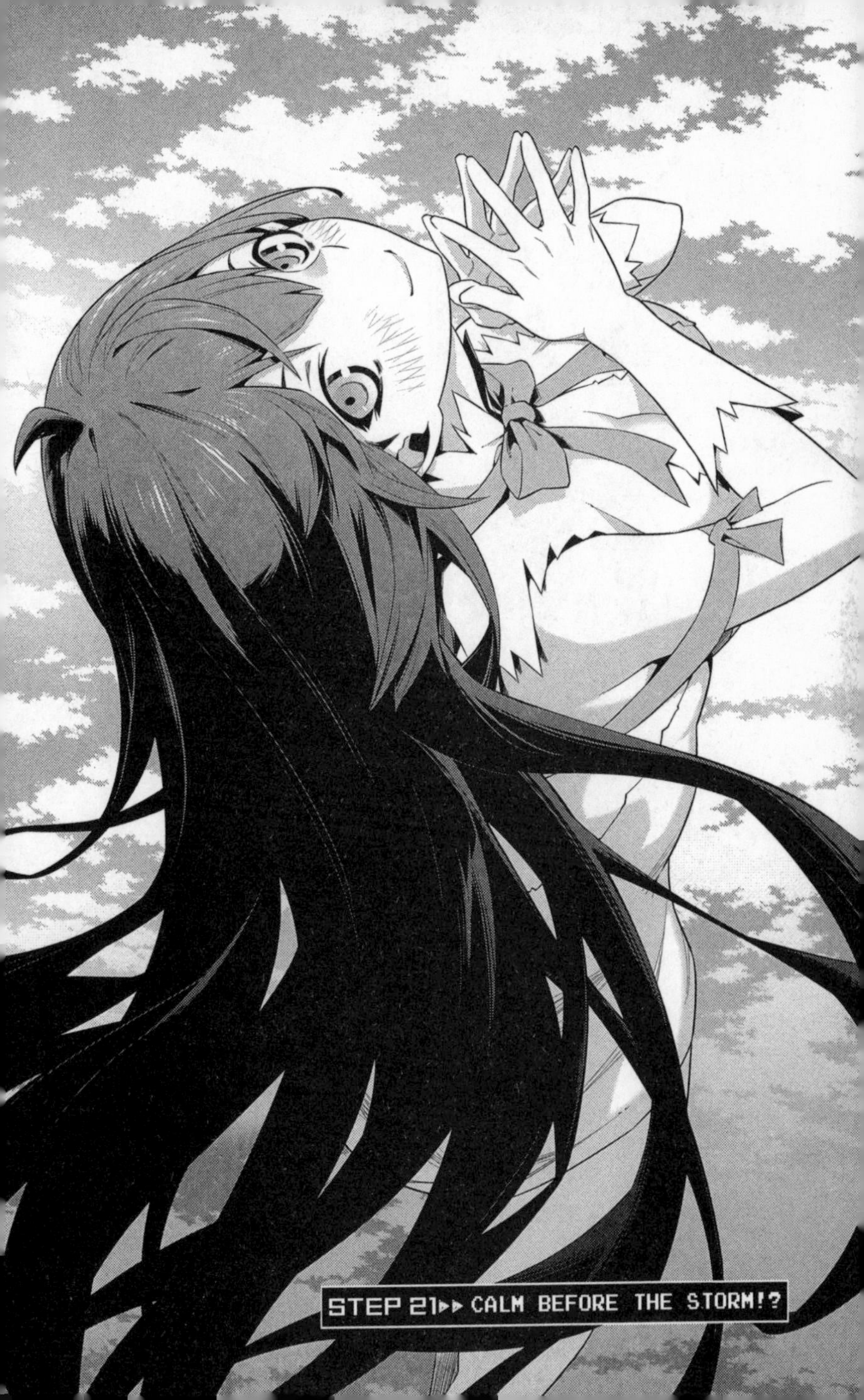
STEP 21▸▸ CALM BEFORE THE STORM!?

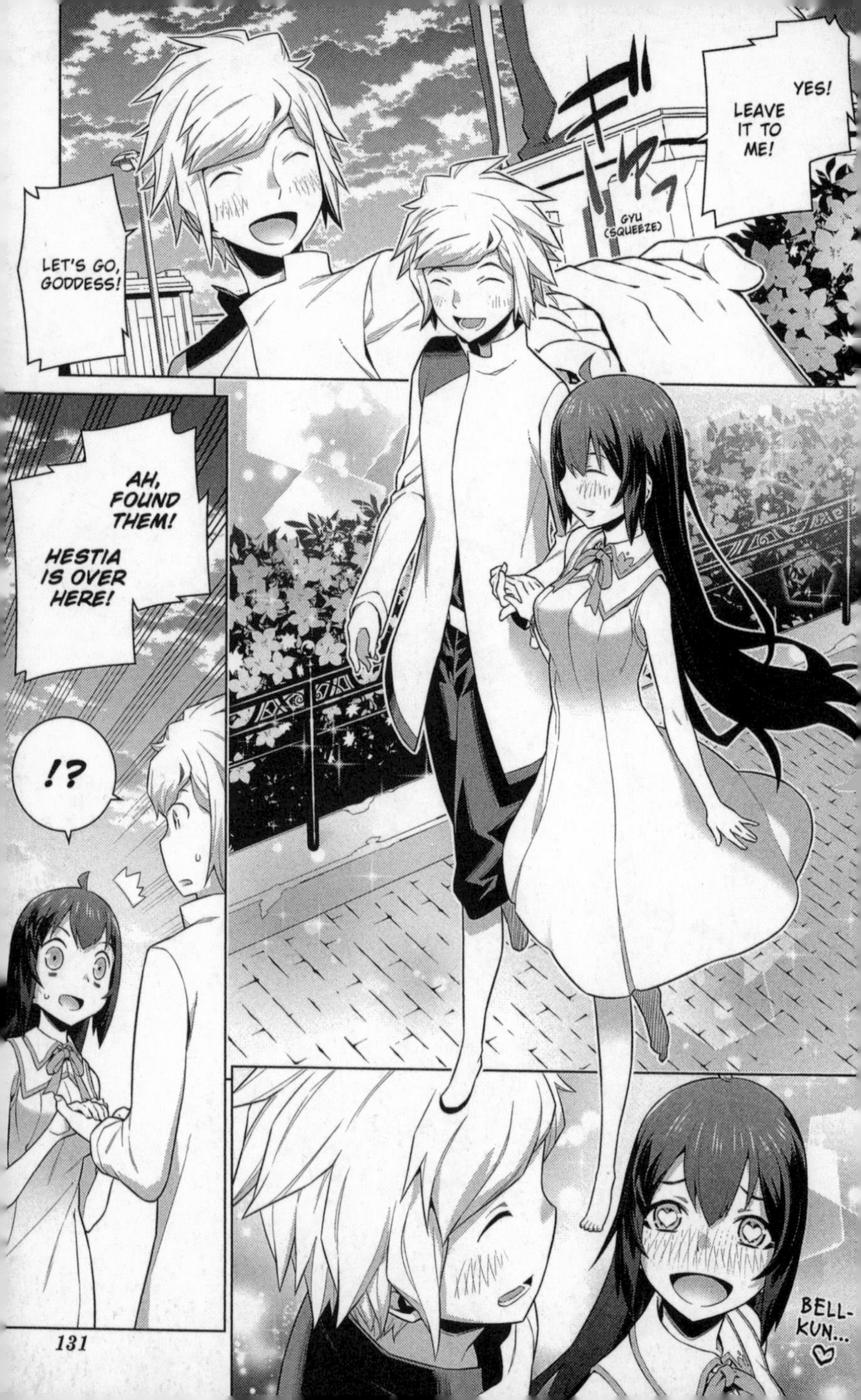
YES! LEAVE IT TO ME!
ギュッ
GYU (SQUEEZE)
LET'S GO, GODDESS!
BELL-KUN... ♡
AH, FOUND THEM! HESTIA IS OVER HERE!
!?

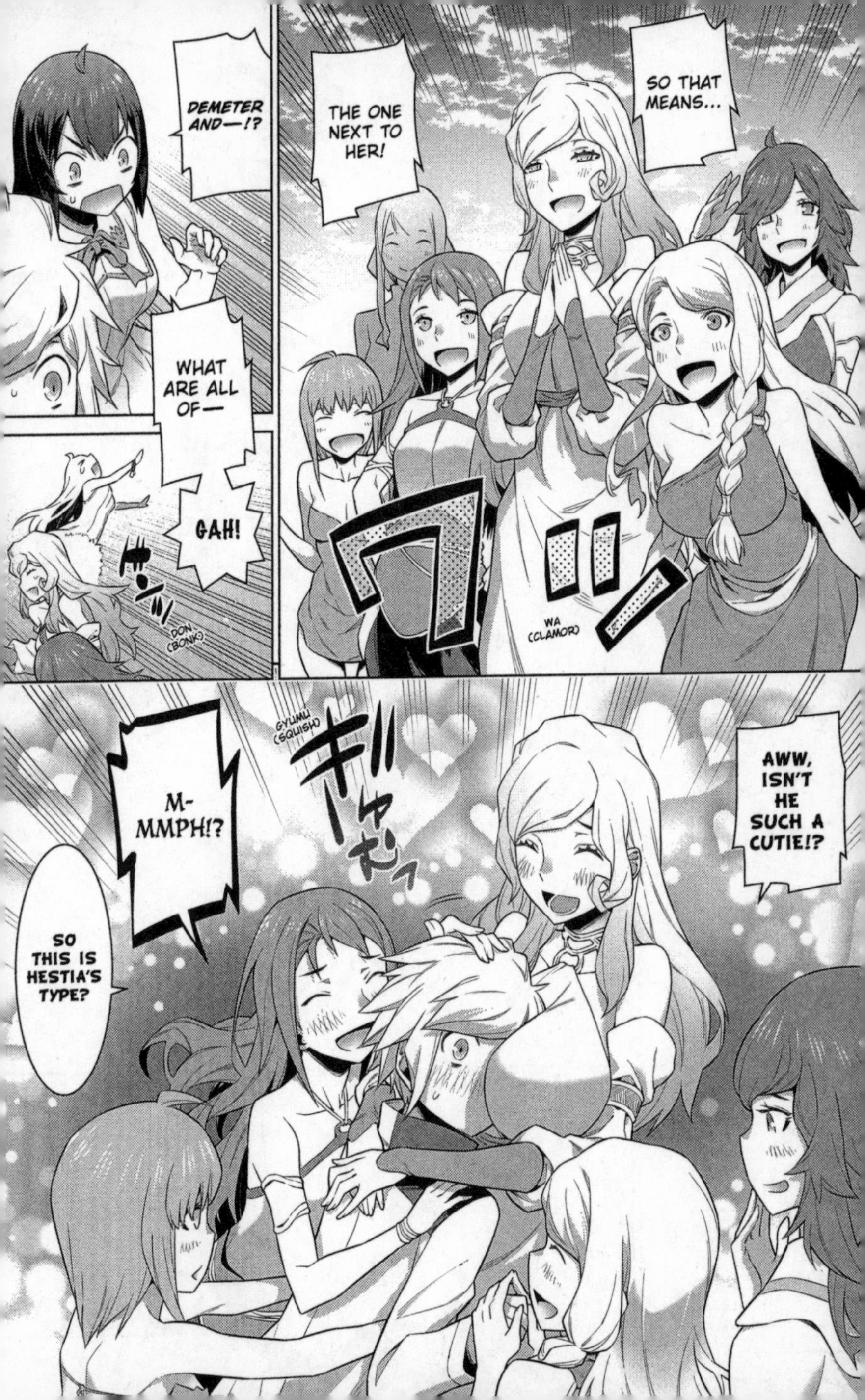

SO THAT MEANS...
THE ONE NEXT TO HER!
WA (CLAMOR)
DEMETER AND—!?
WHAT ARE ALL OF—
GAH!
DON (BONK)
AWW, ISN'T HE SUCH A CUTIE!?
GYUMU (SQUISH)
M-MMPH!?
SO THIS IS HESTIA'S TYPE?

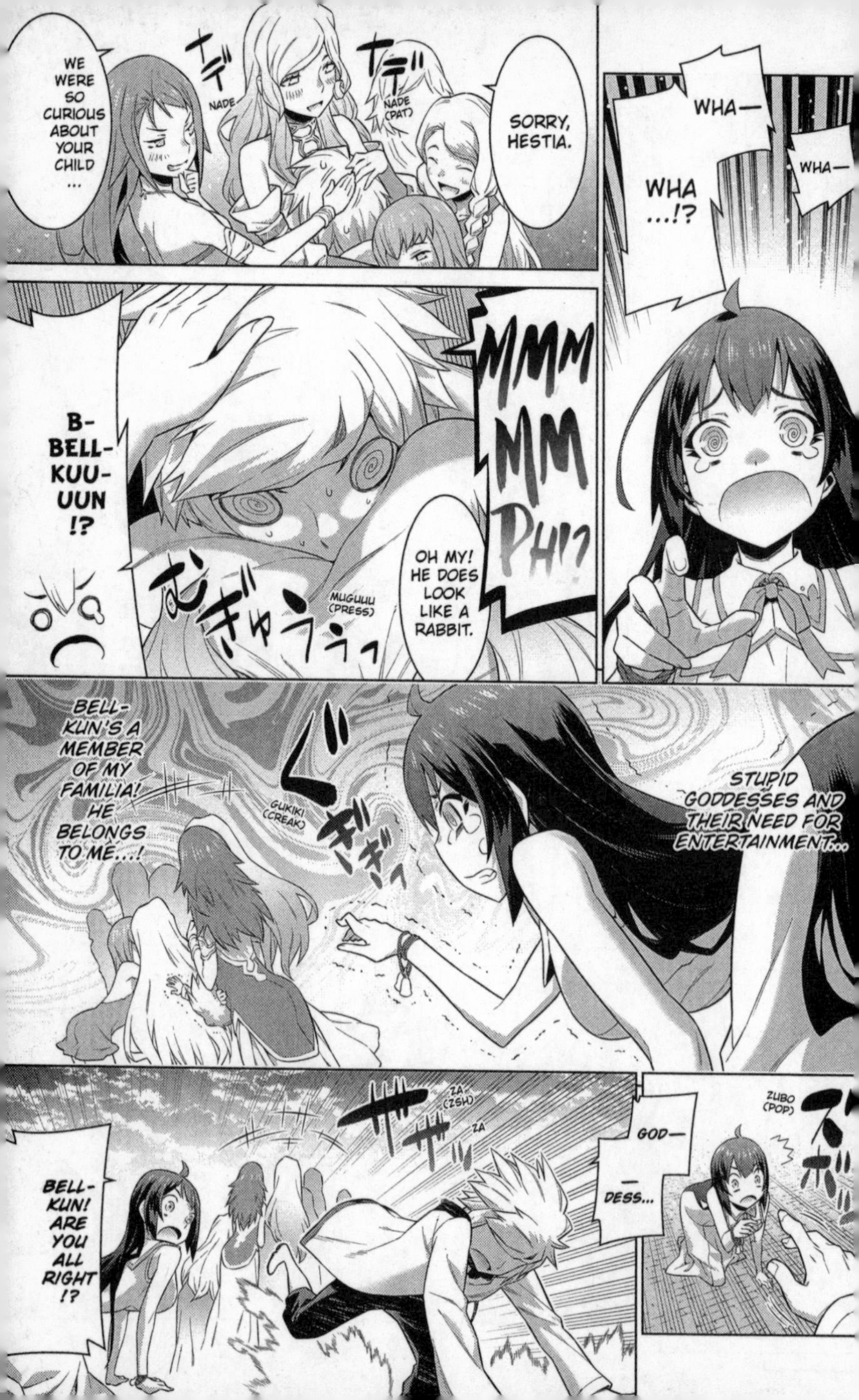

WHA—
WHA—
WHA ...!?
SORRY, HESTIA.
NADE (PAT)
NADE
WE WERE SO CURIOUS ABOUT YOUR CHILD ...
MMMMMPH!?
OH MY! HE DOES LOOK LIKE A RABBIT.
MUGUUU (PRESS)
B-BELL-KUUUUN!?
STUPID GODDESSES AND THEIR NEED FOR ENTERTAINMENT...
GUKIKI (CREAK)
BELL-KUN'S A MEMBER OF MY FAMILIA! HE BELONGS TO ME...!
ZUBO (POP)
GOD—
—DESS...
ZA (ZSH)
ZA
BELL-KUN! ARE YOU ALL RIGHT!?

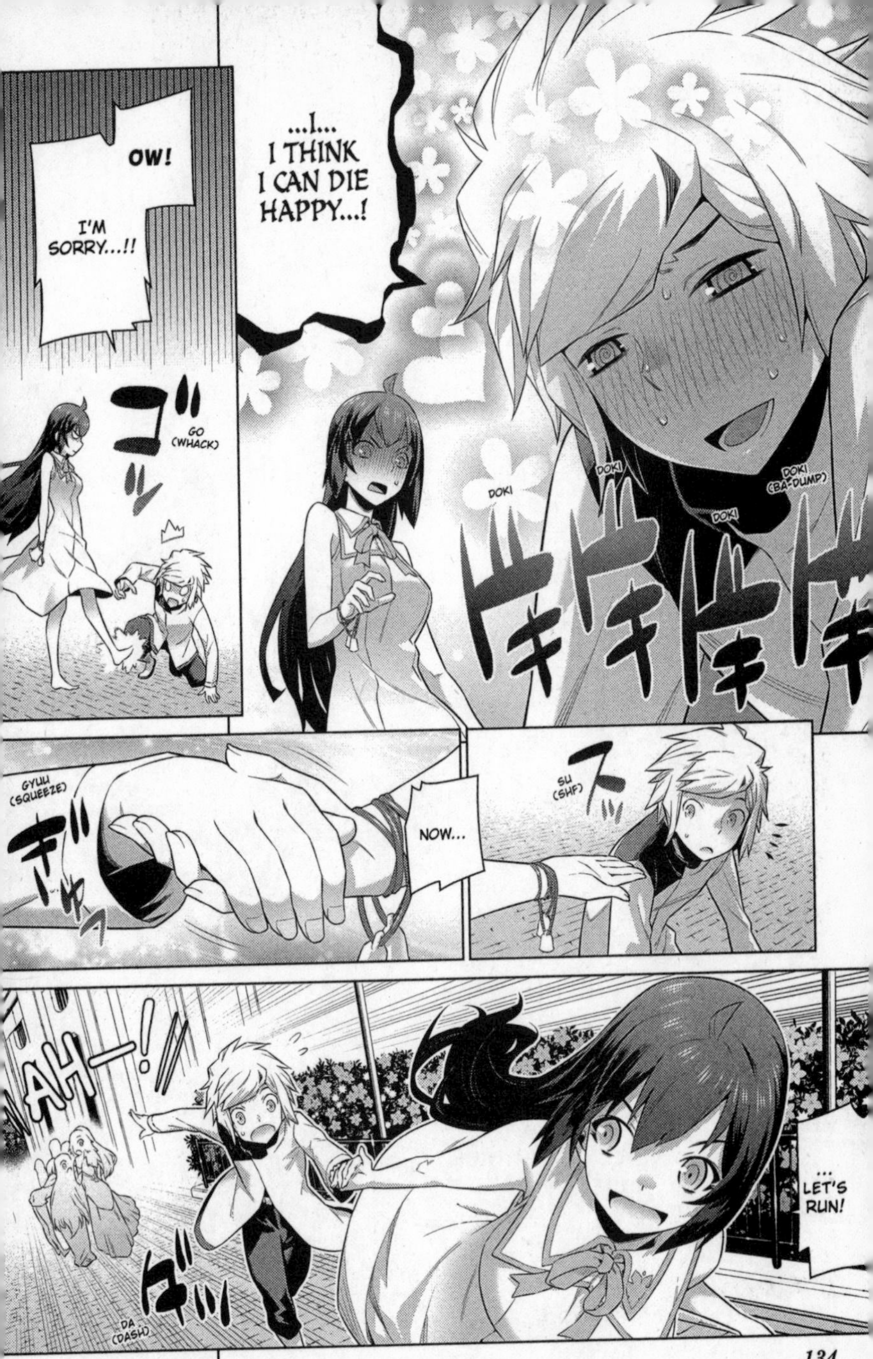
...I...
I THINK
I CAN DIE
HAPPY...!
DOKI
DOKI
DOKI
DOKI (BA-DUMP)
GO (WHACK)
OW!
I'M SORRY...!!
SU (SHF)
NOW...
GYUU (SQUEEZE)
...LET'S RUN!
AH—!
DA (DASH)

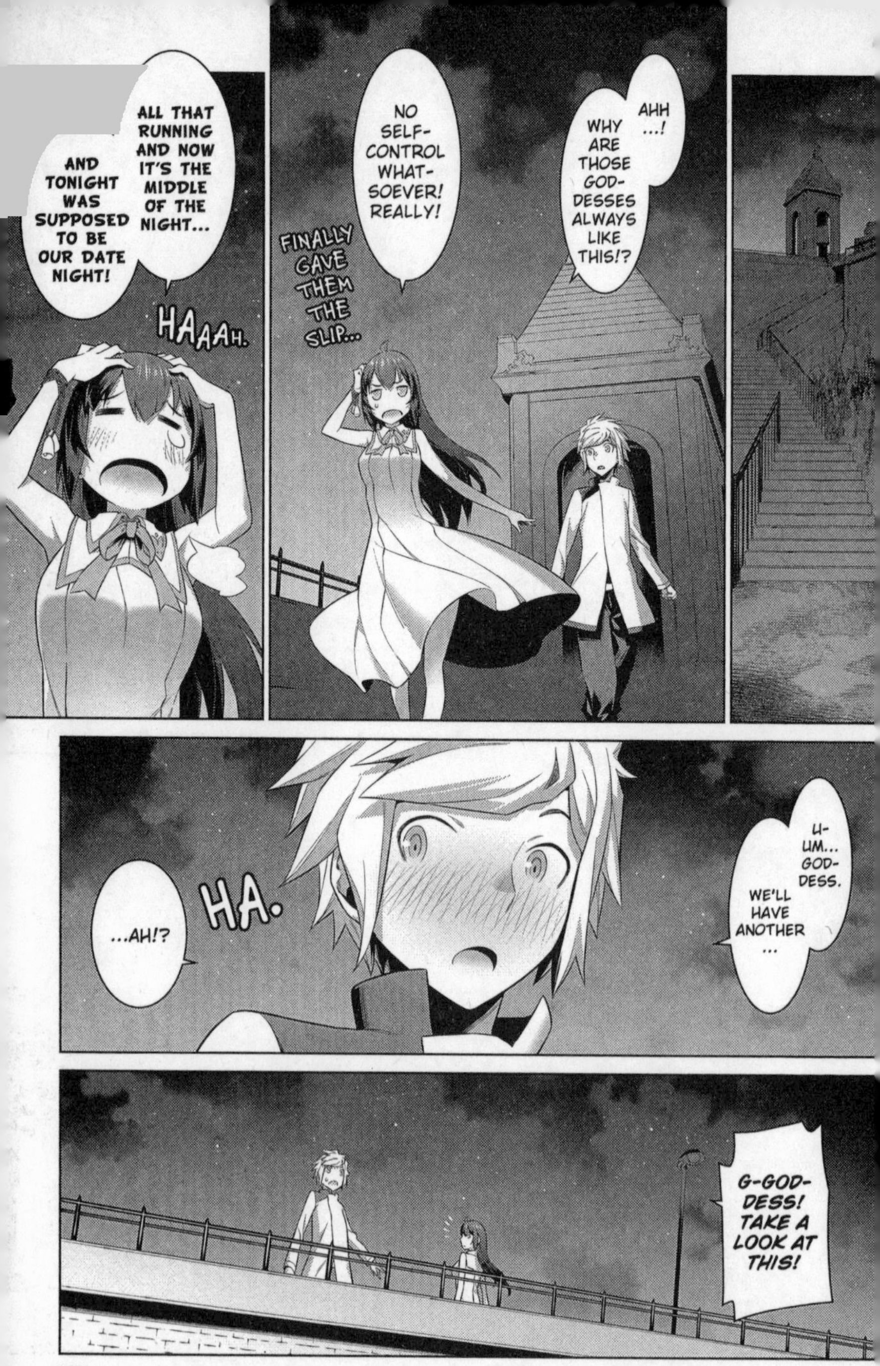
AHH ...! WHY ARE THOSE GOD-DESSES ALWAYS LIKE THIS!?
NO SELF-CONTROL WHAT-SOEVER! REALLY!
FINALLY GAVE THEM THE SLIP...
ALL THAT RUNNING AND NOW IT'S THE MIDDLE OF THE NIGHT...
AND TONIGHT WAS SUPPOSED TO BE OUR DATE NIGHT!
HAAAAH.
U-UM... GOD-DESS. WE'LL HAVE ANOTHER ...
HA.
...AH!?
G-GOD-DESS! TAKE A LOOK AT THIS!

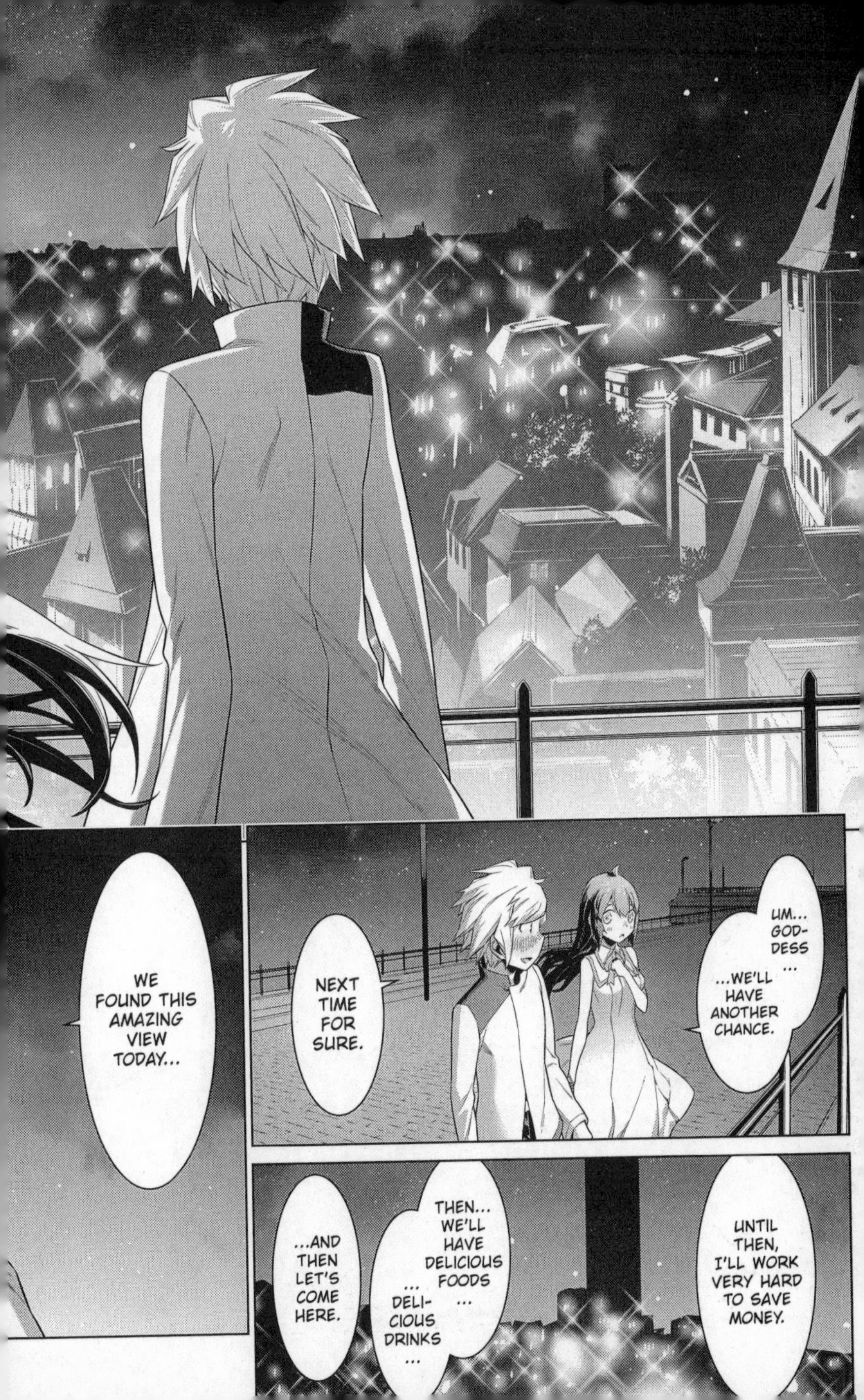
UM... GODDESS ...
...WE'LL HAVE ANOTHER CHANCE.
NEXT TIME FOR SURE.
UNTIL THEN, I'LL WORK VERY HARD TO SAVE MONEY.
THEN... WE'LL HAVE DELICIOUS FOODS ... DELICIOUS DRINKS ...
...AND THEN LET'S COME HERE.
WE FOUND THIS AMAZING VIEW TODAY...

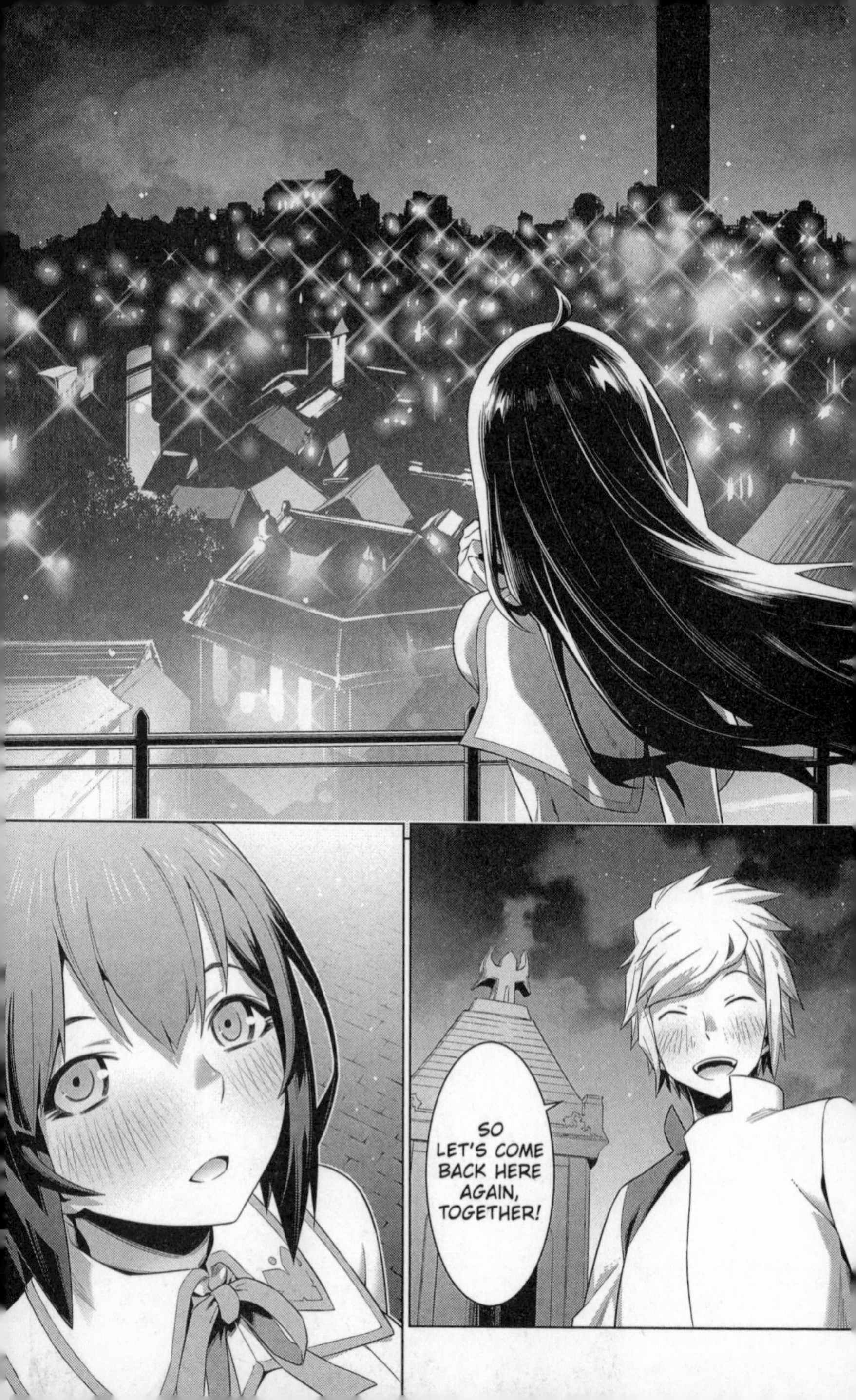
SO LET'S COME BACK HERE AGAIN, TOGETHER!

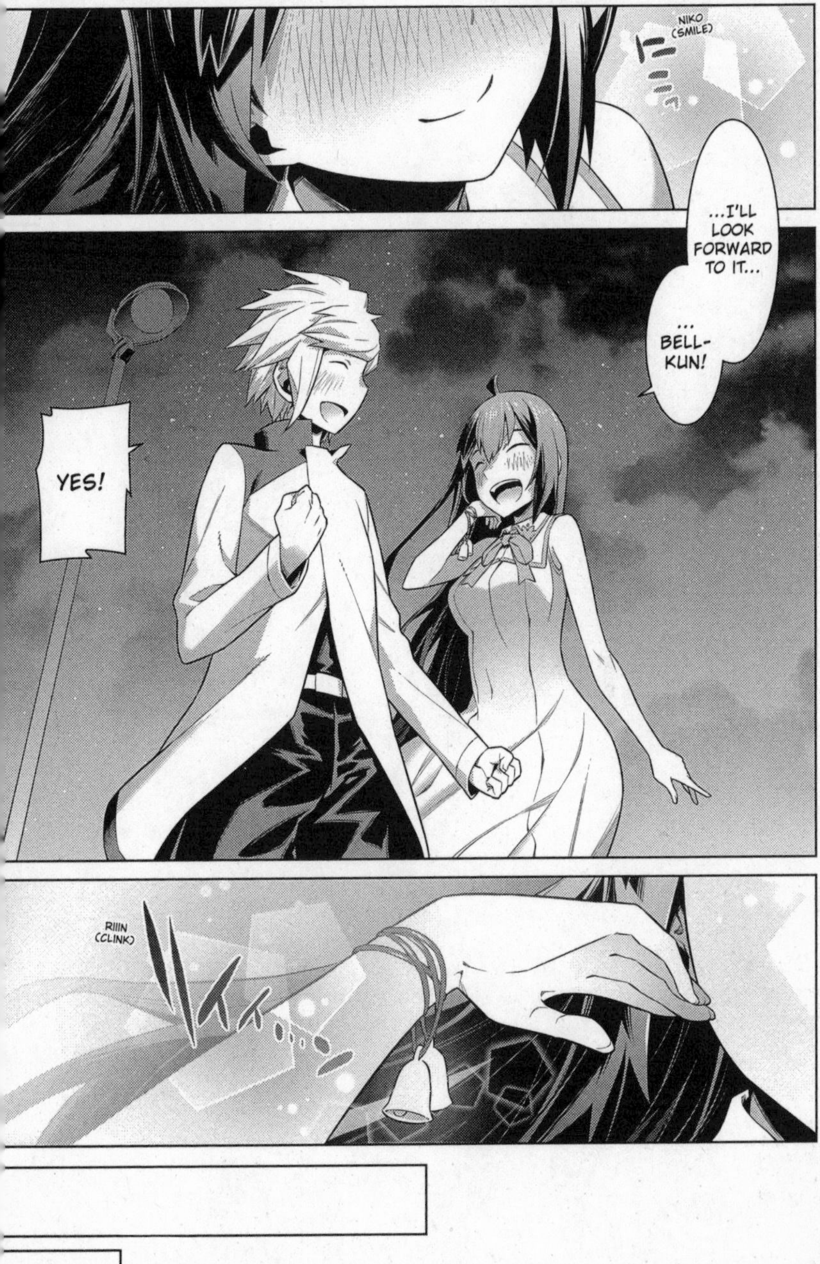
NIKO (SMILE)
...I'LL LOOK FORWARD TO IT...
... BELL-KUN!
YES!
RIIIN (CLINK)

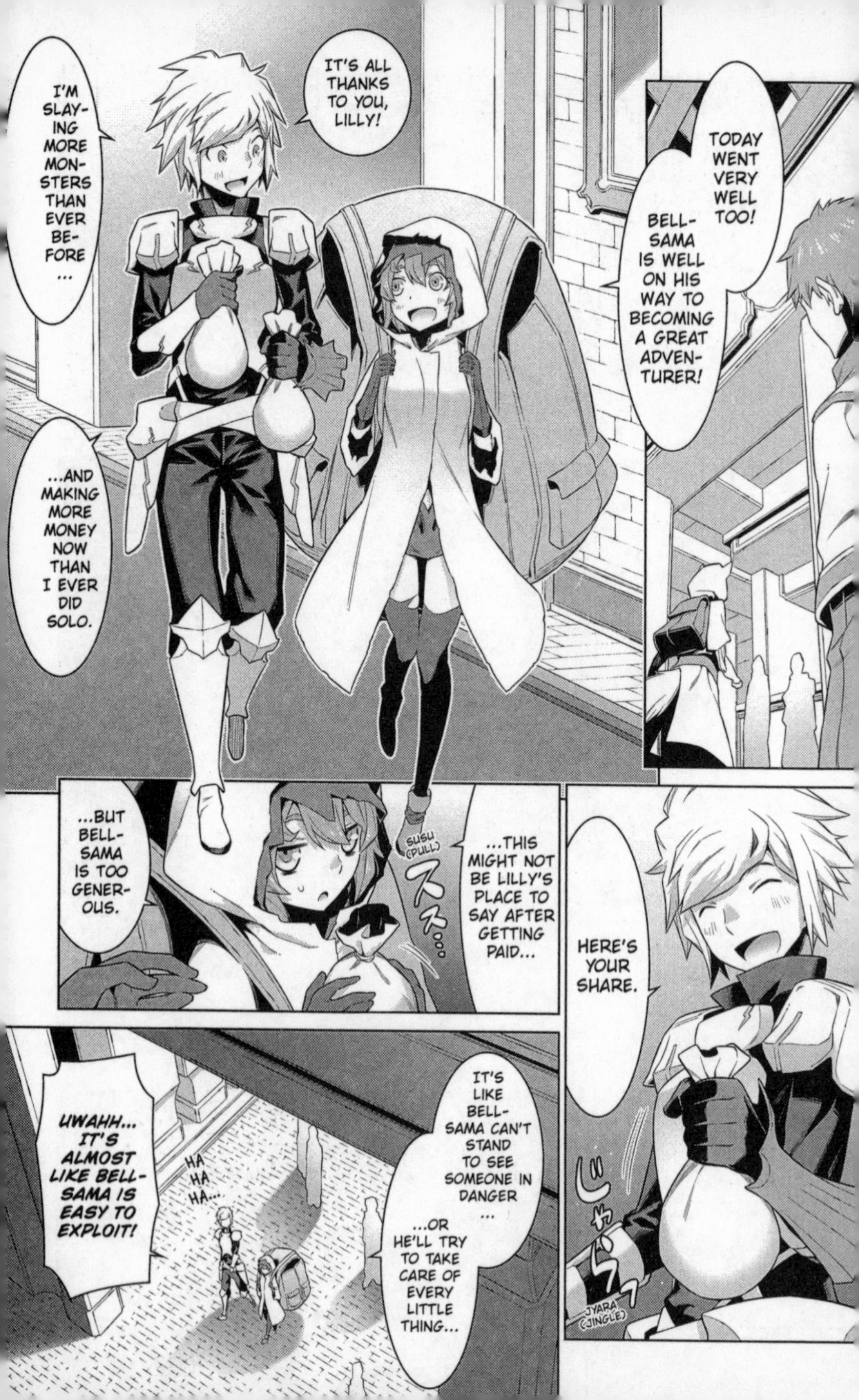

TODAY WENT VERY WELL TOO!
BELL-SAMA IS WELL ON HIS WAY TO BECOMING A GREAT ADVENTURER!
IT'S ALL THANKS TO YOU, LILLY!
I'M SLAY-ING MORE MON-STERS THAN EVER BE-FORE...
...AND MAKING MORE MONEY NOW THAN I EVER DID SOLO.
HERE'S YOUR SHARE.
JYARA (JINGLE)
SUSU (PULL)
...THIS MIGHT NOT BE LILLY'S PLACE TO SAY AFTER GETTING PAID...
...BUT BELL-SAMA IS TOO GENER-OUS.
IT'S LIKE BELL-SAMA CAN'T STAND TO SEE SOMEONE IN DANGER...
...OR HE'LL TRY TO TAKE CARE OF EVERY LITTLE THING...
HA HA HA...
UWAHH... IT'S ALMOST LIKE BELL-SAMA IS EASY TO EXPLOIT!

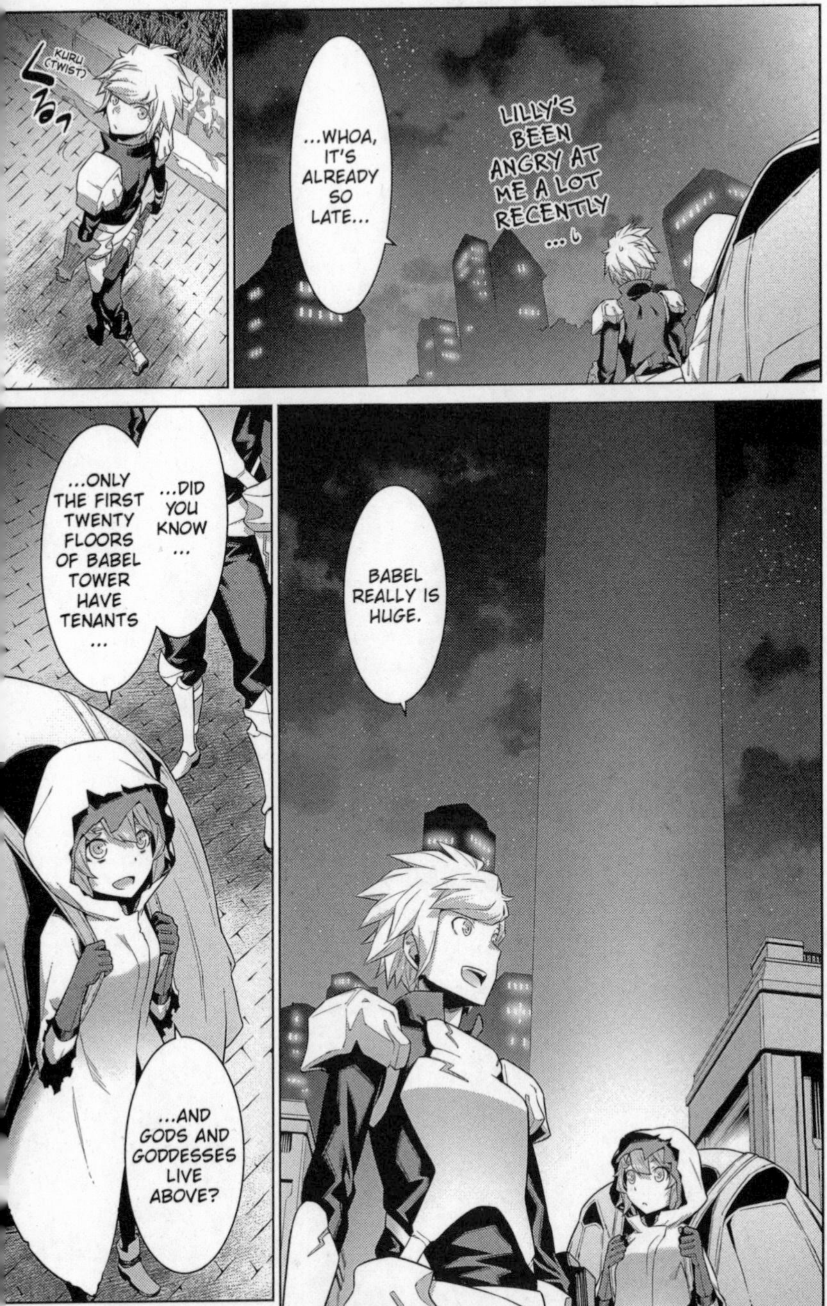
...WHOA, IT'S ALREADY SO LATE...
LILLY'S BEEN ANGRY AT ME A LOT RECENTLY...
KURU (TWIST)
BABEL REALLY IS HUGE.
...DID YOU KNOW...
...ONLY THE FIRST TWENTY FLOORS OF BABEL TOWER HAVE TENANTS...
...AND GODS AND GODDESSES LIVE ABOVE?

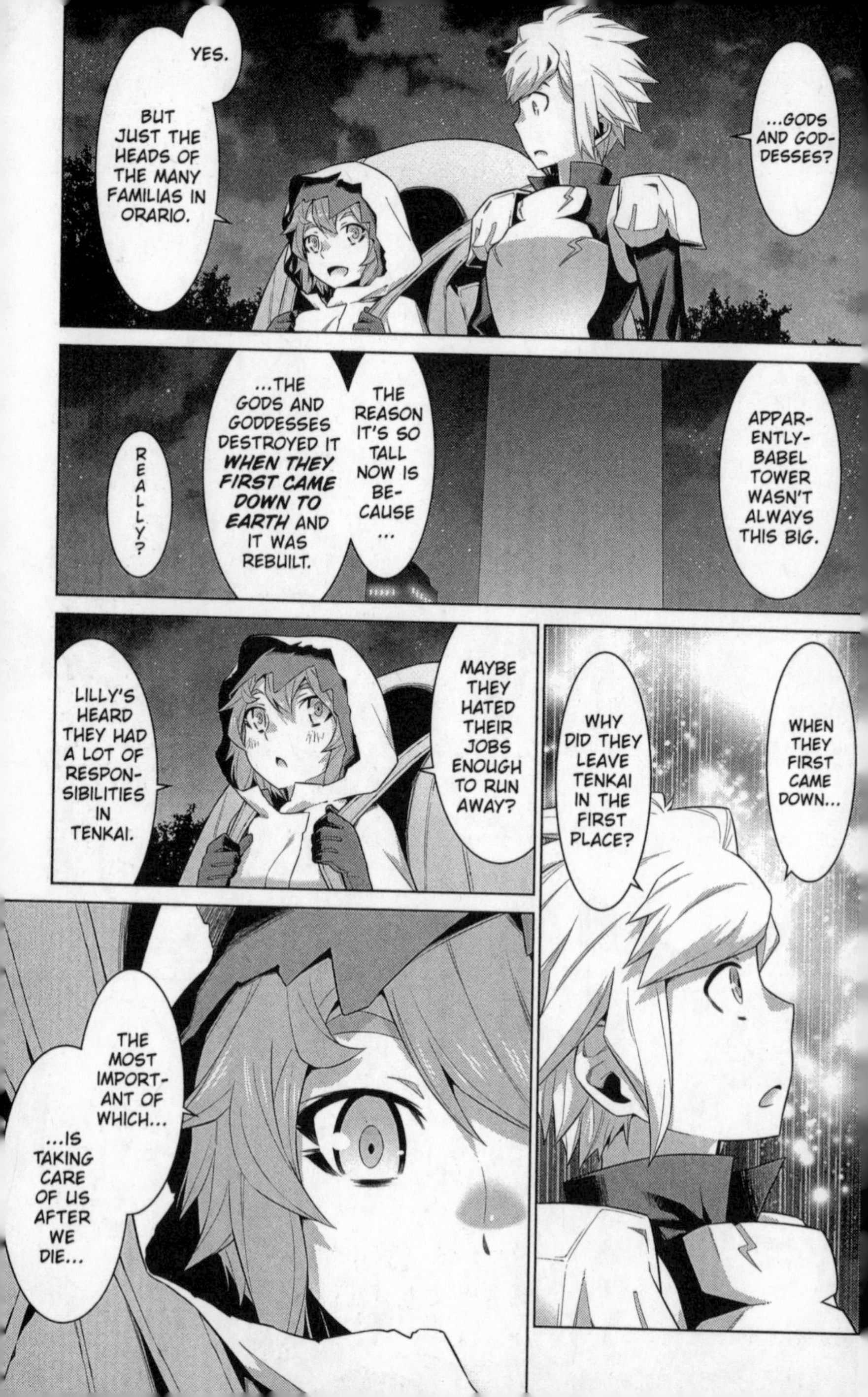
...GODS AND GOD-DESSES?
YES.
BUT JUST THE HEADS OF THE MANY FAMILIAS IN ORARIO.
APPAR-ENTLY-BABEL TOWER WASN'T ALWAYS THIS BIG.
THE REASON IT'S SO TALL NOW IS BE-CAUSE...
...THE GODS AND GODDESSES DESTROYED IT *WHEN THEY FIRST CAME DOWN TO EARTH* AND IT WAS REBUILT.
REALLY?
WHEN THEY FIRST CAME DOWN...
WHY DID THEY LEAVE TENKAI IN THE FIRST PLACE?
MAYBE THEY HATED THEIR JOBS ENOUGH TO RUN AWAY?
LILLY'S HEARD THEY HAD A LOT OF RESPON-SIBILITIES IN TENKAI.
THE MOST IMPORT-ANT OF WHICH...
...IS TAKING CARE OF US AFTER WE DIE...

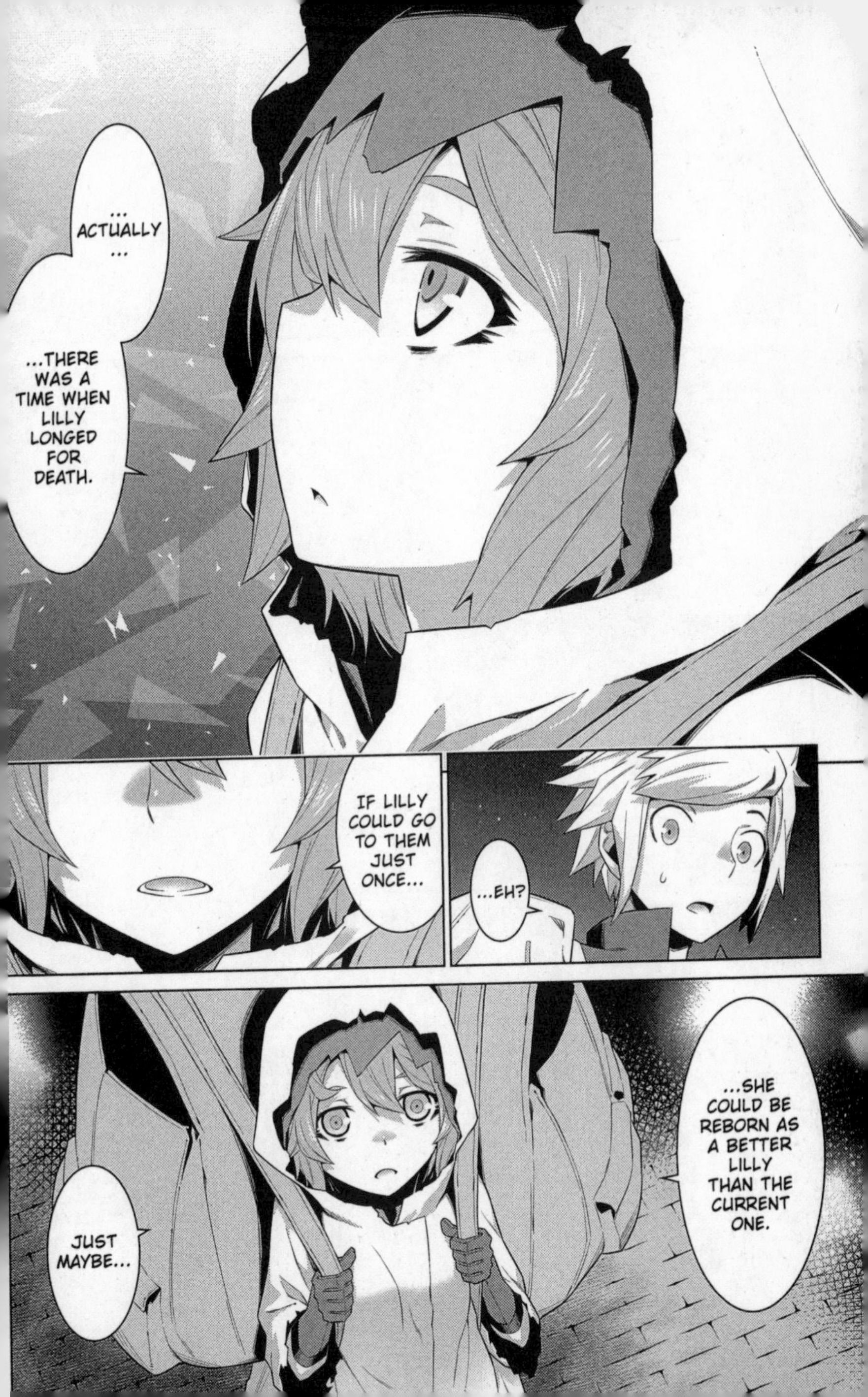
...ACTUALLY...
...THERE WAS A TIME WHEN LILLY LONGED FOR DEATH.
...EH?
IF LILLY COULD GO TO THEM JUST ONCE...
...SHE COULD BE REBORN AS A BETTER LILLY THAN THE CURRENT ONE.
JUST MAYBE...

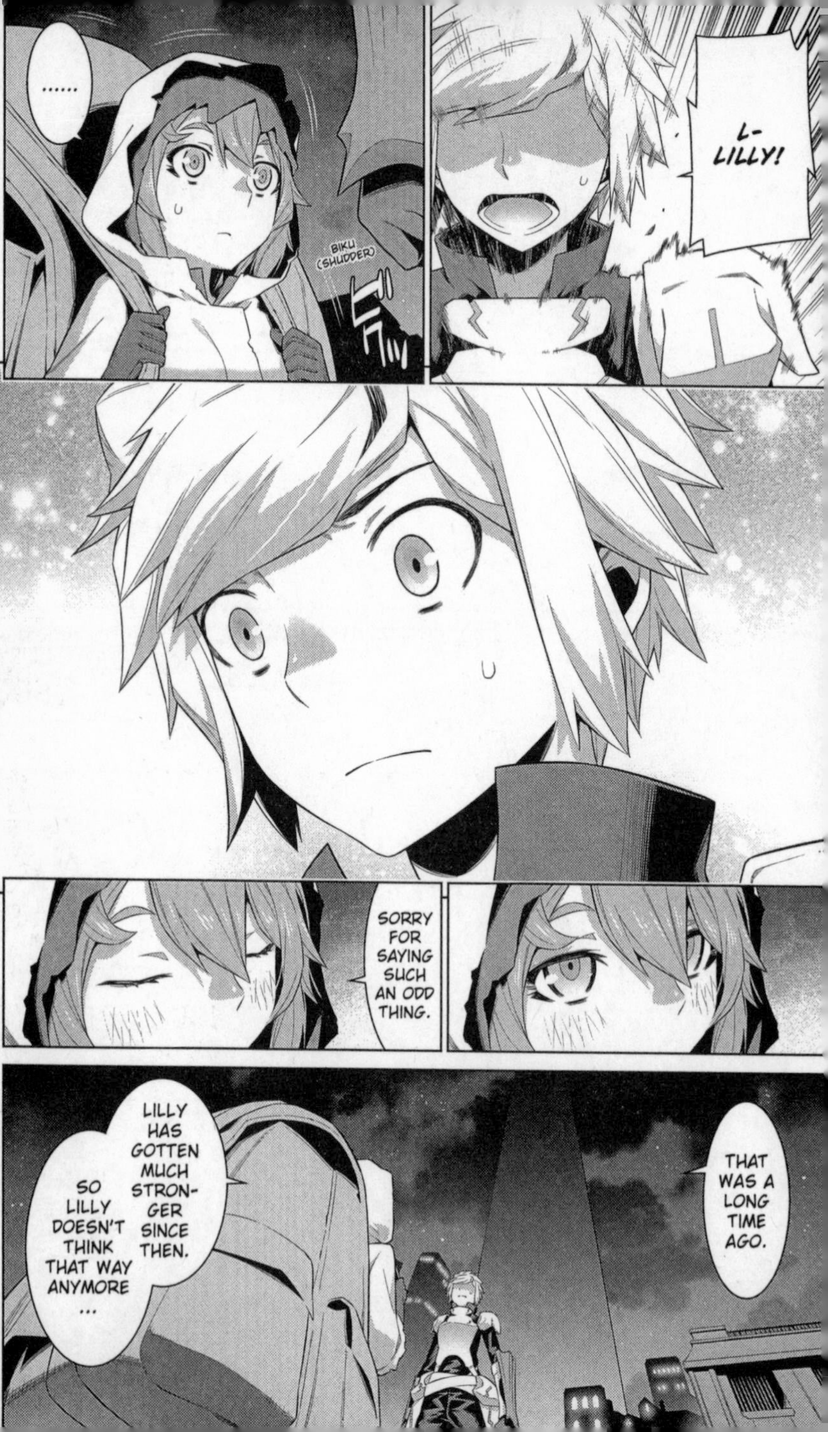
L-LILLY!
......
BIKU (SHUDDER)
SORRY FOR SAYING SUCH AN ODD THING.
THAT WAS A LONG TIME AGO.
LILLY HAS GOTTEN MUCH STRONGER SINCE THEN.
SO LILLY DOESN'T THINK THAT WAY ANYMORE ...

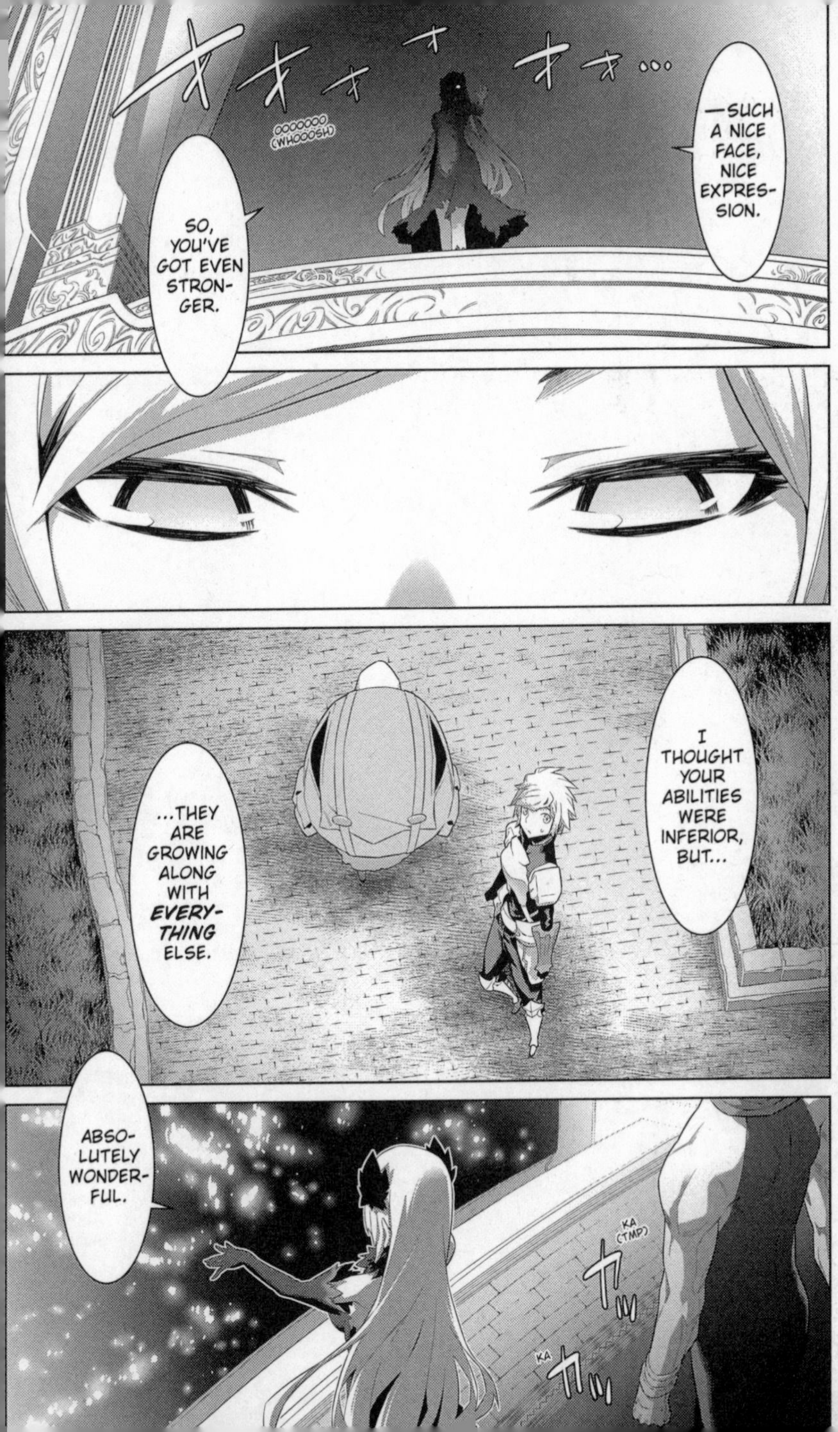
OOOOOOO (WHOOOSH)
—SUCH A NICE FACE, NICE EXPRESSION.
SO, YOU'VE GOT EVEN STRONGER.
I THOUGHT YOUR ABILITIES WERE INFERIOR, BUT...
...THEY ARE GROWING ALONG WITH EVERYTHING ELSE.
ABSOLUTELY WONDERFUL.
KA (TMP)
KA

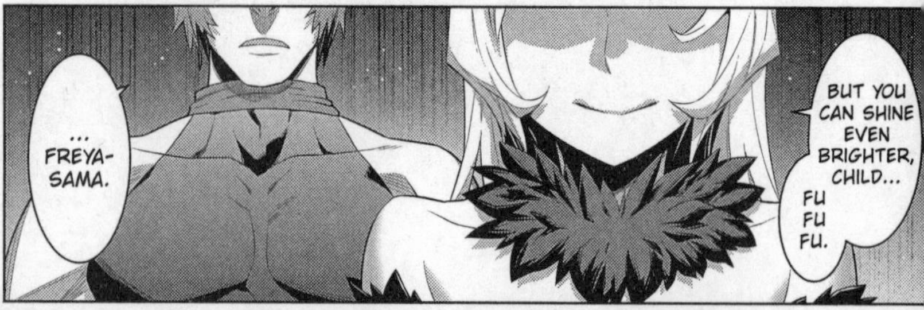
BUT YOU CAN SHINE EVEN BRIGHTER, CHILD...
FU FU FU.
...FREYA-SAMA.
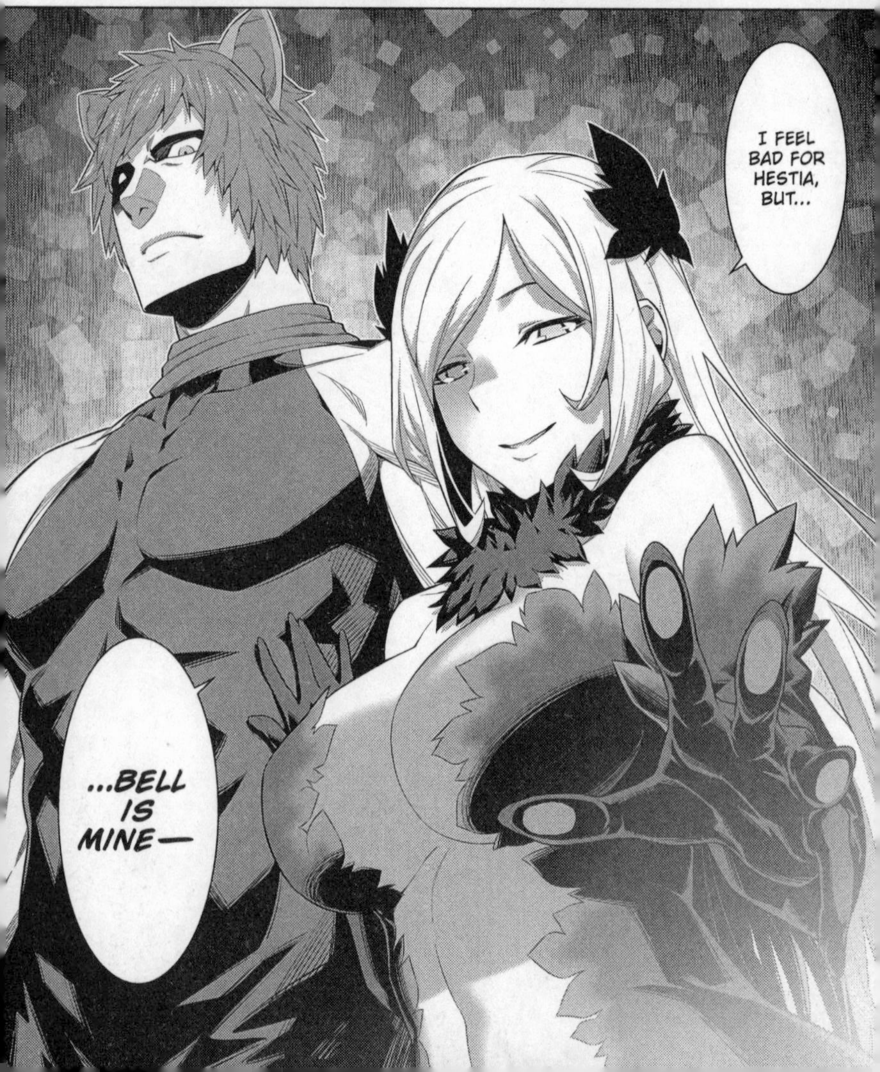
I FEEL BAD FOR HESTIA, BUT...
...BELL IS MINE—

Is it WRONG to TRY to PICK UP GIRLS IN A DUNGEON?

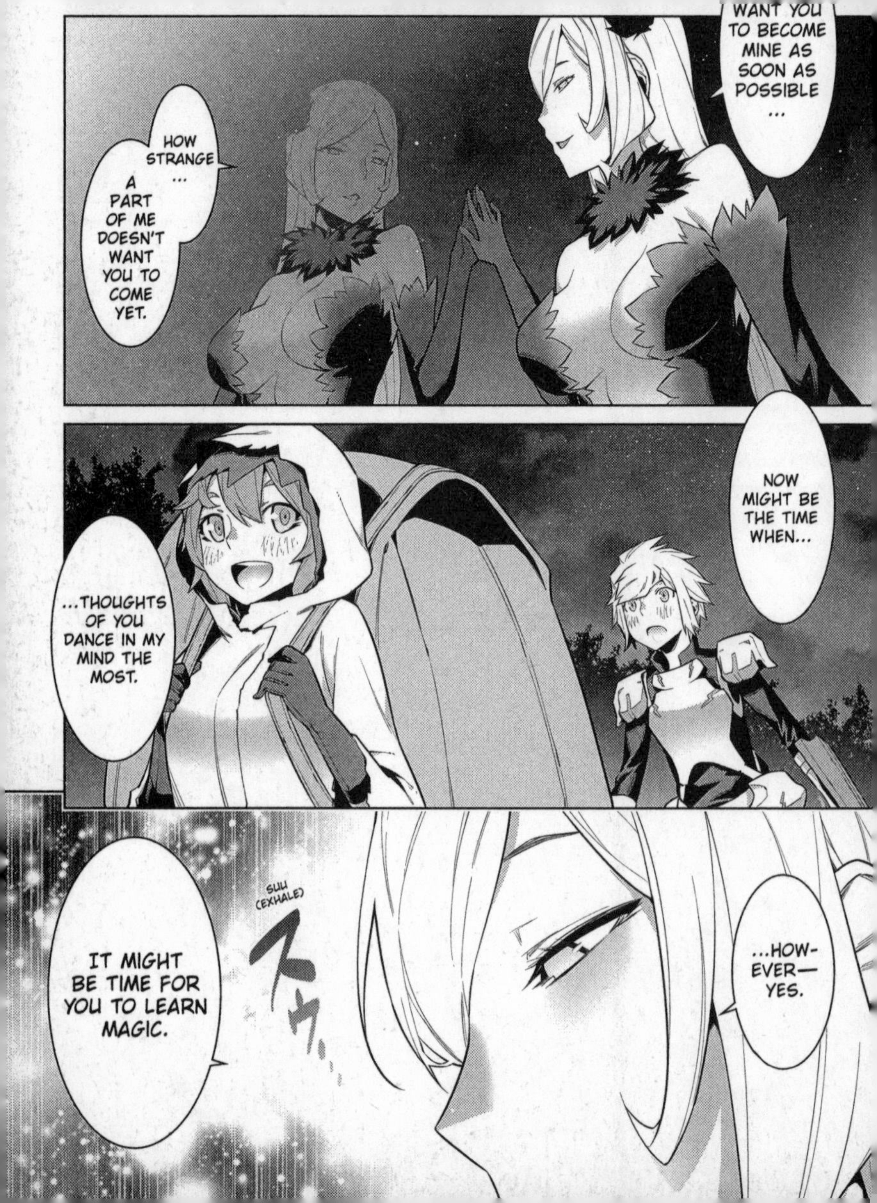
WANT YOU TO BECOME MINE AS SOON AS POSSIBLE...
HOW STRANGE... A PART OF ME DOESN'T WANT YOU TO COME YET.
NOW MIGHT BE THE TIME WHEN...
...THOUGHTS OF YOU DANCE IN MY MIND THE MOST.
...HOW-EVER—YES.
SUU (EXHALE)
IT MIGHT BE TIME FOR YOU TO LEARN MAGIC.

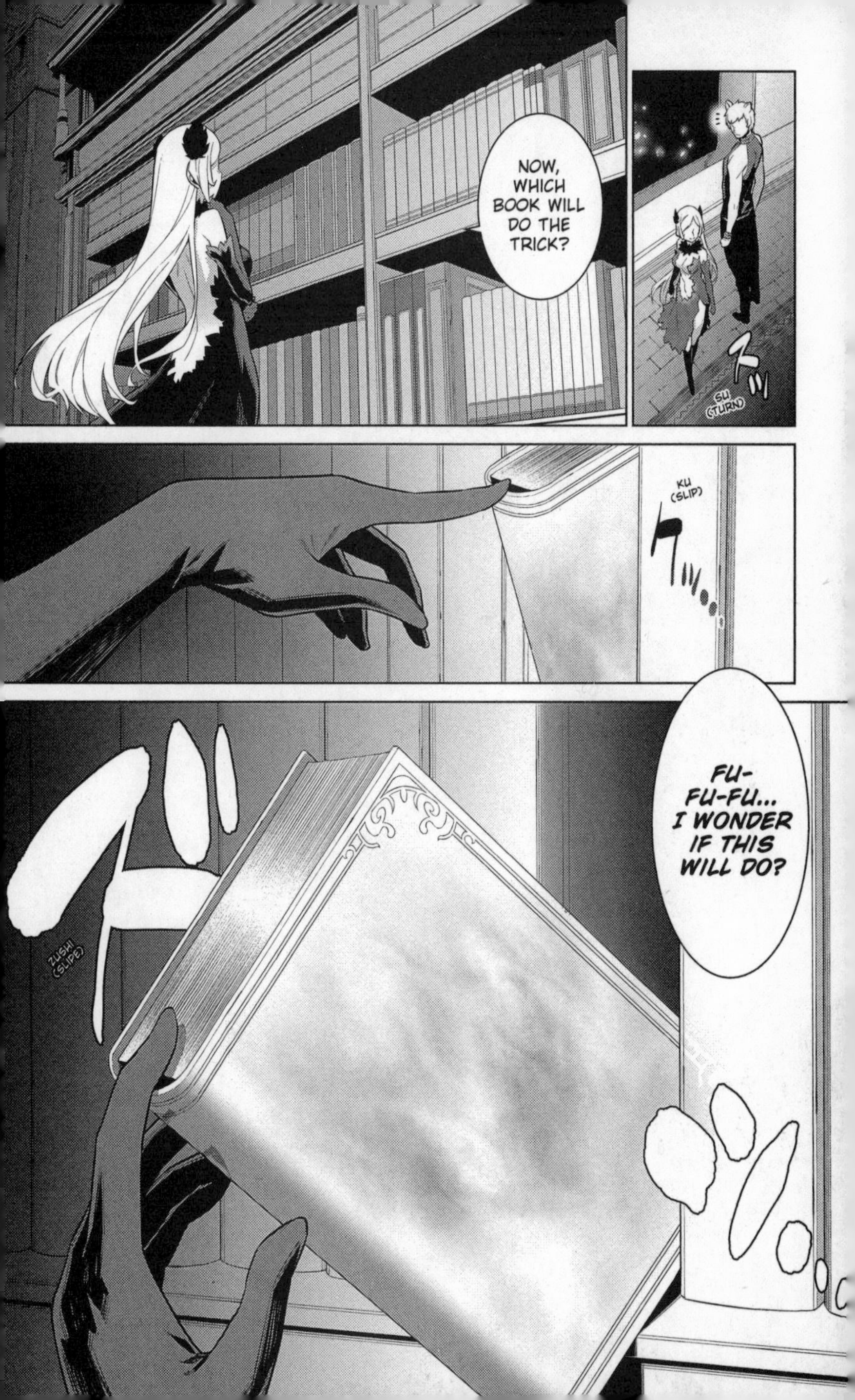
SU (TURN)
NOW, WHICH BOOK WILL DO THE TRICK?
KU (SLIP)
FU-FU-FU... I WONDER IF THIS WILL DO?
ZUSHI (SLIPE)

STEP 22 ▶▶ RECKLESS!?

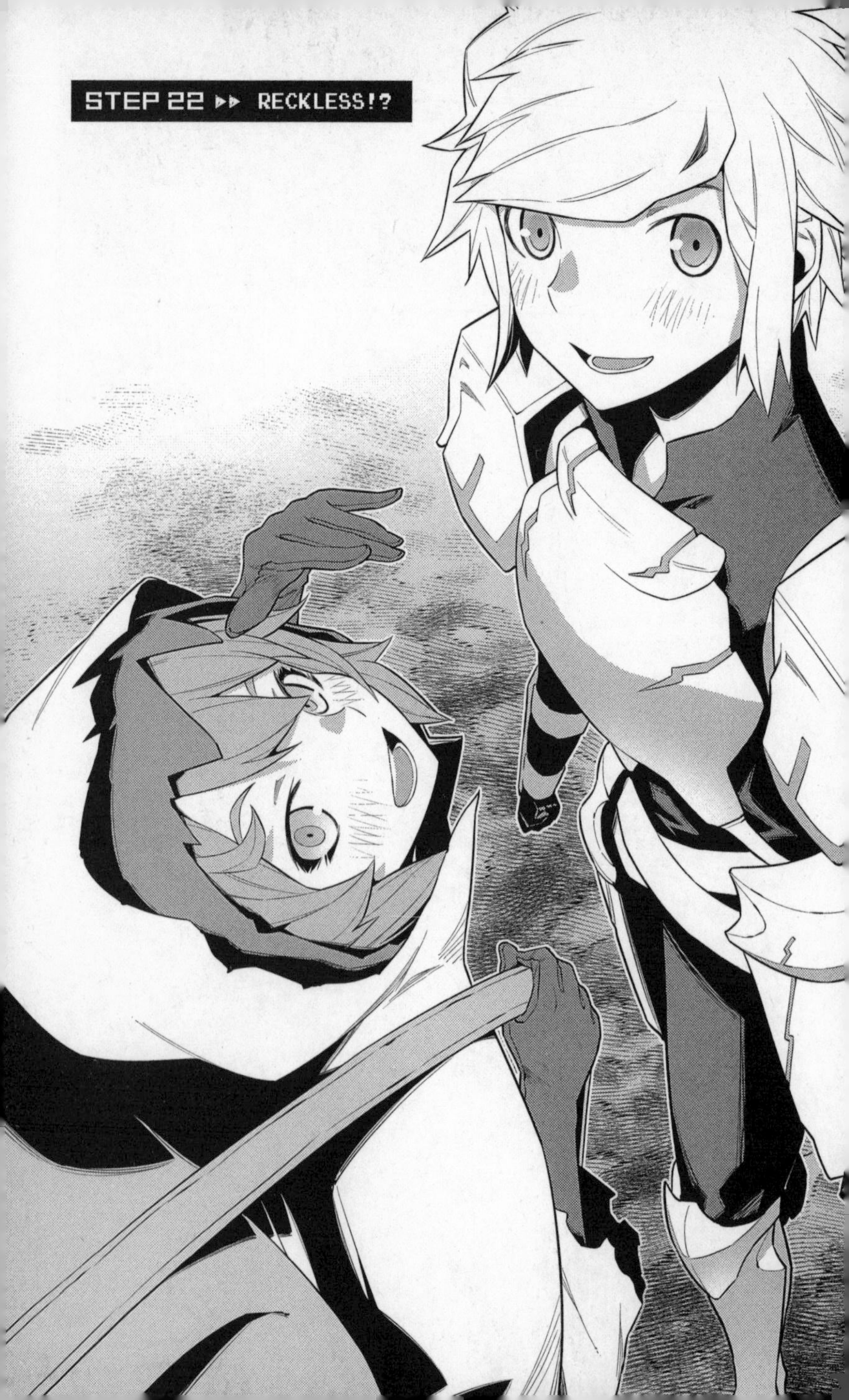

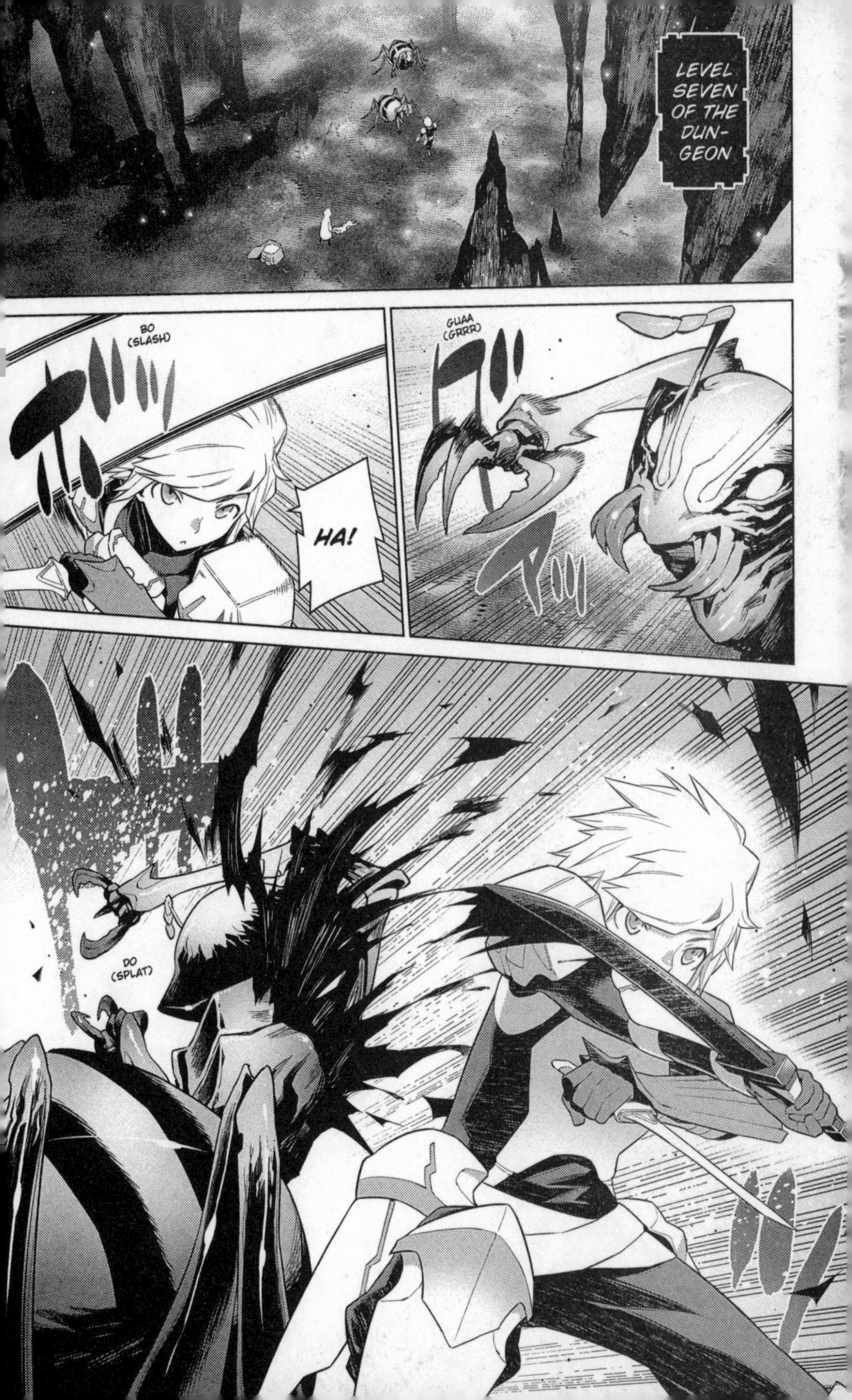
LEVEL SEVEN OF THE DUN-GEON
GUAA (GRRR)
BO (SLASH)
HA!
DO (SPLAT)

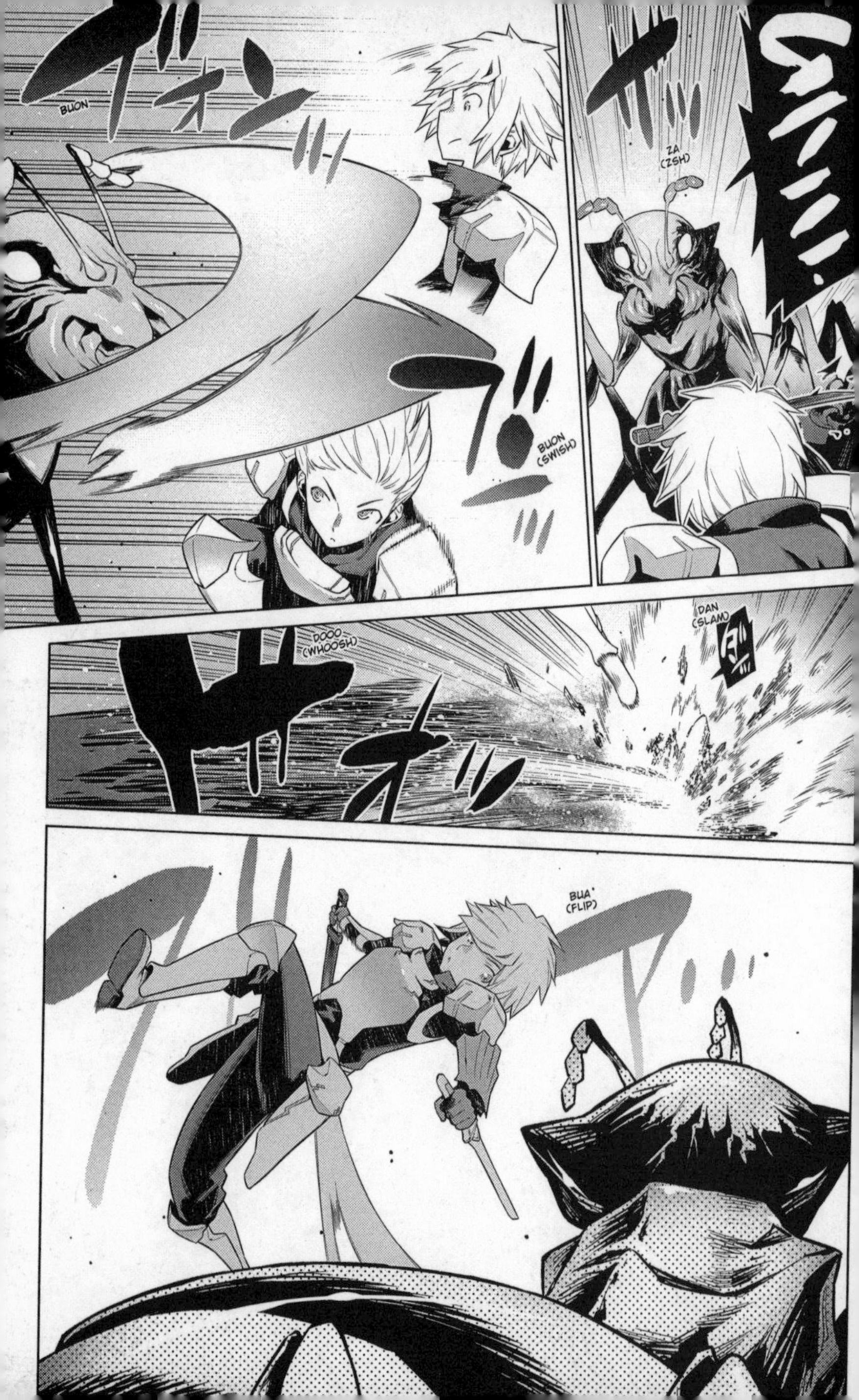
ZA
(ZSH)
BUON
BUON
(SWISH)
DAN
(SLAM)
DOOO
(WHOOSH)
BUA
(FLIP)

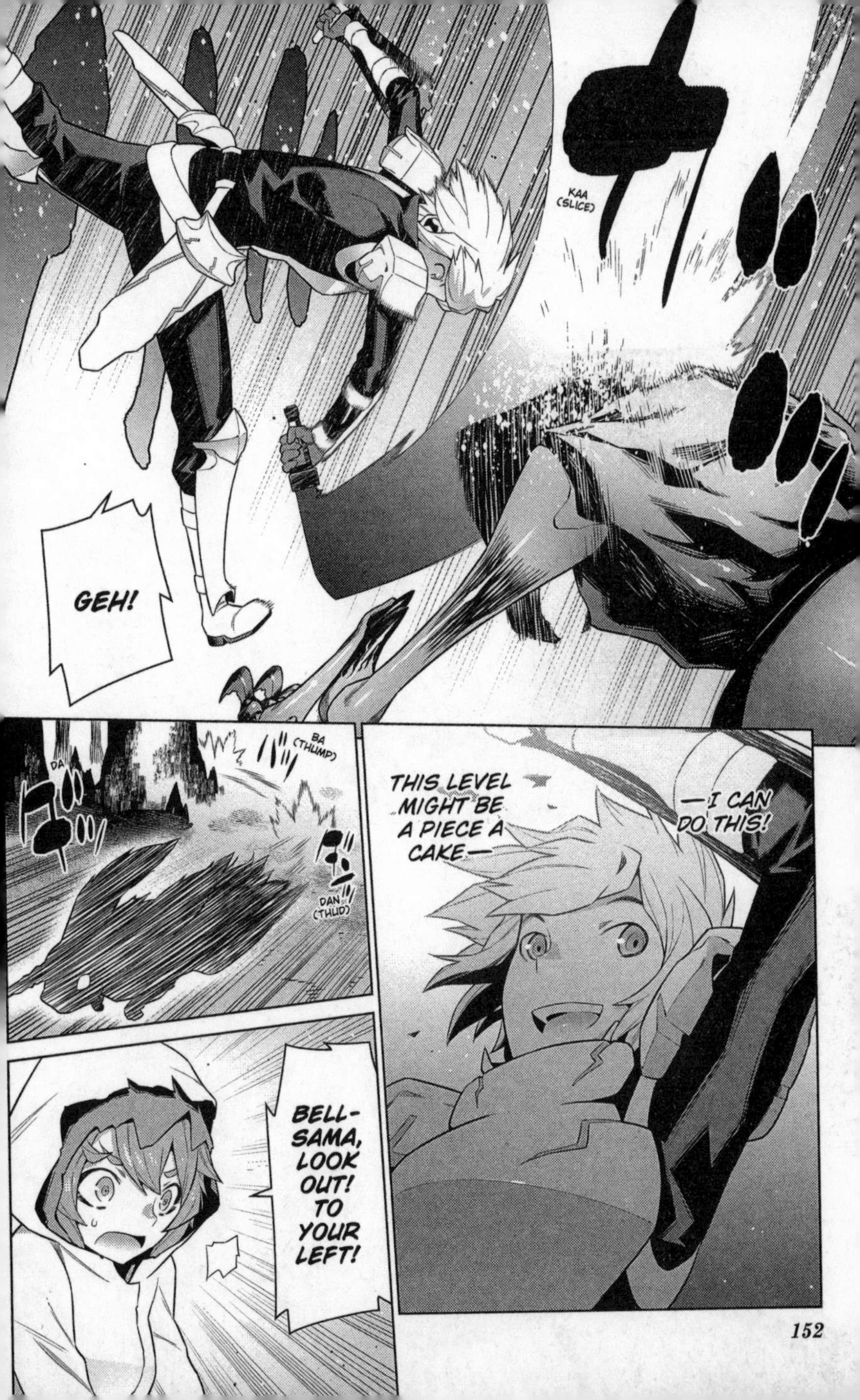
KAA (SLICE)
GEH!
THIS LEVEL MIGHT BE A PIECE A CAKE—
—I CAN DO THIS!
BA (THUMP)
DA
DAN (THUD)
BELL-SAMA, LOOK OUT! TO YOUR LEFT!

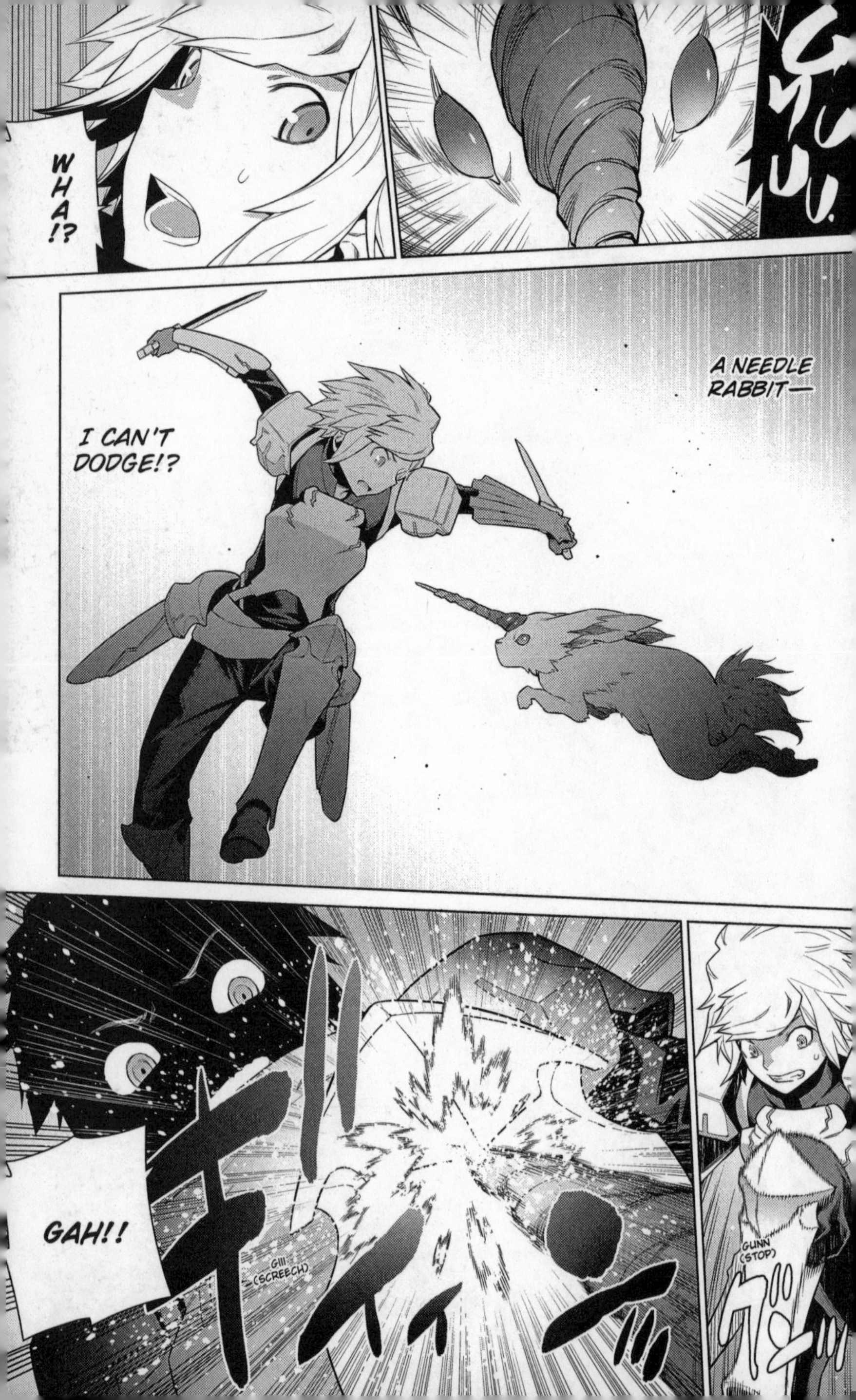
WHA!?
A NEEDLE RABBIT—
I CAN'T DODGE!?
GUNN (STOP)
GIII (SCREECH)
GAH!!

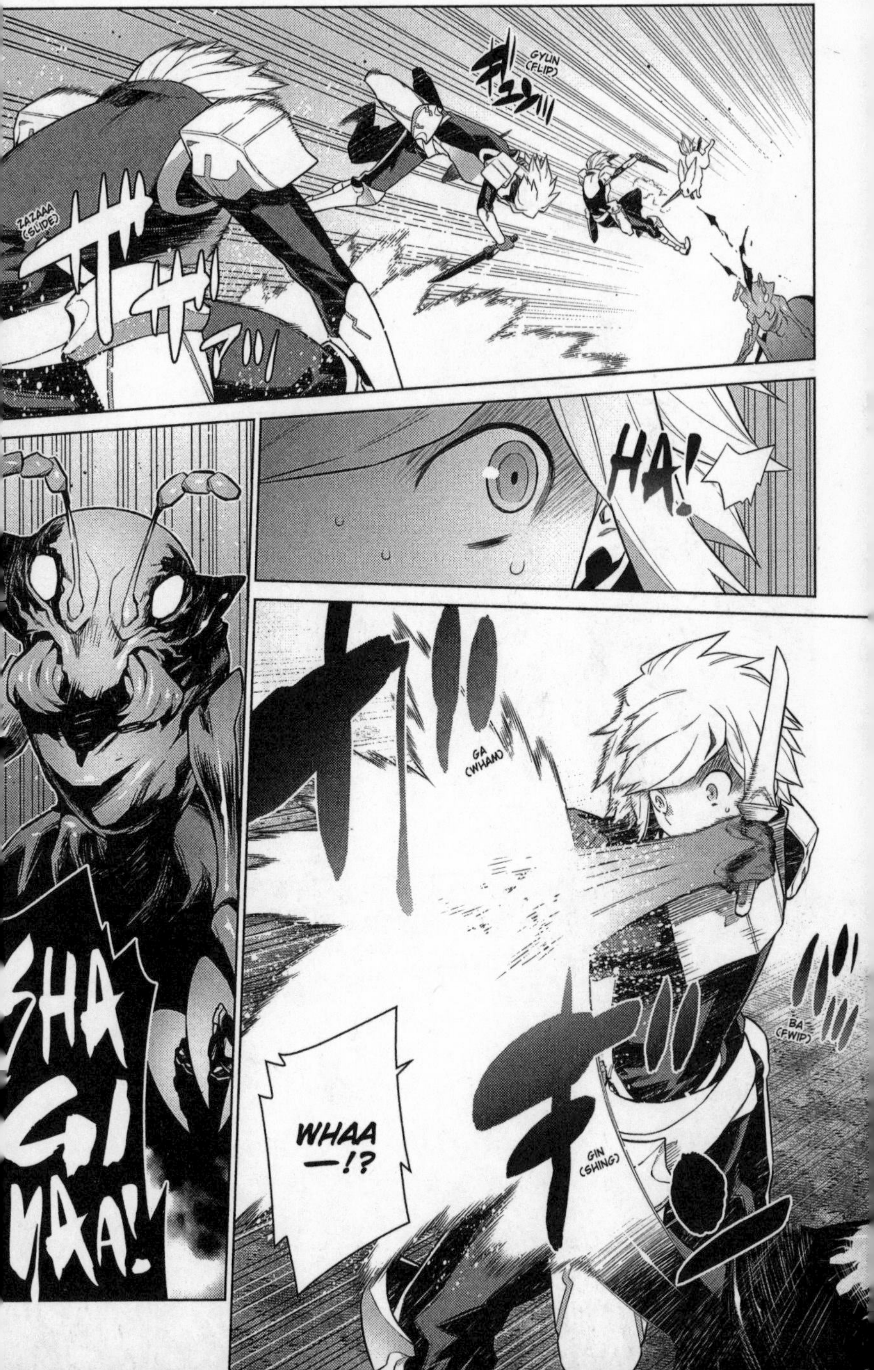
GYUN (FLIP)
ZAZAAA (SLIDE)
HA!
GA (WHAM)
BA (FWIP)
GIN (SHING)
WHAA—!?
SHA GI YAA!

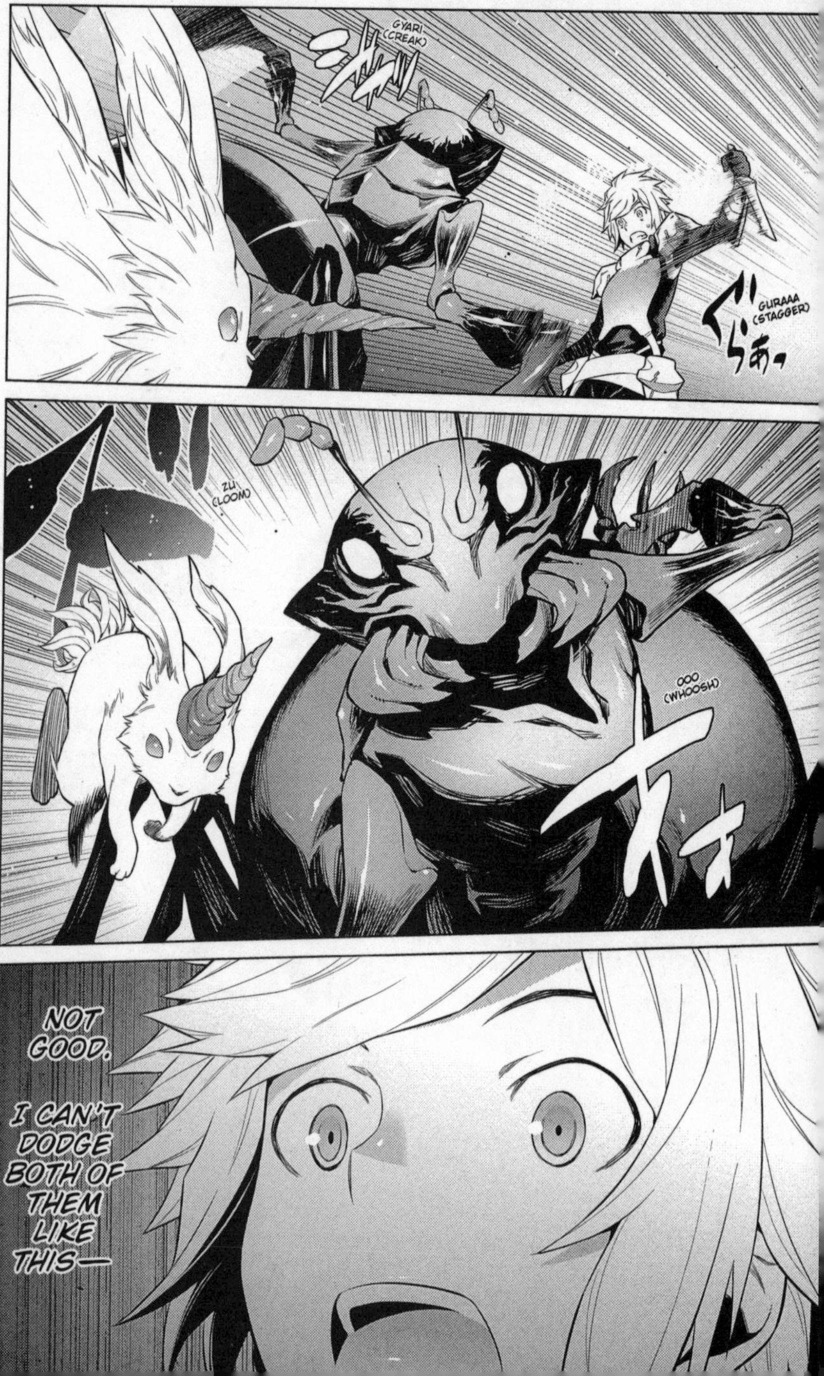
GYARI (CREAK)
GURAAA (STAGGER)
ZU (LOOM)
OOO (WHOOSH)
NOT GOOD.
I CAN'T DODGE BOTH OF THEM LIKE THIS—

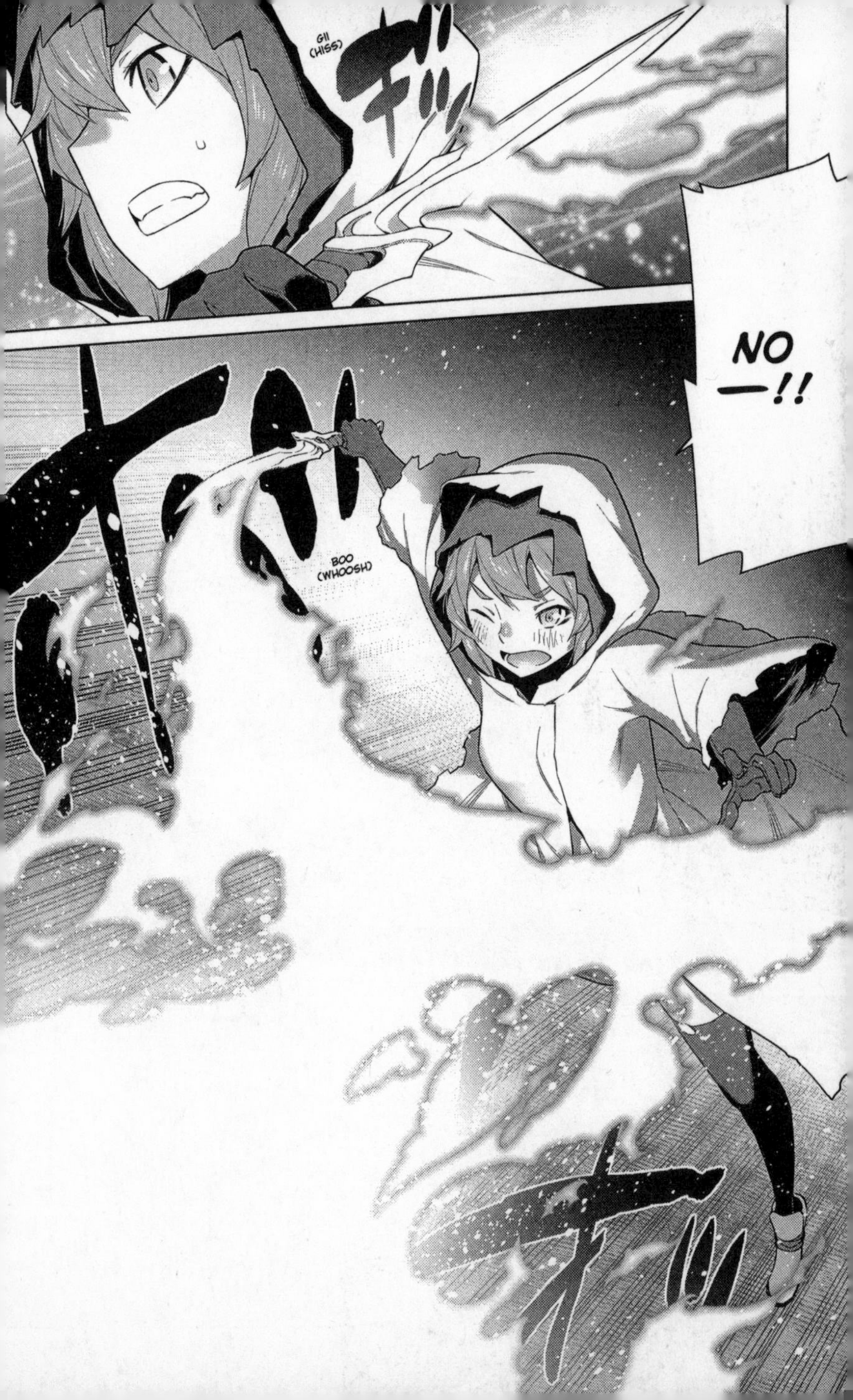
GII (HISS)
NO—!!
BOO (WHOOSH)

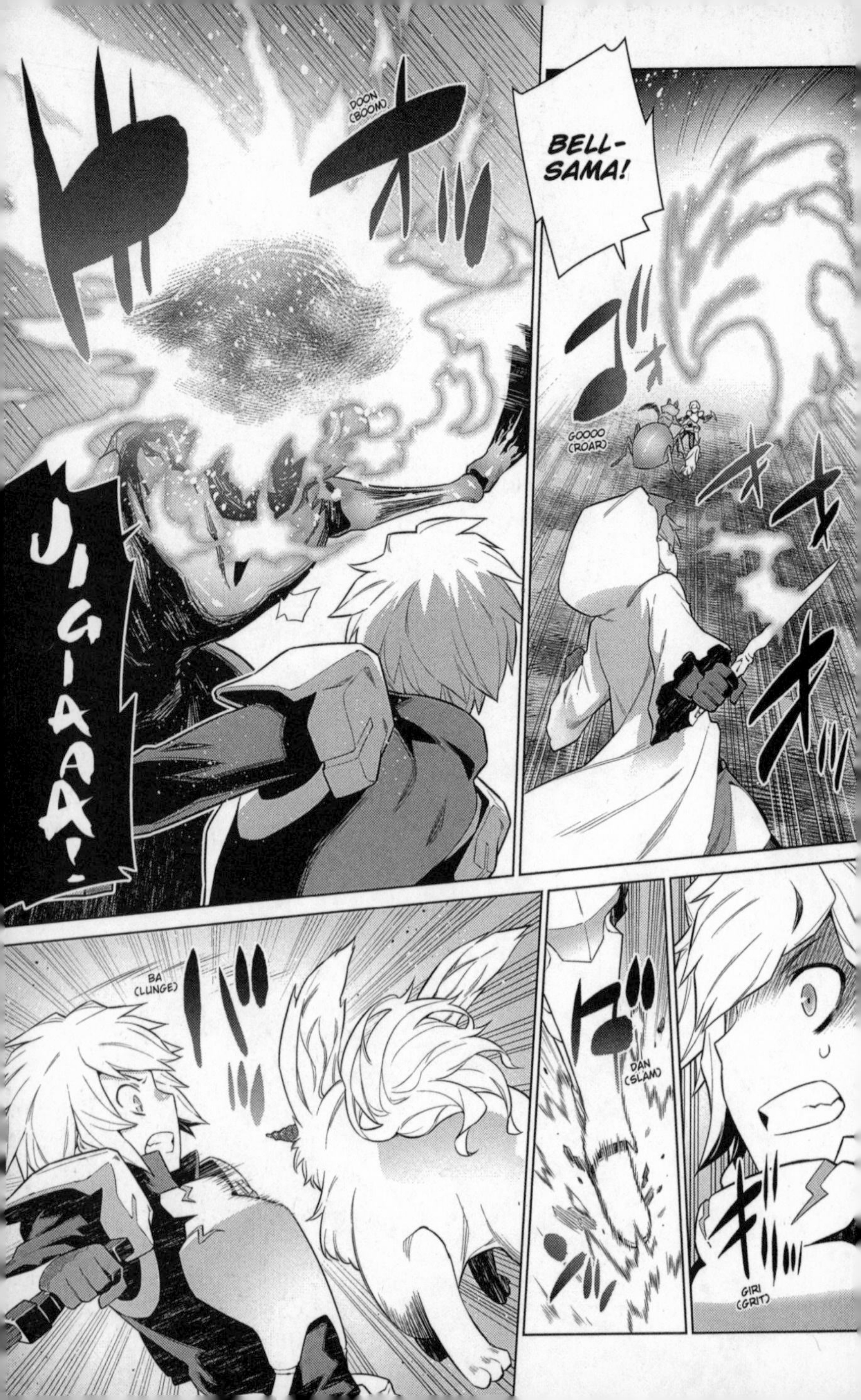
BELL-SAMA!
GOOOO (ROAR)
DOON (BOOM)
JIGIAAAA!
GIRI (GRIT)
DAN (SLAM)
BA (LUNGE)

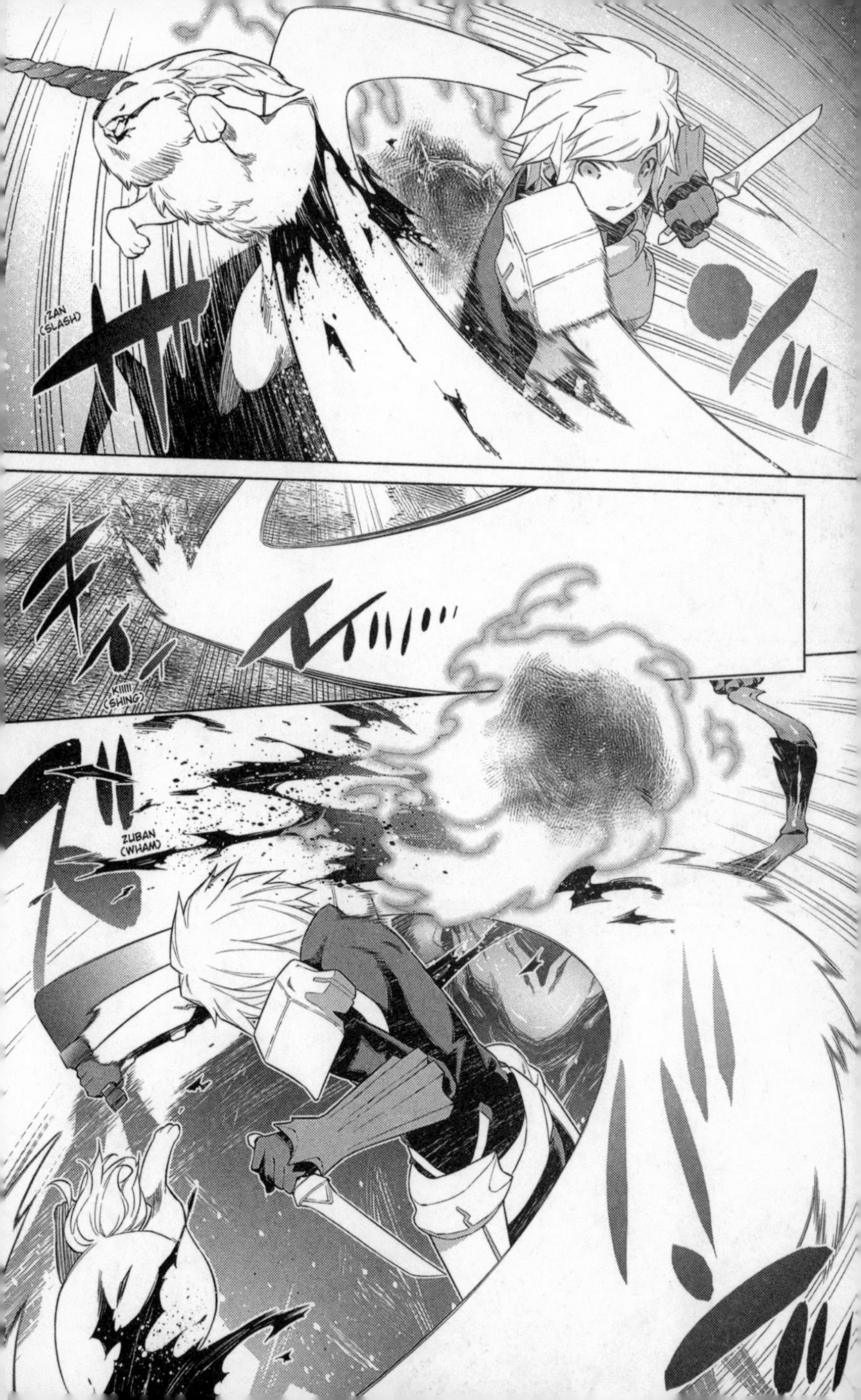

ZAN (SLASH)
KIIIII (SHING)
ZUBAN (WHAM)

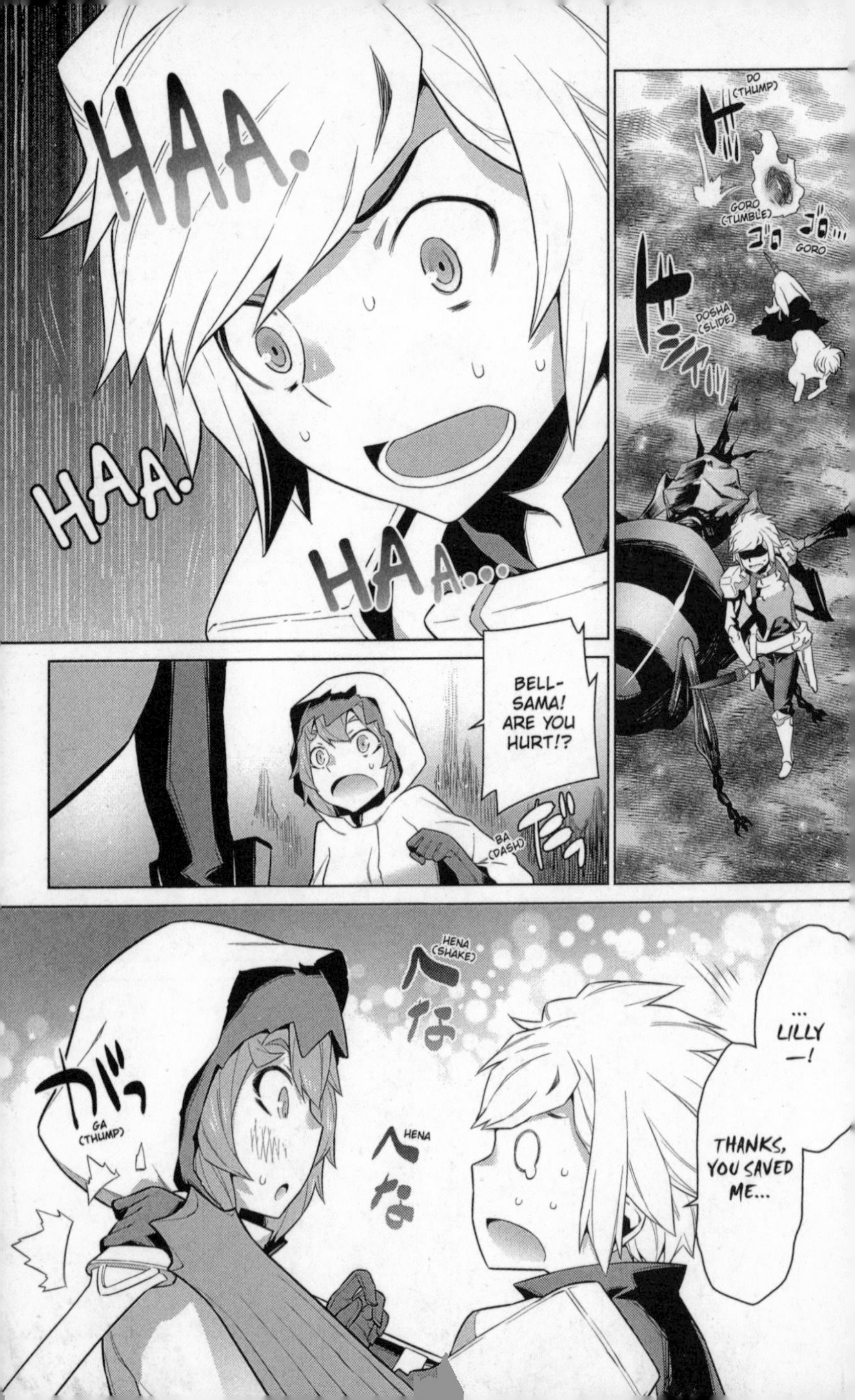
DO (THUMP)
GORO (TUMBLE)
GORO
DOSHA (SLIDE)
HAA.
HAA.
HAA...
BELL-SAMA! ARE YOU HURT!?
BA (DASH)
...LILLY—!
THANKS, YOU SAVED ME...
HENA (SHAKE)
HENA
GA (THUMP)

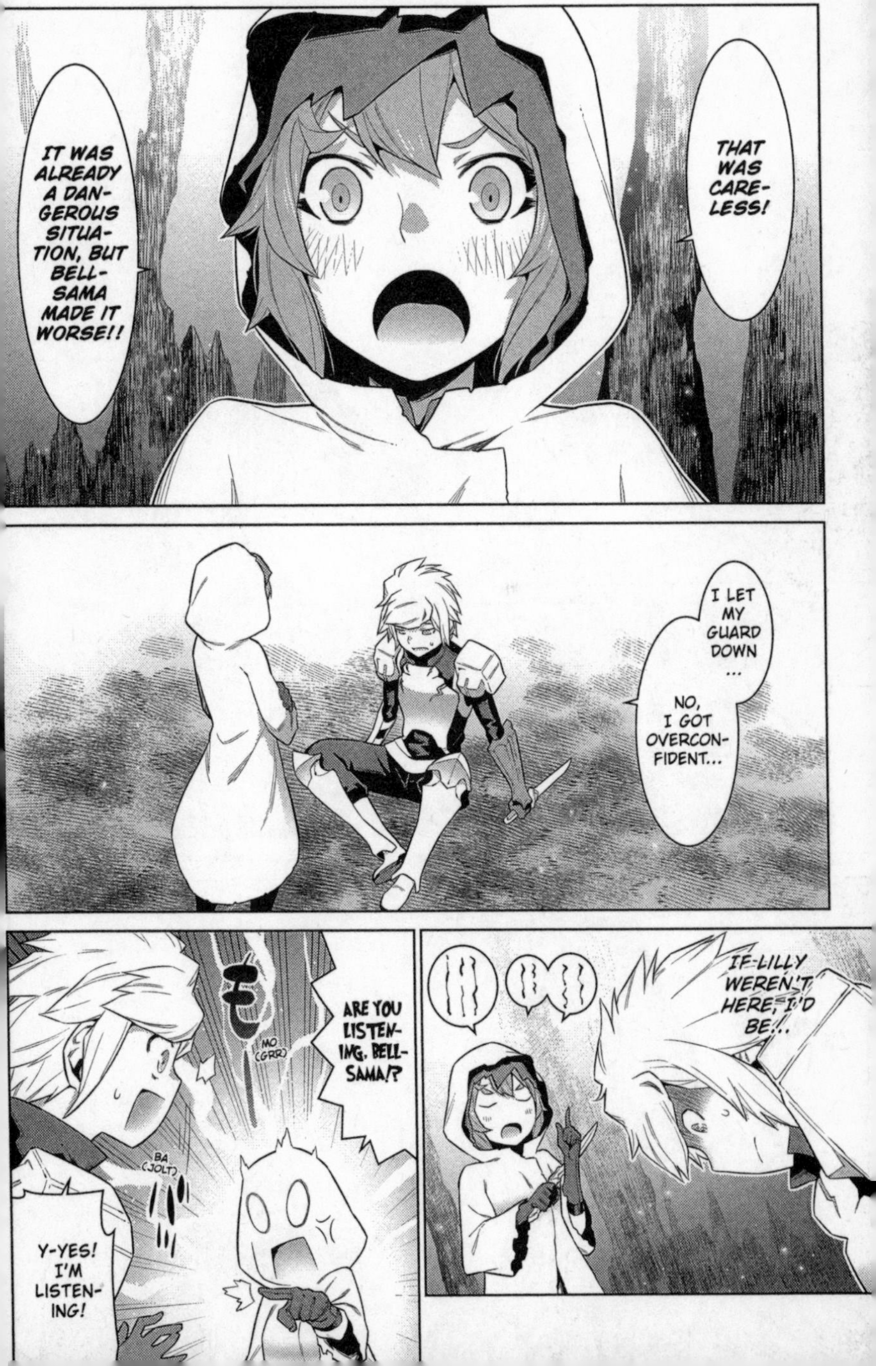
THAT WAS CARE-LESS!
IT WAS ALREADY A DAN-GEROUS SITUA-TION, BUT BELL-SAMA MADE IT WORSE!!
I LET MY GUARD DOWN...
NO, I GOT OVERCON-FIDENT...
IF LILLY WEREN'T HERE, I'D BE...!
ARE YOU LISTEN-ING, BELL-SAMA!?
MO (GRR)
BA (JOLT)
Y-YES! I'M LISTEN-ING!

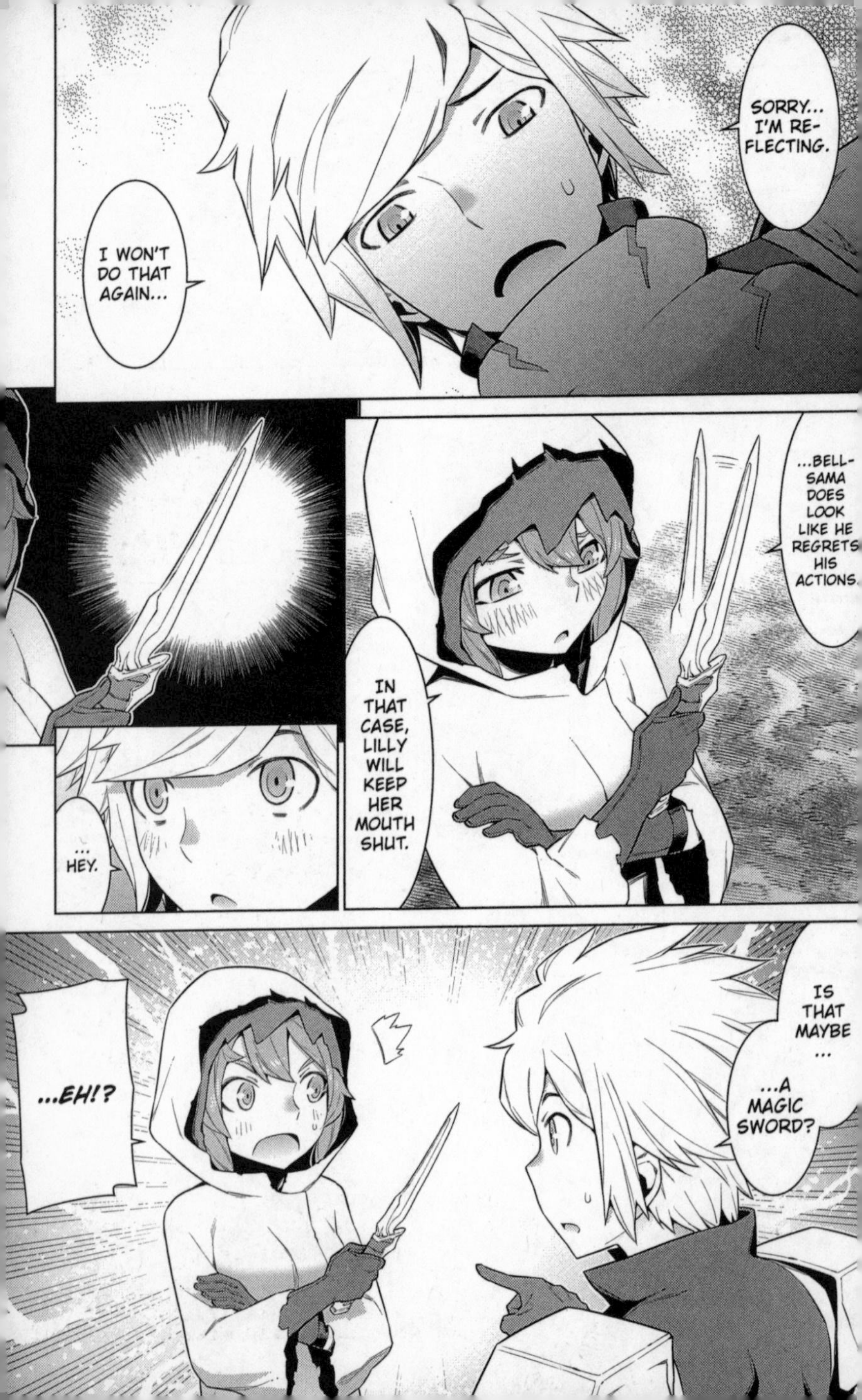
SORRY... I'M RE-FLECTING.
I WON'T DO THAT AGAIN...
...BELL-SAMA DOES LOOK LIKE HE REGRETS HIS ACTIONS.
IN THAT CASE, LILLY WILL KEEP HER MOUTH SHUT.
... HEY.
IS THAT MAYBE ...
...A MAGIC SWORD?
...EH!?

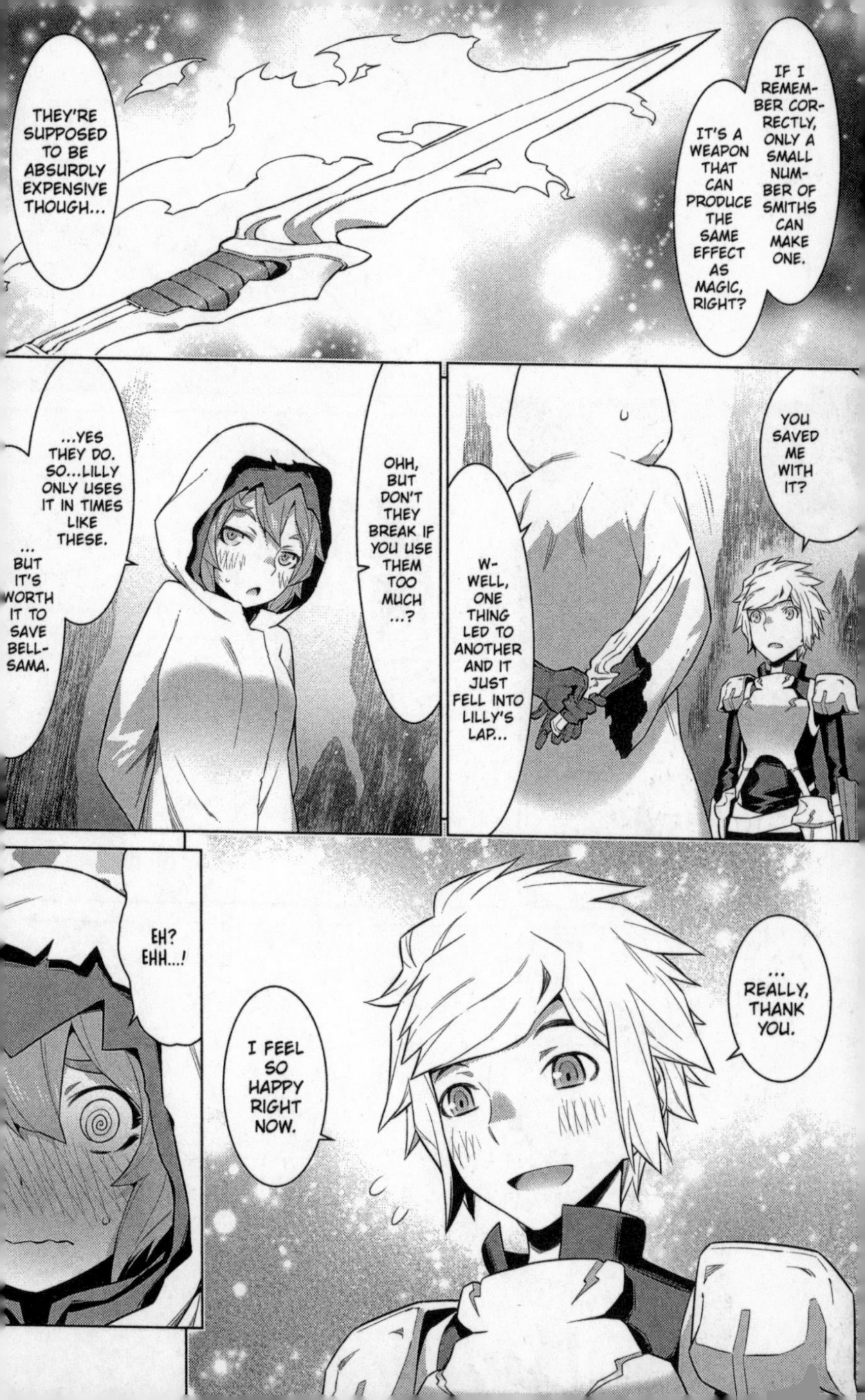
IF I REMEMBER CORRECTLY, ONLY A SMALL NUMBER OF SMITHS CAN MAKE ONE.
IT'S A WEAPON THAT CAN PRODUCE THE SAME EFFECT AS MAGIC, RIGHT?
THEY'RE SUPPOSED TO BE ABSURDLY EXPENSIVE THOUGH...
YOU SAVED ME WITH IT?
W-WELL, ONE THING LED TO ANOTHER AND IT JUST FELL INTO LILLY'S LAP...
OHH, BUT DON'T THEY BREAK IF YOU USE THEM TOO MUCH...?
...YES THEY DO. SO...LILLY ONLY USES IT IN TIMES LIKE THESE.
...BUT IT'S WORTH IT TO SAVE BELL-SAMA.
...REALLY, THANK YOU.
I FEEL SO HAPPY RIGHT NOW.
EH? EHH...!

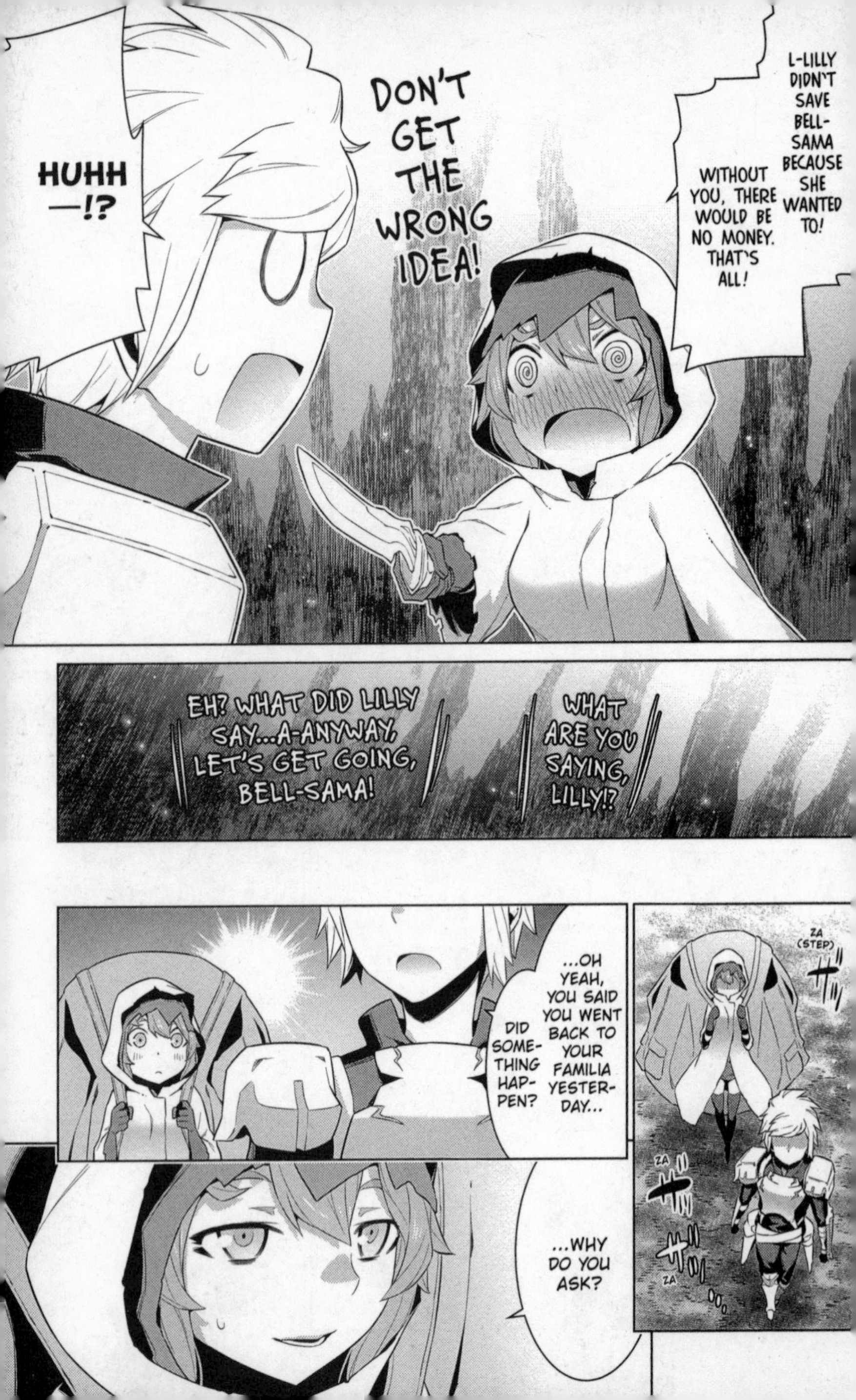
L-LILLY DIDN'T SAVE BELL-SAMA BECAUSE SHE WANTED TO!
WITHOUT YOU, THERE WOULD BE NO MONEY. THAT'S ALL!
DON'T GET THE WRONG IDEA!
HUHH—!?
WHAT ARE YOU SAYING, LILLY!?
EH? WHAT DID LILLY SAY...A-ANYWAY, LET'S GET GOING, BELL-SAMA!
ZA (STEP)
ZA
ZA
...OH YEAH, YOU SAID YOU WENT BACK TO YOUR FAMILIA YESTERDAY...
DID SOMETHING HAPPEN?
...WHY DO YOU ASK?

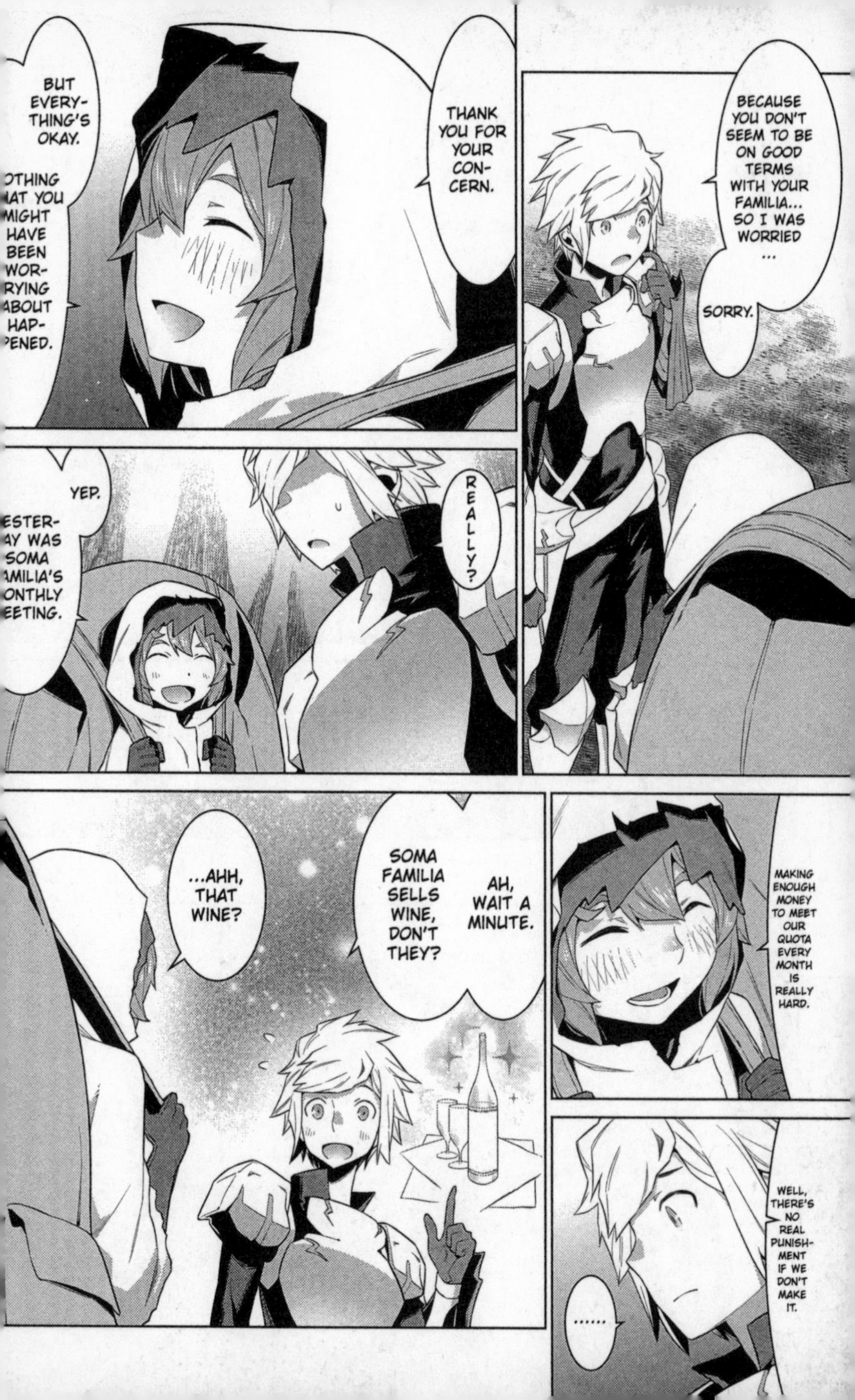
BECAUSE YOU DON'T SEEM TO BE ON GOOD TERMS WITH YOUR FAMILIA... SO I WAS WORRIED ...
SORRY.
THANK YOU FOR YOUR CON-CERN.
BUT EVERY-THING'S OKAY.
OTHING AT YOU MIGHT HAVE BEEN WOR-RYING ABOUT HAP-PENED.
REALLY?
YEP.
ESTER-AY WAS SOMA AMILIA'S ONTHLY EETING.
MAKING ENOUGH MONEY TO MEET OUR QUOTA EVERY MONTH IS REALLY HARD.
WELL, THERE'S NO REAL PUNISH-MENT IF WE DON'T MAKE IT.
......
AH, WAIT A MINUTE.
SOMA FAMILIA SELLS WINE, DON'T THEY?
...AHH, THAT WINE?

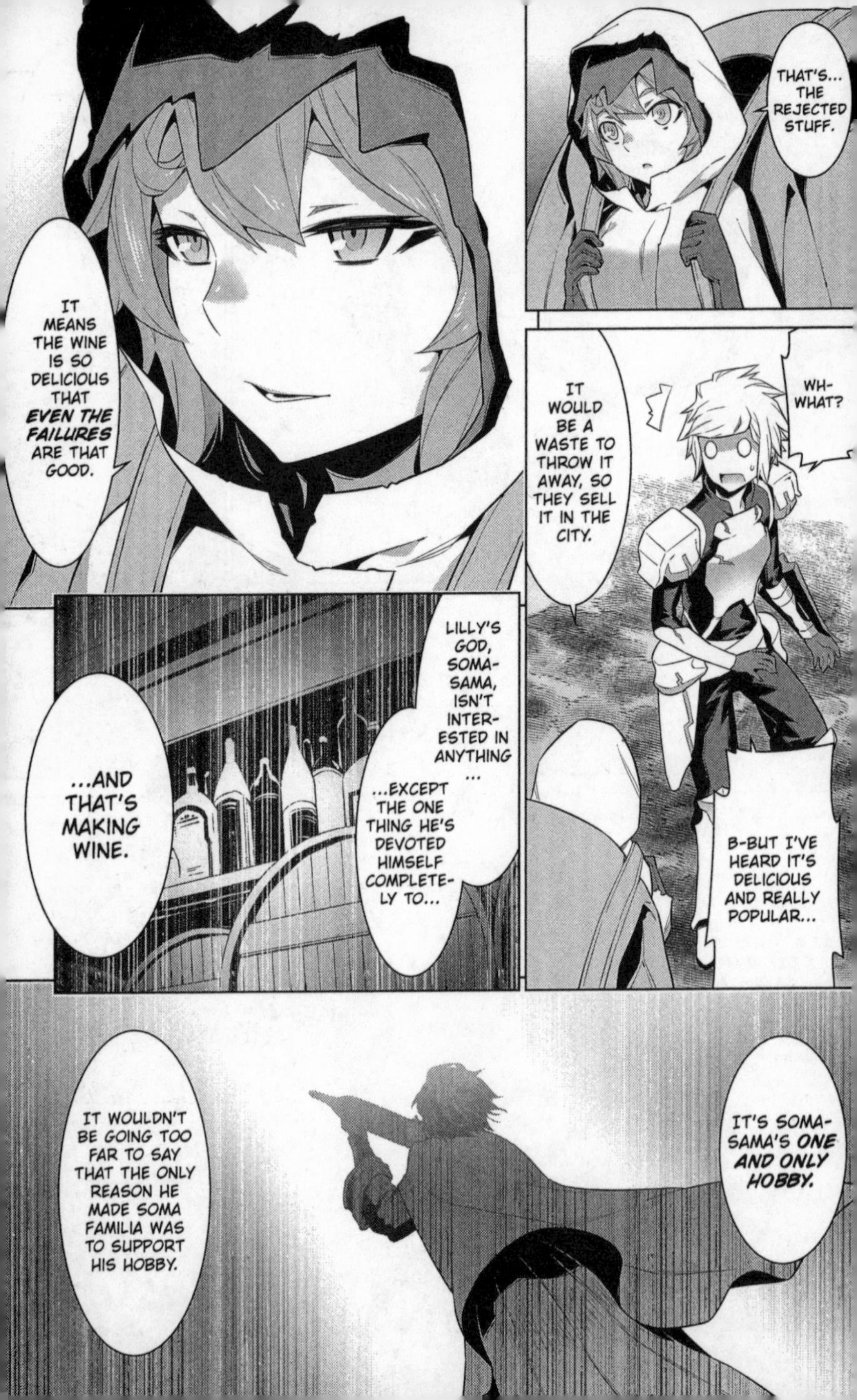
THAT'S... THE REJECTED STUFF.
WH-WHAT?
IT WOULD BE A WASTE TO THROW IT AWAY, SO THEY SELL IT IN THE CITY.
B-BUT I'VE HEARD IT'S DELICIOUS AND REALLY POPULAR...
IT MEANS THE WINE IS SO DELICIOUS THAT ***EVEN THE FAILURES*** ARE THAT GOOD.
LILLY'S GOD, SOMA-SAMA, ISN'T INTER-ESTED IN ANYTHING ...
...EXCEPT THE ONE THING HE'S DEVOTED HIMSELF COMPLETE-LY TO...
...AND THAT'S MAKING WINE.
IT'S SOMA-SAMA'S ***ONE AND ONLY HOBBY.***
IT WOULDN'T BE GOING TOO FAR TO SAY THAT THE ONLY REASON HE MADE SOMA FAMILIA WAS TO SUPPORT HIS HOBBY.

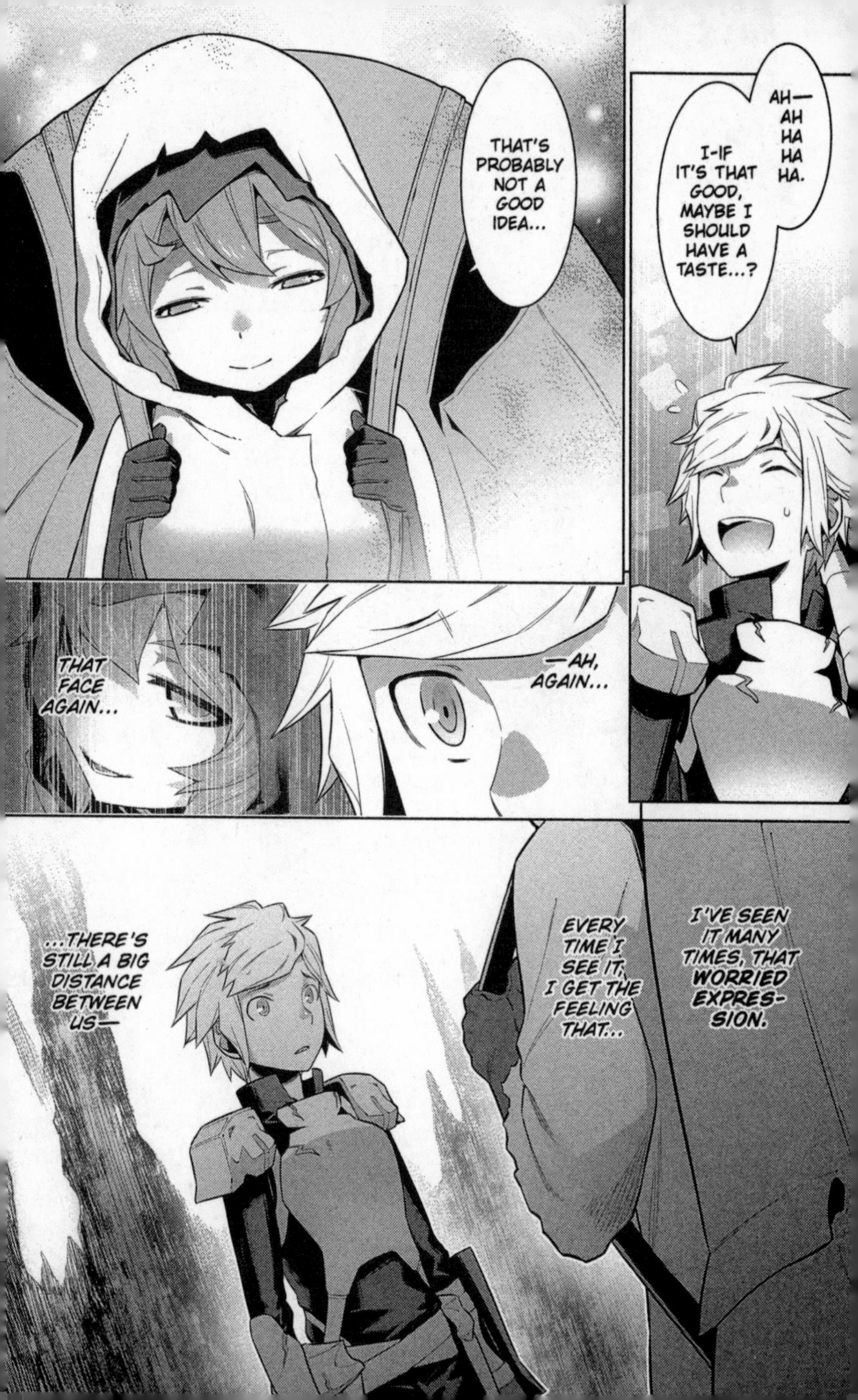
AH— AH HA HA HA HA.
I-IF IT'S THAT GOOD, MAYBE I SHOULD HAVE A TASTE...?
THAT'S PROBABLY NOT A GOOD IDEA...
—AH, AGAIN...
THAT FACE AGAIN...
I'VE SEEN IT MANY TIMES, THAT WORRIED EXPRES-SION.
EVERY TIME I SEE IT, I GET THE FEELING THAT...
...THERE'S STILL A BIG DISTANCE BETWEEN US—

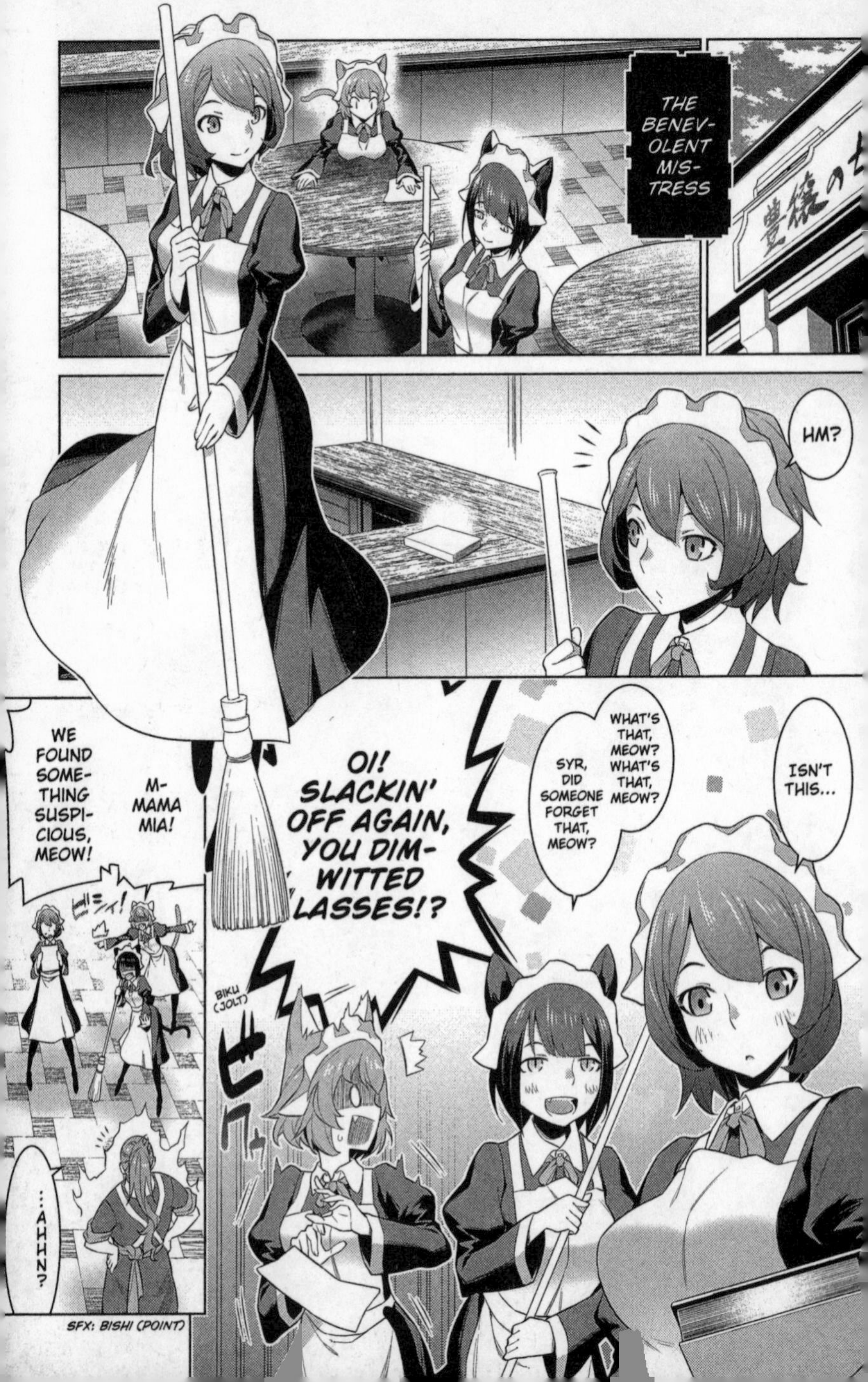
THE BENEVOLENT MISTRESS
HM?
ISN'T THIS...
SYR, DID SOMEONE FORGET THAT, MEOW?
WHAT'S THAT, MEOW? WHAT'S THAT, MEOW?
OI! SLACKIN' OFF AGAIN, YOU DIM-WITTED LASSES!?
BIKU (JOLT)
M-MAMA MIA!
WE FOUND SOMETHING SUSPICIOUS, MEOW!
...AHHN?
SFX: BISHI (POINT)

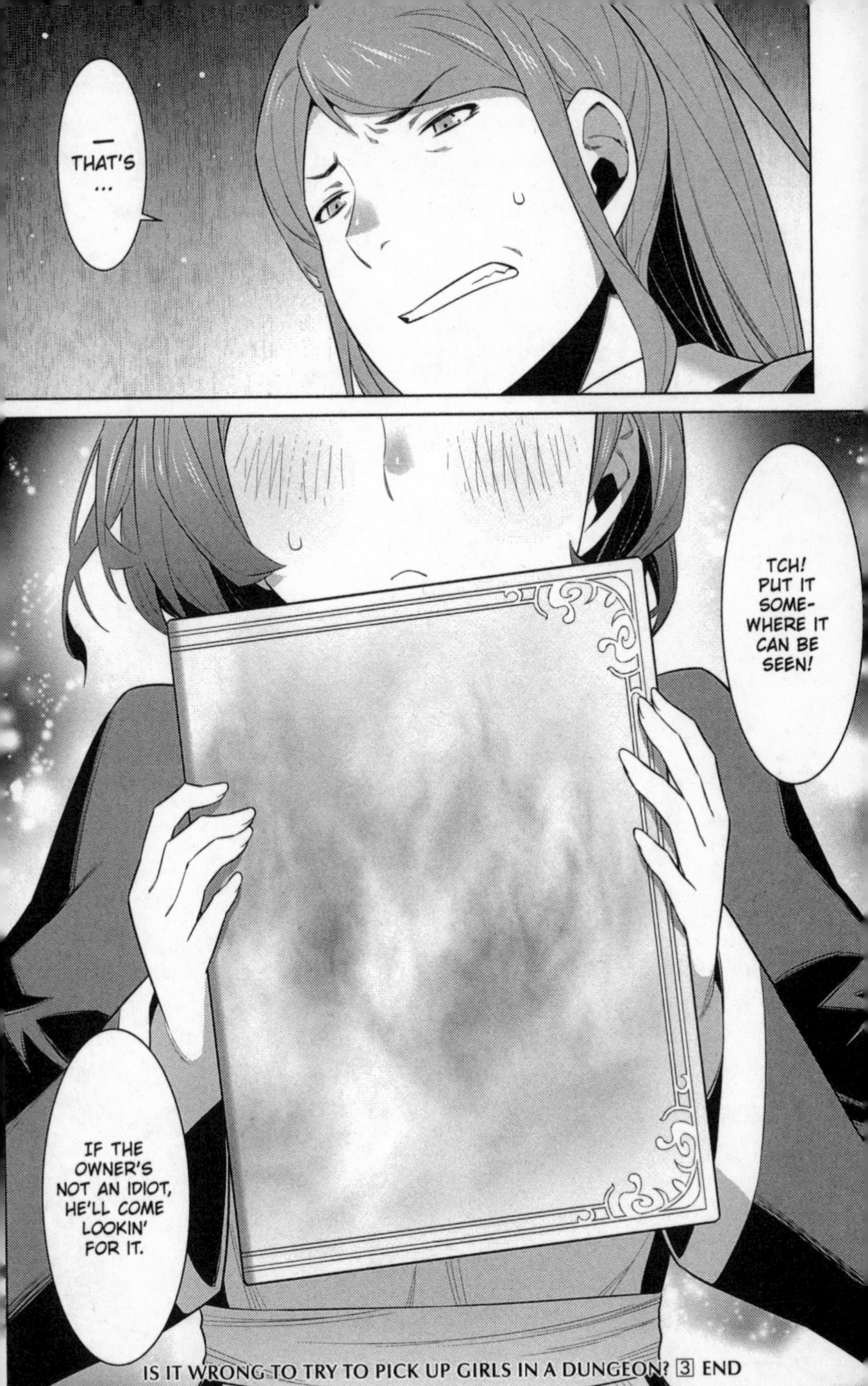
—THAT'S...
TCH! PUT IT SOME-WHERE IT CAN BE SEEN!
IF THE OWNER'S NOT AN IDIOT, HE'LL COME LOOKIN' FOR IT.

IS IT WRONG TO TRY TO PICK UP GIRLS IN A DUNGEON? 3 END

TRANSLATION NOTES

Common Honorifics

no honorific: Indicates familiarity or closeness; if used without permission or reason, addressing someone in this manner would constitute an insult.

-san: The Japanese equivalent of Mr./Mrs./Miss. If a situation calls for politeness, this is the failsafe honorific.

-shi: Not unlike -san; the equivalent of Mr./Mrs./Miss but conveying a more official or bureaucratic mood.

-sama: Conveys great respect; may also indicate that the social status of the speaker is lower than that of the addressee.

-kun: Used most often when referring to boys, this indicates affection or familiarity. Occasionally used by older men among their peers, but it may also be used by anyone referring to a person of lower standing.

-chan: An affectionate honorific indicating familiarity used mostly in reference to girls; also used in reference to cute persons or animals of either gender.

PAGE 16
Prum: One of the races of demi-humans that inhabit the city of Orario, whose most obvious feature is their short stature.

PAGE 73
Falna: A god's blessing on the adventurers in their *Familia*, a Falna is tattooed on the back of every member and, like a character sheet in an RPG, is a record of experience and abilities accrued by the adventurer while in the Dungeon.

PAGE 141
Tenkai: Literally "the heavenly world," this refers to the heavens—the realm from which the gods descended.

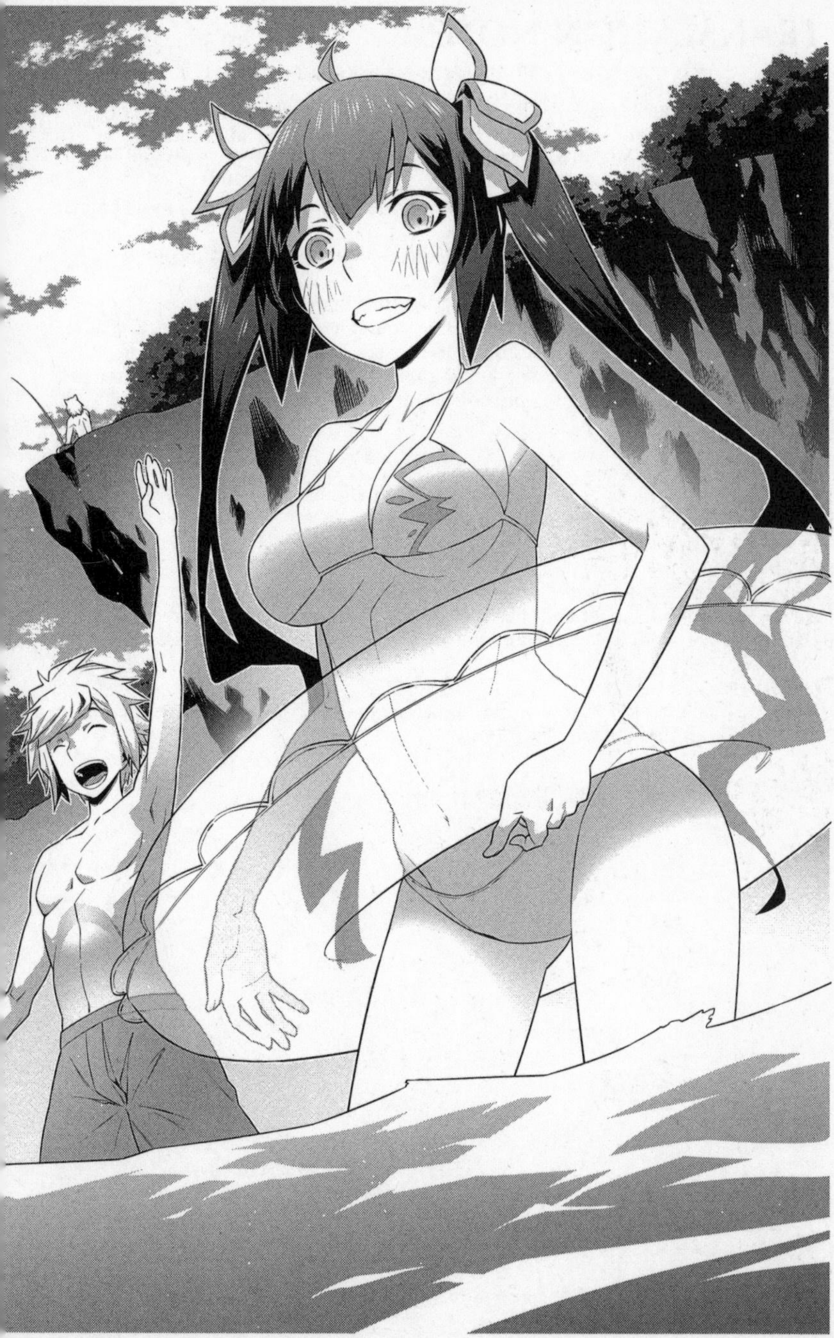

THANK YOU FOR PURCHASING THE THIRD VOLUME OF THIS MANGA!
THERE'S AN ANIME NOW TOO!
I CAN'T HIDE MY EXCITEMENT FOR THE EVER-GROWING WORLD OF *IS IT WRONG TO TRY TO PICK UP GIRLS IN A DUNGEON?*

AS I SIT HERE WRITING THIS, SUMMER HAS PASSED IN THE BLINK OF AN EYE, AND NOW IT'S ALMOST WINTER.
WHILE I'D LIKE TO SAY THAT I ENJOYED THIS SUMMER AS A SUMMER SHOULD BE ENJOYED, THAT'S NOT THE CASE. I WAS ACTUALLY A LITTLE LONELY. SO THE LEAST I COULD DO WAS GIVE BELL AND THE OTHERS THE SUMMER VACATION THEY DESERVE.
I CALL THIS ILLUSTRATION "FUN IN THE WATER."

UNTIL THE NEXT INSTALLMENT.

九二枝
KUNIEDA

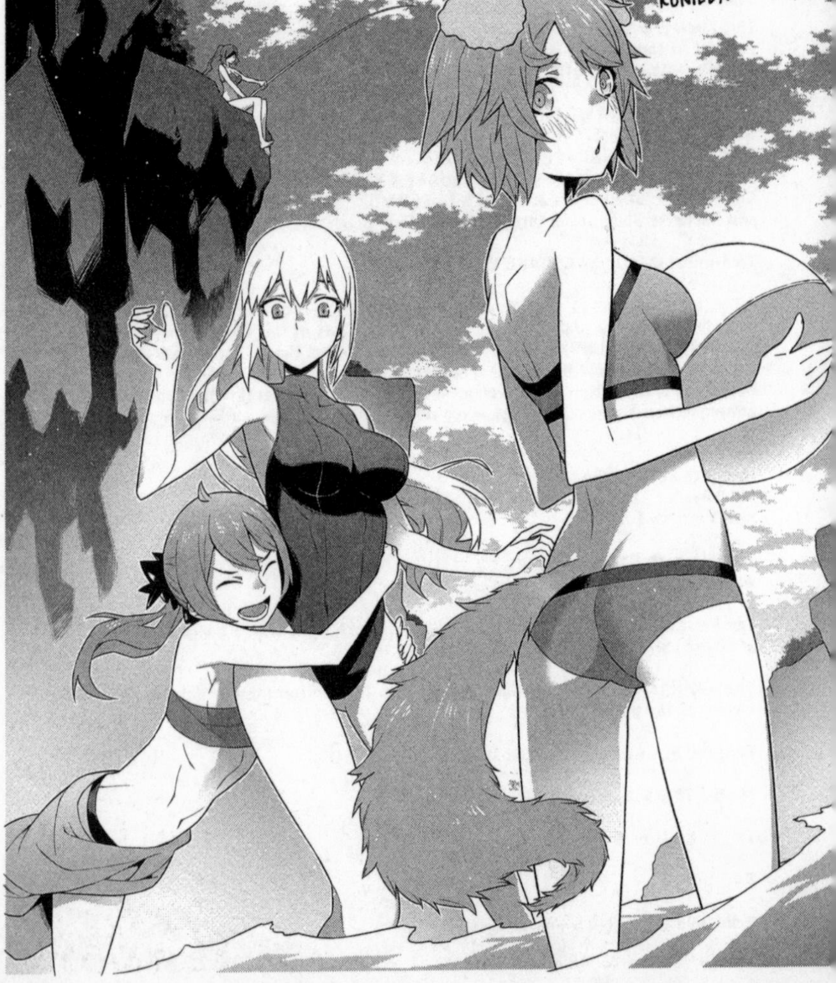

IS IT WRONG TO TRY TO PICK UP GIRLS IN A DUNGEON? ❸

FUJINO OMORI
KUNIEDA
SUZUHITO YASUDA

Translation: Andrew Gaippe • Lettering: Brndn Blakeslee, Lys Blakeslee

DUNGEON NI DEAI WO MOTOMERU NO WA MACHIGATTEIRUDAROUKA vol. 3
© 2014 Fujino Omori / SB Creative Corp.
© 2014 Kunieda / SQUARE ENIX CO., LTD.
First published in Japan in 2014 by SQUARE ENIX CO., LTD.
English Translation rights arranged with SQUARE ENIX CO., LTD.
and Hachette Book Group through Tuttle Mori Agency, Inc.

Translation © 2015 by SQUARE ENIX CO., LTD.

Yen Press
Hachette Book Group
1290 Avenue of the Americas
New York, NY 10104

www.HachetteBookGroup.com
www.YenPress.com

Yen Press is an imprint of Hachette Book Group, Inc. The Yen Press name and logo are trademarks of Hachette Book Group, Inc.

The publisher is not responsible for websites (or their content) that are not owned by the publisher.

First Yen Press Edition: November 2015

ISBN: 978-0-316-35207-9

10 9 8 7 6 5 4 3 2 1

BVG

Printed in the United States of America

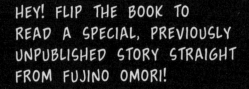

HEY! FLIP THE BOOK TO
READ A SPECIAL, PREVIOUSLY
UNPUBLISHED STORY STRAIGHT
FROM FUJINO OMORI!

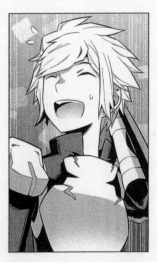